Criminal Law

The Essentials

SUE TITUS REID, J.D., PH.D.
Florida State University

SECOND EDITION

New York   Oxford

OXFORD UNIVERSITY PRESS

*In honor of Mandy Trept, who suffered severe injuries in a fall while raising money
for charity. Thanks, Mandy, for your devotion to others; congratulations on your
extraordinary rehabilitation; and best wishes to you and your devoted family
as you continue to reach for the stars.*

Oxford University Press is a department of the University of Oxford.
It furthers the University's objective of excellence in research,
scholarship, and education by publishing worldwide.

Oxford   New York
Auckland   Cape Town   Dar es Salaam   Hong Kong   Karachi
Kuala Lumpur   Madrid   Melbourne   Mexico City   Nairobi
New Delhi   Shanghai   Taipei   Toronto

With offices in
Argentina   Austria   Brazil   Chile   Czech Republic   France   Greece
Guatemala   Hungary   Italy   Japan   Poland   Portugal   Singapore
South Korea   Switzerland   Thailand   Turkey   Ukraine   Vietnam

For titles covered by Section 112 of the US Higher Education Opportunity Act,
please visit www.oup.com/us/he for the latest information about pricing and
alternate formats.

Published by Oxford University Press
198 Madison Avenue, New York, NY 10016
http://www.oup.com

Library of Congress Cataloging-in-Publication Data
Reid, Sue Titus.
Criminal law : the essentials / by Sue Titus Reid.—2nd ed.
  p. cm.
Includes index.
ISBN 978-0-19-989086-6
1. Criminal law—United States—Cases.
I. Title.
KF9219.R45 2012
345.73—dc23   2012012553

Printing Number: 9 8 7 6 5 4 3 2 1

Printed in the United States of America
on acid-free paper

About the Author

Sue Titus Reid, a professor in the Reubin O'D. Askew School of Public Administration and Policy at Florida State University, Tallahassee, has taught law students, graduate students, and undergraduate students in many states. She has served on the board of the Midwest Sociological Society and the executive staff of the American Sociological Association. She has been a chairperson, associate dean, and dean. In 1977, she was a distinguished visiting professor of law and sociology at the University of Tulsa. In 1985, she held the prestigious George Beto Chair in criminal justice at the Criminal Justice Center, Sam Houston State University, Huntsville, Texas.

Dr. Reid's formal training in criminology began in graduate school, but her interest in the field dates back to her early childhood. She was strongly influenced in her career by her father, who was born in the jail where his father, the under sheriff of a small east Texas county, lived with his family. Her grandmother prepared the inmates' meals. As a child, she helped her father in his grocery store and was quite disturbed when, on three separate occasions, he was victimized by criminals, one an armed robber. In each instance the offender took all the cash and checks; no one was ever apprehended.

Dr. Reid graduated with honors from Texas Woman's University in 1960 and received graduate degrees in sociology (M.A. in 1962 and Ph.D. in 1965) from the University of Missouri-Columbia. In 1972, she graduated with distinction from the University of Iowa College of Law. She was admitted to the Iowa Bar that year and later to the District of Columbia Court of Appeals. She has also been admitted to practice before the U.S. Supreme Court.

Dr. Reid is unique among authors in the criminal justice field because of her distinguished qualifications in both law and the social sciences. She launched her text publishing career with *Crime and Criminology* in 1976, and that text, now in its thirteenth edition, has been widely adopted throughout the United States and in foreign countries. Dr. Reid's other titles include *Criminal Justice: The Essentials,* ninth edition; *The Correctional System: An Introduction*; and *Criminal Law*, ninth edition. She has contributed articles to the *Encyclopedia of Crime and Justice* and the *Encyclopedia of American Prisons*, as well as to other books, in addition to publishing scholarly articles in both law and sociology.

Dr. Reid's contributions to her profession have been widely recognized nationally and abroad. In 1982 the American Society of Criminology elected her a fellow "for outstanding contributions to the field of Criminology." Other national honors include the following: Who's Who Among Women; Who's Who in America; Who's Who in American Education; Who's Who in Criminal Law; 2,000 Notable Women (Hall of Fame for Outstanding Contributions to Criminal Law, 1990); Personalities of America; and Most Admired Woman of the Decade, 1992.

Her international honors include numerous recognitions from the International Biographical Centre (IBC), Cambridge, England, including the prestigious International Order of Merit. The IBC named Dr. Reid an inaugural member as one of the Top 100 Educators—2008, an honor limited by the IBC "to those individuals who, in our belief, have made a significant enough contribution in their field to engender influence on a local, national or international basis." Among the other international honors received by Dr. Reid are the following: International Woman of the Year, 1991–1992; International Who's Who of Intellectuals; International Who's Who of Professionals; International Who's Who of Professional and Business Women; International Order of Merit, 1993; Who's Who in the World; Marquis Who's Who in the World; and the Manchester Who's Who Among Executive and Professional Women.

In 1979, Dr. Reid received the Distinguished Alumna Award from Texas Woman's University, one of the youngest graduates to be awarded that honor. In 2000, she received a university teaching award from Florida State University.

Dr. Reid has traveled extensively to widen her knowledge of criminal justice systems in the United States and in other countries. In 1982, she was a member of the Eisenhower Foundation–sponsored People-to-People Crime Prevention delegation to the People's Republic of China. Her several trips to Europe included a three-month study and lecture tour of 10 countries in 1985.

In August 2010, the Commission on Physical and Mental Disabilities of the 400,000-member American Bar Association featured Dr. Reid in its monthly spotlight on a lawyer or judge who, despite disabilities, has made a significant contribution to the legal profession.

Brief Contents

Contents

Chapter 6   **Assault, Robbery, Rape, and Other Crimes Against the Person   110**

Preface

In the study of criminal law, it is important to analyze the facts of cases and the judicial interpretations of those facts, along with legal terms and statutes and the various reasons for court decisions. It is also important to understand that the principles of criminal law vary from state to state and between states and the federal system. Although it is not reasonable to survey all jurisdictions, this text includes references to federal and state statutes and cases to illustrate the agreement and divergence within criminal law.

This text focuses on *substantive* rather than procedural criminal law. Despite this focus on substantive criminal law, it is necessary to discuss some constitutional principles that relate directly to criminal law, and that is done where applicable.

FEATURES

This text, a shorter one similar in nature to the author's *Criminal Law,* 9th edition, is designed to provide an overview of criminal law for the reader who does not have the time to delve more deeply into the subject. Thus, it does not contain extensive case excerpts or the many statutes included in the larger version. It does, however, include focus boxes, figures, and graphs to enhance the reader's interest while relating general principles and laws to the text.

To help students master the text material and prepare for exams, each chapter contains several study aids. Each begins with an outline, followed by a summary overview of the chapter's contents designed to give students a brief view of that chapter's material. Chapters conclude with study questions to facilitate the combined purposes of mastering and analyzing the chapters' contents, as well as a debate issue designed to generate lively discussion on relevant topics. Throughout the text, key terms are boldfaced. A list of key terms, along with the pages on which they are located, is featured at the end of each chapter, and key terms are defined at the end of the text in a comprehensive glossary.

Each chapter also features an *Internet activity,* which students can use to explore topics on the Web. Case, name, and general indexes enable readers to find information quickly, while Appendix A reprints pertinent sections from the U.S. Constitution to provide easy reference to the portions of that document that are mentioned throughout the text. Appendix B features a legal case citation, along with an explanation of how to read and interpret it.

SECOND EDITION—ORGANIZATION AND CHANGES

All reasonable efforts have been made to keep the text current to the time of publication. But because many of the cases are recent, some will be reversed or altered on appeal after this text is published. Likewise, some of the current events will have had major developments (or even resolutions) since the last opportunity to update the text. Many areas of criminal law have been changing rapidly, and it is reasonable to expect this trend to continue. All data have been updated where possible, including the addition of the FBI's preliminary crime data for 2011.

Chapter 1, An Introduction to Criminal Law, contains an overview of criminal law, which is contrasted with civil law. It encompasses the nature and purposes of punishment and raises the issue of which acts should be covered by the criminal law. The Model Penal Code (MPC) and its influence on U.S. criminal law are discussed, as is the impact of English common law. The sources of criminal law and discretion within criminal law are noted, as are classifications of crimes and related offenses.

The chapter continues with an analysis of the limitations on criminal law, ranging from the void for vagueness and overbreadth doctrines to the right of privacy. Chapter 1 includes an overview of the nature and purpose of U.S. court systems, including a look at the dual court system approach and detailing trial and appellate courts. The establishment of guilt is discussed in the context of the adversary system and includes comments on the burden of proof and the ways in which guilt is determined—that is, by a judge or a jury. The chapter closes with a discussion entitled How to Read and Interpret an Appellate Opinion. That section is illustrated with Focus 1.3, The Evolution of the Right to Counsel, which was revised in this edition.

Among Chapter 1's new information is the Casey Anthony case from Florida; an update on *Kennedy v. Louisiana* (concerning the death penalty for the rape but not murder of a child), which was decided by the U.S. Supreme Court after the publication of the first edition; and a new focus (Focus 1.2, Beyond a Reasonable Doubt: An Example).

Chapter 2, Elements of a Crime, analyzes the elements of criminal liability, including the criminal act (as well as the failure to act), the criminal intent or state of mind, concurring with the act and causation (now featuring the Texas statute on causation), and the attendant circumstances (required for some crimes) that must accompany acts for them to be considered criminal. The chapter closes with a section on the issue of liability without fault, which includes strict liability, vicarious liability, and enterprise liability. The chapter's Internet Activity section focuses on the Penn State sexual abuse scandal.

Chapter 3, Anticipatory Offenses and Parties to Crimes, contains complicated concepts, but an effort was made to simplify the discussions of the crimes of solicitation, attempt, and conspiracy. The elements and defenses for each of these areas of criminal activity are detailed and analyzed before the chapter turns to an analysis of parties to crimes. New to this edition is Focus 3.2 concerning whether an attempt crime is committed by a person who, knowing he or she has the HIV virus or AIDS, has unprotected sex without mentioning that fact to the partner.

Chapter 4, Defenses to Criminal Culpability, covers the more traditional defenses to criminal acts. It discusses the nature of defenses, including an overview of the burden of proof and presumptions. After a brief look at the defenses of ignorance or mistake, duress or necessity, and infancy, the chapter explores the insanity defense in greater detail. That section summarizes the various tests used for deciding whether a defendant is insane. It analyzes the related concepts of guilty but mentally ill and guilty except insane (discussed with reference to the man accused of shooting Congresswoman Gabrielle Giffords and others); and considers jurisdictions that have abolished the insanity defense.

With regard to the defense of infancy, Chapter 4 considers such new information as the U.S. Supreme Court cases on sentencing juveniles (see Focus 4.1): *Roper v. Simmons* (concerning capital punishment of those who committed homicides while they were under age 18) and *Graham v. Florida* (concerning life without parole for juveniles who commit a nonhomicide crime).

Chapter 4 looks at other more traditional defenses, such as automatism, entrapment, outrageous government conduct, the defense of persons and property, and the defense of law enforcement. Brief attention is given to such defenses as intoxication, domestic authority, and consent and condonation. The chapter closes with an enhanced discussion of syndrome and stress disorder defenses. The chapter's Internet Activity includes, among other exercises, a quest for information on how stress defenses might be related to returning veterans and raises the issue of whether stress defenses are related to the forthcoming trial of Major Nidal Malik Hassan, an Army psychiatrist charged with the 2009 shooting massacre at the Army installation at Ford Hood, Texas.

Chapter 5, Criminal Homicide, begins with an overview of violent crimes before focusing on homicide in general (including the important elements of causation and *corpus delicti*) and murder and nonnegligent manslaughter in particular. Murder is considered under common law as well as modern statutory law. The types of murder (intent to kill, intent to inflict great bodily harm, depraved heart, intent to commit a felony, and murder for hire) are explained, followed by the division of murder into degrees of culpability. The concept of lesser included offenses is defined. Mercy killing is considered in the context of whether it is an exception to murder. The discussion on physician assisted suicide (PAS) is enlarged and now includes the Washington State statute, which was enacted after the publication of the first edition of this text. The chapter closes with a detailed discussion of manslaughter, which notes the conviction of Dr. Conrad Murray for the death of his patient, pop star Michael Jackson. It also discusses the conviction in the Arizona sweat lodge case.

Also new to Chapter 5 is a notation of the Federal Bureau of Investigation's revised definition of *rape* to include male victims and female perpetrators as well as what is often called *rape by instrumentation*. Finally, the Internet Activity for Chapter 5 contains information on the 20 July 2012 Colorado massacre, which occurred after the text of the chapter was completed.

Chapter 6 continues the discussion begun in Chapter 5 on crimes against the person, focusing on assault, robbery, forcible rape, and sodomy. After covering these major violent crimes, the discussion turns to a look at domestic violence, including intimate personal violence (IPV), marital rape, date rape, child abuse, and elder abuse. The chapter presents information concerning the crimes of false imprisonment, kidnapping, hate crimes, and stalking.

New to Chapter 6 is a focus on home invasion and bank robbery (Focus 6.1), which involves two very unusual and unsolved Florida cases, along with the highly publicized Connecticut case that resulted in the torture and deaths of three persons; an extended discussion of forcible rape; new data on intimate personal violence; notation of one jurisdiction that repealed its misdemeanor domestic violence ordinance to save money on prosecutions; updates and extensions of the discussion on elder abuse, including the Elder Abuse Justice Act of 2007 that was enacted into law in 2010; and considerably more information on stalking and cyberstalking. Finally, this chapter features a new topic and discussion on bullying, including some of the most recent examples of this crime.

Chapter 7, Property and Related Crimes, includes Figure 7.1, with 2010 data, along with the text discussion of preliminary data for 2011, of the four serious property offenses: larceny-theft, burglary, motor vehicle theft, and arson. The chapter also includes other property crimes, such as embezzlement and fraud, false pretense, forgery, stolen property offenses, malicious mischief, trespass, and extortion or blackmail. In particular, the discussion on fraud was expanded with new sections on fraud against the elderly and mortgage fraud.

This edition features a brief discussion of the Dodd-Frank Wall Street Reform and Consumer Act, signed in 2010, constituting "the greatest overhaul in the regulation of U.S. financial institutions since the Great Depression." There is also a reference to the *Free Enterprise Fund v. Public Company Accounting Oversight Board*, a 2010 case on the constitutionality of the Sarbanes-Oxley Act (SOX).

An analysis of computer crime includes the types of this crime as well as suggested methods for controlling it. The fast-growing and relatively new crime of *identity theft* is featured, followed by a discussion of another relatively recent crime: carjacking.

Chapter 8's title, Crimes Against Public Order and Public Decency, is changed as a result of moving the discussions on the administration of government to Chapter 9. The chapter now features a significantly expanded discussion of alcohol- and drug-related offenses, including driving under the influence (DUI) and offenses relating to minors. The discussion on animal abuse is updated and enlarged and now includes a 2010 U.S. Supreme Court case, *United States v. Stevens,* involving the depiction of animal abuse in videos. The chapter notes the case of animal abuse involving football player Michael Vick. It features a new section on human trafficking (national and international), including Focus 8.3 on that topic.

Chapter 8's enhanced discussion of consensual sodomy includes the 2003 U.S. Supreme Court case, *Lawrence v. Texas,* which declared the Texas statute unconstitutional. Finally, the chapter's discussion of pornography is updated, enlarged, and includes recent cases.

Chapter 9's new title, Crimes Against the Government and Terrorism, reflects the reorganization of Chapter 8 and this chapter. Chapter 9 begins with the crimes of perjury, bribery, official misconduct in office, and obstruction of justice, which were discussed in the previous edition. New to this edition are the following: Focus 9.1, which includes perjury cases involving Martha Stewart, Roger Clemens (who was acquitted), Marion Jones, the Balloon Boy's parents, and Casey Anthony; Focus 9.2, which includes the bribery cases of former Congressman William J. Jefferson; Monica Conyers, former Detroit City Council member and wife of U.S. Representative John Conyers; and a case involving the judiciary. The text includes the latest information on the obstruction of justice case involving baseball player Barry Bonds.

Chapter 9 includes a new section on contempt, which features recent and unusual cases involving jail terms for contempt citations. The discussion of terrorism is, at the recommendation of several reviewers, reduced although updated. Particular attention is still given to the problems of defining *terrorism*. Federal and state attempts to control terrorist acts are also discussed and updated, including illustrative statutes.

Chapter 10, Substance Abuse Crimes, begins with a look at the history and current status of the regulation of alcoholic beverages before turning to an analysis of controlled substances. This section includes discussions on possession of controlled substances and of drug paraphernalia as well as drug trafficking and adds the topic of prescription drug abuse and fetal abuse. Baby Moses laws are discussed and updated. A new section focuses on the economic impact of drug abuse, along with updated information on the impact of illegal drugs, including discussions on the relationship of illegal drugs to other crimes in general and to campus problems in particular. The impact of drugs on criminal justice systems is noted.

Chapter 10 also considers federal and state efforts to control illegal drugs. Prominent in the discussion are the latest White House policies and the changes in the severe drug policies in the state of New York. The discussions of drug treatment and drug courts are expanded. The chapter closes with a section on the controversial topic of legalizing marijuana for medicinal purposes. It updates the list of states that currently permit the practice as well as legal cases challenging it.

Chapter 11, Sentencing, begins with a focus on the approaches to sentencing and how sentences are determined. Sentencing guidelines are assessed at both the federal and state levels and are evaluated. Considerable discussion focuses on recent sentencing reform measures. California's unsuccessful attempts to change that state's "three strikes" law are noted. A new section on the recently enacted Fair Sentencing Act of 2010 is significant, as that statute changed the frequently criticized 100:1 ratio of sentences for the conviction of crack compared to powder cocaine. The discussion includes an analysis of whether this statute would be applied retroactively, noting that the U.S. Supreme Court decided that issue during its 2011–2012 term.

The discussion on capital punishment is updated, as are the constitutional issues in sentencing. Focus 11.5 now features the 2010 U.S. Supreme Court opinion, *Graham v. Florida,* holding that life without parole for juveniles who do not commit a homicide constitutes cruel and unusual punishment and is thus unconstitutional. The chapter also includes a brief reference to *Miller v. Alabama,* decided on 25 June 2012 during the final stages of the production of the text. That case involved the issue of whether mandating a life without parole sentence for juveniles convicted of murder constitutes cruel and unusual punishment.

Finally, the section on Megan's laws is changed to reflect the wider development of such statutes and is now called *Sex Offender Laws* and includes a discussion on civil commitment procedures for sex offenders who have served their criminal sentences but who are still considered dangerous to society.

SUPPLEMENTS

The *Criminal Law: The Essentials—Casebook,* available separately, has been specifically designed to accompany this text. Following this book's contents, chapter for chapter, the *Casebook* provides substantial case excerpts along with review questions. It is designed to supplement this book by providing students with additional exposure to the language of case law.

Instructors interested in an exam copy should contact a sales representative by calling 1-800-280-0280 or visit our website at www.oup.com/us/he

ACKNOWLEDGMENTS

Any text revision is a major effort, but this is particularly the case in criminal law, for the subject matter changes daily and in many jurisdictions. My work on this shorter version of the ninth edition of *Criminal Law* was aided by family, friends, and colleagues, and I am grateful to all of them.

As always, several professional colleagues have contributed significantly to the publication of this text. Dr. David Fabianic of the University of Central Florida has provided almost daily encouragement. Chris Morales gave me advice on international issues, and my long-time friend and college roommate Heidi van Hulst was a frequent correspondent, adding her encouragement and wisdom.

My weekly flights between Dallas, Texas, and Tallahassee, Florida, during the school year present many challenges, but at least my cat, Ashley, is well cared for by her cat nanny, Dorothy Olszewski. Flight problems were eased by my Delta friends. In particular, I am grateful to Jeffrey Penzkowski, Libby Hunt, Michele Patrick, Stanley Strong, Stephen Garrett, Robert Clinard, and many others in Delta's Sky Clubs in the Atlanta Airport. My hand surgeons Dr. Stephen Trigg and his nurse Jackie Bowman, of the Mayo Clinic in Jacksonville, Florida, enabled me to type more easily and with less pain. Thanks to you and your colleagues, especially my internist, Dr. Walter C. Hellinger, his assistant Lynette Kick, and my physiatrist, Dr. Peter T. Dorsher of the Department of Physical Medicine and Rehabilitation.

My move from Jackson, New Hampshire, to Dallas, Texas, during this revision, was aided by the incredible help of my family: Jill Pickett, who spent a week with me in New Hampshire, spent hours unpacking in Dallas, and provided shuttle service as I learned to navigate the roads of the big city; and her husband Roger Pickett, who not only delivered the *New York Times* daily during those first weeks, but also unpacked, moved, installed, and, with Jill, provided excellent meals.

Rhonda Sue Pickett Santoyo, my niece and namesake, and her husband, John Santoyo, flew to New Hampshire for my last week of packing, organizing, and cleaning and drove the car while the cat and I enjoyed relaxing in the back seat. That long trip was memorable, especially due to our helicopter flight over Niagara Falls. My back and leg pain were eased by their driving.

After our arrival in Dallas, my nephew, Clint Pickett, his wife Stephanie, and their daughter Cherith helped with the unpacking and organizing. Cherith, headed for her eighth birthday, entertained me on numerous occasions with her laughter, her love, her piano, ballet, and violin; she is a true joy.

A Florida State University student in the Askew School of Public Administration and Policy assisted me during the revision of this text. John Bailey, MPA candidate, met my classes when I was out for medical or professional reasons and took care of some computer issues. Thanks, John, for easing my burdens.

Finally, my long-time friend and former college roommate, Heidi, and her husband, Karl van Hulst, provided housing and meals during those tiring days of unpacking and organizing after I moved to Dallas. Heidi, a design expert, carefully considered every piece of furniture I planned to move and detailed on paper how it would fit into my living accommodations. She made many arrangements with the persons in charge of my apartment complex. Without her efforts I could not have handled the move and my manuscripts.

Several Oxford University Press (OUP) employees were helpful in the production of this text. Sarah Calabi, my editor, quickly secured the reviews of the previous edition and made her suggestions for this revision. Her assistant, Richard Beck, responded with efficiency and speed to my numerous requests for editorial assistance. Based on my knowledge of his work on a previous manuscript, I welcomed back Keith Faivre, Senior Production Editor of Higher Education at OUP, with great enthusiasm, and I was not disappointed. Thanks, Keith, for your expertise, your professionalism, your understanding, and for your assistance in helping me meet deadlines. My appreciation also to Dorothy Bauhoff for copy editing this edition.

Although the final work is the responsibility of the author, the suggestions for revisions made by the following professors were greatly appreciated: George Coroian, Northern Kentucky University; Jo-Ann Della Giustina, Bridgewater State University; Pamela Everett, Wayne State College; John P. Feldmeier, Wright

State University; Sara Ellen Kitchen, Chestnut Hill College; Shana L. Maier, Widener University; and Peyton Paxson, Middlesex Community College.

Sue Titus Reid, J.D., Ph. D.
Professor
Reubin O'D. Askew School of Public Administration and Policy
Florida State University

An Introduction to Criminal Law

INTRODUCTION

For centuries people have been fascinated by law, particularly by criminal law and violent crimes. Scholars and philosophers have written volumes in an attempt to explain the history and evolution of criminal law and the reasons for criminal behavior, and citizens have made these topics ones of intense political focus. Americans have supported stricter criminal laws and punishments while expressing increased fears of becoming crime victims.

The purpose of this text is to explore the dimensions of criminal law. This chapter introduces the subject by covering the traditional reasons for imposing criminal penalties on those who violate society's laws. It includes a discussion of the extent to which the criminal law should be used to regulate behavior. Specific attention is given to the inclusion in the criminal law of behavior that some people consider private, and the chapter summarizes the nature and impact of the Model Penal Code and English common law on U.S. court systems.

The chapter examines the sources of criminal law, the nature of discretion in criminal law, and the classification of crimes and related offenses. It includes an analysis of the constitutional limitations that are placed on criminal laws in the United States. This chapter summarizes the nature and purpose of U.S. court systems, focusing on both the federal and state systems as well as trial and appellate courts. It contains a brief discussion of the establishment of guilt within the adversary system and concludes with a discussion of how to read and interpret an appellate opinion.

THE EMERGENCE OF LAW

In small groups and societies, formal laws are not necessary because human behavior can be regulated through informal methods of social control. From infancy, children are taught proper behavior by their families and other social institutions, such as churches and schools. These institutions may impose informal penalties against those who violate society's norms. Those penalties range from a disapproving glance or social ostracism to physical expulsion from the community. In most cases, the threat of being banished from the community is sufficient to ensure proper behavior. The key to the success of such informal social controls is the cohesiveness of the group or society. Most members accept and follow the norms; those who do not are easily detected and can be punished swiftly and effectively without formal criminal laws.

As groups and societies become more complex, however, informal social controls become less effective and major social institutions are required to control human behavior. More conflicts arise and a more formal, rationally thought-out method of social control is necessary. Although there is disagreement over how laws evolved, it is clear that at some point law emerged as a formal method by which conflicts are resolved and behavior is controlled. There are many types of laws, but those that are most relevant to this text are classified as **criminal law**, and they must be distinguished from **civil law**.

CIVIL AND CRIMINAL LAW DISTINGUISHED

Both civil law and criminal law are designed to control behavior to protect the interests of society and of individuals. Both prohibit or require specific actions and permit the government to assess penalties, and both may result in social stigma. The two types of law are distinguishable in the following ways:

- A private party brings the lawsuit in a civil case; the state is the accusing party and initiates the charges in a criminal case.
- Different rules of evidence and procedure apply, and those rules are stricter in criminal cases.
- Normally, society's moral condemnation is greater against those who violate the criminal law.
- The emphasis in civil law is on compensating the wronged person; the emphasis in criminal law is on punishing the offender.
- Criminal law carries more serious penalties, such as incarceration or even the death penalty, while civil penalties consist primarily of fines or orders to cease or begin specified actions.

THE NATURE AND PURPOSE OF CRIMINAL LAW

It is important to analyze the punishment philosophies that have provided the historical justification for criminal law. The emphasis on each approach has varied over time, but there has been some consistency in the punishment philosophies advanced to support criminal law.

Criminal Law as Punishment

Punishing individuals through the criminal law is a serious act and should be based on reasons presumed to assist society in meeting worthy goals, such as the maintenance of social solidarity and the protection of citizens. Throughout history the basic punishment goals of criminal law have been **retribution**, **incapacitation**, **deterrence**, and **rehabilitation.**

Retribution

In early times, crime victims were permitted (and expected) to take direct action against criminal offenders, and private acts could even take such extreme forms as murder. The philosophy of retribution permitted victims to inflict on offenders the same acts they had suffered. Today, the philosophy of retribution permits a society's governing body to impose on criminal offenders the punishment they deserve, although that does not always mean that society's punishment may involve the same act that the offender committed.

Incapacitation

Historically, incapacitation was employed literally in some societies. For example, the hands of a thief were cut off to prevent further thefts. This practice is not permitted in U.S. criminal justice systems today. Rather, incapacitation now focuses on removing the offender from the community or restricting that individual's movements within the community.

Deterrence

Deterrence is based on the assumption that behavior is rational and that criminal behavior can be prevented if people fear the penalties. Punishment of a specific offender, or *specific deterrence*, may involve physical restraint or incapacitation, such as incarceration or capital punishment. But deterrence also assumes that people may be prevented from choosing to engage in criminal acts; thus, it is not necessary to amputate a thief's hands to prevent theft. In addition, one person's punishment should deter others (*general deterrence*) from committing the same or similar criminal acts.

It is difficult to prove or disprove that measures aimed at deterrence are effective. Many supporters of the deterrence approach argue from intuition and emotion rather than from scientific data. Some empirical studies fail to distinguish between general and specific deterrence or to measure the perceived swiftness and probability of being punished. Some potential criminals may not be deterred from crime, despite potentially harsh penalties, if they perceive that they will not be apprehended or that the laws will not be enforced.

Rehabilitation

While retribution and deterrence focus on crime, rehabilitation focuses on individual offenders and emphasizes the possibility of changing their behavior. Those who advocate rehabilitation believe that offenders can become law-abiding citizens with proper treatment. Rehabilitation was the dominant focus of U.S. criminal justice systems during the late 1960s and 1970s. In the late 1970s and 1980s, however, the trend shifted. When the public demanded harsher punishments, statutes were changed, as exemplified in the federal system. In 1984, after hearing testimony that rehabilitation had failed and was an outmoded concept on which to base sentences, Congress enacted a comprehensive federal sentencing statute and rejected rehabilitation as the primary basis for determining sentence length.[1]

Rehabilitation remained in vogue in some states, but in most jurisdictions the philosophy was replaced by an emphasis on deterrence and retribution. However, there has been some recent support for rehabilitation, especially in the area of nonviolent drug offenses. Regardless of a jurisdiction's punishment philosophy, the problem of deciding which acts should be considered criminal is an issue of controversy, especially in the area of morality.

Criminal Law and Morality

The debate over whether certain acts should be included within the purview of criminal law involves distinguishing between acts that are *mala in se* (evil in themselves) and those that are considered *mala prohibita* (evil only because they are prohibited by law). The first group includes crimes such as murder, forcible rape, robbery, aggravated assault, burglary, and arson—serious acts that most, if not all, people consider criminal. The second group includes acts that are considered criminal only because statutes have defined them as such. They are not universally regarded as criminal; they may not even be regarded as criminal by most people. Examples might be private sexual acts between consenting adults, use of alcohol and other drugs, prostitution, gambling, and carrying a concealed weapon. When deciding whether such acts should be covered by criminal law, it is important to consider to what extent they involve areas that are of legitimate concern to the public, such as the spread of disease or the commission of other, more serious crimes.

It is also important to consider whether criminal law is an effective way of controlling these behaviors. These decisions may change over time, and the inclusions differ from state to state. This text examines a variety of state laws. In their enactment of law, state legislators are often influenced by the **Model Penal Code (MPC)**.

THE MODEL PENAL CODE (MPC) AND CRIMINAL LAW REFORM

In recent years many states (as well as Congress) have attempted a complete revision of their criminal statutes. They have been assisted in this process by the American Law Institute (ALI), an organization of lawyers, judges, and legal scholars, who author and update a Model Penal Code (MPC) and explanations of that code. States enact their own criminal laws and procedures, and many of them follow the recommended statutes provided by the MPC, at least in part. States and the federal government are also influenced by English common law.

ENGLISH COMMON LAW AND ITS IMPACT

English **common law** provides the basis for much of U.S. civil and criminal law. The term *common law* refers to those customs, traditions, judicial decisions, and other materials that guide courts in decision making but that have not been enacted by the legislatures into statutes or embodied in constitutions. English common law developed after the Norman Conquest in 1066. Prior to that time there was no distinction among law, custom, religion, and morality, and legal decisions differed from community to community. The Normans wanted to establish some unity; to do so, the king employed representatives to travel to the various jurisdictions. These persons kept the king informed about the developments in varying jurisdictions and carried news to each of what was happening in the others. The legal principles began to be similar, or common, throughout England and came to be referred to as *English common law*.

English common law was brought by the colonists to America and became the basis for much of this country's early law.[2] Common law offenses have been kept alive and interpreted by judicial decisions, which are an important part of American law today. Even when state legislatures enact laws to cover common law offenses, the interpretation of those statutes may be made in light of common law decisions. This is seen in federal courts, where a person cannot be punished for a common law crime today unless it is enacted into a statute. But once that occurs and Congress has provided a penalty for the offense, courts can resort to English or American common law for interpretations. This is also true in some states.

SOURCES OF CRIMINAL LAW

Criminal law is derived from four sources: statutes, constitutions, judicial decisions, and administrative regulations.

Statutory Law

Today most states have **codified** their criminal laws, meaning that they have reduced their customs, unwritten laws, common law, and rules to written statutes enacted by their legislatures. Thus, they do not recognize an act as criminal unless it is included within the **statutory law**.

Each state's criminal statutes define the crimes and penalties applicable in that state. Although the names and citations vary, state statutes are recorded officially in publications with such names as the *Criminal Code* or *Penal Code* (or abbreviations such as *Pen Code*), preceded by the name of the state. For example, *Cal Pen Code* refers to the criminal statutes that govern California. Congress is responsible for passing statutes that define federal crimes. These are recorded in the *United States Code*, which is also referred to as the *U.S. Code* or the USCS.

A study of criminal law should also distinguish between **procedural law** and **substantive law**. The latter defines the elements, rights, and responsibilities of law, whereas the former defines the methods by which the law may be enforced. This text is concerned primarily with substantive criminal law and makes reference to procedural law only when that is necessary for an understanding of substantive law.

Constitutions

In the federal and in state systems, criminal laws are generally defined by statute rather than by the relevant constitutions, but the latter may establish an approved framework under which statutes may be enacted and enforced. The U.S. Constitution (see Appendix A) deals primarily with procedural criminal law, but the limits it establishes and the guarantees it provides are important to an understanding of all federal laws. The same is true for state constitutions and state laws. However, federal and state constitutions are viewed as *minimal* protections; federal and state laws and regulations may enhance the constitutional protections provided to individuals by the jurisdictions in which they are recognized. State laws and constitutions may not conflict with the U.S. Constitution and applicable federal laws.

Judicial Decisions and Customs

Laws also come from judicial decisions and customs. As noted earlier, historically, common law referred to England's laws that developed through judicial decisions on a case-by-case basis (leading to the term **case law**) and that influenced the development of English and American law. But common law also applies to unwritten laws in the United States, although as noted, most laws have been codified. It is important to read case law carefully, for case law is real law.

Administrative Law

A final source of law is **administrative law**, which consists of a body of regulations and rules that come from administrative agencies (such as the Internal Revenue Service—the IRS) to which Congress and state legislatures have delegated the power to make and enforce rules and regulations. Most regulations and decisions of administrative agencies concern civil, not criminal, matters, but violations of administrative law may constitute offenses that can be enforced through criminal courts. Thousands of state and federal agencies enact and enforce administrative rules that affect daily lives in many ways and, as a result, administrative law is an important method for controlling behavior. In some instances, it may be more effective than criminal law.

DISCRETION AND CRIMINAL LAW

A key concept in U.S. criminal justice systems is **discretion**. As noted in Focus 1.1, criminal justice systems permit wide discretion, leaving public officials and others the freedom to make independent judgments concerning the disposition of cases. This discretion is the subject of debate, much of which focuses on police discretion to stop, question, search, or arrest a person or seize property or judicial discretion to sentence. But it also involves decisions regarding the definitions and classifications of acts that are covered by criminal statutes, constitutions, and administrative regulations.

Focus 1.1

Discretion and Criminal Law

These criminal justice officials . . .	. . . must often decide whether or not or how to:
Police	• Enforce specific laws • Investigate specific crimes • Search people, vicinities, buildings • Arrest or detain people
Prosecutors	• File charges or petitions for adjudication • Seek indictments • Drop cases • Reduce charges
Judges or magistrates	• Set bail or conditions for release • Accept pleas • Determine delinquency • Dismiss charges • Impose sentences • Revoke probation
Correctional officials	• Assign to type of correctional facility • Award privileges
Paroling authority	• Revoke parole

SOURCE: Bureau of Justice Statistics, *Report to the Nation on Crime and Justice,* 2nd ed. (Washington, D.C.: U.S. Department of Justice, 1988), p. 59.

One type of discretion that is often overlooked but is of particular significance to an understanding of criminal law is *prosecutorial discretion.* The **prosecutor** (or **prosecuting attorney**) is an attorney who represents the state (or federal government, in which case he or she is called a *U.S. attorney*) in a criminal case, in contrast to the **defense attorney**, who represents the accused. After police arrest a suspect, the prosecutor makes the initial decision of whether to pursue the case.

The decision of whether to prosecute is a powerful one for which criminal justice systems provide few checks. When the prosecutor decides to pursue a case, he or she has broad discretion in deciding the offense (or offenses) with which to charge the accused. For example, a person arrested for rape might be charged with rape, aggravated assault and battery, or a lesser sexual offense. The prosecutor may make this decision for one or more legitimate reasons, such as insufficient evidence, the refusal of an alleged victim to cooperate, insufficient resources within the system to devote to a long trial, societal interests, or the welfare of the accused. Some decisions may be made for reasons, such as race or gender, that the law does not permit.

In some cases, prosecutorial charging decisions may be appropriate in terms of the evidence but for other reasons may not lead to a guilty verdict. For example, in Florida in 2011, after Casey Anthony was acquitted in the death of her young daughter Caylee, some legal critics blamed the prosecution for charging her with capital murder, a decision made by the state's attorney general. It was argued that the jury was unlikely to convict Anthony of that most serious charge but might have found her guilty of a lesser charge. The discretion to make the charging decision is obviously immense, and there are few checks on this power.

Discretion also exists in the *classification* of crimes, both in deciding which classifications to use and in how to categorize crimes within those classifications.

CLASSIFICATION OF CRIMES AND RELATED OFFENSES

Before looking at the various classifications of crimes and related offenses, it is necessary to define **crime**. Simply stated, a *crime* is the commission of an act prohibited by criminal law or the failure to act as required by criminal law.

Two basic principles of U.S. criminal justice systems are relevant to an understanding of the definition of crime. The first is that the government may not punish unless there is a *law* (statutory or common) providing that an act (or a failure to act) is a crime. The second is that there is no crime without punishment. This does not mean that a state or the federal government may not decline to prosecute or refuse to punish when a person is found guilty. Rather, it means that unless the state (or the federal government) has defined an act or omission as a crime and has provided a **sanction**, or penalty (or a range of penalties), punishment may not be inflicted just because the act is considered to be harmful to society.

Crimes may be classified in several ways. The most common classification is by the degree of seriousness of the offense.

Grade of Offense

Most criminal codes distinguish between a **misdemeanor**, a less serious crime, and a **felony**, a more serious crime. The distinction was very important under early English common law, which held most felonies punishable by death. Today, in general, felonies are crimes for which offenders may be sentenced to death or imprisoned for a long period, whereas misdemeanors are offenses punishable by fines, work, probation, community service, or short-term incarceration, usually in a jail rather than a state or federal prison. Some statutes add a third category—*petty misdemeanors* or *petty offenses*. Statutes also use the terms *violation* or *infraction* to refer to less serious acts, such as traffic offenses.

In addition to determining punishment, the distinction between felonies and misdemeanors (and petty offenses, where they are classified separately) may determine the court in which the case is heard. The distinction may also have a bearing on the procedures that must be followed in criminal proceedings. Arrest rules may vary, and civil penalties that follow convictions may differ. For example, an offender might lose the right to vote upon conviction of a felony but not upon conviction of a misdemeanor.

Finally, the impact of discretion may be seen in the classification of crimes by seriousness. An act that is viewed as a felony in one state may be classified as a misdemeanor in another. Or an act that is classified as a misdemeanor the first time a person is convicted of that offense may be treated as a felony for subsequent convictions of the same offense.

Moral Turpitude

Crimes may also be classified in terms of moral turpitude, which refers to acts that are base, vile, and immoral. The distinction between crimes that do and those that do not involve moral turpitude is important. Conviction of a crime of moral turpitude may result in the disbarment of a lawyer, the revocation of a doctor's license, the dismissal of a tenured professor, or the deportation of an alien. It may also result in enhanced penalties. In many instances, however, it is difficult to define which acts are included among moral turpitude crimes if that phrase is not defined in the statute, as is frequently the case.

THE LIMITATIONS ON CRIMINAL LAW

Congress and state legislatures are limited in what they may do to define acts as criminal; similarly, courts are limited in their enforcement of criminal law. Many of the limitations are matters of criminal procedure and therefore not covered in this text, but understanding some procedural limitations is necessary for comprehending criminal law.

Void for Vagueness and Overbreadth

U.S. criminal justice systems require that a statute must be declared void if it is vague or too broad. *Vague* means that the statute does not provide sufficient understanding for a person to know what is forbidden or required. A 1926 U.S. Supreme Court decision defined *void for vagueness* as occurring when a law is defined in such terms that people "of common intelligence must necessarily guess at its meaning and differ as to its application."[3]

A law must also be stated narrowly, including only those acts that the government has a right to control. But laws cannot specify every possible circumstance. Laws must, of necessity, be broadly worded, but, according to the U.S. Supreme Court, laws must be drafted so that they focus on the *specific* behaviors to be restricted or prohibited. A law must not "sweep within its ambit other activities that constitute an exercise" of protected rights.[4] For example, some acts, such as viewing pornography, are permitted for adults (as long as the materials do not involve children) but not for minors. A statute designed to prevent minors from securing pornography should be declared void if it is worded so broadly that, in effect, it makes it difficult or impossible for an adult to obtain legally permitted pornographic materials.

Ex Post Facto Laws and Bills of Attainder

The U.S. Constitution provides that "no bill of attainder or *ex post facto* law shall be passed."[5] The U.S. Supreme Court has defined an ***ex post facto* law** as one that "retroactively alter[s] the definition of crimes or increase[s] the punishment for criminal acts."[6] The *ex post facto* doctrine is interpreted to mean that although a state may change its statutes or regulations to benefit a specific person, it may not do so to impose punishment that did not exist at the time an act was committed or to increase the punishment for that act.

In addition to forbidding *ex post facto* laws, the U.S. Constitution prohibits bills of attainder. In 1876, the U.S. Supreme Court defined **bill of attainder** as a "legislative act which inflicts punishment without a judicial trial." Originally, the term referred only to the death penalty, and a bill of attainder involving lesser penalties was called a *bill of pains and penalties*.[7]

The prohibition against a bill of attainder does not mean that the government may not enact a statute with regard to the behavior of a particular person. To illustrate, in 1977, a statute providing for governmental custody of President Richard Nixon's presidential papers was upheld. The statute dealt with the preservation of those materials and was not considered by the U.S. Supreme Court to be punitive. Although Nixon was an identifiable person, the statute did not constitute a bill of attainder.[8]

Repeal or Amendment of a Statute

Another issue arises when a statute is repealed or amended after the accused committed the act but before he or she is tried, raising the issue of whether the suspect may be tried for the offense specified in that statute. Under common law, the accused could not be tried unless the repeal or amendment had a "saving" provision that implied a legislative intent not to eliminate prosecutions of previous offenses. The rule applied to cases in which prosecutions had begun but had not been completed and to cases not yet begun. Prosecutions could continue or start, however, if the new statute or amendment contained a provision that had essentially all the elements of the former statute. For example, a new statute that required the same elements for first-degree sexual assault as those required for a prior rape statute would not preclude prosecution of a defendant charged under the rape statute.[9]

Cruel and Unusual Punishment

The Eighth Amendment of the U.S. Constitution (see Appendix A) prohibits the imposition of **cruel and unusual punishment**, but there is little agreement on the meaning of this phrase. The U.S. Supreme Court has interpreted it in numerous cases, particularly those involving capital punishment. Although some justices disagree, the Court has not declared capital punishment per se to be cruel and unusual, but it may be held to be unconstitutional if the penalty is not proportional to the crime for which it is imposed.[10] For example, the Supreme Court has ruled that capital punishment for rape (but not murder) is not proportional and thus constitutes cruel and unusual punishment. The Court's 1977 ruling on this issue involving an adult female victim was extended in 2008 to include the rape but not murder of a child.[11]

In addition to proportionality, there are other situations to which the prohibition against cruel and unusual punishment might apply. For example, a punishment that tortures or inflicts unnecessary pain is not permitted.

Due Process and Equal Protection

The U.S. Constitution prohibits the federal government (in the Fifth Amendment) and the states (in the Fourteenth Amendment) from depriving persons of life, liberty, or property without **due process** and **equal protection** of the law (see Appendix A). Many cases have been decided by lower courts and by the U.S. Supreme Court in attempts to define these concepts. That body of case law cannot be reviewed here, but a definition and brief interpretation of each term are important.

Due process means that statutes may not be defined or enforced in an unreasonable, capricious, or arbitrary manner. People charged with crimes have a right to be notified, to be heard, and to defend themselves against the charges. Due process refers to other constitutional guarantees before, during, and after a criminal trial. The particulars of the concept may vary from case to case.

Equal protection means that no person or class of persons may be denied the same protection of law that is provided to other persons or classes of persons. The litigation in this area is extensive and frequently arises with respect to race and gender.

The Right of Privacy

The right to privacy is not specified by the U.S. Constitution, although some state constitutions recognize the right specifically. The federal right to privacy was articulated by the U.S. Supreme Court in a 1965 decision in a case that involved the convictions of persons found guilty and fined for violating the Connecticut statute that prohibited the counseling for, sale of, or use of contraceptives. The U.S. Supreme Court held that the statute interfered with the intimate relationships between married persons as well as their relationships with their physicians. The Court held that specific guarantees in the Bill of Rights "have penumbras, formed by emanations from those guarantees that help give them life and substance." The case established a right to privacy that has not only survived but has been enlarged by subsequent U.S. Supreme Court decisions, as further discussions in this text demonstrate.[12]

Other Constitutional Limitations

Criminal laws exist within the framework of other constitutional rights, such as freedom of religion, freedom of speech and the press, the right to assemble peacefully, the right to petition the government for redress, freedom from unreasonable searches and seizures, freedom from compulsory self-incrimination, and numerous rights that defendants have at trial, such as the right to counsel, and the right not to testify against themselves. Any or all of these and other rights may become important in passing and enforcing a criminal statute, and some are demonstrated throughout this text. Courts interpret constitutional rights, and thus, it is important to look at this component of U.S. criminal justice systems.

THE NATURE AND PURPOSE OF U.S. COURT SYSTEMS

The U.S. Constitution provides for three branches of government: executive, legislative, and judicial. All are important for purposes of this text, but the emphasis is on the judicial branch, for that branch has the power of **judicial review**, meaning that appellate courts may interpret the acts and events that occur in the other two branches as well as in lower courts.[13]

The highest court of each state is the final determiner of the constitutionality of ordinances and statutes under that state's constitution and procedural rules; the U.S. Supreme Court is the final determiner of whether the decisions of any lower federal courts violate the U.S. Constitution, federal procedures, and federal statutes. States' rights are considered very important, and the U.S. Constitution provides that the powers that are not delegated to the federal government are reserved for the states. In fact, most crimes are violations of state, not federal, laws (although in recent years Congress has included more crimes within the federal system); consequently, most criminal trials occur in state courts.

The state and the federal court systems are separate systems, but a state statute may not violate the federal Constitution. Statutes that are thought to do so may be appealed to the U.S. Supreme Court.

The Dual Court System

To simplify this discussion, Figure 1.1 provides a simple diagram of this **dual court system**. Note that on the left side of Figure 1.1 the levels of federal courts are listed. In the federal system, cases may move from the lowest level, the U.S. magistrates (judges who are appointed by the district courts to hear some cases) to the district courts. These are the trial courts in the federal system, and most federal cases begin there. Decisions of the district courts may be reviewed by the appropriate circuit court of appeal; those decisions may be heard by the highest court, the U.S. Supreme Court. The state courts are diagramed on the right side of Figure 1.1 and are explained in greater detail in Table 1.1.

Some important concepts should be defined at this point. The lawful right of the legislative, executive, or judicial branch to exercise official authority is called **jurisdiction**. Jurisdiction may be limited by geographical areas or by other classifications, such as subject matter or crime categories. For example, some courts may hear and decide only misdemeanor cases; others may decide only felony cases. Courts may be empowered to decide certain types of cases, such as criminal or civil, domestic or probate (wills and estates), adult or juvenile, and so on. Some courts are trial courts exclusively; others are appellate only. State courts may not decide federal court cases and vice versa. State court decisions may be appealed to the U.S. Supreme Court if a *federal* constitutional or statutory issue is involved.

A court may have *original jurisdiction* (the court that has the power to hear the case first) or more than one court may have *concurrent jurisdiction* (both have the power to try the case). Some courts have only *appellate jurisdiction*, and those courts hear cases that are on **appeal** from other courts. A state court decision may not be appealed to a court in another state. State courts may hear only cases

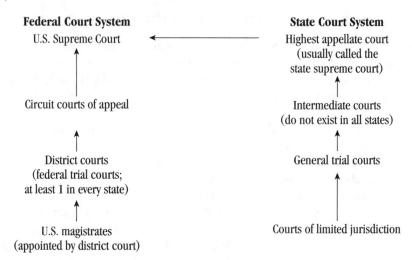

Federal Court System

U.S. Supreme Court

Circuit courts of appeal

District courts
(federal trial courts;
at least 1 in every state)

U.S. magistrates
(appointed by district court)

State Court System

Highest appellate court
(usually called the
state supreme court)

Intermediate courts
(do not exist in all states)

General trial courts

Courts of limited jurisdiction

FIGURE 1.1 **Diagram of the U.S. Dual Court Systems**
Note: The arrows designate the ways in which cases may be appealed to a higher level.
SOURCE: Sue Titus Reid, *Criminal Justice Essentials*, 9th ed. (Boston: Wiley-Blackwell, 2012), p. 202.

involving issues arising from statutes or ordinances within that state, and likewise the federal system with the exception noted. There are some exceptions in civil areas, but they are not of concern in this text. An act may violate both state and federal law, giving both the state and the federal court jurisdiction.

Trial and Appellate Courts

In a criminal case, trial courts hear the facts of a case, and either a judge or a jury determines the ultimate fact: the defendant's guilt or innocence. Trial courts also assess the penalties for defendants who are convicted or who plead guilty. Prior to trial, judges make other decisions, such as whether to grant bail. Trial judges deny or grant motions concerning such issues as whether evidence should be admitted or excluded. A defendant who has an adverse ruling by a trial judge may have grounds to appeal that decision to a higher court. At this point the defendant becomes the **appellant**, who argues that the lower court made a mistake that prejudiced the appellant, who now deserves a reversal of the conviction (or a change in the sentence if that is the issue). The prosecution, now the **appellee**, argues that no mistake was made at trial or, if so, it did not prejudice the appellant.

Trial and appellate courts operate primarily under the criminal laws and procedures of their respective jurisdictions, although, as already noted, state statutes may not violate the federal Constitution or federal laws. However, state statutes may (and many do) provide rights *beyond* those provided in the federal Constitution or in federal statutes.

All procedures in U.S. criminal courts relate to the primary purposes of those courts: the determination of whether the accused are guilty and, if so, how they should be sentenced.

Table 1.1 Structure, Jurisdiction, and Function of State Court Systems

Court	Structure	Jurisdiction
Highest state appellate court (usually called the supreme court)	Consists of five, seven, or nine justices, who may be appointed or elected; cases decided by this court may not be appealed to the U.S. Supreme Court unless they involve a federal question, and then there is no right of appeal except in limited cases.	If there is no intermediate appellate court, defendants convicted in a general trial court will have a right of appeal to this court; if there is an intermediate appellate court, this court will have discretion to limit appeals with few exceptions such as in capital cases.
Intermediate appellate court (also called court of appeals; exists in approximately half of the states)	May have one court that hears appeals from all general trial courts or may have more than one court, each with appellate jurisdiction over a particular area of the state; usually has a panel of three judges.	Defendants convicted in general trial court have right of appeal to this level.
General trial courts (also called superior courts, circuit courts, court of common pleas)	Usually state is divided into judicial districts, with one general trial court in each district, often one per county; courts may be divided by function, such as civil, criminal, probate, domestic.	Jurisdiction to try cases usually begins where jurisdiction of lower court ends, so this court tries more serious cases; may have appellate jurisdiction over cases decided in lower courts.
Courts of limited jurisdiction (also called magistrate's courts, police courts, justice of peace courts, municipal courts)	Differs from state to state; some states divide state into districts, with each having the same type of lower court; in other states, courts may be located in political subdivisions, such as cities or townships, in which case the structure may differ from court to court; may not be a court of record, in which case the system will permit trial de novo in general trial court; particularly in rural areas, magistrates may not be lawyers and may work only part-time	May be limited to specific proceedings, such as initial appearance, preliminary hearing, issuing search and arrest warrants, setting bail, appointing counsel for indigent defendants; jurisdiction of cases is limited to certain types, usually the lesser criminal and civil cases; some jurisdictions may hear all misdemeanors—others are limited to misdemeanors with minor penalties.

SOURCE: Sue Titus Reid, *Criminal Justice Essentials*, 9th ed. (Boston: Wiley-Blackwell, 2012), p. 203.

THE ESTABLISHMENT OF GUILT

Although much of the law applying to the establishment of guilt in a criminal case is procedural and thus not the subject matter of this text, some points must be covered for an adequate understanding of criminal law. The next section considers the basis of U.S. criminal justice systems, its adversary nature, and how that differs from other systems.

The Adversary System

U.S. criminal justice systems are adversarial rather than inquisitorial. In the **inquisitorial system,** defendants are presumed guilty and must prove their innocence. In the **adversary system**, the prosecutor (representing the state and the victim) and the defense counsel (representing the defendant) oppose each other in a trial if they are unable or unwilling to dispose of the case prior to a trial, and the defendant is presumed innocent. The state must prove guilt, and that is a heavy burden because of the standard of proof required in a criminal case, as noted in the next section.

The Burden of Proof

In a trial, one party has the **burden of proof** on certain issues. In a civil case, the person who brings the action must prove his or her case, usually by the standard of a *preponderance of the evidence*. In a criminal trial, the prosecution brings the case and must prove all of the elements of the charges **beyond a reasonable doubt**.[14] In some instances the defendant in a criminal case may have a burden of proof, although that never applies to any of the legal elements of the offense charged. For example, in some jurisdictions the defendant may be required to sustain the burden of proof for an **affirmative defense** (defenses are discussed in Chapter 4 of this text), but generally, the standard of proof for those defenses will be by a preponderance of the evidence, rather than the more stringent standard of beyond a reasonable doubt.

The standard of beyond a reasonable doubt is illustrated by a hypothetical offered by a trial attorney. The details are provided in Focus 1.2.

Determining Criminal Culpability: The Judge and the Jury

In a criminal case, the determination of whether the defendant is guilty is a question of fact to be made by the jury (or by the judge if the case is not tried before a jury).

This chapter noted previously that considerable discretion exists within criminal justice systems. The roles of the trial judge and the jury illustrate this discretion. If the trial judge believes that the prosecution has not proved its case beyond a reasonable doubt, he or she may grant a defense motion for the judge to enter a verdict of not guilty. The judge has wide discretion in this and other decisions at the trial stage. In addition, during the proceeding or after all evidence is presented, the judge may dismiss the case for lack of evidence.

If procedural rules are violated; if the jury is unable to reach a verdict; if inadmissible evidence is introduced; if jurors, attorneys, or others in the courtroom misbehave or any of the participants in the trial become ill or cannot attend; or if any number of other reasons occur, the judge may declare a **mistrial**, which is an incomplete trial. After a mistrial, the case may be tried again before another jury (or judge), or the charges may be dismissed.

Focus 1.2

Beyond a Reasonable Doubt: An Example

A noted law professor, Jim McElhaney, published an article about reasonable doubt. In that article, he quoted the following example originally presented by another lawyer. The facts pertain to an effort to establish reasonable doubt in the minds of jurors when there is only circumstantial evidence.

> Suppose that you take a mouse and put him in a box. Now take a cat and put him in the box with the mouse. Then take the lid and cover the box. Now tie up the box with string so the lid can't come off.
>
> Leave the room for half an hour. When you come back, untie the string, take off the lid and look inside. There is no mouse, but there is one happy cat.
>
> Do you know what happened? You weren't there, there are no eyewitnesses. All you have is circumstantial evidence. But you know beyond any reasonable doubt what happened to that mouse.
>
> Let's do it again. Put the mouse in the box. Put the cat in the box with the mouse. Put on the lid. Tie it down. Leave the room for half an hour. Come back into the room. Untie the string. Take off the lid and look inside.
>
> There is the cat. No mouse.
>
> But look—there in the corner of the box. There is a hole, just big enough for a mouse.
>
> That hole is reasonable doubt. Now let's look at the holes in the prosecution's case.

In recounting the story, McElhaney concludes, "Then by implication, every problem in the government's case is not just a hole; it is a reasonable doubt."

source: Jim McElhaney, "The Burden of Reasonable Doubt," *American Bar Association Journal* 97 (October 2011): 22–23; quotation is on p. 23. McElhaney is referring to the words of the late Peter M. deManio of Sarasota, Florida. Reprinted with the permission of the American Bar Association.

Even if there are no procedural problems and the evidence suggests guilt beyond a reasonable doubt, the jury may refuse to return a guilty verdict—a process called **jury nullification**. Many people were upset by the verdict in the Casey Anthony case, mentioned earlier, as they thought the evidence was sufficient to establish the murder of her child beyond a reasonable doubt. But the jury found otherwise and acquitted the defendant of that charge, and the jury has that power.

Jury nullification often occurs in cases that involve **mercy killings**, in which an individual takes the life of one who asks for death as possibly the only relief from pain. The law does not permit such actions, but even if all of the elements of murder are proven beyond a reasonable doubt, many juries do not convict defendants in such cases. Finally, juries also often decline to convict defendants who kill persons (such as a parent or a spouse) who have allegedly battered them for a long period of time.

The critical question is whether juries have a *right* to ignore evidence or whether it is just a reality that they might do so. Their deliberations are secret; so theoretically we would never know why they reached their conclusions. Still, many jurisdictions recognize jury nullification, although few, if any, judges inform juries of their right to nullify.

HOW TO READ AND INTERPRET AN APPELLATE OPINION

Law is based on the reading and interpreting of appellate opinions written in decided cases and applying new fact patterns to the holding and reasoning of those cases. Appendix B details how to read a court citation, and this discussion presents some general points to consider in reading and analyzing an appellate opinion.

To begin, consider some terminology that is crucial to reading legal opinions. First is the principal of **stare decisis**, which literally means "let the decision stand." *Stare decisis* means that although the law must be flexible and change with the times, it must also be stable and predictable, and courts are reluctant to make changes. Thus, appellate opinions make frequent references to other cases, or *precedent cases*, although in this text some of those references and footnotes have been deleted to simplify the opinions.

Second, the decision of an appellate court is usually announced and explained in the majority opinion, but some of the justices who voted with the majority may write their own opinions. Those who dissent from the majority vote may also write opinions. Justices may write opinions that agree with some points of other opinions in the case while disagreeing with other opinions or points within specific opinions. In reading these opinions, it is critical to distinguish between the *rule of law* or the *holding* of the case—that is, the actual decision based on the facts of the case—and the *dicta*, or comments, that the judges might make verbally or in writing but that are not part of the actual holding of the case. In their written opinions, judges and justices may make comments that represent their own views and have little or nothing to do with the holding of the case. Those comments do not constitute the law of the case, although they may be meaningful to interpreting future cases.

Another important concept is *legal reasoning*, which means that lawyers read the facts of decided cases and present the facts of undecided cases in light of those decisions—arguing that the law as decided either does or does not apply to the new fact pattern. The facts are crucial, for technically, a court decision applies only to the facts of that case.

Consider this example. Recall the previous discussion of the Connecticut contraception case. The persons who received contraceptives in that case were married. A subsequent challenge heard by the U.S. Supreme Court and decided in 1972[15] arose under a Massachusetts statute that provided a five-year prison term for anyone who gave away "any drug, medicine, instrument or article whatever for the prevention of conception." Excluded from the statute were registered physicians, who were permitted to "administer to or prescribe for any married person drugs or articles intended for the prevention of pregnancy or conception."[16] Registered pharmacists who were actually engaged in the pharmacy business were permitted under the law to fill those prescriptions, but they could not do so for single persons. Married persons could get the contraceptives even if their purpose in securing them was to engage in illicit sexual relations. The U.S. Supreme Court held that the privacy right for married persons, articulated in 1965, also applies to single persons. As subsequent discussions in this text show, the U.S. Supreme Court later extended the right of privacy beyond these cases. The contraceptive cases also illustrate that the law evolves over time—in some instances, such as the right to counsel, discussed in Focus 1.3, over many years.

Focus 1.3

The Evolution of the Right to Counsel

The right to counsel, a critical right of defendants, is specified in the Sixth Amendment to the U.S. Constitution (see Appendix A), which states, "In all criminal prosecutions, the accused shall enjoy the right . . . to have the Assistance of Counsel for his defense." This right has been litigated frequently, but a brief look at a few key cases decided by the U.S. Supreme Court emphasizes the long period of time over which the right evolved through judicial decisions. This discussion also demonstrates the issue, discussed in the text, of the importance of reading cases carefully.

Throughout most of our history, the Sixth Amendment right to counsel meant that counsel was permitted only if a defendant could afford to retain an attorney. In 1932, the U.S. Supreme Court upheld the right to appointed (paid for by the government) counsel.[1] The case involved three Scottsboro, Alabama, African American male youths (among others), who were accused of raping two young white women. The situation was volatile, and the state militia was ordered in to protect the defendants. The judge appointed the entire Scottsboro bar to represent the youths at their arraignments and later stated that he assumed some of those counsel would represent the defendants, who entered not guilty pleas, at their trials, each of which was completed in only one day. There was no record of any attorneys appointed to represent these young defendants. All were convicted. Alabama law required that the jury assessed the penalty, which could range from 10 years to death; they imposed death in each case. These decisions were affirmed on first appeal. The U.S. Supreme Court considered only one of the issues appealed: whether the appellants had counsel, and if not, whether they were denied due process.

The U.S. Supreme Court recognized the "special circumstances" of this case: the youth, illiteracy, and low mentality of all the defendants. The Court considered these circumstances and the seriousness of the crime in question and held that the state had a duty to appoint effective assistance of counsel. Ten years later, the U.S. Supreme Court refused to extend the right to appointed counsel to an adult defendant who was intelligent and had an

(Continued)

Focus 1.3 (*Continued*)

average education. According to the Court, the fact that the defendant was indigent was not sufficient to warrant appointed counsel.[2]

In 1963, the U.S. Supreme Court held that the right to appointed counsel extended to all felony cases. The defendant, Clarence Earle Gideon, who was charged with a felony in Florida, had maintained that he was entitled to appointed counsel despite Florida's statute, which extended that right only in death penalty cases. The Court's opinion noted that in criminal cases, lawyers are not luxuries but necessities, overruled its prior case, and extended the right to appointed counsel to all felony cases in which the defendant is indigent.[3]

Subsequently, the right to appointed counsel was extended beyond felony cases, and the U.S. Supreme Court decided several cases concerning the right to effective assistance of counsel, along with numerous decisions involving when and under what circumstances the right to counsel attaches.

[1]*Powell v. Alabama,* 287 U.S. 45 (1932).
[2]*Betts v. Brady,* 316 U.S. 455 (1942), overruled by *Gideon v. Wainwright,* 372 U.S. 335 (1963).
[3]*Gideon v. Wainwright,* 372 U.S. 335 (1963).

SUMMARY

This chapter provided a brief overview of criminal law. In earlier times, when societies were less complex and everyone knew everyone else, human behavior could be controlled by informal means. Even the criminal law permitted people to engage in private retribution, which usually was a successful method for apprehending and punishing those who did not behave within the norms. As societies grew and became more complex, informal controls were replaced with a formal system of state action; in criminal law, private retribution was replaced by government retribution.

A brief general distinction between civil and criminal law was followed by a more extensive discussion of the nature and purpose of criminal law. Legal punishment is a serious intrusion into private lives; thus, the state needs reasonable justifications for its imposition. The reasons for criminal punishment—retribution, incapacitation, deterrence, and rehabilitation (or reformation)—were viewed historically and discussed as the basis for punitive government action against criminal offenders.

Another issue in criminal law is the difficult question of which acts to include as crimes. Courts and legislators continue to debate the issue of whether certain types of behavior—such as private sexual behavior between consenting adults or the use and abuse of alcohol and other drugs—should be criminal. This chapter looked at the historical basis for the inclusion of morality within the criminal law and raised the general question of how extensive the criminal law should be. Subsequent chapters look in more detail at particular areas of concern.

The chapter then looked at the Model Penal Code, its meaning, and its impact on criminal law in the United States. English common law, which has also been influential in the development of modern U.S. criminal law, was noted and discussed.

Law comes from several sources, and brief attention was given to them: statutory law, judicial decisions and customs, constitutions, and administrative law. Because the processing of criminal law involves wide discretion, the chapter discussed the importance of discretion in U.S. criminal justice systems and focused on the extent and nature of prosecutorial discretion. Such discretion cannot and should not be eliminated, but more attention should be given to judicial review of it.

Crimes are classified in several ways; the distinctions are not always agreed on, but they are important for several reasons. The categories of felony and misdemeanor; crimes that are evil intrinsically compared to acts that are crimes primarily because they are defined as such; crimes of moral turpitude and infamous crimes; and acts, such as those committed by juveniles, that are processed in separate hearings, are important in determining procedures that must be followed and in assessing punishment.

An important discussion in this chapter focused on some of the constitutional limitations on criminal law in the United States. Statutes that are vague or too broad may not be enforced against the accused. Suspects may not be convicted for acts that were not defined as crimes when they were committed. Nor is it permissible to pass statutes aimed at criminal punishment for particular categories of persons to the exclusion of others; categories such as race, ethnicity, and gender are examples. In addition, attention must be paid to statutes that have been repealed or amended and the circumstances, if any, under which people may be prosecuted in these instances.

A criminal statute may not impose cruel and unusual punishment or punishment that is considered excessive in comparison to the crime for which it is imposed. In both substantive and procedural criminal law, due process and equal protection of the law must be observed. Other constitutional rights—such as the right to privacy, the right to free speech, and freedom of religion—may give way to criminal prosecutions in instances that endanger the public welfare.

To set the stage for future discussions, this chapter included an overview of courts and their functions, noting in particular the dual court nature of U.S. criminal justice systems. Trial and appellate courts were distinguished. The establishment of guilt in an adversary system was analyzed. In U.S. criminal justice systems, the accused does not have to prove innocence; rather, the prosecution is required to prove all elements of the charges beyond a reasonable doubt. Unless that is done, the defendant should not be convicted. Even when that burden of proof is met by the prosecution, the defendant may be entitled to an acquittal if the defense provides proof by a preponderance of the evidence that he or she had an adequate defense in the commission of the alleged crime.

Even if the prosecutor presents sufficient proof of all of the elements of a crime, U.S. criminal justice systems permit a jury (or a judge if the case is not tried before a jury) to decide against criminal culpability.

The chapter closed with a brief overview of how to read and interpret an appellate opinion.

Chapter 2 focuses in greater detail on the elements of a crime.

STUDY QUESTIONS

1. Why do we have a formal system of criminal law, and what are its advantages and disadvantages when compared with an informal system?
2. Distinguish civil law from criminal law.
3. Have criminal justice systems progressed or regressed by deemphasizing rehabilitation? Why or why not? Is retribution a reasonable justification for imposing criminal law? If not, why not? If so, how far would you carry the concept?
4. Distinguish crimes that are evil in themselves from those that are considered evil primarily because the law defines them as such.
5. What is the importance of the Model Penal Code (MPC)?
6. Define *English common law*, and discuss its importance in U.S. criminal law systems.
7. Explain the meaning and importance of case law, statutory law, and procedural law.
8. What is administrative law, and why is it important to a study of criminal law?
9. Articulate a plan for curbing prosecutorial discretion, and explain why your plan is a good one.
10. Why is it important to classify crimes, and in what ways may that be done?
11. Why do U.S. criminal justice systems provide that a statute is void if it is vague or too broad?
12. Distinguish between an *ex post facto* law and a *bill of attainder*.
13. Do you think capital punishment is cruel and unusual? Would your answer differ if you were comparing adults and juveniles?
14. Explain due process and equal protection.
15. What is the basis for a right to privacy?
16. What is meant by this statement: "The United States has dual court systems"?
17. Distinguish between trial and appellate courts.
18. Distinguish the adversary and the inquisitorial systems.
19. What do you understand the phrase *beyond a reasonable doubt* to mean?
20. If you were a criminal defendant, would you prefer to have your case decided by a judge or a jury? Give reasons for your answer.
21. What is meant by the holding or the rule of law of a case?
22. Define *legal reasoning*, and explain the importance of the facts to the interpretation of a court decision.
23. Summarize the evolution of the right to appointed counsel in felony cases.

FOR DEBATE

This chapter discussed various ways to attempt to control behavior. This text is about criminal law, but that law may not always be the most efficient, just, or reasonable way to approach a problem. This group debate topic should foster a lively discussion on the use of criminal law to control behavior.

RESOLVED: Criminal law, compared to administrative law and civil law, is a more effective way to control the following behaviors:

a. Gambling
b. Prostitution
c. The use of marijuana
d. Wearing seatbelts
e. Wearing helmets while motorcycling or bicycling
f. The use of cocaine
g. Consensual, private sex between adults
h. Language

KEY TERMS

administrative law   7
adversary system   16
affirmative defense   16
appeal   13
appellant   14
appellee   14
beyond a reasonable doubt   16
bill of attainder   11
burden of proof   16
case law   7
civil law   3
codified   6
common law   5
crime   9
criminal law   3
cruel and unusual punishment   11
defense attorney   8
deterrence   4
discretion   7
dual court system   13
due process   12

equal protection   12
ex post facto law   10
felony   9
incapacitation   4
inquisitorial system   16
judicial review   13
jurisdiction   13
jury nullification   17
mala in se   5
mala prohibita   5
mercy killings   17
misdemeanor   9
mistrial   16
Model Penal Code (MPC)   5
procedural law   6
prosecutor or prosecuting attorney   8
rehabilitation   4
retribution   4
sanction   9
stare decisis   18
statutory law   6
substantive law   6

INTERNET ACTIVITY

1. Go on line to FindLaw, http://caselaw.lp.findlaw.com (accessed 7 May 2012) and check to see what you can find out about the *void-for-vagueness* doctrine, due process and equal protection; and the right of privacy.
2. Check out http://www.uscourts.gov/ (accessed 7 May 2012) and locate your region on the U.S. map. Name the states that are included within your federal circuit court of appeals. What can you find out about the U.S. Supreme Court from this site?

NOTES

1. See the Sentence Reform Act of 1984, USCS, Title 18, Section 3551 *et seq.*; and USCS, Title 287, Sections 991-998 (2012).
2. Oliver W. Holmes Jr., *The Common Law* (Boston: Little, Brown, 1881), pp. 1–2.
3. *Connally v. General Construction Co.*, 269 U.S. 385 (1926).
4. *Thornhill v. Alabama*, 310 U.S. 88, 97 (1940).
5. U.S. Constitution, Article I, Section 9(3).
6. *Collins v. Youngblood*, 497 U.S. 37 (1990).
7. *Cummings v. Missouri*, 71 U.S. (4 Wall.) 277 (1867).
8. *Nixon v. Administrator of General Services*, 433 U.S. 425 (1977).
9. See, for example, *State v. Babbitt*, 457 A.2d 1049 (R.I. 1983).
10. See *Weems v. United States*, 217 U.S. 349 (1910).
11. See *Coker v. Georgia*, 433 U.S. 584 (1977); *State v. Kennedy*, 554 U.S. 407 (2008).
12. The case was *Griswold v. Connecticut*, 381 U.S. 479 (1965). The statute was Conn. Gen. Stats., Sections 53-32 and 54-196 (1965).
13. The power of judicial review was established by the U.S. Supreme Court in the case of *Marbury v. Madison*, 1 Cranch 137 (1803).
14. *In re Winship*, 397 U.S. 358, 363–364 (1970).
15. *Baird v. Eisenstadt*, 405 U.S. 438 (1972).
16. Mass. Gen. Laws Ann., Chapter 272, Section 21 (1972).

CHAPTER 2

Elements of a Crime

INTRODUCTION

This chapter discusses the **elements of a crime** that are applicable to criminal acts in U.S. criminal justice systems. Subsequent chapters consider the elements of specific crimes.

THE ELEMENTS OF A CRIME

In general, for an act to be a crime in U.S. criminal justice systems, four elements must be present:

1. A criminal act
2. A criminal state of mind
3. Concurrence of a criminal act and a criminal state of mind
4. Causation

The four general elements of a crime are diagrammed in Figure 2.1.

A Criminal Act

Although it may appear simplistic to state that a crime involves a criminal act, the matter is complex. The term *criminal act*, or **actus reus**, is open to interpretation. Technically, it means a wrongful deed that, if combined with the other elements of a crime, may result in the legal arrest, trial, conviction, and punishment of the accused. But what constitutes an act? Some scholars and statutes include involuntary acts, but most require a *voluntary* act.

The Exclusion of Involuntary Conduct

Although it is true that involuntary actions may, and often do, affect the health and welfare of others, these acts are usually not considered criminal but may result in *civil* liability. The concept of *criminal* **culpability** is illustrated by cases involving defendants who claimed that they were sleepwalking when they committed the alleged criminal acts for which they were charged. Two such cases are summarized in Focus 2.1.

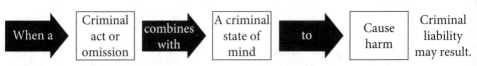

FIGURE 2.1 Elements of a Crime
Note: Some crimes also require the proof of attendant circumstances as one or more of the elements of the crime.

Proof of an Act

It is not always easy to determine the difference between a voluntary act and an involuntary act. Likewise, it may be difficult to prove that an act occurred even when it did. Despite this difficulty, there must be sufficient evidence to prove, beyond a reasonable doubt, the existence of a criminal act, along with all of the required elements of that act.

Focus 2.1

Acts Committed by Sleepwalkers: Excusable or Criminal?

One of the elements of a crime is that the defendant must have engaged in a voluntary act. Involuntary acts are excluded, but experts disagree on the meaning of the terms. For example, should a defendant be responsible for an otherwise criminal act committed while he or she is sleepwalking? U.S. Supreme Court Justice Clarence Thomas referred to the hypothetical case of a sleepwalker who took money forcefully as behavior that should be considered "innocent, if aberrant activity."[1] Consider the following actual cases.

The issue of whether sleepwalking is a defense to a criminal act was raised successfully by a defendant who was acquitted of sexual assault and attempted aggravated sexual assault against a seven-year-old sleeping girl. The acts allegedly occurred while Richard Overton, 43, was sleepwalking. Overton testified that he was a chronic sleepwalker and that he did not recall anything about the alleged crimes. His testimony was bolstered by that of a sleep disorders expert, who claimed that Overton may have been unconscious when the alleged acts occurred. Overton was, however, convicted of child endangerment and child abuse.[2]

In June 2002, Adam Kieczykowski, 19, was acquitted of charges resulting from his actions on Spring Fling weekend at the University of Massachusetts at Amherst in May 2001. The defendant testified that his body may have hopped in and out of elevators on 13 floors of a campus dorm but that he did not recall any of the alleged acts, ranging from sexual assault to theft, for which he was charged. The defendant claimed he was sleepwalking, and after only one hour of deliberation, the jury agreed and acquitted Kieczykowski on all 18 charges. Whether the sleepwalking defense was successful, however, might be debated. Some jurors said they decided the case on the basis of the inconsistent testimony of the witnesses. Still, some attorneys hire experts in sleepwalking to testify for the defense in cases in which the information may be admitted as relevant to the defendant's actions at the time of the alleged crime.[3]

[1] *Carter v. United States*, 530 U.S. 255 (2000).
[2] "Sleepwalker Gets Mixed Verdict," *National Law Journal* (1 January 2001), p. 6.
[3] "Jury Acquits 'Sleepwalker' in UMass Sex Assaults," *Boston Globe* (8 July 2002), p. 1B.

Possession as an Act
An act might include possession of illegal goods, such as narcotics, alcohol, or stolen property. Possession is considered an act; however, as with other acts, possession alone may not be sufficient for a successful criminal prosecution. Generally, when a criminal statute defines *possession* as a crime, the word is interpreted to mean *conscious* possession, although there may be some exceptions. Young people may be familiar with the charge of *minor in possession* (MIP) of alcohol or other illegal drugs in an automobile. All occupants of the car may be charged with MIP even though some claim they did not know that the illegal goods were in the vehicle.

Criminal Failure to Act
Omission or failure to act may also constitute an *act* for purposes of criminal culpability, but only when there is a **legal duty** to act, such as the duty imposed on parents to come to the aid of their minor children, on physicians to aid their patients, or any duty imposed by a contract, such as marriage, employment, or custody, or by a statute or ordinance. A legal duty might also exist when a person takes affirmative action that creates a situation of danger to a person to whom no duty was previously owed. The failure to exercise due care in this situation may constitute a **tort**, which literally means a wrong. In law, that wrongful act may result in legal civil liability. Some torts are also crimes.

The fact that under most criminal statutes there is no general affirmative duty to prevent crime is illustrated by the highly publicized case featured in Focus 2.2. The moral outrage at hearing that some people not only watched but cheered during a gang rape in New Bedford, Massachusetts, led some states to consider legislation to criminalize the failure to act to help prevent a crime.

It is important to understand that requiring people to take affirmative action to aid others creates problems, such as how much action should be required and what provisions should be made in the event that a bystander, required by law to act to prevent a crime, is injured or killed by taking preventive action.

A Criminal Intent
To be criminal, an act requires a criminal mind or criminal **intent** (the state of mind referring to the willful commission of an act or the omission of an act one has a legal duty to perform). The legal term for intent, ***mens rea***, means "a guilty mind." The statement that *mens rea* is a required element of a crime, however, is misleading if taken literally. As this chapter notes below, some acts involving fault but unaccompanied by a guilty mind may constitute crimes.

The intent element required for criminal culpability is one of the most difficult to interpret and apply. Historically, intent was divided into *general intent* and *specific intent*. Those concepts, however, are difficult to distinguish. Simply stated, *general intent* refers to the willful commission of an act (or the omission of an act that one has a legal duty to perform); *specific intent* requires more. The

---

Focus 2.2

Should Failure to Report or Stop a Crime Be a Crime?

In the spring of 1983, four men raped a young woman repeatedly in a New Bedford, Massachusetts, bar. They were indicted along with two men who were arrested for encouraging them while holding the woman down on the bar table where the acts occurred. Numerous witnesses observed the gang rape without calling the police, some reportedly yelling, "Go for it." The incident and subsequent trial received considerable media attention. The trial resulted in two acquittals and two convictions.

Public outrage at the New Bedford case led to attempts to enact statutes to require bystanders, under penalty of civil or criminal law, to come to the aid of crime victims. It was argued that, at a minimum, the law should require witnesses to call the police. Some advocates said that the law should require affirmative action to intervene when alleged criminal acts are observed.[1]

The refusal of bystanders to come to the aid of the New Bedford rape victim was reminiscent of the widely publicized 1967 case of Kitty Genovese, whose New York neighbors refused to come to her aid while she was stabbed repeatedly. In discussing these and other cases, criminologist Gilbert Geis stated, "It's becoming a much more anonymous society, a much more uncaring society." Many bystanders do not want to become involved in any way in alleged criminal activity. Even as a witness, a person may be threatened; it is easier to avoid involvement.[2]

Legally the issue is not whether bystanders should go to the aid of others but whether the law should require them to do so.

[1]Summarized by the author from media accounts.
[2]"Silent Crime: Bystanders Who Say, Do Nothing," *Orlando Sentinel* (11 May 1993), p. 5.

---

difference may be illustrated by the common law crime of larceny-theft, one of the four serious property crimes (as recorded by the Federal Bureau of Investigation [FBI]) and the most frequently committed of those crimes. To establish that the defendant committed larceny-theft, the prosecution must prove that the defendant took the property of another *and* intended to carry it away, which implies a general intent to commit the forbidden act.

An additional element of larceny-theft is a specific intent, usually stated as the intent to steal the property. That is, the prosecution must prove that the defendant intended to deprive the owner of the property permanently or for an unreasonable length of time, not just that the property was taken away intentionally. Theoretically, a person could intend to take property away from its lawful owner without intending to steal it.

Some scholars have suggested that because of this confusion, the terms *general intent* and *specific intent* should be abandoned. One solution is illustrated by the Model Penal Code (MPC) provision concerning the general requirements of culpability, which are presented in Focus 2.3. The MPC utilizes four levels of culpability: purposely, knowingly, recklessly, and negligently. It defines each level of intent, ranging from the highest level (purposely) to the lowest (negligently).

Focus 2.3

General Requirements of Culpability

MODEL PENAL CODE, SECTION 2.02

(1) *Minimum Requirements of Culpability.* Except as provided in Section 2.05, a person is not guilty of an offense unless he acted purposely, knowingly, recklessly or negligently, as the law may require, with respect to each material element of the offense.

(2) *Kinds of Culpability Defined.*

  (a) *Purposely.* A person acts purposely with respect to a material element of an offense when:

    (i) if the element involves the nature of his conduct or a result thereof, it is his conscious object to engage in conduct of that nature or to cause such a result; and

    (ii) if the element involves the attendant circumstances, he is aware of the existence of such circumstances or he believes or hopes that they exist.

  (b) *Knowingly.* A person acts knowingly with respect to a material element of an offense when:

    (i) if the element involves the nature of his conduct or the attendant circumstances, he is aware that his conduct is of that nature or that such circumstances exist; and

    (ii) if the element involves the result of his conduct, he is aware that it is practically certain that his conduct will cause such a result.

  (c) *Recklessly.* A person acts recklessly with respect to a material element of an offense when he consciously disregards a substantial and unjustifiable risk that the material element exists or will result from his conduct. The risk must be of such a nature and degree that, considering the nature and purpose of the actor's conduct and the circumstances known to him, its disregard involves a gross deviation from the standard of conduct that a law-abiding person would observe in the actor's situation.

  (d) *Negligently.* A person acts negligently with respect to a material element of an offense when he should be aware of a substantial and unjustifiable risk that the material element exists or will result from his conduct. The risk must be of such a nature and degree that the actor's failure to perceive it, considering the nature and purpose of his conduct and the circumstances known to him, involves a gross deviation from the standard of care that a reasonable person would observe in the actor's situation.

In categorizing levels of culpability, the MPC distinguishes between *purposely* and *knowingly*. Both involve knowledge, but *purposely* is a stronger, more culpable intent because the defendant *consciously* intended to engage in the criminal act or to bring about a particular result, as distinct from having been "practically certain" that particular results would follow the act.

Both *purposely* and *knowingly* are to be distinguished from *recklessly*, which involves serious risks and which, according to the MPC comments, "resembles acting knowingly in that a state of awareness is involved, but the awareness is of risk, that is of a probability less than substantial certainty."[1]

To constitute *recklessness*, the risk must be substantial *and* unjustified. The substantial risk taken by a surgeon who is aware that a proposed operation *may* be fatal, but who also knows that the patient will die without that operation, does not constitute reckless behavior under this code. The MPC comments indicate that there is no way to make the definition of recklessness more specific; the jury must analyze the facts of each case in determining whether the behavior at issue was reckless.

There is some disagreement over the inclusion within the criminal law of acts that only involve **negligence**, the fourth level of culpability in the MPC. In tort law, *negligence* refers to acts that a reasonable person would not do or the failure to do something that a reasonable person would do under the same or similar circumstances. Negligence in tort law does not require a criminal intent, but in criminal law, a negligent act may be considered a crime if it is *grossly* negligent.

To illustrate the difference between *ordinary negligence*, which is sufficient to establish a cause of action in civil law, and *gross negligence*, required in criminal law, consider the following: A surgeon who operates on a patient's left foot when permission had been given only for surgery on the right foot has committed an unauthorized act, which is considered an act of negligence. This negligence may sustain a civil action for which the patient could receive monetary damages, but in all probability no attempt would be made to prosecute the doctor under a criminal statute, even though technically the act constitutes a battery, which is a crime as well as a civil wrong. If, however, the surgeon had performed the surgery while under the influence of alcohol, criminal charges might be filed.

Problems of Interpretation

The MPC provisions for criminal culpability have been widely adopted, in some cases with modifications, but there are problems with interpretation of the levels of culpability. Because interpretation problems are extensive in case law, it is important to understand the impossibility of stating what is meant by the *intent* in criminal law. Rather, it is necessary to analyze carefully the prior interpretations of a statute before concluding how that statute might apply to the facts of a new case. Furthermore, it is necessary to consider the intent element in terms of state and federal constitutional law.

Proving Criminal Intent

Proving that a defendant intended to commit a crime is not always an easy task, but the law permits an **inference** of intent from relevant facts. Thus, if A fires a loaded pistol at B, intending to kill B, but kills C instead, it is reasonable to infer an intent on the part of A sufficient to charge A with the murder of C. But how may one prove that A intended to kill B, particularly as it is unlikely that A will admit that intent when questioned? Suppose A intended only to wound or scare B? These are factual issues that must be determined by the jury, or by the judge if the case is not tried before a jury. If sufficient **circumstantial evidence** (direct evidence—such as eyewitness testimony—of facts other than those on which proof is needed but from which deductions or inferences may be drawn concerning the facts in dispute) is presented, the jury may be permitted to infer intent from that evidence.

Intent must be distinguished from **motive**, which refers to the *why* of a defendant's actions. Hungry parents who steal bread from a local store may do so to feed their families, but that motive does not negate the crime, although in some cases necessity might be a defense (such as breaking into a structure to use a phone to report an emergency; one might not be charged with a crime but probably would have to pay for the cost of the resulting property damage). In general, the state is not required to prove a bad motive to get a conviction, although it may be helpful to do so.

The Concurrence of a Criminal Act and a Criminal Intent

It is a general principle of U.S. criminal laws that the state of mind, or *mens rea*, and the act, *actus reus*, must coincide. In addition, there must be evidence that the criminal act is the result of the *mens rea*. If A intends to kill B, buys a gun, fires at B, misses, and then decides not to make another attempt to kill B but later does so accidentally, A has not committed murder. The criminal state of mind required for murder did not coincide with the act that caused B's death.

Causation

Even if all of the elements discussed so far are proved beyond a reasonable doubt, defendants should not be held criminally responsible unless it can be shown that their acts *caused* the injury, death, or property damage sustained by the victim(s). **Causation** is a complicated term. In criminal law, the search for cause is not easy, but generally, a court is looking for the *legal* cause of the harm, which technically means the act that is nearest in the order of causation. This does not necessarily mean that the alleged criminal act occurred closest to the resulting personal injury or property damage. For example, a criminal act committed against a victim who later dies may be followed by other noncriminal acts that contribute to the victim's death. But, if the criminal act is a **substantial factor** (one that a reasonable person might conclude was sufficient to support the resulting injury or death) contributing to that death, it may be judged the *legal* cause.

In contrast, an **intervening act** (one that occurs after an alleged criminal act) may be judged the legal cause—or at least a contributing cause—of the death. For example, a person with the *mens rea* for murder, who fires a gun at the victim, misses the heart (for which the bullet was aimed), and hits the arm should not be charged with murder when the victim subsequently dies of cancer. The actor may, however, be charged with attempted murder. He or she had the requisite intent and committed the criminal act, even if that act was not the cause of death. If, however, the victim is taken to the hospital after being shot in the arm, and death ensues as the result of negligently performed surgery, the actor who fired the shot may be held criminally responsible for murder unless the doctor's actions are grossly negligent or intentional. In this hypothetical case, the doctor's acts may be considered an independent intervening cause, relieving the original actor of criminal responsibility for murder because his criminal act did not cause the death. The doctor's act, however, would not relieve the criminal actor of a charge of *attempted* murder.

Texas statutes contain the following requirements for causation in criminal law:

(a) A person is criminally responsible if the result would not have occurred but for his conduct, operating either alone or concurrently with another cause, unless the concurrent cause was clearly sufficient to produce the result and the conduct of the actor clearly insufficient.

(b) A person is nevertheless criminally responsible for causing a result if the only difference between what actually occurred and what he desired, contemplated, or risked is that:

(1) a different offense was committed; or

(2) a different person or property was injured, harmed, or otherwise affected.[2]

It is also possible that an act not caused by an offender may combine with the offender's act(s) to produce a harmful result. The other causes may be the result of the negligence or criminal activities of other parties or of natural causes, such as a storm. For example, a fire caused by a storm (or another party) might join a fire started maliciously by the defendant to form a raging fire that destroys property and causes death. When multiple causes occur, it may be difficult to determine whether the offender should be held criminally responsible for some or all of the harmful results.

ATTENDANT CIRCUMSTANCES

Some crimes have an additional element (or elements) that must be proved. **Attendant circumstances** are facts surrounding an event. This means that a criminal act may not be prosecuted as a crime—even if the guilty mind is present and the act caused the injury, death, or property loss—unless the specified circumstances coexist with the act and guilty mind. For example, under the common law a man could not be prosecuted for raping his wife. Rape statutes excluded marital sexual relations even when they involved force. Thus, to prove rape, it was necessary to prove (in addition to other elements of the crime) that the defendant raped someone who was not his wife. This common law approach to rape has been changed in England and in many U.S. jurisdictions.

LIABILITY WITHOUT FAULT

Criminal culpability is imposed in some situations even though no fault or evil intent can be shown on the part of the accused. The three categories of liability without fault discussed in this section are justified on the grounds that:

- In many cases in which they are applied, only minor penalties are assessed.
- Proof of intent is difficult if not impossible to obtain.
- Criminal culpability is essential for compensation of victims as well as for deterrence of others.

Strict Liability

The first type of liability without fault, **strict liability,** is illustrated by the provision in most jurisdictions that selling alcoholic beverages to a minor is a strict liability crime. It is not necessary to prove a criminal intent to sell to a minor or even that the seller knew the buyer was a minor. Proof that the liquor was sold to the minor is sufficient to establish liability.

Statutory rape (sexual intercourse, or, in some jurisdictions, other sexual acts as well, with an underage person even though that person allegedly consented) is also a strict liability offense in most jurisdictions. Historically, it made no difference that the minor victim appeared to be of age or that she initiated the activity. The crime of statutory rape was intended for the protection of girls considered to be too young to consent to sex. Today many jurisdictions include boys in their definitions of statutory rape victims.

Over the years, the rationale that young people need to be protected from sexual experiences has been questioned in cases involving alleged victims close to the age (usually 16) at which they may legally consent to sex. Today, some exceptions are made to the strict liability approach to statutory rape prosecutions, with a few courts allowing the defense that a reasonable person would have thought the alleged victim was of legal age. In other jurisdictions, legislatures have defined the seriousness of the crime and the extent of the penalties in terms of the difference between the ages of alleged victims and of those who offend them. Because prison sentences for statutory rape may be long, the use of the strict liability approach in this crime is an exception to the rationale that most convictions for strict liability crimes result in relatively minor penalties and usually do not involve incarceration in a penal institution.

Vicarious Liability

The second type of liability without fault, **vicarious liability,** "in contrast to strict liability, dispenses with the requirement of the *actus reus* and imputes the criminal act of one person to another."[3] For example, an employer who engages in negligent hiring by employing a person without conducting an adequate background check may be held liable when that individual, a registered sex offender, attacks another employee. Whether the employer could be held responsible in criminal as well as civil (tort) law is determined by the law of the jurisdiction in which the employment occurred and the specific facts of the case.

Enterprise Liability

The third type of liability without fault is **enterprise liability**. Under common law, corporations could not be charged with crimes. This position rested on the argument that corporations had no mind (thus there could be no intent) and no bodies (thus there could be no imprisonment). As the criminal law broke away from that position, the first impositions of criminal responsibility on corporations or other business enterprises resulted in criminal fines. The charges were limited to situations such as the mislabeling of drugs or the packaging and distribution of adulterated products. Today, most courts rule that corporations or business enterprises may be held criminally culpable for the criminal acts (or omissions) of their agents who are acting on behalf of the enterprise that employs them.

The U.S. Supreme Court has upheld the constitutionality of criminal laws that impute the acts of agents to their corporations, holding the latter responsible. The Court said, "The act of agent, while exercising the authority delegated to him . . . may be controlled, in the interest of public policy, by imputing his act to his employer and imposing penalties upon the corporation for which he is acting."[4] This has been interpreted to mean that the mental state as well as the act(s) of the agent(s) may be imputed to the corporation.

There are limitations to enterprise liability. Corporations are held responsible for the criminal acts of their agents only when those agents are acting within the scope of their corporate employment. Further, if the statute in question provides only for the punishments of death or imprisonment, corporations cannot be held liable, as those punishments would not be applicable. Some courts have ruled that crimes that may be considered inherently personal, such as rape, murder, or bigamy, are not included within enterprise liability.

One final point regarding enterprise liability is that the previously successful argument by corporations that they should be liable only for property crimes has been challenged. For example, one lower federal court emphasized the potential harm to society of personal crimes committed by corporate agents. The court emphasized the economic benefits that corporations might enjoy if they were not responsible for damages and personal injuries (or deaths) caused by their defective products. The court reasoned, "To get these economic benefits, corporate management may shortcut expensive safety precautions, respond forcibly to strikes, or engage in criminal anticompetitive behavior."[5]

With the increasing number of serious injuries and deaths caused by defectively designed products, it is reasonable to expect more prosecutions under the enterprise theory of criminal culpability. The arguments against criminal culpability are, however, quite strong. In addition to giving serious consideration to the policy aspect of enterprise liability in criminal law, society should consider whether the use of the criminal law is a deterrent in these cases. If not, perhaps enterprise liability cases are best left to civil law.

SUMMARY

This chapter focused on the four general elements of criminal responsibility: a criminal act, a criminal intent, the concurrence of the act and the intent, and causation. Some crimes also require attendant circumstances in addition to these four elements. All crimes must involve a criminal act or a failure to act where there is a legal duty to act. Individuals may not be prosecuted for criminal thoughts, but criminal culpability may exist once they take a substantial step toward a criminal act. Involuntary reflexes or convulsions, bodily movements during sleep or unconsciousness, or conduct during hypnosis are not considered voluntary acts, as they do not occur with the volition of the actor. Some voluntary acts may be criminal but may not result in criminal culpability because of recognized defenses, which are discussed in Chapter 4.

The second general element of a crime is that a criminal intent, or *mens rea*, must be proved. The problems with interpreting and proving criminal intent were discussed.

The third element of a crime requires concurrence of the criminal act and the criminal intent. The fourth general element requires that the criminal act and intent, occurring together, must have *caused* the result in question. All intervening variables must be excluded.

In addition to these four elements, some crimes require proof of attendant circumstances. Normally these circumstances are specified by the statute establishing the crime, and they may not always require the same level of criminal intent as that required to prove the act, the state of mind, and causation.

The final section of this chapter discussed those acts in criminal law that involve liability without fault. Some acts are considered so important that the criminal law imposes liability even when the actors do not realize they are violating a law, such as an adult who engages in sex with an underage person who allegedly consents. This section discussed the three types of liability without fault: strict liability, vicarious liability, and enterprise liability.

Even if all of the elements of a crime are proved beyond a reasonable doubt, the jury (or judge if the case is not tried before a jury) may return a verdict of not guilty, as Chapter 1 noted. In addition, by presenting an adequate defense, the defendant may avoid (or reduce the level of) criminal responsibility, despite the prosecution's successful presentation of sufficient evidence of all elements of the crime. Defenses in criminal law are discussed in Chapter 4. First, however, it is necessary to look at anticipatory offenses and parties to crimes, the focus of Chapter 3.

STUDY QUESTIONS

1. Explain the meaning of the terms *actus reus* and *mens rea*.
2. When is a behavior not an act in the criminal law? Explain.
3. Distinguish between failure to act (or omission) and an act.
4. List the four levels of intent or culpability in the Model Penal Code (MPC), and define each.

5. Illustrate the difficulties in trying to prove criminal intent.
6. What is meant by the following quote from the U.S. Supreme Court: "The law presumes that a person intends the ordinary consequences of his voluntary acts"?
7. How does *motive* differ from *intent* in criminal law?
8. What is meant by *causation* in criminal law?
9. How does the concept of intervening causes influence legal causation? How does multiple causation affect criminal responsibility?
10. What is meant by *attendant circumstances*, and how do you know when they exist?
11. Distinguish strict liability, vicarious liability, and enterprise liability. Would you exclude any of these from the criminal law? Why or why not?

FOR DEBATE

Discuss the issues surrounding the following debate topics, giving special attention to the reasons for (or the lack of) such statutes historically, along with the societal changes that might make it reasonable to revise or abolish (or create) the statutes.

RESOLVED: All persons who witness a crime should be required to report that incident to law enforcement officials as soon as reasonably possible. Proof of failure to do so should constitute a crime.

RESOLVED: Laws that criminalize sexual behavior between adults and consenting teenagers between the ages of 12 and 16 should be abolished.

KEY TERMS

actus reus   26
attendant circumstances   33
causation   32
circumstantial evidence   32
culpability   26
elements of a crime   26
enterprise liability   35
inference   32
intent   28
intervening act   32
legal duty   28
mens rea   28
motive   32
negligence   31
statutory rape   34
strict liability   34
substantial factor   32
tort   28
vicarious liability   34

INTERNET ACTIVITY

1. *Mens rea* is a crucial element of a crime, but it has different meanings, depending on the nature and definition of the crime. Go to the Crime Library, a collection of nonfiction feature stories on major crimes, criminals, trials, forensics, and

criminal profiling, http://www.trutv.com/library/crime/index.html (accessed 7 May 2012). Select five crimes or criminals, and see what you can find out about the intent requirement for each. Also look for a motive. Although motive is not an element of a criminal offense, it may provide powerful evidence in getting a conviction in a given case.

2. Criminal law does not require everyone to take affirmative action to try to prevent a crime. The New Bedford rape case was discussed in Focus 2.2. In 2011, numerous allegations of sexual abuse were made against Jerry Sandusky, former assistant football coach at Penn State University. Assistant coach Michael McQueary testified before the grand jury (and later at trial) that he witnessed Sandusky sexually abusing a young boy in the shower in the men's locker room in 2002 and that he reported this to longtime Penn State football coach Joe Paterno. Paterno reported the allegations to university officials but went no further when no legal action was taken against Sandusky. Sandusky was charged with multiple felonies, and Paterno was fired, along with the university's president, vice president, and athletic director. As this book was in its final production stages in July 2012, Louis Freeh, former judge and former FBI director, issued his findings and conclusions based on his 7-month investigation of the actions of all persons with knowledge of the events. The report accuses these and others of showing a "total and consistent disregard" for the victims and working together to conceal evidence of their abuse and to prevent the abuse of other children.

   In 2012, Sandusky was convicted of multiple counts involving ten victims, nine of whom were victimized after university officials were informed that Sandusky was allegedly abusing young boys. Go online to discern the latest findings in the ongoing case. Which university officials have been charged with crimes? Have they been tried and, if so, what are the results? Joe Paterno died prior to the release of the Freeh report. Had he lived, should he have been charged in criminal or civil court or both?

   Should the Penn State case result in criminal charges against any other persons? Discuss the case in terms of a legal duty (or a lack thereof) to take affirmative action to prevent a crime. Consider that Pennsylvania has a statute requiring certain persons to report suspected child abuse (see Pa.C.S., Title 23, Section 6311).

NOTES

1. Commentary to Section 2.02, Model Penal Code (1985).
2. Tex. Penal Code, Title 2, Section 6.04 (2012).
3. *State v. Beaudry*, 365 N.W.2d 593 (Wis. 1985).
4. *New York Central and Hudson River Railroad Co. v. United States*, 212 U.S. 481 (1909).
5. *Granite Construction Co. v. Superior Court*, 149 Cal. App. 3d 465 (5th Dist. 1983).

CHAPTER 3

Anticipatory Offenses and Parties to Crimes

CHAPTER OUTLINE
Introduction
Solicitation
    Elements of Solicitation
    Defenses to Solicitation
Attempt
    Elements of Attempt
    Defenses to Attempt
Conspiracy
    The Problem of Definition
    Elements of Conspiracy
        The Act or Agreement
            The Problem of Multiple Agreements
            The Requirement of an Act Plus an Agreement
        The Intent
    Limitations on Parties to Conspiracy
    Defenses to Conspiracy
    Other Issues in Conspiracy
Parties to Crimes
    Elements of Accomplice Liability
    Other Issues in Accomplice Liability
        The Wharton Rule
        Defenses to Accomplice Liability
        The Scope of Accomplice Liability
Summary
Study Questions
For Debate
Key Terms

Internet Activity
Notes

INTRODUCTION

Chapters 1 and 2 introduced criminal law, including the required elements of a crime, such as an act. It is possible, however, that individuals may engage in behaviors that are dangerous to society because those acts imply an *inclination* to commit a crime even though the target crime is never accomplished. For example, an attempt to commit rape is a serious threat to the potential victim and to society even though the rape is not committed. Anticipatory, uncompleted, or incipient crimes are called **inchoate crimes**. These crimes are important because they are threatening and may lead to other crimes.

It is also important to consider whether all persons who are involved in a crime should have the same criminal responsibility. Thus, the role of various parties to crimes is another focus of this chapter, which begins with a discussion of solicitation.

SOLICITATION

The asking, inciting, ordering, urgently requesting, or enticing of another person to commit a crime is known as **solicitation**. The target crime does not have to be committed for solicitation to occur. Perhaps most familiar among these crimes are soliciting for a bribe or for prostitution, but the act may involve soliciting for murder or other violent crimes.

Solicitation statutes recognize that when one person entices another to commit a crime, that act constitutes sufficient danger to society that the criminal law should be applied.

Elements of Solicitation
The crime of solicitation has essentially two elements:

1. An act: commanding, encouraging, or demanding that another person engage in conduct that constitutes a crime
2. An intent: having the purpose of promoting or facilitating that person to commit a crime

Thus, criminal solicitation requires a purpose to promote or facilitate the commission of a crime as well as a command, encouragement, demand, request, or other means of enticing another to commit the crime. That incitement may be directed at a group or crowd and not just a particular individual. Some statutes require that the solicited crime must be a serious one—for example, a felony—whereas others include any crime.

Penalties for solicitation vary, with some statutes providing a lesser penalty for solicitation than for the solicited crime. Others provide the same penalty as that for the most serious crime solicited, with the exception of capital crimes and first-degree felonies. In those cases, the attempt may be punished as a second-degree felony. Some jurisdictions require corroboration of witnesses or circumstances to substantiate the intent for solicitation.

To commit the crime of solicitation, it is not sufficient to joke to another about committing a crime, even if that person commits the crime suggested. The communication must be made with the intent to entice the target party to commit the crime.

Defenses to Solicitation

Some criminal statutes permit the defense of renouncing solicitation, while others require that for renunciation to be acceptable, the solicitor of the crime must persuade the solicitee not to commit the crime or must in some other way prevent the crime from occurring. Presumably this action means that the solicitor is no longer dangerous to society and therefore punishment is not necessary.

ATTEMPT

Most jurisdictions have statutes criminalizing attempts to commit crimes. The nature of the statutes varies. Some refer to *any* crime, while others limit the crime to an attempt to commit a serious crime, a felony, or any one of an enumerated list of serious crimes. Many jurisdictions have one statute that covers all attempt crimes, while some include a separate statute for each crime (attempted rape, attempted robbery, and so on).

Elements of Attempt

The crime of attempt has two elements:

1. A criminal intent
2. A criminal act

The first element of **attempt** is that the defendant must have had the requisite *mens rea*, or criminal intent. The intent required for attempt is a *specific intent*. It is not sufficient that the defendant had a general criminal intent. As one court concluded, "One cannot attempt to commit an act which one does not intend to commit."[1] Legally, a person cannot attempt to commit a crime that does not require a specific intent. Thus, criminal attempt excludes crimes that are the result of a general intent, negligence, or recklessness.

The Model Penal Code (MPC) definition of *criminal attempt*, reprinted in Focus 3.1, emphasizes the intent requirement by requiring that the intent must be made *purposely*. Notice also that under the MPC, criminal attempt includes an omission, or failure to act, where there is a legal duty to act.

One problem with the intent requirement occurs when the defendant has been charged with attempted murder but the victim has not died. A person may be convicted of murder without proof of a specific intent to kill a particular victim. And a conviction is appropriate in some cases in which the defendant has not exhibited an intent to kill but has engaged in reckless behavior reflecting

===== Focus 3.1 =====

Criminal Attempt: The Model Penal Code (MPC)

Section 5.01. Criminal Attemp

(1) *Definition of Attempt.* A person is guilty of an attempt to commit a crime if, acting with the kind of culpability otherwise required for commission of the crime, he:

   (a) purposely engages in conduct which would constitute the crime if the attendant circumstances were as he believes them to be; or

   (b) when causing a particular result is an element of the crime, does or omits to do anything with the purpose of causing or with the belief that it will cause such result without further conduct on his part; or

   (c) purposely does or omits to do anything which, under the circumstances as he believes them to be, is an act or omission constituting a substantial step in a course of conduct planned to culminate in his commission of the crime.

(2) *Conduct Which May Be Held Substantial Step Under Subsection (1)(c).* Conduct shall not be held to constitute a substantial step under Subsection (1)(c) of this Section unless it is strongly corroborative of the actor's criminal purpose. Without negating the sufficiency of other conduct, the following, if strongly corroborative of the actor's criminal purpose, shall not be held insufficient as a matter of law:

   (a) lying in wait, searching for or following the contemplated victim of the crime;

   (b) enticing or seeking to entice the contemplated victim of the crime to go to the place contemplated for its commission;

   (c) reconnoitering the place contemplated for the commission of the crime;

   (d) unlawful entry of a structure, vehicle or enclosure in which it is contemplated that the crime will be committed;

   (e) possession of materials to be employed in the commission of the crime, which are specially designed for such unlawful use or which can serve no lawful purpose of the actor under the circumstances;

   (f) possession, collection or fabrication of materials to be employed in the commission of the crime, at or near the place contemplated for its commission, where such possession, collection or fabrication serves no lawful purpose of the actor under the circumstances;

   (g) soliciting an innocent agent to engage in conduct constituting an element of the crime.

(3) *Conduct Designed to Aid Another in Commission of a Crime.* A person who engages in conduct designed to aid another to commit a crime which would establish his complicity under Section 2.06 if the crime were committed by such other person, is guilty of an attempt to commit the crime, although the crime is not committed or attempted by such other person. . . .

SOURCE: *Model Penal Code.* Copyright ©1985 by the American Law Institute. Reprinted with the permission of the American Law Institute.

indifference to human life or has manifested an intent to inflict only great bodily harm, not to kill, but death resulted. With these same facts and a victim who does not die, a charge of attempted murder is inappropriate.

Under these facts, attempted murder requires a higher intent than would be required for a murder conviction had the victim died. This situation has been questioned because of the threat to individuals and to society that may result when people who are grossly negligent in their conduct escape criminal responsibility because the attempt statutes do not cover their acts. Consider, for example, the case discussed in Focus 3.2.

The second element of attempt is that there must be a criminal act. Usually courts require that the defendant went beyond preparation and moved toward perpetration of the crime. The difference between *preparation* and *perpetration*

Focus 3.2

AIDS and Sex: Attempted Crime?

A critical question in criminal attempt law is whether a person who knows that he or she is HIV positive or has AIDS, who has been told of the dangers of transmitting the disease during unprotected sex, and who proceeds to engage in unprotected sexual acts without telling the partner can be charged with and convicted of attempted battery or even murder. There is no cure for AIDS, although modern medicines are effective in controlling it. The treatment is expensive, however, and not all persons who have AIDS have the financial means or insurance to cover treatment costs.

A Maryland appellate court held that the intent required for attempted second-degree murder could not be inferred from the following facts. An HIV-positive defendant had been told that if he had unprotected sex he could transmit the condition to his victims. Dwight Ralph Smallwood, who was accused of raping and robbing three women, entered guilty pleas to some of the charges but successfully challenged those for attempted second-degree murder based on the fact that he did not use protection during the attacks. In reversing Small's convictions for assault with intent to commit murder and attempted murder, the appellate court distinguished Small's case from those in which defendants expressed a desire to kill by transmitting the HIV virus. According to the court, "Without such evidence, it cannot fairly be concluded that death by AIDS was sufficiently probable to support an inference that Smallwood intended to kill." The court continued as follows:

> [T]he state in this case would allow the trier of fact to infer that Smallwood exposed his victims to the risk that they might contract HIV. Without evidence showing that such a result is sufficiently probable to support this inference, we conclude that Smallwood's convictions for attempted murder and assault with intent to murder must be reversed.[1]

[1]*Smallwood v. State*, 680 A.2d 512 (Md. 1996).

is of critical legal significance in that unless perpetration has occurred, there is no criminal attempt. One does not have to be the active participant to constitute perpetration; he or she can **aid or abet** in committing the criminal act. To aid or abet means to assist or facilitate the commission of a crime.

Focus 3.3 contains quotations from several courts that have drawn the line between preparation and perpetration. A close reading of those statements shows the difficulty in distinguishing the two concepts.

One final point on the act element for attempt crimes is that the offender's act does not have to be the last act in the chain of causation to constitute an attempt.

Defenses to Attempt

Two defenses recognized in attempt cases are:

1. Abandonment
2. Impossibility

Focus 3.3

Preparation or Attempt? Courts Seek a Definition

Courts devise tests to determine whether a defendant goes beyond preparation and commits an act sufficient to constitute an attempt crime. The following are a few of the guidelines articulated by various courts over the years:

1. "The act must reach far enough towards the accomplishment of the desired result to amount to the commencement of the consummation."[1]

2. "[W]here the intent to commit the substantive offense is . . . clearly established . . ., acts done toward the commission of the crime may constitute an attempt, where the same acts would be held insufficient to constitute an attempt if the intent with which they were done is equivocal and not clearly proved."[2]

3. "Acts in furtherance of a criminal project do not reach the stage of an 'attempt' unless they carry the project forward within dangerous proximity to the criminal end to be attained."[3]

4. "The question whether an accused is guilty of an attempt to commit a crime is determined by his intentions and actions, and is unaffected by the circumstance that by reason of some unforeseen obstacle he was prevented from achieving his purpose. He is guilty if he has with criminal intent made some positive steps, beyond mere preparation, looking to the performance of an act which, if perpetrated, would be a crime."[4]

[1]*People v. Miller*, 42 P.2d 308, 309 (Cal. 1935).
[2]*People v. Berger*, 280 P.2d 136, 138 (Cal.Ct.App. 1955).
[3]*People v. Ditchik*, 41 N.E.2d 905 (N.Y. 1942), citations omitted.
[4]*People v. Sullivan*, 75 N.E. 989, 992 (N.Y. 1903).

Some courts recognize *abandonment* as a defense if there is evidence that it is voluntary and complete. Most courts do not recognize this defense when abandonment is the result of getting caught. When the defense is allowed, it is interpreted strictly, and most defendants do not succeed with it.

A more plausible defense to attempt is **factual impossibility** (meaning there are circumstances, unknown to the actor, that prevented the commission of an attempt) or **legal impossibility** (no crime would have been committed even if the defendant's intentions had been fully performed or set in motion).

Most U.S. courts hold that a defendant may be charged with an attempt crime when physical or factual impossibility exists, but not when legal impossibility exists.

The intent requirement for attempt crimes is complicated and often difficult to prove, as is the next crime discussed.

CONSPIRACY

Like solicitation and attempt, **conspiracy** is an inchoate crime. *Conspiracy* means agreeing with another to join together for the purpose of committing an unlawful act or agreeing to use unlawful means to commit an act that would otherwise be lawful. The unlawful act does not have to be committed; the crime of conspiracy involves the *agreement* to engage in the unlawful act.

Unlike the other inchoate crimes, conspiracy permits criminal prosecution for the behavior of others as well as for one's own acts. A further distinction between attempt and conspiracy is that, unlike attempt, which merges into the crime (thus, a defendant cannot be convicted of both attempt to commit robbery and robbery of the same person), in most jurisdictions a defendant can be convicted of conspiracy and of the crime that was its object. Some jurisdictions do not permit two convictions.

Conspiracy may also be distinguished from attempt in that attempt requires an *act* of preparation, whereas the agreement may be sufficient to constitute the act requirement in conspiracy. Therefore, it is possible that a defendant could be convicted of conspiracy to commit robbery under circumstances that would not justify a conviction for attempted robbery.

The role that conspiracy charges can play in today's world is illustrated in Focus 3.4, which discusses a U.S. Supreme Court case on conspiracy.

The Problem of Definition

Students may become frustrated by the lack of agreement in law. Conspiracy is no exception to this situation. It would be a misrepresentation of the facts to suggest a simple and definite statement defining the crime.

A good starting point is a brief look at common law conspiracy. Conspiracy was not a recognized crime in early common law. When it emerged, it was defined narrowly, but over the years the definition was expanded. For purposes of this discussion, an 1832 definition is significant. In that year, an English lord stated that an indictment for conspiracy required that a defendant must be charged

---

Focus 3.4

The U.S. Supreme Court Looks at Conspiracy

In 2003, the U.S. Supreme Court decided *United States v. Recio*,[1] which focused on a drug transaction in which four men were charged and convicted of illegally transporting cocaine and marijuana. Government officials seized a truck they suspected of containing a large amount of illegal drugs. They arrested two men, who then cooperated with law enforcement and drove the truck to their original destination, at which point the truck was taken over by Jimenez Recio and Adrian Lopez-Meza, the other two alleged conspirators. Recio and Lopez-Meza were arrested, charged, and convicted of conspiracy to possess with intent to distribute a controlled substance. Recio was also convicted of possession with intent to distribute.

Recio and Lopez-Meza argued successfully to the Ninth Circuit Court of Appeals that their conspiracy convictions should be reversed because, based on a precedent case decided by that court, a conspiracy ends when it becomes impossible to achieve the object of that conspiracy because of intervention by law enforcement officials. Here, the government had already seized the truck when the appellants took possession; thus, they argued, they could not continue with the "object" of the alleged conspiracy.

The Ninth Circuit agreed, but the U.S. Supreme Court reversed and remanded the case, holding that a conspiracy does not end because its "object" is thwarted by law enforcement officials. The U.S. Supreme Court noted that it has "repeatedly said that the essence of a conspiracy is 'an agreement to commit an unlawful act.'" The agreement is a "distinct criminal evil," which is punishable.[2]

[1]*United States v. Jimenez Recio*, 258 F.3d 1069 (9th Cir. 2002), *rev'd., remanded*, 537 U.S. 270 (2003).
[2]*United States v. Jimenez Recio*, 537 U.S. 270 (2003).

---

either with conspiracy "to do an unlawful act or a lawful act by unlawful means."[2] Although the word *unlawful* could have been understood as meaning *criminal*, the English and American courts interpreted it more broadly, to include acts that are "corrupt, dishonest, fraudulent, immoral, and in that sense illegal, and it is in the combination to make use of such practices that the dangers of this offense consist."[3]

Some jurisdictions retain this common law definition even though they have codified the law. Where that occurs, *conspiracy* is defined broadly as an agreement (or combination or confederation) to engage in an unlawful act or to engage in a lawful act by unlawful means. Some jurisdictions specify that the conspiracy must be to commit a crime, whereas others specify the type of crime. In general, conspiracy statutes are broad, but despite this, many courts have upheld them. The broad language gives prosecutors greater latitude to prosecute in this area, but the U.S. Supreme Court has held that a statute prohibiting conspiracies "to commit any act injurious to the public health, to public morals, or to trade, commerce or for the perversion or obstruction of justice or the due administration of the law" is vague unless narrowed by the state court.[4]

Some statutes divide conspiracy into degrees. Regardless of the definition, however, it is the involvement of more than one person that makes conspiracy more serious than other inchoate crimes.

Elements of Conspiracy

Conspiracy consists of two essential elements:

1. A criminal act, which may be an agreement (some statutes require an act plus an agreement)
2. A criminal intent

The Act or Agreement

The first element of conspiracy is that there must be a criminal act. The act may be the agreement, which is the essence of conspiracy. The agreement does not have to be a written one; usually it is not. It may be inferred from the facts and circumstances of the case.

Proving the existence of an agreement may be difficult. One method is the objective standard, articulated by one court as whether any *rational* trier of fact (e.g., a judge or juror) could conclude beyond a reasonable doubt that an agreement existed. The objective standard may be distinguished from the subjective test, which asks whether the actual trier of fact(s) could conclude that there was an agreement.[5]

Careful analysis of the alleged agreement is important to determine the several crucial issues in litigating the crime of conspiracy.

The Problem of Multiple Agreements. Another issue in conspiracy is whether more than one agreement was in effect. If the prosecutor charges defendants with more than one conspiracy but can prove only one, or charges only one and there is evidence of more than one agreement, the defendants may be entitled to an acquittal. The number of agreements may also be important in the imposition of punishment.

The Requirement of an Act Plus an Agreement. In those jurisdictions that do require an act plus the agreement, there must be an overt (open, public) act. When that is the case, normally the requirement is not as stringent as that required for an attempt. Often this requirement is intended to give any of the actors in the conspiracy a chance to abandon their participation and avoid prosecution. An example of a sufficient overt act is the purchase of stamps to carry out a conspiracy to commit murder by poison sent through the mail.

Some states specify that an act in addition to an agreement is required only for *some* conspiracy crimes. When an overt act is required, it is not always necessary that all co-conspirators engage in the overt act; an act on the part of one may be sufficient to establish this element of the crime.[6]

The Intent

In prosecuting conspiracy, it is not sufficient to show that the defendants intended to agree. It must be proved that they intended to accomplish an unlawful (or criminal) objective, which was the object of the conspiracy. The elements of the objective must be met. Consider the following example: Suppose A and B plan to bomb a building to destroy the structure. They know that there are people inside and that in all probability, those people will be killed by the explosion. A and B do not intend to kill the occupants, so they do not have the intent required for murder. If they bomb the building and people inside die as a result, under many statutes A and B may be convicted of murder. But they may not be convicted of conspiracy to commit murder, only of conspiracy to bomb the building.[7]

Another problem that exists with regard to the intent requirement of conspiracy is what to do with alleged conspirators who merely provided goods or services that were used by others for unlawful (or criminal) purposes. Conspiracy requires intent, not just knowledge; so it would seem that knowledge that the goods and services would be used for unlawful purposes would not be sufficient to support a conspiracy charge.

One final intent requirement in conspiracy cases in some jurisdictions is that the parties must have had a corrupt *motive,* which refers to the reason for the defendant's action(s). Thus, if the parties did not know they were violating a statute, they might argue successfully that they were not guilty of conspiracy, which, by definition, implies that the agreement "must have been entered into with an evil purpose, as distinguished from a purpose to do the act prohibited, in ignorance of the prohibition."[8]

Not all courts agree, however, noting that normally ignorance of the law is not an excuse. Others take the position that if the conspiracy is to commit an act that is not generally agreed to be a crime but has been defined as such, the corrupt motive doctrine applies. This is based on the assumption that a person should be aware that there are laws against the more serious acts (such as murder, rape, robbery) but might not be aware that acts such as gambling or using some drugs are crimes.

Limitations on Parties to Conspiracy

The law establishes four limitations on parties to conspiracy. Some jurisdictions do not accept all of these limitations.

- Wharton rule
- Husband-and-wife rule
- Two-or-more rule
- Corporation rule

The **Wharton rule**, named after its author, Francis Wharton, specifies that when individuals engage in crimes that by definition require more than one person, they may not be prosecuted for conspiracy to commit those crimes; a third party must be involved for a conspiracy to exist. Crimes that qualify under this rule are acts such as adultery, bigamy, and incest. Some jurisdictions have rejected this rule.

A second limitation is the *husband-and-wife rule*. Under common law, a husband and wife were considered to be one person, and because conspiracy requires two or more persons, they could not conspire to commit a crime. This position was accepted in the United States in earlier days, based primarily on the assumption that the husband "owned" his wife, who was under his control. As other laws concerning the relationship between husband and wife have changed, so has the law of conspiracy. Today, a wife may legally act independently of her husband, so the two of them may commit conspiracy.

A third limitation on parties to conspiracy is the *two-or-more rule*, requiring that for a conspiracy to exist, two or more persons must be involved. Although it is obvious that the definition of conspiracy precludes one person from conspiring alone, courts have taken different positions on what happens if, for example, one of two alleged conspirators is acquitted. Technically, if there are only two alleged conspirators and one is acquitted, the other may not be convicted, as there would be only one party to the conspiracy. Some courts have taken this position, while others look to the reason that a second alleged co-conspirator was not convicted. For example, if one defendant was acquitted in a separate trial or granted immunity in exchange for testifying against the second co-conspirator, a conspiracy conviction may be upheld for the other defendant.

Although it might seem unfair to uphold the conspiracy conviction of a defendant whose alleged co-conspirator was granted immunity or acquitted in a separate trial but not to uphold the conviction if the acquittal occurred in the same trial, the argument for taking this position is that it is necessary to maintain internal consistency. Logically, the same jury could not acquit one of two alleged conspirators and convict the other, for, under those circumstances, the second defendant would not have had anyone with whom to conspire. But if two juries reach different conclusions, internal consistency is not compromised. These issues are not problems, of course, in those jurisdictions that do not recognize the two-or-more rule.

A similar issue arises when the person charged with conspiracy allegedly conspired with a person who had no intention to carry out the conspiracy—for example, a police officer. Modern cases have held that this situation does not preclude a conspiracy conviction against the party with the criminal intent.

The fourth limitation on parties to conspiracy is the *corporation rule*. Corporations may commit conspiracy with other corporations or with a natural person, although there are problems with the two-or-more rule. When two corporations and an officer of each are charged, there is no problem, for there are two or more separate persons involved in the conspiracy. Likewise, when a corporation is indicted for conspiracy, along with one of its officers and an officer from another corporation, the two-or-more requirement is met.

The problem arises when a corporation and one of its officers are charged with conspiracy. Very early cases established that this does not constitute a conspiracy.[9] Nor is there a conspiracy in a case involving two corporations and one agent acting for both corporations. In both of these cases, only one human actor is involved, so there can be no agreement between two or more persons.

The two-or-more requirement also arises when two or more agents of the same corporation are involved. Courts have differed on whether this situation meets the two-or-more requirement for conspiracy.

Defenses to Conspiracy

Most courts hold that impossibility is not a defense to conspiracy. Some, using the analogy of attempt, hold that legal but not factual impossibility is a defense. Some statutes permit withdrawal or renunciation as a defense to conspiracy.

Renunciation or abandonment of a conspiracy might be difficult to prove. Jurisdictions differ on their statutory requirements to prove this defense, and courts vary on their interpretations of the statutes.

Other Issues in Conspiracy

An important issue that arises in conspiracy cases is the extent to which the actor is responsible for the crimes of his or her co-conspirators. In the leading case of *Pinkerton v. United States,* the U.S. Supreme Court established that a co-conspirator may be held accountable for the acts of fellow conspirators even though the requirements of criminal culpability for the acts of accomplices, discussed later in this chapter, are not met.[10]

The **Pinkerton rule** has been criticized as one that could result in gross distortions. If anyone who becomes involved in a conspiracy is responsible for all criminal acts of co-conspirators, a relatively uninvolved person could become criminally culpable for many crimes. Some courts dodge this problem by limiting criminal culpability for crimes of co-conspirators to reasonably foreseeable acts.

Another issue concerns the duration of a conspiracy. Culpability for the crimes of co-conspirators lasts only as long as the conspiracy. Thus, a conspiracy continues until the agreement is abandoned or succeeds. In a particular case, that point might be hard to determine, but it is important, as a number of procedural issues are affected by the time at which the conspiracy ends. Both the duration of the conspiracy and the extent of criminal culpability for the crimes of co-conspirators, in the case of a particular defendant, are affected by whether that defendant withdraws successfully or abandons the conspiracy. Statutes concerning the duration of a conspiracy vary.

One final point of importance in conspiracy cases is that they may be (and usually are) extremely complicated. Frequently, conspiracy charges are combined with charges for substantive crimes, many of which involve illegal drug sales. There may be multiple defendants (even scores of them in some instances), which means multiple attorneys if the cases are tried together. In addition, numerous substantive crimes may be alleged, with the criminal charges differing by defendants. These cases may take weeks, even months, to try, resulting in enormous expense to the government and to the defendants, along with inconvenience to all parties involved in the trials.

PARTIES TO CRIMES

The law has long recognized criminal culpability for people other than those who commit criminal acts. Individuals may assist, aid and abet, incite, or encourage others to commit criminal acts. The word **complicity** means association in a wrongful act. Thus, a person who shares in the guilt, even though he or she did not engage in the crime, is an **accomplice** to the crime, meaning that the individual shares in the responsibility for the crime but not in the criminal act itself. Such a person assumes criminal culpability in terms of the degree of involvement in the criminal act. Various terms are used to describe the type and degree of accomplice involvement. Not all jurisdictions have all of these categories, and they may differ in definitions as well.

Under common law, a **principal** was the person who committed the crime, in contrast to the **accessory**, who assisted in the crime or who encouraged another person to commit a crime. Most modern statutes do not make this distinction. Both the principal and the accessory are treated as principals, and accessories may be convicted even if the principal has not been convicted. Some jurisdictions, however, distinguish between types of principals. A **principal in the first degree** is one who perpetrates a crime either through his or her own act or by use of inanimate objects or innocent people. A **principal in the second degree** incites or abets the commission of a crime and is present actually or constructively. A person is present constructively when, without being present, he or she assists the principal of the first degree at the moment the crime is being committed. In many crimes, it is common for the principal in the second degree of a bank robbery to be posted away from the bank, ready to signal when the coast is clear.

An **accessory before the fact** incites or abets but is not present actually or constructively when the crime is committed. An example is someone who provides information or tools used in the commission of a crime. An **accessory after the fact** is one who, knowing that a felony has been committed, receives, relieves, comforts, or assists the perpetrator of the criminal act for the purpose of hindering the apprehension and conviction of that person. Most modern statutes do not distinguish between principals of either degree and accessories before the fact; all three are treated as principals.

Accessories may be convicted even if the principal has not been convicted, although there are some exceptions. Many current statutes simply specify that an accomplice is accountable legally for the conduct of another, without referring to any of the categories used historically and defined here.

Elements of Accomplice Liability
In general, there are three elements to accomplice liability.

1. Whether it is necessary to find the principal guilty before convicting the accomplice
2. The act
3. The mental state

Often a fine line is drawn between doing and not doing enough to constitute the act required for accomplice liability. The easier cases are those in which the alleged accomplice provides a hotel room for a prostitute or a gun for a murderer, drives the getaway car for a robber, or supplies the necessary technological information for a computer thief. More difficult is the person who is present and appears to approve and who has some legal duty to act but does not do so. Each case must be decided on its unique facts.

Jurisdictions also differ regarding the intent requirement of complicity. Generally, alleged accomplices are required to have the intent required for the offenses for which they are alleged to be accomplices. In addition, most jurisdictions specify that the criminal acts must be accompanied by an intent to aid in the commission of the crime, although in many cases it is difficult to distinguish between one who intends only to sell a product or a service and one who intends to do that to facilitate a crime. For example, if a motel owner rents rooms to individuals knowing that they intend to use those rooms for illegal purposes, has the owner intended to facilitate a crime as well as to engage in a financial transaction?

Few cases have been decided on this issue, and the two leading ones disagree. One case, decided in 1940, provides that the "seller may not ignore the purpose for which the purchase is made if he is advised of that purpose, or wash his hands of the aid that he has given the perpetrator of a felony by the plea that he has merely made a sale of merchandise."[11] However, an earlier case, decided in 1938, concluded, "All the words used—even the most colorless, "abet"—carry an implication of purposive attitude towards" the crime.[12]

Several ways to solve the conflict between these two positions have been suggested. Accomplice liability may be limited to instances in which there exists "the purpose of promoting or facilitating the commission of an offense." Thus, it must be shown that the accomplice affirmatively desired to encourage or assist the principal.[13]

Second, some courts have held that it is sufficient that accomplices *know* that their acts will assist in the commission of crimes, although they do not necessarily *desire* that result. Third, some jurisdictions permit finding that accomplices have the requisite criminal intent if they act recklessly, knowing that their behavior will facilitate the commission of a crime. These people may be just as dangerous to society as those who intend the harmful result. Some courts acknowledge this scenario only in the case of serious crimes.

Some jurisdictions have specified other conditions that must be considered, such as what stake the accomplice has in the outcome of the venture. For example, a defendant who will share in the financial proceeds of the venture presumably would have the intent to aid.

One other approach to the intent issue in accomplice liability is to enact a statute for criminal **facilitation**, which means to make it easier for another person to engage in a criminal act.

A final point with regard to complicity is that the penalty may be assessed in terms of the seriousness of the target crime. For example, the penalty for facilitating a misdemeanor is less than that for facilitating a felony.

Other Issues in Accomplice Liability

Three other issues regarding accomplice liability are as follows:

- Whether the Wharton rule applies
- Defenses
- The scope of the crime

The Wharton Rule

In most cases of accomplice liability, an individual is not held criminally culpable as an accomplice when he or she assists a principal to commit a crime that by definition requires two people, such as prostitution, which requires a prostitute and a customer.

Defenses to Accomplice Liability

Generally, abandonment is recognized as a defense to accomplice liability, but to sustain this defense, the defendant must show that the complicity was abandoned in a timely manner.

The Scope of Accomplice Liability

Traditionally, an accomplice has been held criminally responsible for all crimes that might reasonably result in complicity, even though the principal's crimes go beyond those crimes contemplated by the accomplice. It may be argued, however, that this position extends criminal culpability beyond the requirement of a criminal state of mind; consequently, some jurisdictions reject the traditional rule.

SUMMARY

After two chapters that discussed the meaning and purpose of the criminal law and the general culpability of persons for criminal acts, this chapter focused on anticipatory crimes and the criminal responsibility of people who are connected to crimes but who are not participants in the traditional sense. An understanding of the crimes discussed in this chapter provides additional reasons for thinking about the meaning and purpose of criminal law and for reexamining how far that law should go to deter, to promote justice, to punish, or to accomplish any other relevant purpose.

Some of the crimes discussed in this chapter may be categorized as inchoate or anticipatory in that the actual crime is never committed. Inchoate crimes are important, however, for in many cases they lead to the commission of other crimes. An individual who is thwarted in an attempted robbery may try again—and may succeed. But even the failures are threats to society, as well as to potential victims.

The crime of solicitation permits punishing people who are the instigators of crimes but who do not commit those crimes. The solicitor may be the prime reason that the crime is committed. Because of the potential seriousness of solicitation, some jurisdictions have strict requirements for a successful abandonment or renunciation defense.

It is not always easy to distinguish *solicitation*, which involves preparation, from *attempt*, which involves perpetration along with the required criminal state of mind. The facts of each case must be analyzed carefully to determine whether there is any direct movement toward committing a crime—in other words, whether there is an attempt.

Abandonment and legal impossibility are two defenses that may be permitted in attempt cases. Both require careful consideration of the facts. Frequently it is difficult to determine whether the accused abandoned the attempt or just failed to achieve the goal of committing a crime successfully. Likewise, it may be difficult to determine the difference between factual impossibility, which usually is not a defense, and legal impossibility, which may be a valid defense.

Conspiracy occupied a significant portion of this chapter, for it is a crime that is prosecuted frequently today and, most recently, has involved noted executives in large corporations. Because some jurisdictions permit prosecution and conviction for a substantive crime (such as murder) and conspiracy (such as conspiracy to commit murder), conspiracy is a very important tool for prosecutors. Conspiracy is important, too, because this crime may be prosecuted successfully even when the crime for which the accused conspired did not occur. Thus a person may be found guilty of conspiracy to commit burglary even though the burglary was not committed. Conspiracy statutes are defined broadly. Most are precise enough to pass constitutional scrutiny but sufficiently broad to encompass a wide range of acts.

Conspiracy requires an agreement between two or more parties. In most jurisdictions, the agreement is sufficient to constitute the act required for a crime, but some jurisdictions require an overt act in addition to the agreement. The agreement required for conspiracy is not an easy element to prove. It does not have to be a written agreement; in fact, conspiracy agreements are seldom written. Nor does the agreement have to be communicated to each person in the alleged conspiracy.

Conspiracies may be limited by the Wharton rule, referring to crimes that require a specific number of people. Adultery, for example, requires two people; therefore, if only two people are involved, under the Wharton rule, they cannot conspire to commit adultery. Although in the past, husbands and wives could not conspire to commit an unlawful act (or a crime) because legally they were considered to be one person, most jurisdictions have changed that rule.

Corporations may be charged with conspiracy provided the two-or-more rule is not violated. The key is to determine whether one or two human actors were involved in the alleged criminal agreements. Although any alleged conspiracy may have begun with more than one party to the agreement, that may change when one party is acquitted. If only one party is left without an acquittal, that individual may not be tried for conspiracy in many jurisdictions. Exceptions may be made, depending on the nature of the acquittal.

The intent requirement for conspiracy presents problems. The conspirators need to have not only an intent to agree but also an intent to accomplish the criminal purpose. Usually the degree of intent required is that required for the substantive crime. Intent may be inferred, however, from the alleged conspirator's knowledge of the situation. In addition, some jurisdictions require an evil purpose or motive.

Conspiracy statutes permit punishment of individuals for crimes committed by others, and some of these crimes may go beyond the original agreement. This rule, called the *Pinkerton rule*, has been criticized. Some jurisdictions handle the Pinkerton rule problem by limiting criminal liability of an individual for the criminal acts of a co-conspirator only if those acts are reasonably foreseeable.

The last section of this chapter focused on parties to crimes. Jurisdictions differ in how they categorize such crimes, but generally the following categories exist: principal in the first degree, principal in the second degree, accessory before the fact, and accessory after the fact. Today most jurisdictions do not distinguish among either degree of principals and accessories before the fact; all three are treated as principals.

As with other crimes included in this chapter, defining the elements of a principal may be difficult. An act is required. Usually courts look for affirmative acts in contrast to mere acquiescence to an act. The intent required for a principal may be hard to determine, but usually it will require at least the level of intent required for the offense to which the actor is an alleged accomplice. Some jurisdictions require proof of an intent to aid. Some look to see what stake the accomplice has in the outcome of the illegal venture. Others try to avoid these problems by drafting a separate statute to cover criminal facilitation.

All of the crimes discussed in this chapter may be related to the rest of a jurisdiction's criminal code. It is important to check that code carefully before deciding how anticipatory crimes and parties to crimes are applied. The crimes discussed in this chapter may also be related to the crimes covered in subsequent chapters, such as violent crimes, property crimes, drug trafficking, terrorism, and so on.

STUDY QUESTIONS

1. Why does a criminal code need to include solicitation?
2. Comment in detail on this statement: A person charged with solicitation to burn a house may not be convicted of that crime if the house does not burn.
3. Discuss the elements and the defenses for solicitation.
4. Distinguish between solicitation and attempt.
5. Explain how the act and intent elements of a crime relate to the crime of criminal attempt. Explain what is meant by the "substantial step" requirement imposed by some attempt statutes or judicial interpretations of those statutes.
6. What must occur for a defendant to establish the defense of abandoning an attempt? What is the difference between voluntary and involuntary abandonment?
7. What is meant by *impossibility* in criminal law? Distinguish between factual impossibility and legal impossibility.
8. Why are prosecutors so fond of conspiracy statutes?
9. Discuss the requirement of an act as an element of conspiracy.
10. What is meant by the *Wharton rule*? Should it be abolished?
11. Under what circumstances may corporations be prosecuted for conspiracy?
12. Briefly discuss the problems with requiring a criminal intent for conspiracy.
13. To what extent may conspirators be held criminally responsible for the crimes of their co-conspirators? How does the Pinkerton rule apply to this question? Do you think this rule should be followed? Why or why not?

14. How long does a conspiracy last? How do you know when it ended? Why are conspiracy cases so complicated?
15. Explain the differences among the following: principal in the first degree, principal in the second degree, accessory before the fact, and accessory after the fact. Should any of these categories be abolished? Why or why not?
16. Explain the elements in accomplice liability crimes.

FOR DEBATE

Later in this text, the crimes of drug trafficking and terrorism are discussed. In both of these areas of criminal activity, some persons may be involved only indirectly, but their participation is still important. This chapter's debate topic is based on this area of concern.

RESOLVED: That federal and state prosecutors should pursue vigorously the prosecution of all persons involved indirectly, along with those having direct involvement, in crimes related to drug trafficking, terrorist acts, or other major crimes, if there is *any* evidence that those persons may have been involved in acts of complicity.

KEY TERMS

accessory 51	factual impossibility 45
accessory after the fact 51	inchoate crimes 40
accessory before the fact 51	legal impossibility 45
accomplice 51	Pinkerton rule 50
aid or abet 44	principal 51
attempt 41	principal in the first degree 51
complicity 51	principal in the second degree 51
conspiracy 45	solicitation 40
facilitation 52	Wharton rule 48

INTERNET ACTIVITY

1. Defense attorneys have expressed concern about the indictment of their colleagues who represent terrorists. Go to the Internet and see what you can find about the case of Lynne Stewart, long-time civil rights attorney, who was convicted of aiding her clients who were charged with terrorist acts. What did she do that led to prosecution and conviction? What sentence was she given, and do you think it is reasonable?
2. Famed football player Michael Vick was involved in a dog fighting conspiracy. What were the charges, and why do you think Vick entered a guilty plea although plea bargains were available? Do you think it is reasonable for the prosecution to seek plea deals by one or more persons in an alleged conspiracy in order to get information on another person? Vick was sentenced to a 23-month prison term. After his release from prison, he returned to playing

football. Do you agree with the decision to permit him to do so? Search the Internet to discern the facts concerning Vick's crime, his imprisonment and release, and his subsequent employment.

NOTES

1. *People v. Terry*, 479 N.Y.S.2d 278, 279 (N.Y.App.Div. 1984).
2. *Rex v. Jones*, 110 Eng. Rep. 485 (1832).
3. *State v. Burnham*, 15 N.H. 396 (N.H. 1844).
4. *Musser v. Utah*, 333 U.S. 95 (1948).
5. *United States v. Brown*, 776 F.2d 397 (2d Cir. 1985), *cert. denied*, 475 U.S. 1141 (1986).
6. *United States v. Robinson*, 503 F.2d 208 (7th Cir. 1974), *cert. denied*, 420 U.S. 949 (1975).
7. See Model Penal Code comment to Section 5.03, p. 403.
8. *People v. Powell*, 63 N.Y. 88 (1875).
9. *Union Pacific Coal Co. v. United States*, 173 F. 737 (8th Cir. 1909).
10. *Pinkerton v. United States*, 328 U.S. 640 (1946).
11. *Backun v. United States*, 112 F.2d 635, 637 (4th Cir. 1940).
12. *United States v. Peoni*, 100 F.2d 401, 402 (2d Cir. 1938).
13. Model Penal Code, Section 2.06(3)(a).

CHAPTER 4

Defenses to Criminal Culpability

CHAPTER OUTLINE

Internet Activity

Notes

INTRODUCTION

In U.S. criminal justice systems, the prosecution is required to prove beyond a reasonable doubt that the defendant is guilty of the crime (or crimes) charged. All elements of the crime must be proved. The prosecution must prove that a particular defendant committed a specified criminal act, with the requisite intent; that any attendant circumstances required by the statute were present; and that the act was the legal cause of the harm in question. It is possible, however, that proof on all of these elements may not be sufficient for a conviction.

In criminal law, a successful **defense** may result in a reduced charge or an acquittal. A *defense* is a legal challenge by the defendant. It may consist of a denial of the factual allegations of the prosecution, or it may offer new facts in an effort to negate the charges, in which case it is called an *affirmative defense*. For example, a defendant might respond that in effect, yes, I committed that crime, but I did not have the requisite intent for the act because I was insane.

Defenses are very important, but they are not always easily understood. Nor is there agreement on the vast array of defenses. Some defenses utilized today were accepted historically; others are relatively new. Some, such as insanity, are highly controversial but are used infrequently and are rarely successful.

The chapter begins with a look at the role of the burden of proof regarding defenses.

THE BURDEN OF PROOF AND PRESUMPTIONS

Chapter 2 discussed the *elements* of a crime that the prosecution must prove to sustain a conviction. These elements include an act and a criminal state of mind that concur to produce a harmful result. In addition, some crimes require proof of attendant circumstances. All elements must be proved beyond a reasonable doubt, a standard that requires evidence that is fully satisfactory, entirely convincing, and true to a moral certainty. The defense has the burden of proving any defenses that may be offered, and that standard of proof is usually a **preponderance of the evidence**, a lower standard meaning that, on the whole, the evidence supports the fact or facts in question.

A defense may be *partial,* meaning that it reduces the charge, or *complete*, in which case it defeats the charge. A partial defense to the charge of murder might result in a manslaughter conviction because it defeats one of the elements of murder. A complete defense, such as insanity, may lead to an acquittal.

Although it is tempting to make statements such as "The prosecution must prove all elements of a crime beyond a reasonable doubt" and "The defense must prove all defenses by a preponderance of the evidence," in reality the issues are more complicated because of the concept of **presumption**. A *presumption* is an assumption of a fact that is based on other facts; it is not a fact but an inference from a fact. The most well-known is perhaps the presumption of innocence; a defendant is presumed to be innocent, and the state must prove guilt. Thus if the prosecution presents sufficient evidence, the presumption of innocence is refuted or overcome, and the defendant is found guilty. Some presumptions cannot be refuted, although this is rare. One such *conclusive presumption* in criminal law is that children under a specific age, such as the age of 7 years under common law, are incapable of committing a crime. Thus, if a 6-year-old child fires a gun and kills another human being, that child cannot be charged with a crime.

The presumption of innocence may be used to illustrate some of the problems that arise in allocating the burden of proof between the prosecution and the defense. The prosecution has the difficult burden of proving beyond a reasonable doubt all of the required elements of the crime or crimes charged. To ease the prosecutor's burden, the legislature could draft a statute that would shift the burden of proof on an element of the crime from the prosecution to the defense. That is not permitted constitutionally, but the problem arises when a statute does so by the use of presumptions.

This situation is illustrated by a U.S. Supreme Court case in which the Court considered the issue of a jury instruction that could lead a juror to conclude that the defendant had the burden of proof on intent, a required element of a crime, which must be proved by the prosecution. The misleading instruction was that "a person of sound mind and discretion is presumed to intend the natural and probable consequences of his acts, but the presumption may be rebutted." The Supreme Court held that this instruction is an unconstitutional violation of due process because it sounds like a command. Jurors were not instructed that they were not required to infer intent, and they may have mistakenly thought that they had to do so. The Court emphasized that the prosecution must prove all elements of a crime beyond a reasonable doubt and stated:

> This "bedrock, 'axiomatic and elementary' [constitutional] principle," prohibits the State from using evidentiary presumptions in a jury charge that has the effect of relieving the State of its burden of persuasion beyond a reasonable doubt of every essential element of a crime.[1]

TYPES OF DEFENSES

In studying defenses, it is important to recall the meaning and purpose of criminal law. The moral or blameworthy element of punishment through the criminal law is critical to the topic of defenses, for recognizing defenses means that some criminal acts will not be punished or that punishment may be reduced because of a defense. As with most issues in criminal law, the lines are difficult to draw in particular cases. Likewise, jurisdictions differ in their statutory definitions and judicial interpretations of these defenses.

Ignorance or Mistake

Ignorance is generally not a legally acceptable reason for violating a law, but under some circumstances, a **mistake** defense is permitted. This defense pertains to situations in which actors engage in acts that they claim that they would not have committed had they known that their behavior was criminal. Such lack of knowledge may constitute a *mistake of law* or a *mistake of fact*. These concepts may be distinguished as follows:

> Mistake and ignorance of *fact* involve perceptions of the world and empirical judgments derived from those perceptions. Mistake and ignorance of *law* involve assessment of whether, given a certain set of acts, the actor would or would not be violating the law.[2]

The mistake defense may be used to negate a mental element of a crime, such as the knowledge or belief requirement. For example, a good-faith belief with regard to an income tax deduction may negate the federal statute's requirement of *willful* as an element of income tax evasion.

The mistake defense may be applied in two situations. In the first, individuals do not know that the law exists. Normally this is not an excuse, although in rare cases it may be, as illustrated by a landmark case decided by the U.S. Supreme Court in 1957, in which the Court invalidated a Los Angeles municipal ordinance that forbade any convicted person to be or to remain in the city for more than five days without registering. The Supreme Court emphasized that although "ignorance of the law will not excuse," the law requires reasonable notice. Because most people would not expect a registration ordinance of the nature involved, actual knowledge of the duty to register and meet other requirements of the ordinance would be required for the ordinance to be constitutional. "[O]therwise, the evil would be as great as it is when the law is written in print too fine to read or in a language foreign to the community."[3]

The second type of mistake occurs when individuals are mistaken about an additional element, such as the legality of a previous divorce, which causes them to misunderstand the legal significance of their conduct, such as remarrying. Although bigamy (marriage between two parties, one or both of whom is already legally married) is a strict liability crime in most jurisdictions, some jurisdictions recognize an honest and reasonable mistake as a partial or complete defense to bigamy.

The use of mistake of fact as a partial rather than a complete defense may be applicable to statutory rape cases in some jurisdictions. Others permit the mistake of fact (to age) as a defense but restrict the use of the defense to specific ages. However, as noted in Chapter 2, many jurisdictions retain the position that statutory rape is a strict liability crime and that a reasonable mistake of fact regarding the age of the victim is not a defense.

Duress or Necessity

Defendants may succeed in defending their criminal acts if they can show that they acted under **duress**. *Duress* refers to a condition in which an individual is coerced or induced by the wrongful act of another to commit a criminal act. To succeed with a duress defense, defendants must prove that they were threatened by unlawful force when they committed the crimes for which they are advancing the defense. Most courts hold that the force must be such that it would cause serious bodily injury or death, and the threat of harm must be imminent. Most statutes require that the threat is to the actor rather than to a third party, although a few permit a duress defense for defendants whose close relatives are threatened. A defendant must have acted reasonably to assert the duress defense, which is usually not permitted in murder cases.

The duress defense may not be available when defendants recklessly place themselves in positions in which it is probable that they will be subjected to duress. In addition, this defense may not be available for persons who negligently place themselves in such circumstances if negligence is the basis of culpability for the crime in question.

In criminal law, the concept of **necessity** refers to an act that, though criminal in other circumstances, may not be considered criminal because of the compelling force of the circumstances. Necessity may constitute a defense, which is similar to that of duress, with the exception that in most cases, the coercive forces in a successful necessity case are forces of nature rather than of humans. In actual cases, however, the distinction is not always clear. Like duress, the necessity defense is based on the assumption that a person ought to be free to commit some crimes in order to prevent greater harm. Thus, breaking into the home of another to secure shelter or food or to telephone the police during an emergency may constitute a defense to breaking and entering, although the person who commits this act may be required to pay for the resulting damages.

Unlike duress, a successful necessity defense need not be based on avoiding human injury or death; avoiding property damage may be acceptable. In rare cases, the defense permits serious crimes, such as intentional homicide, when that act is necessary to avoid a greater harm, such as killing one person to avoid the deaths of two others. The actor must have the intent to avoid a greater harm. The decision regarding whether a greater or lesser harm was avoided is left to the court, not to defendants.

Two final points regarding the necessity defense are important. First, a defendant is not permitted to use the defense if another alternative is available that would prevent the greater harm and would still be legal. For example, it is not permissible to steal clothes for needy children if free clothing may be secured from local agencies. Second, the necessity defense is not available to defendants who created the necessity to choose between two evils, although the defense may be permitted to prevent a greater evil.

Infancy

As noted, English common law provided that children below the age of 7 could not be convicted of a crime because of a conclusive presumption that they were not capable of forming the requisite criminal intent. This presumption could be refuted in cases involving children who were between the ages of 7 and 14, with the exception that boys under age 14 were conclusively presumed incapable of rape. A **rebuttable presumption** of criminal intent existed for children age 14 and over, and they could be charged as adults provided enough evidence was presented to overcome the presumption.

Although most U.S. jurisdictions retain some of these distinctions, they are less important now than under common law because of the prevalence of the juvenile court, which has jurisdiction over children of specified ages. Many states, however, permit waivers to adult criminal courts of juveniles who are accused of serious crimes. Some limit waivers to serious violent crimes. Jurisdiction may also be waived when it appears to be in the best interests of society, when the children are thought to be beyond rehabilitation, or when they have committed several serious crimes. Some states specify by statute that juveniles who are accused of committing serious crimes may be tried in criminal courts without the requirement of waiver hearings and procedures.

In recent years, the U.S. Supreme Court has faced the infancy issue in several cases. Most recently, the Court held that the execution of a person who was 17 when he committed murder and the imposition of life without parole for a 17-year-old juvenile who committed a noncapital crime constitute cruel and unusual punishment, thus giving support to the infancy defense. Focus 4.1 contains the facts of these cases.[4]

Focus 4.1

The Infancy Defense: A Glimpse at the Sentencing of Juveniles

The text notes that, traditionally, infancy has been a recognized defense to criminal behavior and mentions that the U.S. Supreme Court has faced this issue with regard to capital punishment and a life without parole sentence for a juvenile who commits a noncapital crime. This focus features the two recent cases on the issue. Chapter 11 discusses them in greater detail, along with a 2012 related case.

In 2005, in *Roper v. Simmons*,[1] the U.S. Supreme Court held that capital punishment of a person who was under 18 when he committed murder constitutes cruel and unusual punishment and thus is unconstitutional. Christopher Simmons, age 17, told two friends (ages 15 and 16) that he wanted to commit murder and that they would get away with it because they were minors. Simmons' proposal was to break and enter a home during the night, bind a victim, and throw that person off a bridge to drown.

The three teens met about 2 a.m. the night of the crimes, but the 16-year-old left before the other two committed the acts. Simmons and the 15-year-old selected a home, reached through an open window, unlocked the back door, and attacked Shirley Crook. Simmons recognized Crook from a previous car accident involving the two of them. Simmons later told friends that he killed a woman "because the bitch seen my face." The assailants wrapped Crook's face in duct tape, bound her hands, drove her in her car to a state park, reinforced the bindings, tied her hands and feet together, and threw her off the bridge. Her body was found the next day by fishermen. Simmons was convicted of murder and sentenced to death.

In *Roper v. Simmons*, the U.S. Supreme Court held as follows:

The Eighth and Fourteenth Amendments forbid imposition of the death penalty on offenders who were under the age of 18 when their crimes were committed.

In this 5–4 decision, the majority opinion discussed the history of capital punishment, emphasizing that this most severe punishment "is reserved for a

(Continued)

Focus 4.1 (*Continued*)

narrow category of crimes and offenders." The Court gave three reasons that juveniles under 18 are not in that category.

- They are characterized by a lack of maturity and "an underdeveloped sense of responsibility."
- They are "more vulnerable or susceptible to negative influences and outside pressures."
- Their character "is not as well formed" as that of adults, and their personality traits are more transitory.

In 2010, the U.S. Supreme Court held that sentencing a juvenile to life without parole (LWOP) for committing a nonhomicide crime constitutes cruel and unusual punishment in violation of the Eighth Amendment (see Appendix A) and thus is unconstitutional. *Graham v. Florida*[2] involved a 17-year-old, Terrance Jamar Graham, who was charged with armed burglary with assault or battery, a first-degree felony carrying a maximum penalty of life in prison without the possibility of parole; and attempted armed robbery, a second-degree felony carrying a maximum penalty of 15 years in prison. Graham accepted a plea bargain but violated the terms of his probation and was charged with committing additional crimes. He was found guilty of those crimes as well as the charge of armed robbery, which had been deferred when he was placed on probation. He was sentenced to life in prison without the possibility of parole.

In holding that imposing LWOP on a teen who did not commit a murder, the Court cited its holding and reasons in *Roper v. Simmons*, emphasizing the three reasons enumerated above, and concluded:

> These salient characteristics mean that "[i]t is difficult even for expert psychologists to differentiate between the juvenile offender whose crime reflects unfortunate yet transient immaturity, and the rare juvenile offender whose crime reflects irreparable corruption."

[1]*Roper v. Simmons*, 543 U.S. 551 (2005).
[2]*Graham v. Florida*, 130 S.Ct. 2011 (2010), citations omitted. See also *Sullivan v. Florida*, 130 S.Ct. 2059 (2010).

Insanity

The **insanity** defense (a defense involving a state of mind or mental condition that negates a defendant's responsibility for his or her actions) is a controversial defense, despite the fact that it is used in less than 1 percent of all felony cases, and most defendants who assert the defense are not successful.

Technically, *insanity* is a social and legal term, but often it is assumed to be a medical term synonymous with *mental illness*. When used successfully in criminal law, the insanity defense results in an acquittal. But, unlike other defenses, the successful use of the insanity defense does not always result in the release of a defendant. Most defendants found not guilty by reason of insanity are confined to a mental hospital for treatment, as illustrated by the case of John W. Hinckley Jr., discussed in Focus 4.2.

Focus 4.2

The Insanity Defense in the Spotlight

On 30 March 1981, John W. Hinckley Jr. stepped from behind a crowd of on-lookers watching President Ronald Reagan leave a Washington hotel. He lev-eled a handgun at Reagan, and in one last, desperate attempt, tried to blast his way into the heart of actress Jodie Foster. Hinckley shot and wounded Rea-gan; Reagan's press secretary, James Brady; a Secret Service agent; and a Dis-trict of Columbia police officer.

An estimated 100 million Americans watched as newscasts replayed the scene of the boyish-looking 25-year-old Hinckley firing shots at the presiden-tial party and of Secret Service agents wresting the gun from Hinckley's hands while Reagan was rushed from the scene. The public thought this case would be an easy one for the prosecutor to win; there was little doubt about Hinck-ley's actions.

At Hinckley's trial, however, the defense presented evidence from psychi-atric examinations to show that Hinckley was legally insane at the time of the shootings. The most sensational evidence, and the cornerstone of Hinckley's defense, was the revelation of his obsession with the 1976 movie *Taxi Driver*.

Jurors watched as TV monitors replayed *Taxi Driver*, in which Jodie Foster plays the part of a 12-year-old prostitute. The lead character is a lonely taxi driver who becomes so obsessed with the prostitute that he stalks a U.S. sen-ator with a gun to gain publicity and the attention of the character played by Foster. At the end of the movie, the taxi driver kills the prostitute's pimp and becomes a hero.

After watching *Taxi Driver* several times, Hinckley became obsessed with the plot and with Foster, whom he had never met. The defense argued that Hinckley plotted to kill the president, thinking that it was the only way to get Foster to notice him. Other less drastic attempts to win her attention had failed. The defense presented evidence that attempted to show that Hinckley was psychotic and depressed and that he suffered delusions. A federal jury deliberated for over four days before finding Hinckley not guilty by reason of insanity.

Hinckley remains confined in St. Elizabeth's Psychiatric Hospital in Wash-ington, D.C. In 2005, the court gave Hinckley permission to visit his parents in their D.C. area home. In 2006, Hinckley was given permission to visit his parents in their home 200 miles away, but he was required to see a psychia-trist while he was on those visits. In June 2007, a federal court granted more freedom to hospital authorities in terms of the advance notice they must give Secret Service agents before they take Hinckley on local outings. Since that time, Hinckley's time away from St. Elizabeth's has been increased.

(Continued)

Focus 4.2 (*Continued*)

In 2011, the family asked for additional release time, and in January 2012, Washington, D.C., U.S. District Judge Paul Friedman began hearings on whether Hinckley should be granted additional leave time. Officials at St. Elizabeths Hospital proposed granting Hinckley two unsupervised 17-day visits with his mother at her home in Kingsmill, Virginia. Those visits would then be followed by six 24-day visits with her. Hinckley's attorneys predicted that these 8 visits would be completed within 8 to 10 months after which Hinckley should be given a convalescence leave. Federal prosecutors maintain that Hinckley remains a threat to society, has lied to his treatment personnel, and has low socialization skills. Thus they objected to the proposals. The judge stated that he was not likely to agree to the convalescence leave without another full hearing.[1]

The average stay at St. Elizabeth's is five years. With assassins or attempted assassins the rule appears to be different. Perhaps Hinckley's fate will be no different from that of other would-be presidential assassins. The man who attempted to assassinate President Andrew Jackson used the insanity defense successfully but spent the rest of his life in a mental institution. An attempted assassin of President Theodore Roosevelt, who claimed that he had been operating under the instructions of the ghost of President William McKinley, spent the last 31 years of his life in a mental ward. No attempted presidential assassin who has used the insanity defense successfully has left custody alive.[2]

[1]"Hearing To Resume on Greater Freedom for Reagan Gunman," *Los Angeles Times* (23 January 2012), p. 2.
[2]See James W. Clarke, *American Assassins: The Darker Side of Politics* (Princeton, NJ: Princeton University Press, 1982).

Insanity Tests

Over the years, several tests have been developed to define and measure insanity. The elements of these tests are stated in Focus 4.3, and each test is discussed briefly in the text.

The traditional, most frequently used insanity test, the **M'Naghten rule**, or the *right-versus-wrong test*, comes from an 1843 English case. Under this rule, a defendant may be found not guilty by reason of insanity if it can be shown that, as a result of a defect of reason from disease of the mind, the defendant (1) did not know the nature and quality of the act committed, or (2) did not know that the act was wrong.[5]

In the English case, defendant Daniel M'Naghten was found not guilty by reason of insanity after he argued successfully that the criminal act for which he was charged was caused by his delusions. M'Naghten was accused of shooting and killing the British prime minister's secretary. He argued that he thought the secretary was the prime minister, whom he believed was heading a conspiracy to kill him.

Focus 4.3

Insanity Tests

M'Naghten Rule: The Right-versus-Wrong Test
A defendant may be found not guilty by reason of insanity if, as the result of a defect of reason from disease of the mind, the defendant either:

- Did not know the nature and quality of the act committed or
- Did not know that the act was wrong

The Irresistible Impulse Test
The defendant's state of mind is such that he or she may know the nature and quality of an act and that it is wrong but cannot forbear from committing the act.

The Durham Rule: The Product Rule
If the unlawful act was the product of mental disease or defect, the accused is not criminally responsible for his or her conduct.

The ALI Test of the Model Penal Code: The Substantial Capacity Test

Section 4.01. Mental Disease or Defect Excluding Responsibility

(1) A person is not responsible for criminal conduct if at the time of such conduct as a result of mental disease or defect he lacks substantial capacity either to appreciate the criminality [wrongfulness] of his conduct or to conform his conduct to the requirements of law.

(2) As used in this article, the terms "mental disease or defect" do not include an abnormality manifested only by repeated criminal or otherwise antisocial conduct.

The main problems with the M'Naghten rule have centered on definitions. There is little case law on the meaning of the phrase *disease of the mind*. Most courts have not seemed too concerned about the issue and, without defining the phrase, tell the jury that they must find that the defendant suffered from a mental disease. The meaning of the word *know* is a more serious problem. Does it mean that the defendant has cognitive (pertaining to memory, reasoning, judgment, in contrast to emotion) knowledge or that he or she has a moral understanding of the nature and quality of the act? Again, most courts do not decide; the M'Naghten rule is stated without a definition of *know*.

The M'Naghten rule has other words and phrases that may also present interpretation problems, such as *nature and quality of the act* and *wrong*. Does the former mean that the defendant understands both the physical nature and the physical consequences of an act—for example, that putting a match to kerosene will cause a fire that will burn a building and kill people sleeping inside? Does *wrong* mean knowing that an act is legally wrong, morally wrong, or both? For these and other reasons, the M'Naghten rule is criticized.

Some argue that the M'Naghten rule emphasizes the cognitive part of the personality to the exclusion of the emotional elements, but that the ability to control one's behavior is not determined solely by cognition. It is also argued that the M'Naghten rule presents psychiatrists with impossible questions that must be answered when they testify at trial and that the test is not an adequate way to identify defendants who should not be subjected to criminal punishments.

A second insanity test is the **irresistible impulse test**, which provides that defendants may be found not guilty by reason of insanity if they were unable to control their criminal acts even though they knew that the acts were wrong. Some states have adopted this approach either by statute or by court decision.

The definition of irresistible impulse varies, with one case stating that the phrase means that a defendant would commit a crime even if there were a "policeman at his [or her] elbow."[6] It is suggested, however, that this instruction is too restrictive. Some people might be able to exercise self-control in the presence of a police officer but be unable to control their behavior in other circumstances.

The third insanity test, the **Durham rule**, comes from a 1954 District of Columbia case, *Durham v. United States,* which stated: "An accused is not criminally responsible if his unlawful act was the product of mental disease or mental defect."[7] The Durham rule became known as the *product rule.*

The *Durham* case distinguished *disease*, which is "capable of either improving or deteriorating," from *defect*, a "condition which is not considered capable of either improving or deteriorating and which may be either congenital, or the result of injury, or the residual effect of a physical or mental disease." It was thought that the Durham rule would assist in eliminating from criminal culpability those people who are not punishable in U.S. criminal justice systems because they lack moral blame.

The Durham rule was not widely adopted. Critics argued that the test permitted mental health experts too much influence and juries too much discretion. In addition, no standards were set by the court. In 1972 the *Durham* case was overruled in the District of Columbia, where it originated.[8]

A fourth insanity test is the **substantial capacity test**, which was developed by the scholars of the American Law Institute (ALI), who drafted the Model Penal Code. The ALI rejected the Durham rule and proposed a modified version of the M'Naghten and irresistible impulse tests. The substantial capacity test provides as follows:

(1) A person is not responsible for criminal conduct if at the time of such conduct as a result of mental disease or defect he lacks substantial capacity either to appreciate the criminality [wrongfulness] of his conduct or to conform his conduct to the requirements of law.

(2) As used in this article, the terms "mental disease or defect" do not include an abnormality manifested only by repeated criminal or otherwise antisocial conduct.[9]

The ALI test is broader than the M'Naghten rule in its substitution of *appreciate* for *know*. Thus, under the ALI test, a defendant who knows the difference between right and wrong but who does not appreciate that difference may be successful using an insanity defense. It is appropriate to introduce **expert testimony**, such as that provided by psychiatrists and psychologists, to provide evidence of the defendant's emotional and intellectual capacity. The ALI test appears to be a compromise between what can be viewed as the total impairment requirement of the M'Naghten and irresistible impulse tests and the apparent requirement of only slight impairment in the Durham rule.

The second paragraph of the ALI test was written to exclude sociopathic or psychopathic personalities (these terms are difficult to distinguish, but both refer to the lack of the development of a moral sense, i.e., an antisocial personality) because of disagreement among authorities over whether people with these personality types suffer from a mental disease. The paragraph is controversial and has been rejected by some jurisdictions, but it has been adopted by most jurisdictions that use the ALI test.

These four insanity tests and other issues, such as the jury verdict of not guilty by reason of insanity in the trial of John W. Hinckley Jr., led to strong public support for changes in the insanity defense. Some jurisdictions followed the Michigan plan, discussed next.

Guilty but Mentally Ill (GBMI)

Since 1975, a defendant who raises the insanity defense in Michigan, in addition to being found guilty, not guilty, or not guilty by reason of insanity, may be found **guilty but mentally ill (GBMI)**.

The Michigan statute distinguishes insanity from mental illness and provides for a finding of GBMI if the jury is convinced beyond a reasonable doubt of *all* of the following:

1. That the defendant is guilty of an offense
2. That the defendant was mentally ill at the time of the commission of that offense
3. That the defendant was not legally insane at the time of the commission of that offense[10]

Under the Michigan statute, a defendant who pleads guilty or who, after a trial, is found to be mentally ill, may receive the sentence that could be imposed under a guilty plea alone. The difference is that a verdict of GBMI obligates the Department of Mental Health to provide psychiatric treatment while the defendant is under its jurisdiction.

Guilty Except Insane

Other states have adopted various versions of the Michigan statute. For example, Arizona's statute provides for a finding of *guilty except insane*. A finding under this statute could result in confinement in a state mental health facility or the psychiatric facility of the correctional system. The constitutionality of portions of this statute were upheld by the U.S. Supreme Court in 2006.[11]

The Arizona statute may become relevant if Arizona brings state charges against Jared Lee Loughner, who is facing 49 federal felonies, including murder and attempted murder, for the shooting spree in Tucson, Arizona, on 8 January 2011. Six people, including a federal judge, were killed, and 13 people, including Congresswoman Gabrielle Giffords, were wounded. Loughner was being held in a federal mental health facility in Springfield, Missouri, in March 2012, when a federal court held that he could be forcibly medicated because he was a threat to himself and to others. As of this writing, Loughner had not yet been ruled mentally competent to stand trial.[12]

Congresswoman Giffords was making remarkable recovery from serious wounds, but in January 2012, she resigned her position to devote more time to her rehabilitation.

Abolition of the Insanity Defense

Dissatisfaction with the insanity defense has led some jurisdictions to abolish it. The Idaho Code states: "Mental condition shall not be a defense to any charge of criminal conduct." The code does, however, permit the admission of expert testimony to negate the intent required for the charged offense.[13] Some states permit evidence of mental illness to be admitted only for the purpose of determining the appropriate sentence.

Diminished Capacity or Partial Responsibility

Some defendants who do not wish to pursue an insanity defense may attempt to establish the similar defense of diminished capacity or partial responsibility. This defense is available when it can be shown that the defendant's mental illness, though not sufficient to establish insanity, caused such a lack of capacity that the defendant could not have achieved the requisite intent at the time of the crime. For example, defendants charged with first-degree murder may use this defense to show that they did not have the requisite intent for that crime, although they might reasonably be convicted of the lesser crime of manslaughter. Some jurisdictions abolished the defense of diminished capacity.

Automatism

The automatism defense may be raised by defendants who can offer evidence that they were unconscious or semiconscious when they acted. For example, a physical problem—such as an epileptic seizure, a concussion, or an unexplained blackout—that results in an accident that kills someone might support a complete defense for a driver charged with manslaughter. However, if the driver knew or should have known that the physical problem existed, the defense probably would not be applicable.

Emotional trauma might be another acceptable reason for the automatism defense, but brainwashing is not a sufficient basis for asserting the defense. Nor is unconsciousness caused by voluntary intoxication sufficient.

From the defendant's point of view, automatism as a defense is to be preferred over that of insanity because an acquittal based on the automatism defense is complete and the defendant is released, although civil commitment proceedings might follow.

Entrapment

The **entrapment** defense, which applies only to actions by government agents or their employees, may be used when a government agent induces a defendant to commit a crime that he or she would not have been inclined to commit without that inducement. A successful entrapment defense requires proof of two elements:

1. A government agent induced the defendant to commit the crime.
2. The defendant was not otherwise predisposed to commit the crime.

It is obvious that one of the best ways for police to gather evidence against offenders is to be present when the crimes are committed. Since this rarely occurs, police may go undercover or may use informants to gain information about criminal activity. Both practices are acceptable as long as government agents do not go too far in their activities. In a 1932 decision, the U.S. Supreme Court stated, "Society is at war with the criminal classes, and courts have uniformly held that in waging this warfare the forces of prevention and detection may use traps, decoys, and deception to obtain evidence of the commission of crime."[14]

There are limits to what the government may do without committing entrapment. According to the U.S. Supreme Court, "To determine whether entrapment has been established a line must be drawn between the trap for the unwary innocent and the trap for the unwary criminal."[15] That line was drawn in a case decided by the U.S. Supreme Court and discussed in Focus 4.4.

Focus 4.4

U.S. Supreme Court Rebukes Government Action: Nebraska Farmer Wins on Entrapment Defense

In 1992, in *Jacobson v. United States*,[1] the U.S. Supreme Court reversed a Nebraska farmer's conviction for violation of the Child Pornography Act of 1984, which criminalizes the knowing receipt through the mails of a "visual depiction [that] involves the use of a minor engaging in sexually explicit conduct." The following excerpt outlines the basic facts and conclusions of law of this case.1

Jacobson v. United States

In February 1984, petitioner, a 56-year-old veteran-turned-farmer who supported his elderly father in Nebraska, ordered two magazines and a brochure from a California adult bookstore. The magazines, entitled *Bare Boys I* and *Bare Boys II*, contained photographs of nude preteen and teenage boys. The contents of the magazines startled petitioner, who testified that he had expected to receive photographs of "young men 18 years or older."…The young men depicted in the magazines were not engaged in sexual activity, and petitioner's receipt of the magazine was legal under both federal and Nebraska law. Within three months, the law with respect to child pornography changed; Congress passed the Act illegalizing the receipt through the

(Continued)

Focus 4.4 (*Continued*)

mails of sexually explicit depictions of children. In the very month that the new provision became law, postal inspectors found petitioner's name on the mailing list of the California bookstore that had mailed him *Bare Boys I* and *II*. There followed over the next 2½ years, repeated efforts by two Government agencies, through five fictitious organizations and a bogus pen pal, to explore petitioner's willingness to break the law by ordering sexually explicit photographs of children through the mail....

[The Court described the government's actions in detail.]

There can be no dispute about the evils of child pornography or the difficulties that laws and law enforcement have encountered in eliminating it. Likewise, there can be no dispute that the Government may use undercover agents to enforce the law....

In their zeal to enforce the law, however, Government agents may not originate a criminal design, implant in an innocent person's mind the disposition to commit a criminal act, and then induce commission of the crime so that the Government may prosecute....

By the time the petitioner finally placed his order, he had already been the target of 26 months of repeated mailings and communications from Government agents and fictitious organizations. Therefore, although he had become predisposed to break the law by May 1987, it is our view that the Government did not prove that this predisposition was independent and not the product of the attention that the Government had directed at petitioner since January 1985.

[1]*Jacobson v. United States*, 503 U.S. 540 (1992), cases and citations omitted.

Outrageous Government Conduct

A defense similar to entrapment is that of *outrageous government conduct*. This defense is based on the assumption that some behavior is so offensive and so outrageous that when it is committed by a government agent, it cannot be the basis for legally collecting evidence to convict a defendant. The behavior in question "must be shocking, outrageous, and clearly intolerable."[16]

A lower federal court has held that the outrageous conduct prohibition would not preclude a government agent from supplying *some* drugs to addicts while working under cover, but that

[a]t a certain threshold, the government's conduct would violate due process. For instance, we speculate that if a government agent entered a drug rehabilitation treatment center and sold heroin to a recovering addict, and the addict was subsequently prosecuted for possession of a controlled substance, the outrageous government conduct defense might properly be invoked.[17]

Another lower federal appeals court ruled that the outrageous government conduct defense does not exist. The U.S. Supreme Court refused to review the case, thus permitting the lower court's ruling to remain in effect.[18]

Defense of Persons and Property
The law permits people to defend themselves, other people, and property under certain circumstances. The defense of persons or property is one of the most controversial defenses today, as more people are buying guns and using them defensively. Defense of self, defense of others, and defense of property may not be separated in all cases; some cases involve all three. To the extent that these defenses are separable, the rules differ with regard to acts that are permitted.

Self-Defense
The defense of self and of others is permitted under some circumstances. The general rule on self-defense is that a person is permitted to use force to repel the actions of another under the following circumstances, which constitute the elements of self-defense:

1. The individual has an honest and reasonable belief that he or she is
2. Facing an unlawful threat of imminent death or serious bodily injury (which could justify the use of deadly force in self-defense)
3. By an aggressor (i.e., no provocation on the part of the one who asserts self-defense) and
4. The force used was reasonable under the circumstances.

In the first and fourth elements, the word *reasonable* is important, for it establishes an *objective* rather than a *subjective* test, meaning that the accused acted as a reasonable person would have acted under the circumstances. If the belief was a reasonable one, it would not matter that it was inaccurate. That is, if it can be shown that most people would reasonably believe that they were in danger of immediate physical harm, use of force is justified.

In some jurisdictions the rules regarding self-defense may be different for police officers, who may be held to a subjective rather than an objective standard, in which case the issue is whether *that* officer believed he or she was in danger, not whether a reasonable person would have that belief. Finally, the threatened harm must be imminent and unlawful, and the actor must not have provoked the attack.

The right to use force does not always include the right to use **deadly force**. The use of deadly force to protect oneself or others may be limited to situations in which the actors have reasonable beliefs that deadly force is necessary to protect them from harm that might cause serious bodily injury or death. The Model Penal Code (MPC) permits the use of deadly force when "the actor believes that such force is necessary to protect himself against death, serious bodily injury, kidnapping, or sexual intercourse compelled by force or threat." The MPC does not permit the use of deadly force as a defense if, in the same encounter, the actor provoked the incident that led to the threat of harm or death.[19]

Some jurisdictions require a person to retreat before using deadly force, although some limit that duty to situations in which retreat can be accomplished with safety. The MPC requires retreating if it can be done with "complete safety," although, with a few exceptions, the code does not require actors to retreat within their own homes.[20] The exclusion of the home from the duty to retreat is known as the *castle doctrine*, recognized in most U.S. jurisdictions and meaning that a person who is threatened inside his or her home is *not* required to retreat. The castle doctrine was utilized on New Year's Eve in 2011, when a teen widow shot and killed one of two intruders who forced their way past a sofa at the door and into her mobile home where she lived with her infant. Sarah McKinley's husband had died of lung cancer on Christmas Day. McKinley called law enforcement and asked if she could shoot the intruder(s). The dispatcher said she could not tell McKinley that she could do that, "but you do what you have to do to protect your baby." The intruder died clutching a knife; his alleged accomplice later turned himself in.[21]

In recent years, some jurisdictions have retreated from the castle doctrine and other restrictions and given more leeway to persons who use force to protect themselves and others. An example is the Florida statute, which provides as follows:

> A person is justified in using force, except deadly force, against another when and to the extent that the person reasonably believes that such conduct is necessary to defend himself or herself or another against the other's imminent use of unlawful force. However, a person is justified in the use of deadly force and does not have a duty to retreat if:
>
> (1) He or she reasonably believes that such force is necessary to prevent imminent death or great bodily harm to himself or herself or another or to prevent the imminent commission of a forcible felony; or
> (2) Under those circumstances permitted pursuant to [another statute, which is concerned with protection of oneself within the home].[22]

This statute became the focus of national protests in 2012 after George Zimmerman shot and killed Trayvon Martin, aged 17 and unarmed, inside a small gated community in Sanford, Florida. Zimmerman was eventually arrested and charged with second-degree murder after the state's governor appointed a special prosecutor to investigate the case. It appeared that Zimmerman's defense would be the *stand your ground* statute. Critics challenged its applicability to the facts as reported in the media. The trial had not occurred as of this publication.

Finally, some jurisdictions have extended the castle doctrine to social guests.

Defense of Others

The rules governing the use of force to protect others are similar to those for self-defense. The actor is justified in using force to protect others if conditions exist that would justify the use of force for self-defense for the actor and for the threatened person and if the actor reasonably believes that it is necessary to use force to protect the other person. Generally, it is not required that a special relationship exist between the parties before the use of force is justified to protect another.

Defense of Property

Even though defense of property is permitted, the rules are more stringent than those for self-defense or for the defense of others. Some of these rules differ among the jurisdictions, although it is well accepted that unless property occupiers need to protect themselves, they are not privileged to use deadly force to protect property. Otherwise, if it is reasonably necessary to use force to protect property from the immediate criminal acts of others, reasonable force is permitted. The force is limited to the amount needed to prevent the criminal acts; it is not reasonable to use any force if the acts can be prevented by asking the intruder to stop.

A property owner is not privileged to use force against a **trespasser** (one who has no legal or implied right to be on the property of another), if that person would be placed in substantial danger of serious bodily injury upon being excluded from the property. This rule prohibits the use of booby traps or other such devices designed to cause serious bodily harm or death.

In most instances, the use of devices that are not designed to cause serious bodily injury or death is justified for the protection of property. Devices that are not designed to cause serious bodily injury or death may be used if they are reasonable under the circumstances and if those devices are used customarily or if reasonable care is taken to inform potential intruders that the devices are present.

Law Enforcement

Another defense against criminal conduct is that of law enforcement. Conduct that is criminal under most circumstances may be justified and therefore not criminal when committed by a law enforcement officer or by a private citizen attempting to enforce the law. However, there is a limit to the otherwise criminal acts that law enforcement may commit to gain evidence of other crimes. For example, it would not be permissible for an officer to engage in sexual intercourse with a prostitute, commit an armed robbery, or hire someone to commit a murder.

Force, including deadly force, may be used by private citizens as well as by law enforcement officers in certain circumstances without incurring criminal responsibility. Officers and people aiding them may use force to effect an arrest or to prevent an escape under some circumstances. The most critical issues arise over the use of deadly force.

Under common law, law enforcement officers were permitted to shoot any **fleeing felon**—a person who had committed a felony and was eluding arrest. This rule existed when all felonies were capital offenses and apprehending criminals was difficult. Felons were likely to get away if they were not apprehended quickly. Many states followed this common law rule in establishing their criminal codes, although some limited the shooting to fleeing felons who were accused of serious felonies, such as murder or forcible rape. This was changed as the result of a 1985 U.S. Supreme Court decision from Tennessee, in which police dispatched to a "prowler inside call" were told by a neighbor that she heard a glass break in the house next door. An officer went to the back of the house, heard a door slam, and saw a man running toward the fence. The officer, with the aid of his flashlight, saw the person's face and hands and said that he appeared to be about 17 or 18 years old and about 5 feet 5 inches to 5 feet 7 inches tall. The suspect was actually 15 years old and 5 feet 4 inches tall. The officer yelled, "Police, halt," but the suspect did not stop. The officer testified that, although apparently the suspect was not armed, he thought that if the suspect got over the fence, he would elude the officers. The officer fired, hit the suspect in the back of the head, and killed him. The Tennessee statute permitted the officer to fire after giving a warning.

After acknowledging the importance of crime prevention, the U.S. Supreme Court ruled that the Tennessee statute was unconstitutional in its application to the facts of this case (although it might be constitutional when applied to other facts). The Court gave reasons and guidelines for the use of deadly force when police are attempting to arrest a suspect. In brief, the Court stated as follows:

> Where the officer has probable cause to believe that the suspect poses a threat of serious physical harm, either to the officer or to others, it is not constitutionally unreasonable to prevent escape by using deadly force. Thus, if the suspect threatens the officer with a weapon or there is probable cause to believe that he has committed a crime involving the infliction or threatened infliction of serious physical harm, deadly force may be used when necessary to prevent escape and when some warning has been given where feasible. Applied in such circumstances, the Tennessee statute would pass constitutional muster.[23]

Under restricted conditions (usually a requirement that the suspect committed a serious felony, such as murder), a private person may use deadly force to effect an arrest. Most statutes permit people who are not assisting peace officers to use deadly force only when they are protecting themselves or others.

Intoxication

The law recognizes a limited **intoxication** defense. *Intoxication* refers to the condition that exists when a person consumes alcohol or other drugs to the extent that his or her mental or physical abilities are significantly affected. The defense is permitted in some instances in which there is evidence that intoxication created a state of mind similar to that of an insane person, and thus the defendant could not form the requisite intent required for that crime. In jurisdictions that recognize the irresistible impulse test, for example, the intoxication defense may be used when defendants offer evidence that as a result of intoxication they were unable to control themselves and thus engaged in criminal behavior although they knew that behavior was wrong. The intoxication defense is not recognized in situations in which intoxication is an element of the crime, as, for example, in the case of driving while intoxicated.

The intoxication defense is divided into two types: involuntary and voluntary. **Involuntary intoxication** (intoxication without choice or will, such as that which occurs when someone slips drugs into the food or drink of an unsuspecting person) is appropriate when a defendant has acted under intoxication that was compelled or coerced by another or when a defendant became intoxicated as the result of deception, mistake, or ignorance. The latter category might involve a defendant who is allegedly unaware of the side effects of a prescription drug, as illustrated by the Pittman case discussed in Focus 4.5.

================ **Focus 4.5** ================

Should Prescription Drug Use Be a Legal Defense to Illegal Behavior?

In recent years, considerable attention has been given to the impact that pre-scription drugs have on behavior. In particular, defense attorneys have sought to introduce the possible effects as reasons to explain the violent behavior of their clients, especially in cases in which the prosecution must prove a specif-ic intent to commit the crime in question. Thus it is argued that, in effect, the drugs prevented the defendant from having the mental capacity to develop that specific intent.

To illustrate, in a widely publicized murder trial in February 2005, defense attorneys argued that their client, Christopher Pittman, who was only 12 when he killed his grandparents, was unable to control his actions because of the effect of Zoloft, an antidepressant drug, which had been prescribed for him shortly before the killings. The defense argued that Pittman did not have the specific intent required for first-degree murder.

The Pittman case is significant because the federal Food and Drug Ad-ministration (FDA) had recently issued an order requiring a warning label on all antidepressants, stating that such drugs might carry an increased risk of suicidal thoughts when taken by young people.

Pittman's defense requested, and the judge granted, a jury instruction on the defense of involuntary intoxication. The jury was told that for this defense to be successful, the defense must prove all of the following:

- The defendant must have been unaware of the potentially intoxicating effect of Zoloft.
- The defendant was taking Zoloft under a doctor's prescription.
- The drug Zoloft rendered the defendant unable to tell the difference between right and wrong.

The essential facts of the Pittman case were as follows. Pittman's mother left him when he was a child. He lived with various relatives, including briefly with his father; his mother reappeared and then disappeared again, after which Pittman ran away. He was placed in a Florida behavioral facility, where he was taking Paxil, an antidepressant drug. He was released from that facility and went to live with his grandparents in South Carolina, enrolled in school, and began taking Zoloft under a physician's prescription. Prosecutors argued that Pittman shot his grandparents after his grandfather disciplined him for getting into trouble at school, set the house on fire, and stole their car. The jury convicted Pittman of two counts of first-degree murder; he was sentenced to two concurrent 30-year prison terms without the possibility for parole.

When questioned after the trial, some jurors said they thought the drug Zoloft may have influenced Pittman's behavior but that it did not cause him to murder his grandparents. Despite the lack of success of the Zoloft defense in the Pittman case, it is significant that the trial judge permitted the defense, as have other judges. This sends mixed signals to the public. On the one hand, even the FDA is suggesting a careful look at this and other antidepressant drugs before prescribing them for young people. On the other hand, many

(Continued)

Focus 4.5 (*Continued*)

people suffering from depression, including young persons, have been helped by Zoloft and other drugs.[1]

On appeal, Pittman's attorneys raised several issues, all of which were rejected by the state supreme court. In 2008, the U.S. Supreme Court refused to review the case.[2] In 2010, Circuit Judge Roger Young ordered a new trial after finding that the defense team committed several errors during Pittman's trial.[3]

A Michigan defendant was found not guilty by reason of insanity after he claimed that he shot his estranged wife because of the influence of the prescription drug Halcion. In his first trial in 1990, John Caulley was convicted of first-degree murder and sentenced to life in prison. He was granted a retrial after an appellate court ruled that the jury should have been permitted to consider the effect of Halcion on his behavior. Caulley claimed the drug, which he took as a sleeping aid, caused him to shoot his wife.[4]

[1] "Boy's Murder Case Entangled in Fight over Antidepressants," *New York Times* (23 August 2004), p. 1; "Boy Who Took Antidepressant Is Convicted in Killings," *New York Times* (16 February 2005), p. 12.
[2] *Pittman v. South Carolina*, 647 S.E.2d 144 (S.C. 2007), *cert. denied*, 552 U.S. 1314 (2008).
[3] "Judge Orders New Trial in S.C. Zoloft Case," *Boston Globe* (28 July 2010), p. 2.
[4] "Man Who Killed His Wife Found Insane: Had Blamed Sleep Aid," *Phoenix Gazette* (21 October 1993), p. 10; *State v. Caulley*, 494 N.W.2d 853 (Mich.App. 1992), *appeal denied*, 502 N.W.2d 39 (Mich. 1993).

In most jurisdictions, **voluntary intoxication**, which refers to intoxication brought on by free will, is not a defense. Voluntary intoxication is a defense in some jurisdictions if it negates an element of the offense, but at best it is only a partial defense, meaning that it cannot negate general intent but may negate specific intent. For example, it might result in reducing a first-degree murder charge to that of second-degree murder or manslaughter. In most jurisdictions, voluntary intoxication cannot negate recklessness or negligence when those elements, rather than purpose or knowledge, are required for the crime.

Domestic Authority

The defense of *domestic authority* stems from ancient laws that gave husbands the legal right to discipline their wives with a "whip or rattan no bigger than [a] thumb, in order to enforce the salutary restraints of domestic discipline."[24] The husband's right to administer such discipline is not recognized under modern common or statutory law. The law does, however, recognize the right of parents to discipline their children. Under some circumstances, those acting in the place of parents may do likewise, under the doctrine of *in loco parentis* (literally, in the place of a parent).

Teachers may also discipline their students. Discipline falls under the domestic authority provision, but the discipline must be reasonable. Some states specify by statute that teachers may not use corporal punishment. Simply stated, Nebraska provides that "Corporal punishment shall be prohibited in public schools."[25] The state's supreme court upheld the constitutionality of that statute, ruling that it is not vague because reasonable people know the meaning of corporal punishment and thus can abide by the statute.[26] Nebraska does provide, however, that teachers and administrative personnel

> may take actions regarding student behavior . . . which are reasonably neces-
> sary to aid the student, further school purposes, or prevent interference with
> the educational process. Such actions may include, but need not be limited to,
> counseling of students, parent conferences, rearrangement of schedules, re-
> quirements that a student remain in school after regular hours to do addition-
> al work, restriction of extracurricular activity, or requirements that a student
> receive counseling, psychological evaluation, or psychiatric evaluation upon
> the written consent of a parent or guardian to such counseling or evaluation.[27]

The U.S. Supreme Court has ruled that the discipline of schoolchildren may include paddling. According to the Court, the Eighth Amendment's prohibition against cruel and unusual punishment (see Appendix A) applies to criminals, not to school students. The Court emphasized that any punishment that goes beyond that which is reasonably necessary to maintain discipline in the classroom may result in civil and criminal culpability.[28]

Domestic authority exists in other situations as well. Persons in charge of trains, theaters, boats, airplanes, and other similar places have the right to use reasonable force to control persons who are disruptive. Prison officials may discipline inmates, but they may not inflict punishment that violates the Eighth Amendment's prohibition against cruel and unusual punishment. Ship captains, service officers, and others may discipline those who serve under them. In all of these situations the discipline must be reasonable.

Two other defenses that have been used historically are consent and condonation.

Consent and Condonation

Usually a person's consent to a crime or forgiveness of that act is not a defense. The issue of consent arises frequently in cases of **euthanasia**, a term applied to the act of killing someone, often at that person's request, because of a terminal illness, considerable pain, or a debilitating handicap. Frequently the person killed is a relative (often a spouse) who has allegedly begged the actor to end his or her pain and misery with death. The law does not permit this cooperation and agreement to negate the criminal act, just as the law does not permit a patient to agree to the malpractice of a medical person, or a sports star to agree to bribery in a game.

In some cases, consent may negate an element of a crime. For example, by definition, *forcible rape* is sexual intercourse without the victim's consent. If the victim consents, the act is not forcible rape. However, if the alleged victim is not of legal age and thus does not have the legal capacity to consent, the act constitutes a crime.

Consent may also be a defense to less serious acts, such as those that might occur in a lawful sports activity, in which a person might be hurt by the nature of the game. The consent must have been given voluntarily (not the product of force, duress, or deception) and knowingly by a legally competent person.

Condonation, or forgiveness of a criminal act by an alleged victim, is not generally a defense to a crime in the United States, although in other countries it may be. For example, a few countries drop forcible rape charges against men whose alleged victims agree to marry them. But in the United States, a victim's forgiveness does not eliminate the criminal responsibility of the perpetrator, for crimes are considered offenses against society as well as against individual victims. Under some circumstances, however, victims of less serious crimes are permitted to negotiate a civil settlement with their assailants, after which the court may dismiss the criminal charges.

Syndrome and Stress Disorder Defenses

A number of mental health syndromes and disorders associated with stress are recognized by courts as partial or complete defenses to criminal acts. The more frequently used ones are discussed.

The **battered person syndrome** defense is somewhat analogous to self-defense, discussed earlier in this chapter. The difference is that evidence of the battered person syndrome is permitted in some courts as a defense to criminal acts even though the element of imminent danger, required for self-defense, is not present.

The battered person syndrome arises from a cycle of abuse by a special person, often a parent or a spouse, that leads the victim to perceive that violence against the offender is the only way to end the abuse. Most commonly, the *term battered woman syndrome* is used, but the extension of the concept to others, such as adult males as well as children who murder their parents after years of alleged physical or sexual abuse, has led to the use of the more neutral term *battered person syndrome*. Evidence of long-term battering may be introduced in court to support a defense to a criminal act or to reduce the defendant's sentence after conviction. Such evidence, provided by expert witnesses, was first permitted in 1979, and the number of courts that permit it are increasing.[29] The evidence is offered to help jurors understand why a battered person, especially a battered adult, would remain in a relationship. In essence, the battered person may develop the belief that he or she is threatened with serious bodily harm and death when, in fact, that may not be the case.

Another stress-type defense is illustrated by an Oregon statute concerning *extreme emotional disturbance*, which may constitute a partial defense to some types of murder. According to the Oregon statute,

> It is an affirmative defense to murder . . . that the homicide was committed under the influence of extreme emotional disturbance when such disturbance is not the result of the person's own intentional, knowing, reckless or criminally negligent act, and if there is a reasonable explanation for the disturbance. The reasonableness of the explanation for the disturbance must be determined from the standpoint of an ordinary person in the actor's situation under the

circumstances that the actor reasonably believed them to be. Extreme emotional disturbance does not constitute a defense to . . . any other crime.[30]

Another category of defenses related to stress are those grouped under the concept of **posttraumatic stress disorder (PTSD). PTSD** is a disorder in which stress is experienced by people who have suffered severe trauma, such as during war or rape. Symptoms include nightmares, feelings of guilt, disorientation, and reliving the traumatic event(s). It is argued that victims of this disorder should not be held accountable for their criminal acts because they cannot control their behavior. Symptoms include nightmares, guilt, disorientation, and reliving the traumatic event(s). PTSD can cause anxiety disorders, depression, substance abuse, poor physical health, or psychological impairment.

Approximately 10 million Americans will develop PTSD at some point in their lives. Among women, the most frequent cause is rape or other sexual trauma. Among military women, the most frequent cause is war.[31]

Several stress syndromes are included within PTSD. The *war combat syndrome* is a prominent one. The most frequent use of the PTSD defense in a criminal case involving defendants who experience combat has been by those who fought in Vietnam. In that war, compared to previous ones, stress problems were magnified by new types of warfare that killed or maimed quickly, but advances in medical technology saved many soldiers, who would have died in previous wars. Multiple amputees, paraplegics, and veterans with other problems returned home. One result was a greater understanding of stress syndromes during and after the Vietnam War, and treatment became available.

In recent years, more reports have surfaced about increased stress within the military. On 13 July 2012, the Institute of Medicine of the National Academy of Sciences released a 400-page report of a long-term study mandated by the U.S. Congress and sponsored by the Defense Department and the Department of Veterans Affairs. The report estimated that "as many as one in five of the 2.6 million service members who have deployed to Iraq or Afghanistan since 2001" are affected by PTSD.[32] Within days of the publication of this report, Pentagon officials issued a statement that they were reviewing the report and had already implemented some of its recommendations.[33]

Officials at the Army's installation at Fort Hood, Texas, one of the largest in the world and included in this study, had previously reported noting more signs of war stress, including more requests for marriage counseling for spouses, especially when their loved ones volunteered for additional tours of combat duty. An Army survey revealed that soldiers were 50 percent more likely to report posttraumatic stress if they served more than one tour of duty. The Army also reported that in recent years soldiers had exhibited a 30 percent increase in binge drinking, a doubling of the use of illegal drugs, and close to a doubling of suicides in Iraq and Kuwait. Equipment shortages for training at Fort Hood, along with housing issues and redeployments, create additional stress.[34]

In cases involving combat stress, PTSD expert testimony may be admitted to show that the defendant was in a dissociative state. For example, one defendant claimed that he believed he was in North Vietnam when he shot a police officer.

Another, who escaped from prison, testified that he thought he was in Vietnam and that he was running back home.[35]

In May 2008, the philanthropic and education arms of the American Psychiatric Association (APA) outlined a major expansion of efforts to offer mental health services to military persons returning from Iraq and Afghanistan. According to the announcement,

> Efforts will be made to create a large, national, volunteer network over the next three years to address postwar mental health issues such as post-traumatic stress disorder (PTSD), traumatic brain injury (TBI), drug abuse, anxiety and depression. . . . [The goal is to recruit] 10 percent of the 400,000 mental health professionals in the United States by 2015 to assist in this effort.[36]

In 2009, however, the Pentagon announced that it would not award the Purple Heart to war veterans who suffered PTSD but were without a physical wound. A spokeswoman stated, "Historically, the Purple Heart has never been awarded for mental disorders or psychological conditions resulting from witnessing or experiencing traumatic combat events." It was concluded that PTSD is too difficult to diagnose "as objectively and routinely as would be required for this award at this time."[37]

Another type of stress disorder that is recognized by some courts as a defense is the **rape trauma syndrome (RTS)**, which is a type of PTSD that follows forced sex. Evidence of RTS may be sufficient to convince juries that complainants are telling the truth when they testify that they submitted to sexual acts to avoid more serious injuries or death. This is important because jurors may not believe that a person was raped unless there is evidence of a serious fight.

The use of RTS evidence is not limited to female victims. There is also evidence that men who are raped may suffer from the RTS. One corrections journal reported a study that focused on male inmate rape victims. The researchers concluded, "These rapes are unimaginably vicious and brutal. . . . Gang assaults are not uncommon and victims may be left beaten, bloody and, in the most extreme cases, dead." Some of the symptoms that male rape victims reported were "nightmares, deep depression, shame, loss of self-esteem, self-hatred and considering or attempting suicide."[38]

So, if men and women who have been raped suffer posttraumatic stress, should evidence of such be admitted if they are tried for subsequent crimes? In other words, should RTS be a recognized defense? In a case involving a 21-year-old woman with an IQ of 70 who shot and killed her alleged rapist whom she had known for years as a friend, an appellate court reversed the conviction on several grounds, including the trial court's refusal to permit the introduction of evidence of RTS. The court stated:

> Post-traumatic stress disorder is a psychological reaction to an extreme traumatic event such as rape. Those suffering from PTSD are said to typically exhibit symptoms such as the re-experiencing of the trauma through memories, nightmares and flashbacks, feelings of numbness or detachment, and insomnia, irritability, impaired concentration, and hypervigilance. . . . Courts in

New York have recognized . . . that rape is a stressor that may cause PTSD. PTSD is an accepted ground for asserting a defense of extreme emotional disturbance under [the N.Y. statute] and a "mental disease or defect" defense under [another N.Y. statute] the latter of which, if accepted by a jury, constitutes a complete defense to a crime.[39]

Another PTSD defense is the **postpartum depression (PPD) syndrome** defense. *Postpartum depression* is a disorder that some women experience after giving birth. Mothers who kill their children may use a variety of reasons in their defenses, but those who kill shortly after their babies are born may have a case for using the PPD syndrome defense.

The American Psychiatric Association reports that approximately three-fourths of all women suffer "baby blues" after giving birth, but most women recover in a few days. Between 10 and 20 percent of women experience depression for a longer period after giving birth. Only approximately one or two of every 1,000 new mothers experience extreme PPD, but an assistant professor of obstetrics and psychiatry at Duke University referred to PPD as "the most under-recognized, under-diagnosed, and under-treated obstetrical complication in America."[40]

SUMMARY

This chapter discussed the major defenses that may be raised to negate a crime or some element of a crime. These defenses are very important, but they are complicated. This chapter gave definitions and some examples, but the case law on defenses is immense, and new challenges continue to arise in the interpretations of long-used defenses as well as the introduction of new ones.

The introduction, which set the stage for discussing individual defenses, presented material concerning the burden of proof, the existence of presumptions and defenses to crimes, and the allocation of the burden of proof regarding those defenses. The chapter illustrated that it is not easy to distinguish some defenses from elements of a crime and that the allocation of the burden of proof is not a simple matter.

Although it is not possible to write a simple statement or draft a list of what can and cannot be done on these issues, it is possible to make general statements. It must be understood, however, that these principles may lead to different legal conclusions, depending on particular fact patterns.

With these limitations in mind, we may state that, generally, the prosecution must prove all elements of a crime beyond a reasonable doubt, and the defense must prove all affirmative defenses by a preponderance of the evidence. Defenses must be defined so that they do not shift from the prosecution to the defendant the burden of proof on any element of a crime.

The section on types of defenses began with a discussion of ignorance or mistake. Despite the commonly held belief that ignorance of the law is no excuse, the law recognizes some circumstances of mistake and ignorance. In addition, the law acknowledges that some otherwise criminal acts are committed under duress; in those cases the actors are not criminally responsible. In other circumstances, someone may need to commit an otherwise criminal act to prevent a greater harm, in which case the defense of necessity is permitted.

Infancy is another factor in determining criminal culpability. Children are not normally held to criminal liability even when they commit serious crimes. Statutes differ on how they define *juvenile* and *adult*. All states have a juvenile court system that differs significantly from adult criminal court systems. More and more states are changing their statutes to permit the prosecution to try juveniles in adult criminal courts when they are charged with serious felonies such as robbery, rape, or murder.

The insanity defense, although used infrequently, is one of the most controversial defenses, particularly because the defense of not guilty by reason of insanity was successful in the trial of John Hinckley Jr., who attempted to assassinate President Ronald Reagan.

Several tests are used to define insanity. The one used most frequently, the M'Naghten rule, is referred to as the *right-versus-wrong* rule. It permits finding a defendant not guilty by reason of insanity if it can be shown that, at the time the crime was committed and as the result of a defect of reason caused by a disease of the mind, the defendant did not know the nature and quality of the act or did not know that the act was wrong.

There was dissatisfaction with the M'Naghten rule because it did not apply to defendants who knew the nature, quality, and illegality of their acts but could not control themselves and keep from committing the crimes. Some jurisdictions combined the M'Naghten rule with the irresistible impulse test, which was drafted to include this situation.

Dissatisfaction with both of these rules led to the Durham rule, which is also called the *product rule*. The test of insanity under the Durham rule is whether the defendant's act is the product of mental disease or mental defect. The difficulty of defining *product, mental disease*, and *mental defect* led to the abolition of the Durham rule, which was never widely adopted.

The substantial capacity test has been widely adopted in those jurisdictions that permit an insanity defense. This test permits the defense in cases in which mental disease or defect results in the lack of a substantial capacity to appreciate the criminality of an act or to conform to the law. This test, in substituting the word *appreciate* for the word *know*, is broader than the M'Naghten rule.

Dissatisfaction with the insanity defense has led a few jurisdictions to legislate a provision for the defense of guilty but mentally ill (GBMI). Michigan led the way with this approach, which applies to a person who is convicted of a crime but is considered mentally ill but not insane when the offense was committed. A defendant found GBMI may receive the same sentence as a defendant found guilty, but the state is obligated to provide psychiatric treatment. Some jurisdictions have adopted variations of Michigan's GBMI, while others have abolished the insanity defense.

The diminished capacity or partial responsibility defense is similar to the insanity defense and may be used by defendants who are not insane but who suffer from such mental impairment that they cannot form the required criminal intent for a particular crime. The defense of automatism is available to defendants who are not in control of their actions because of either unconsciousness or semiconsciousness.

One of the most litigated defenses is entrapment. Despite numerous attempts to define the term, case law illustrates that it remains unclear when the defense is applicable. In general, the defense may be used by defendants who can prove that their criminal acts were the result of inducement by a government official or employee and that they were not otherwise predisposed to commit the crimes. The use of the entrapment defense occurs most frequently in cases involving alleged drug or sex crime violations. The defense may be distinguished from the less frequently used defense of outrageous government conduct, which focuses on the actions of the government official rather than on the predisposition of the offender.

Individuals are permitted to defend themselves or other persons, although this defense is generally permitted only when a person is threatened with unlawful force that would cause immediate harm. The actor may only use as much force as is reasonably necessary for protection. Deadly force is permissible only when there is a threat of serious bodily injury or death. The defense of property is also permitted, although in more restricted circumstances than the defense of persons, and the use of deadly force is not permissible.

Law enforcement officers are permitted to use deadly force in some instances without incurring criminal responsibility. The common law rule that permitted officers to shoot and kill a fleeing felon was changed by ordinances and statutes in some jurisdictions prior to the U.S. Supreme Court's 1985 ruling. Today, law enforcement officers and private persons may not use deadly force except under restricted conditions (usually those involving a dangerous felony).

Intoxication is recognized as a partial defense in some situations, particularly when it negates a specific intent required to prove the crime in question. The intoxication defense is not recognized when intoxication is an element of the crime.

Acts that would be criminal in other circumstances may not be so when committed under domestic authority, such as a parent disciplining a child or a teacher disciplining a pupil. In some cases, consent or condonation may provide a defense to criminal acts. Technically, one cannot consent to be killed. Consent may negate an element of a crime, as in the case of rape, one element of which is lack of consent.

The chapter closed with a discussion of numerous stress- and syndrome-related defenses. The battered person syndrome defense recognizes the lack of appropriateness of the traditional self-defense approach when serious injury or murder occurs after repeated acts of domestic violence over an extended period. In such cases, when the perpetrator is not threatened with imminent harm, some defense attorneys have been successful in their arguments that a person who has suffered abuse over a long period of time may reasonably believe that he or she is in danger of imminent harm or death. Because this is not a matter of common knowledge, some jurisdictions permit experts to testify concerning the battered person syndrome. This evidence informs the jury of how a person may react to the violence. The battered person syndrome may be a complete or partial defense.

Various other stress disorders are being advanced as defenses today. Extreme emotional disturbance is one example. Other defenses are those included within posttraumatic stress disorders (PTSD). The return of many Vietnam War veterans with psychological and emotional problems led to a greater awareness of PTSD. As a result, courts have been more receptive to admitting expert testimony on this disorder. This chapter also looked at combat stress with regard to veterans who returned from Iraq and Afghanistan. Another form of PTSD is rape trauma syndrome (RTS). Expert testimony on this condition is recognized in an increasing number of jurisdictions.

One of the fascinating and challenging aspects of the law is that it changes so much. One might say that there are fads and fashions in criminal law and in criminology, just as there are in clothing and other areas of life. Defenses that are used frequently today may not be as popular in the future. Furthermore, the specific uses of any given defense may change, and the laws regarding those uses continue to develop and grow. It is important in the practice or enforcement of law to be aware of the latest changes in one's jurisdiction.

With the conclusion of this examination of criminal defenses to crime, the text turns in the following chapters to an analysis of the major acts covered by criminal statutes.

STUDY QUESTIONS

1. Why is it necessary to distinguish elements of a crime from defenses to a crime?
2. How does the standard of proof required of the prosecution differ from that required of the defense?
3. How might a presumption affect the burden of proof?
4. When would ignorance or mistake be a defense? Should a reasonable mistake of age be a defense to statutory rape?
5. Should the age of an accused person have any bearing on society's reaction to serious crimes that the person is alleged to have committed?
6. Define and compare the major tests of insanity, and contrast the insanity defense and the irresistible impulse defense. Do you think either of these defenses should be abolished? Is guilty but mentally ill an improvement over the traditional defenses involving mental illness? How about guilty except insane?
7. Define *diminished capacity* and *partial responsibility* as defenses.
8. Distinguish the defense of automatism from that of duress or necessity.
9. What are the key elements of an entrapment defense? Should law enforcement officials ever engage in such activities as drug trafficking and prostitution to catch criminals?
10. Distinguish the outrageous government conduct defense from the entrapment defense. Should either be abolished?
11. Under what circumstances may one defend person or property, and how much force may be used?

12. Compare the position taken by the U.S. Supreme Court today to the traditional common law approach to the use of deadly force by police officers.

13. Discuss the nature and extent of the intoxication defense, and indicate whether you agree with the current general legal position with regard to this defense.

14. Under what circumstances, if any, should condonation and consent be defenses to criminal behavior?

15. Discuss the meaning of the battered person syndrome, along with the extent to which you think it should or should not constitute a defense to a criminal act, such as murdering a spouse, lover, child, friend, or parent. Do you think the law should distinguish any categories of battered persons? Should the defense extend to psychological battering? If so, where would you draw the line?

16. What is the relationship between the battered person defense and self-defense?

17. Should extreme emotional disorder be a defense? Discuss.

18. Evaluate the stress-disorder defenses. Indicate which ones you think should be permitted and why.

FOR DEBATE

When the law states that sex with an underage person is a crime even if that person *appears* to be of legal age and is the aggressor, a perpetrator who has sex with the underage person may be convicted of a sex crime, sent to prison, and required to register (perhaps even for life) as a sex offender within the community. Consider whether this approach to sexual behavior should be continued by debating this issue.

RESOLVED: A reasonable and good-faith belief that a consensual sexual partner is of legal age should be a complete defense to the crime of statutory rape.

It has been argued that in today's U.S. criminal justice systems, defendants have too many freedoms and do not take sufficient responsibility for their acts. It is the tradition of our systems, however, that people who do not have control over their acts should not be held criminally culpable for them. Consider both sides of this issue in the following debate topic.

RESOLVED: U.S. courts should not permit defenses associated with the use of prescription drugs or related to emotional factors.

KEY TERMS

automatism   70

battered person syndrome   80

condonation   80

deadly force   73

defense   59

duress   61

Durham rule   68

entrapment   71

euthanasia   79

expert testimony   69

fleeing felon   75
guilty but mentally ill (GBMI)   69
insanity   64
intoxication   76
involuntary intoxication   76
irresistible impulse test   68
mistake   60
M'Naghten rule   66
necessity   62
postpartum depression (PPD)
   syndrome   83

posttraumatic stress disorder
   (PTSD)   81
preponderance of the evidence   59
presumption   59
rape trauma syndrome (RTS)   82
rebuttable presumption   62
substantial capacity test   68
trespasser   75
voluntary intoxication   78

INTERNET ACTIVITY

1. The American Psychiatric Association (APA) has a website, http://www.psych.
   org (accessed 10 May 2012). Locate this site and read what it says about various
   stress-related disorders. Check the Web for information on the presence of stress
   disorders among returning veterans. Can you find any information that might
   be relevant to the trial of Major Nidal Malik Hasan, psychiatrist at the Army
   installation in Ft. Hood, Texas, who is charged with 13 counts of premeditated
   murder and 32 counts of premeditated attempted murder at that base in 2009?
2. Using your favorite search engine, check the Web to see what you can find
   about Andrea Yates, the Texas woman who admitted that she drowned her
   five children in the bathtub of their home. What do you think of her defense?
   Where is she now?

NOTES

1. *Francis v. Franklin,* 471 U.S. 307 (1985).
2. Kenneth W. Simons, "Mistake and Impossibility, Law and Fact, and Culpability: A Speculative Essay," *Journal of Criminal Law & Criminology* 81 (Fall
   1990): 469, emphasis in the original.
3. *Lambert v. California,* 355 U.S. 225 (1957).
4. See *Roper v. Simmons,* 543 U.S. 551 (2005); *Graham v. Florida,* 130 S.Ct. 2011
   (2010); and *Sullivan v. Florida,* 130 S. Ct. 2059 (2010).
5. *M'Naghten's Case,* 8 Eng. Rep. 718, 722 (H.L. 1843).
6. *United States v. Kunak,* 5 U.S.C.M.A. 346 (1954).
7. *Durham v. United States,* 214 F.2d 862 (D.C.Cir. 1954), *overruled in part, United States v. Brawner,* 471 F.2d 969 (D.C.Cir. 1972).
8. *United States v. Brawner,* 471 F.2d 969 (D.C.Cir. 1972).
9. Model Penal Code, Section 4.01.
10. MCLS, Section 768.36 (2012).
11. See *Clark v. Arizona,* 548 U.S. 735 (2006). The Arizona statute is codified at
    A.R.S., Section 13-502 (2012).
12. *United States v. Loughner,* 672 F.3d 731 (9th Cir. 2012).

13. Idaho Code, Section 18-207 (2012).

14. *Sorrells v. United States,* 287 U.S. 435, 453-454 (1932).

15. *Sherman v. United States,* 356 U.S. 369 (1958).

16. *United States v. Mosley,* 965 F.2d 906, 910 (10th Cir. 1992).

17. *United States v. Harris,* 997 F.2d 812, 818 (10th Cir. 1993).

18. *United States v. Tucker,* 28 F.3d 1420 (6th Cir. 1994), *cert. denied,* 514 U.S. 1049 (1995).

19. Model Penal Code, Section 3.04(2)(b).

20. Model Penal Code, Section 3.04(2)(b)(ii)(A).

21. "Mother, 18, Hailed for Fatal Shooting," *Sun-Sentinel* (Fort Lauderdale, Florida) (6 January 2012), p. 7. The Oklahoma castle doctrine is codified at Okl. St., Title 21, Section 733 (2011).

22. Fla. Stats. 776.012 (2012).

23. *Tennessee v. Garner,* 471 U.S. 1 (1985).

24. *Bradley v. State,* Walker 156, 157 (Miss. 1824).

25. R.R.S. Neb., Section 79-295 (2012).

26. *Daily v. Board of Education of Merrill School District,* 588 N.W.2d 813 (Neb. 1999).

27. R.R.S. Neb., Section 79-258 (2012).

28. *Ingraham v. Wright,* 430 U.S. 651 (1977).

29. See *Ibn–Tamas v. United States,* 407 A.2d 626 (D.C.Cir. 1979).

30. ORS, Section 163.135 (2011).

31. *Today's School Psychologist* 4 (5 July 2001): n.p.

32. Institute of Medicine of the National Academies, *Report: Treatment for Posttraumatic Stress Disorder in Military and Veteran Populations: Initial Assessment* (13 July 2012), http://www.iom.edu/ (accessed 17 July 2012).

33. "Review Urges Defense Dept. to Broaden P.T.S.D. Help," *New York Times* (14 July 2012), 9A.

34. "Pressed by the Demand of Two Wars, Plus Mandates to Expand, Reorganize, and Modernize, the Army Is Nearing Its Breaking Point," *National Journal* (7 April 2007), n.p.

35. *State v. Felde,* 422 So.2d 370 (La. 1982); and *Miller v State,* 338 N.W.2d 673 (S.D. 1983).

36. American Psychiatric Foundation, http://www.psychfoundation.org/ (accessed 25 June 2008).

37. "Purple Heart Is Ruled Out for Traumatic Stress," *New York Times* (8 January 2009), p. 1.

38. "Progression to Sexual Slavery," *Corrections Professional* 6 (4 May 2001): n.p.

39. *People v. Pulinario,* 720 N.Y.S.2d 382 (2d Dep't. 2001), *appeal denied,* 754 N.E.2d 214 (2001), *and habeas corpus granted, Pulinario v. Goord,* 291 F. Supp. 2d 154 (E.D.N.Y. 2003), *aff'd.,* 2004 U.S. App. LEXIS. 26803 (2d Cir. 2004).

40. "Bye Bye Blues: Falling Apart and Picking Up the Pieces with Postpartum Depression," *San Antonio Current* (25 April–1 May 2002), n.p.

CHAPTER 5

Criminal Homicide

CHAPTER OUTLINE
Introduction
An Overview of Violent Crimes
Homicide
    General Definitional Issues
        Another Human Being Requirement
        The Definition of Death
    Causation
        The Year-and-a-Day Rule
        Multiple Causation
    Corpus Delicti
Murder
    Elements of Murder
    Common Law Murder
    Types of Murder

        Intent to Kill

        Intent to Inflict Great Bodily Harm
        Depraved Heart
        Intent to Commit a Felony
        Murder for Hire
    Degrees of Murder
    Lesser Included Offenses
    Mercy Killing: An Exception or Murder?
Physician Assisted Suicide (PAS)
Manslaughter
    Voluntary Manslaughter
        Heat-of-Passion Manslaughter
        Manslaughter in Domestic Relations

INTRODUCTION

This chapter discusses homicide, the most serious, although not the most frequent, **violent crime**. Homicide is a crime featured and dissected extensively by the media and one that gains the attention of a wide audience, as movies and television shows portray real and fictional episodes involving the killing of human beings.

The chapter focuses on the legal aspects of homicide, looking carefully at the elements that constitute the crimes of murder and manslaughter, traditional categories of homicide, along with that of a relatively new crime, physician assisted suicide (PAS). This is the text's first chapter on violent crimes, and it therefore begins with an overview of them.

AN OVERVIEW OF VIOLENT CRIMES

In the United States, crime data come from various sources, but the primary source is that of the Federal Bureau of Investigation (FBI), which requests (and is dependent on) the cooperation of states in reporting crimes. The FBI's annual publication, *Crime in the United States: Uniform Crime Reports*—usually referred to as the *Uniform Crime Reports*, or the *UCR*, reports the national data—the FBI has acquired. The *UCR* recording system includes four crimes in the category of serious violent crimes. For convenience, the four serious violent crimes and their definitions are reprinted in Focus 5.1.

Data on individual violent crimes are noted where appropriate. To set the stage for the discussions and data on specific crimes in this and the following chapters, it is helpful to look at the violent crime scene as a whole. Figure 5.1 graphs the trends in violent crimes in the United States between 2006 and 2010, showing a decline during that period with significant increases during the two most recent years. These decreases followed a rise in violent offenses between 2004 and 2006 after significant decreases between 2002 and 2004. Violent crimes increased by 1.9

Focus 5.1

Uniform Crime Report (UCR) Definitions of Serious Violent Crimes

Murder and Nonnegligent Manslaughter
[T]he willful (nonnegligent) killing of one human being by another.

Forcible Rape
[T]he carnal knowledge of a female forcibly and against her will. Assault or attempts to commit rape by force or threat of force are also included; however, statutory rape (without force) and other sex offenses are excluded.[1]

Robbery
[T]he taking of or attempting to take anything of value from the care, custody, or control of a person or persons by force or threat of force or violence and/or by putting the victim in fear.

Aggravated Assault
[A]n unlawful attack by one person upon another for the purpose of inflicting severe or aggravated bodily injury.... [T]his type of assault is usually accompanied by the use of a weapon or by other means likely to produce death or great bodily harm. Attempted aggravated assault that involves the display of—or threat to use—a gun, knife, or other weapon is included in this crime category because serious personal injury would likely result if the assault were completed. When aggravated assault and larceny-theft occur together, the offense falls under the category of robbery.

[1]This is the official definition of *forcible rape* used by the FBI for 80 years. It was under attack as under inclusive and was changed in 2011 but still appears as this on the FBI's Webpage. The issue is discussed in Chapter 6 of this text.

SOURCE: Federal Bureau of Investigation, *Crime in the United States: Uniform Crime Reports, 2010* (September 2011), http://www.fbi.gov (accessed 11 May 2012).

percent between 2005 and 2006. In 2012, the FBI released preliminary crime data for that year, showing an overall drop in violent crime of 4.0 percent.[1]

The FBI records both the volume and the rate of serious crimes. The **crime rate** refers to the number of crimes per 100,000 in the population. The *UCR* reports **crimes known to the police**, which means all serious violent and property offenses that have been reported to the police and for which the police have sufficient evidence to believe were actually committed. The *UCR* also reports arrest data on serious violent and property crimes as well as on less serious crimes. Definitions of these crimes are noted when appropriate throughout the text.

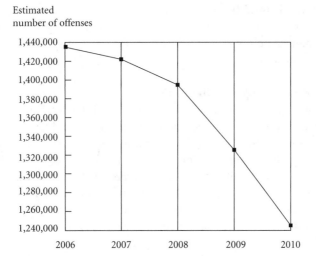

FIGURE 5.1 **Violent Crime in the United States, 2006–2010**
SOURCE: Federal Bureau of Investigation, *Crime in the United States: Uniform Crime Reports, 2010* (September 2011), http://www.fbi.gov/stats-services/crimestats (accessed 11 May 2012).

HOMICIDE

The most serious of all violent acts is that which results in the death of a human being. The term that refers to all cases in which a human being kills another human being by his or her own act, omission, or procurement is **homicide**. Not all killings or homicides carry criminal culpability. A killing committed in self-defense, or by accident or any other circumstance that the law permits, is called an **excusable homicide**. Excusable homicides involve some fault but not enough that the law considers them worthy of criminal culpability, although one that involves extreme (or gross) negligence might be culpable.

The killing of another human being may also be classified as a **justifiable homicide,** which is a killing that is intentional but carries no evil intent and is permitted by law, such as one involving capital punishment or a killing by a law enforcement officer in the line of duty when attempting to prevent a felony.

Some jurisdictions do not use those terms. They may use only one term, such as *criminal homicide,* which may be further divided into categories, such as *murder* and *manslaughter.* Some jurisdictions define criminal homicide along the lines used by the Model Penal Code, with the intent categories of purposely, knowingly, recklessly, or negligently causing the death of another human being (see again Focus 2.3). Other jurisdictions use the term *intentionally,* in place of *purposely,* but the result is essentially the same: a categorization of murder by the seriousness of the act.

General Definitional Issues

Jurisdictions differ in how they define *homicide* and its categories, but there are some common definitional issues, two of which are analyzed in detail in the following sections.

Another Human Being Requirement

The first issue is that of *another human being*. Use of the word *another* precludes listing suicide within the definition of homicide. The second term, *human being*, has been interpreted to be a *living* human being, but these words must be defined and interpreted. The requirement of a living human being becomes an issue when a fetus dies as the result of a crime against a pregnant woman. Under common law the fetus was not considered to be a person or a human being, and it had to be born alive before its death could be classified as a homicide. Most U.S. statutes followed this rule, although that is changing, with many now including the fetus as a person for purposes of murder.

But what does it mean to be born alive? Some jurisdictions require that the fetus be expelled from the mother's body and be breathing on its own. Others require that the baby cry or that the umbilical cord be severed.

The born-alive requirement may affect other crimes, such as **infanticide**, which refers to killing a child at or soon after its birth. Historically, infanticide was acceptable in some societies; parents were permitted to kill deformed children and, in some cases, female children, since male children were preferred. Where infanticide has been a crime, it has not been considered as serious as murder.

Decriminalizing abortion has resulted in a problem when, during an abortion process, a fetus is born alive. To cover this situation, some statutes require health care professionals to take reasonable efforts to save the life of the fetus who is born alive during an abortion.

The decision regarding the status of a fetus has religious, moral, and ethical as well as legal implications. Some jurisdictions have made statutory changes in the common law requirement of being born alive and now include a fetus within their murder statutes. In others, a pregnant woman might be charged with a criminal offense, such as first-degree reckless injury, after giving birth to a baby with **fetal alcohol syndrome**, which refers to a cluster of abnormalities that a fetus may have due to the fact that its mother consumed alcohol during her pregnancy. The effects include growth deficiencies, facial abnormalities, and mental retardation. Similar medical problems may be caused by a pregnant woman who uses drugs other than alcohol.

In 2004, the U.S. Congress passed, and President George W. Bush signed, the Unborn Victims of Violence Act of 2004. This act is also known as Laci and Connor's Act, named in honor of Laci Peterson, who was murdered, resulting in the death of her unborn son, Connor. Scott Peterson is under a death sentence in California for his conviction for capital murder of his wife, Laci. He was convicted of second-degree murder for Connor's death. The California statute provides that under specified circumstances, one who causes injury or death to a fetus in utero commits a separate murder, but it does not carry the death penalty.[2]

Some jurisdictions have established by law a system permitting persons to leave their unwanted newborns at *safe places* without being subject to criminal prosecution. Some allow only 72 hours after birth; others permit 30 days after the infant's birth for turning him or her over to medical or other designated personnel. These **Baby Moses laws** are gaining ground in the United States, but there are problems. For example, Nebraska's original statute did not contain a time limitation for leaving babies at safe havens. Some parents dropped off their teenagers, after which Nebraska amended its statute to limit the procedure to 30 days after a child's birth.[3] Texas provides 60 days from time of birth to deliver an unwanted child to a safe haven.[4] All states have some form of safe haven law, although critics argue that it is impossible to know whether the laws actually save lives or only account for babies whose parent(s) would have put them in safe places anyway. The fact is that many infants are still abandoned and left to die.[5]

The Definition of Death

A second issue that homicide statutes raise is the definition of *death*. Historically, the term was not defined legally, and that was not an issue because there was general agreement that death meant the cessation of breathing and heartbeat. Today, however, the definition of *death* has become a critical issue in many homicide cases, in part because of doctors' ability to keep patients functioning with the aid of life-support systems. Further, organ transplantation has created a need to define when death occurs. For some organs to be viable for successful transplants, they must be removed before all body functions have ceased, and they must be preserved carefully until quick transplantation occurs.

The problem of when death occurs is further complicated by the growing number of living wills. These documents are written statements made by legally competent individuals about the action they want taken if they require life-support systems or organ transplants in order to live. The statutes vary, but if these documents are properly executed, the termination of life-support systems that result in a person's death will generally not constitute homicide.

The resolution of issues regarding the definition of death and the right to terminate life are critical not only for religious and ethical reasons but also for legal reasons, particularly regarding the causation element of homicide.

Causation

An important element the prosecution must prove in homicide cases is that the alleged crime and not some other act *caused* the victim's death. One approach to this issue is illustrated by common law rules.

The Year-and-a-Day Rule

Because of the difficulties in determining the cause of death, common law provided that if the victim's death did not occur within a year and a day, the alleged offender could not be convicted of criminal homicide. Some jurisdictions incorporated that rule into their statutes. Others, in moving from common law to statutory law, did not mention the year-and-a-day rule. Failure to include the rule in a statute may be interpreted as an abandonment of the rule.

Some jurisdictions retained the *theory* of the year-and-a-day rule but expanded the time period. For example, California provides that if a death occurs after three years and a day,

> there shall be a rebuttable presumption that the killing was not criminal. The prosecution shall bear the burden of overcoming this presumption. In the computation of such time, the whole of the day on which the act was done shall be reckoned the first.[6]

Multiple Causation

The year-and-a-day (or similar) rule does not always solve the causation problem because a victim who dies within that time period may have been subjected to more than one cause of death. Assume, for example, that a person who is injured by a criminal act is taken to the hospital, where a doctor performs surgery required by the injury, and the doctor commits medical malpractice. The patient dies two days after being stabbed. Who is responsible for the death?

Usually, if a person commits a *criminal* act, after which another person commits a *negligent* act affecting the same individual, the criminal actor may be charged with criminal homicide if his or her act was a *substantial factor* in causing the victim's death.

Causation also presents problems when two or more parties commit separate acts, neither one of which would have been sufficient to cause the victim's death. In those cases, courts look carefully at the intent of the individuals who committed the acts, as well as at the nature of each act. If the prosecution can prove that a defendant intended to cause death, most courts find that evidence sufficient for a conviction for criminal homicide unless the second act clearly broke the chain of causation between the defendant's act and the victim's death.

Corpus Delicti

Another legal concept important to all crimes but especially to homicides is **corpus delicti**, which literally means the "body of the crime" and refers to the body or other material substance of a crime that constitutes the foundation of that particular crime. The remains of a burned house might be the *corpus delicti* in an arson case. In criminal homicide cases, *corpus delicti* includes much more than the body of the deceased, although to prosecute a defendant for any category of criminal homicide, theoretically the prosecutor must produce the dead body or evidence that one exists.

The *corpus delicti* is required as **corroborating evidence** that the crime occurred. Corroborating evidence provides additional data to support the crime charged, especially in rape and other cases in which there were no witnesses to the alleged act, and it is crucial to proving a case. Thus, even if the accused confesses to a murder, if the body cannot be found or there is no evidence of a dead person, that confession is not sufficient for a conviction. In many cases the prosecutor will not file charges until the body is found. There are some exceptions to the *corpus* *delicti* requirement. Some courts have abandoned this requirement because it is difficult if not impossible to get a tangible *corpus delicti* for some crimes. Examples would be attempt crimes, conspiracy, and income tax evasion.

MURDER

As noted in Focus 5.1, the FBI combines **murder** and nonnegligent manslaughter and defines the crimes as the "willful (nonnegligent) killing of one human being by another." The FBI states that it does not include the following: "deaths caused by negligence, suicide, or accident; justifiable homicides; and attempts to murder or assaults to murder, which are scored as aggravated assaults."[7]

The FBI reported that the volume of the combined crimes of murder and nonnegligent manslaughter, 14,748 in 2010, was 4.2 percent lower than in 2009, 14.8 percent lower than in 2006, and 8.0 percent lower than in 2001. In 2010, these crimes constituted 1.2 percent of the serious violent crimes committed that year, making it the least frequent of the four violent crimes measured by the FBI. The FBI's preliminary data for 2011 showed a decline in murder of 1.9 percent over that period for the previous year.[8]

This chapter discusses nonnegligent manslaughter separately, but first will present a closer look at murder.

Elements of Murder

Regardless of the definition, all acts classified as *murder* generally require the following elements:

1. There must be an unlawful act (or omission) committed by a human being.
2. The act must be accompanied by the requisite *mens rea*.
3. The act must be the legal cause of the victim's death.
4. The victim must be a living human being. (As noted earlier, some jurisdictions now include a fetus.)
5. Death must occur within a reasonable period (usually specified, such as a year-and-a-day under common law; now extended under some modern statutes).

Most of these elements were discussed in Chapter 2. Some—for example, the year-and-a-day rule—were discussed earlier in this chapter. Others, such as the *mens rea* requirement, need further elaboration, and that may be done in the context of the common law development of murder.

Common Law Murder

The common law crime of murder developed over several centuries and referred to the unlawful killing of another human being with **malice aforethought**. Some U.S. jurisdictions follow this definition. Others have modified it (e.g., to include the killing of a fetus). There is so much confusion over the meaning of the crime of murder, however, that some commentators have suggested that, rather than dwelling on the common law definition, jurisdictions should emphasize categories or types of murder. That is the approach this chapter takes, but first, it is important to understand the traditional approach and its influence on current statutes.

Under common law and many modern statutes, murder requires the element of *malice aforethought*, which means that the killing must have been predetermined and intentional and without legal justification or excuse. Malice aforethought, however, is not used literally, and over time the concept has eroded. Common law judges interpreted the term so differently that in many cases it bore no resemblance to its ordinary usage. A typical traditional murder statute that includes the concept provides that malice may be *express* or *implied*. Those terms are distinguished in the California statute as follows:

> It [malice aforethought] is express when there is manifested a deliberate intention unlawfully to take away the life of a fellow creature. It is implied, when no considerable provocation appears, or when the circumstances attending the killing show an abandoned and malignant heart.[9]

Defendants who claim that because they had no malice toward anyone in the area they should not be charged with murder after firing into a crowd at a shopping center will find judges unsympathetic to their arguments. Malice may be inferred from such facts. As one court stated, "Malice aforethought may be inferred from the intentional use of a deadly weapon in a deadly and dangerous manner."[10]

Some jurisdictions have abandoned the malice aforethought requirement in favor of categories that define the various types of murder in terms of the type of mental element or intent involved. They may retain the term *malice aforethought*, however, to distinguish between first- and second-degree murder. Other jurisdictions avoid the use of this confusing terminology altogether.

Types of Murder

Jurisdictions vary in the ways in which they categorize murder. A few categories are distinguished here. The names of these categories are used to describe the type of murder. Some states use the types but give them different names.

Intent to Kill

The most common murders involve the intent to kill. If there are no mitigating circumstances to reduce the murder charge to manslaughter and if the act is not excusable or justifiable, the defendant who intended a killing may be charged with and convicted of murder. Intent-to-kill murders do not require acts; omissions are sufficient, provided there is a legal duty to act. The intent to kill may be shown when the killing takes place under circumstances that would likely result in a death, as well as in those rare cases in which the defendant articulates an intent to kill.

The intentional (as opposed to negligent) use of a deadly weapon may be introduced as evidence from which the jury may draw an inference of an intent to kill, although the defendant may successfully refute that inference. It is possible, for example, that a person might shoot at another person with the intention of scaring, not killing. The real intent, of course, may not be known. The jury must infer intent or lack of intent by analyzing the evidence presented at the trial.

The common law provision that the intent to kill had to be premeditated is no longer required. For this type of murder, it is sufficient to show an unpremeditated intent to kill.

Intent to Inflict Great Bodily Harm
Death that results from serious bodily injuries may be murder when it can be shown that the defendant intended to inflict serious or great bodily harm, even though there was no intent to kill. The phrase *great bodily harm* means harm greater than plain bodily injury (which must be interpreted) but less than death. This is to avoid murder convictions when death occurs from simple injury.

Depraved Heart
Depraved heart murders are killings resulting from extremely reckless conduct. This type of murder is said to be the result of a depraved mind, an abandoned and malignant heart, or wickedness. For depraved heart murder, the defendant must create the risk, but courts differ in their holdings concerning whether the defendant must be aware of the risk (the subjective test) or whether it is sufficient that a reasonable person would have been aware of the risk (the objective test). The risk required for a depraved heart murder must be greater than that required in negligence cases, with some jurisdictions requiring circumstances that manifest "extreme indifference to the value of human life." The firing of a loaded gun into an occupied automobile that results in the death of one or more persons is an example of creating a risk that exhibits extreme indifference to the value of human life.

Intent to Commit a Felony
An unintended death resulting from the commission of a felony may be classified as a **felony murder**. Under common law, these deaths were considered murders, but over the years the felony murder doctrine developed by statute, and it differs among the jurisdictions. Some specifically limit felony murder to deaths resulting from the more serious felonies (such as forcible rape) or state that the doctrine is limited to an inherently dangerous felony (such as armed robbery). Others limit the time period involved; some are more restrictive on legal cause. Still others require that the killing be independent of the felony. Focus 5.2 contains several examples of cases involving felony murders.

Murder for Hire
A final type of murder is *murder for hire*, in which a person hires another to commit a murder. It is not uncommon that a murder for hire is referred to by another name, such as *aggravated first-degree murder*, with a statutory definition that makes it clear that this type of murder involves paying another person to commit the act.

Focus 5.2

Felony Murder Cases

The legality of felony murder statutes has been tested in several cases. The first discussed here occurred in Maryland, where one spring morning William Henry Jackson and James Wells Jr. set out to rob a jewelry store in Baltimore. Apparently the plan was to take as much jewelry as possible and then get away; there were to be no killings.

Acting on a tip, police surrounded Jackson and Wells in the store. In a desperate attempt to escape, the two robbers took the owners hostage. Using them as shields, Jackson and Wells escaped temporarily when they commandeered a police car. A lengthy car chase ended in a hail of gunfire at a police roadblock. During the shoot-out one of the store owners was killed accidentally by police gunfire.

Jackson and Wells were convicted of first-degree murder under the Maryland felony murder statute. The Maryland Court of Appeals, in affirming the conviction, found that the acts of Jackson and Wells "established such a causal relationship with respect to the death as to make them criminally liable therefor."[1]

This case contrasts with the decision reached by the California Supreme Court in a case in which the defendant, a chiropractor, persuaded a couple to remove their daughter from a hospital where she was scheduled to undergo cancer surgery. He assured the parents that he could cure their daughter without surgery. After the daughter died, the state charged the chiropractor, who had received $500 in compensation, with felony grand theft and felony murder. The California Supreme Court struck down the defendant's murder conviction, holding that grand theft was not an inherently dangerous crime and therefore could not be the basis for a felony murder conviction.[2]

In *Tison v. Arizona,* a felony murder case decided by the U.S. Supreme Court, two brothers helped free their father and another convict from prison. When their car broke down, one of the brothers stopped another car. Both brothers watched and did nothing to stop their father from killing the four members of the family in the other car. The brothers and their father were convicted of capital murder and sentenced to death. The Tison brothers appealed to the U.S. Supreme Court, claiming that their participation in the murders was so minor that the imposition of the death penalty would not serve its purposes of retribution and deterrence. The Supreme Court responded that the brothers' participation was "anything but minor" but that even if a defendant's participation in a crime is minor and his mental state is one of "reckless indifference," the death penalty is not precluded.[3]

In an earlier case, *Enmund v. Florida,* the U.S. Supreme Court had considered facts similar to those in *Tison.* In *Enmund* the petitioner received the death sentence despite the fact that he had done nothing more than drive a getaway car. The lower court held that it was irrelevant to this case that when the killings took place the petitioner was not present and that he did not anticipate or intend the killings. The Supreme Court reversed the lower court, holding that the death penalty should be imposed only in situations where the defendant "intended, contemplated or anticipated that lethal force would or might be used or that life would or might be taken in accomplishing the underlying felony."[4]

The differences between *Tison* and *Enmund* may be explained by a closer examination of the facts in the two cases. In *Tison* the brothers looked on and made no effort to prevent their father from killing the victims. In *Enmund* the petitioner sat in a car alongside the road, unaware that the victims were being executed. His involvement in the murders was too remote to justify capital punishment.

[1]*Jackson v. State,* 408 A.2d 711 (Md. 1979).
[2]*People v. Phillips,* 414 P.2d 353 (Cal. 1966).
[3]*Tison v. Arizona,* 481 U.S. 137 (1987).
[4]*Enmund v. Florida,* 458 U.S. 782 (1982).

Degrees of Murder

Although English common law had no degrees of murder, most modern U.S. statutes divide murder into at least two categories (first-degree murder and second-degree murder) in order to assess different penalties. Some jurisdictions have a separate category for murders that carry the death penalty, often referred to as *capital murder.*

First-degree murder includes deliberate, premeditated, intent-to-kill murders, as well as felony murders committed during the commission of dangerous felonies such as forcible rape, arson, robbery, or kidnapping. Some states include as first-degree murder those murders committed by use of poison, lying in wait, or bombing. More recently, some states have included murders that involve torture and terrorism; in some jurisdictions, those acts may be defined as separate crimes.

One of the key elements of first-degree murder is **premeditation**, which refers to the act of planning, deliberating, designing, or thinking out in advance an intention to kill another person. The time required for premeditation for murder may be short, and courts differ on their interpretation of this concept.

Generally, *second-degree murder* is defined as any murder not included in first-degree murder. It includes intent-to-kill murders that are not deliberate or premeditated; felony murders that are not considered first-degree murders (such as killings committed during larceny-theft); depraved heart murders; and intent-to-inflict-serious-bodily-harm murders, whether or not they are premeditated or deliberate.

Lesser Included Offenses

Some jurisdictions provide that in addition to an instruction regarding the crime with which the defendant was charged, the jury may be instructed on a **lesser included offense,** which is a crime that is less serious. It has some but not all of the elements of the charged offense but must not include any element not required for that offense. The prosecutor (or the grand jury) has the discretion to decide which charges to bring, and some will bring lesser included charges than murder (or lesser charges that may not be included within murder) when they have sufficient evidence to file a murder charge. The defense may request an instruction for a lesser included offense; the judge makes the final decision. As a matter of strategy in a first-degree murder case, for example, the defense may not ask for an instruction on second-degree murder or manslaughter, gambling that the jury will not return a guilty verdict for first-degree murder. This strategy may backfire, however, and the jury may find the defendant guilty of first-degree murder.

Mercy Killing: An Exception or Murder?

In some cases the deceased may have begged to be killed because of a terminal illness, considerable and uncontrollable pain, or a severe disability. Killing a person in such circumstances is called *mercy killing or euthanasia.* Technically, however, such killings meet the requirements for murder and are illegal, although often either the cases are not prosecuted or, if prosecuted, juries do not convict. In some countries euthanasia is legal but under restricted circumstances. In the United States the practice is illegal.

PHYSICIAN ASSISTED SUICIDE (PAS)

It is obvious that society does not agree on how mercy killings should be handled despite the fact that in most cases the state can prove the elements required for a murder conviction. One solution is to legalize euthanasia at least in some form. Physician assisted suicide (PAS) is one way to do this, but in 1997, the U.S. Supreme Court upheld the right of states to prohibit PAS.[11] The Court ruled that it is not a violation of federal due process or equal protection for a state to prohibit PAS, but the Court left open the possibility that states may provide for PAS if they choose.

Oregon had already become the first state to enact a statute permitting physicians to assist patients to commit suicide. The Oregon statute, enacted in 1994 and referred to as the *Death with Dignity Act,* permits physicians to prescribe lethal drugs to persons with less than six months to live, provided those persons request the drugs, make an informed decision, and meet other requirements.[12]

On 4 November 2008, the voters of Washington adopted that state's Death with Dignity Act, to become effective 5 March 2009, thus becoming the second state to permit PAS.[13]

In 2009, the Montana Supreme Court refused to reach the issue of whether the state constitution's provision for individual dignity encompasses a right to die with dignity, but it did hold that a patient's consent to a physician who prescribes a drug for PAS constitutes a defense if the physician is charged with homicide.[14]

Massachusetts voters were to vote on PAS in the 2012 elections.

MANSLAUGHTER

A second category of homicide is **manslaughter**, which traditionally has been defined as an unlawful killing without malice aforethought. Generally, *manslaughter* encompasses homicides that are not considered as serious as those that constitute first- or second-degree murder, but in many cases it is difficult to distinguish murder from manslaughter.

Under common law, manslaughter was divided into two types for the purpose of distinguishing different kinds of conduct but not for the purposes of differential punishment. Some jurisdictions have retained these categories, while others define manslaughter in terms of degrees; still others use only the single term *manslaughter*. The types of manslaughter are examined more closely in the following sections.

Voluntary Manslaughter

An unlawful killing that does not involve malice aforethought but that occurs after adequate provocation may be classified as **voluntary manslaughter,** in which the killing must occur after such provocation by the victim that even reasonable people could be expected to react violently. It must be proved that the particular defendant was provoked, that a reasonable person would not have cooled off between the time of the provocation and the killing, and that the defendant did not cool off.

Heat-of-Passion Manslaughter

Voluntary manslaughter may be called heat-of-passion homicide or heat-of-passion voluntary manslaughter. *Heat of passion* was the term used under common law (and followed by some states) to describe this type of voluntary manslaughter. Some states also include extreme emotional or mental disturbance within this form of manslaughter.

Manslaughter in Domestic Relations

The difficulty of drawing the line between murder and voluntary manslaughter is illustrated by the approach taken by common law and by many modern statutes to cases in which a husband killed his wife when he caught her engaging in the act of adultery. It was assumed that seeing one's wife in such a compromising situation was sufficient provocation for killing the lover or the wife.

A few jurisdictions extended this rule to women who caught their husbands in the act of adultery and killed the husband or his lover, but most considered these acts murder. These provisions are no longer in existence. A 1977 Georgia decision explains why: "Any idea that a spouse is ever justified in taking the life of another—adulterous spouse or illicit lover—to prevent adultery is uncivilized."[15]

Despite the demise of adultery as a condition for reducing murder to manslaughter, other circumstances may warrant a manslaughter rather than a murder charge. Words, fights, and other situations that would lead a reasonable person to kill may suffice, depending on the jurisdiction's statutes and case law. In these circumstances, the law does not imply that it is permissible to kill (as in self-defense), but, rather, that it is reasonable to be provoked to kill under circumstances that do not warrant justifiable or excusable homicide. The *reasonable person* (or objective) *standard* is utilized to determine whether a killing was provoked. The rationale is that reasonable people, when sufficiently provoked, will react without thinking. If they kill, they should be responsible for the death, but not to the extent of murder. The jury is to look at all the facts and determine whether, based on those facts, it was reasonable for the defendant to kill.

Some jurisdictions have extended voluntary manslaughter to killings that occur in other situations, such as when provocation results from assault and battery, mutual combat, injury to third parties, illegal arrest, or fighting words.

As with most crimes, attempt crimes are permissible with voluntary manslaughter (although not with involuntary manslaughter, which by definition is not an intentional killing).

Involuntary Manslaughter

The crime of **involuntary manslaughter** is a killing that is committed recklessly but unintentionally, as when a person is under the influence of alcohol or other drugs. Usually this category of manslaughter applies to a killing that results when the defendant is engaged in a criminal act that is less serious than a felony, but that is not always the case, as illustrated by the discussion in Focus 5.3.

Focus 5.3

Probation or Prison when Unintended Death Results?

Two cases of significant interest nationally and internationally culminated in late 2011 in prison terms for professionals—one motivational speaker and one cardiologist—both of whom engaged in negligent behavior that led to deaths. Defense attorneys in both cases argued for probation; both defendants were sentenced to prison.

The first case involved self-help author James Arthur Ray, who presided over a sweat-lodge ceremony in Arizona that led to the deaths of three participants. At the end of his four-month trial, Ray was convicted of three counts of negligent homicide[1] and was sentenced to two years for each, the sentences to run concurrently. Ray was originally charged with manslaughter, but that charge required a finding of reckless behavior, and the jury rejected that element. Ray was also ordered to pay over $57,000 in restitution. The prosecutors asked the judge to impose the maximum sentence of nine years.

The second case involved cardiologist Dr. Conrad Murray, who was hired as the personal physician for pop star Michael Jackson. Dr. Murray was accused of negligence in administering a sedative outside of a hospital setting, in leaving Jackson alone in his bedroom after he administered the drug, and in his response to his patient when he showed signs of stress. Jackson died 25 June 2009. Dr. Murray was convicted of involuntary manslaughter and sentenced to four years in prison, which is the maximum term for that crime in that jurisdiction.

In sentencing Murray, trial judge Michael Pastor said the defendant had shown no remorse and that he had ordered a "staggering amount" of Propofol, a powerful sedative that he administered to Jackson, who desired the drug for sleep. Judge Pastor admonished Dr. Murray for taping Jackson when he was drugged, suggesting that was Murray's insurance policy to use for bribery in case his lucrative relationship with Jackson ended. According to the judge, "Of everything I heard and saw during the course of the trial, one aspect of the evidence stands out the most, and that is the surreptitious recording of Michael Jackson by his trusted doctor."[2]

Dr. Murray will probably serve no more than two years of his four year sentence due to overcrowding in California's correctional facilities. He could be released earlier.

[1] The Arizona criminal code, A.R.S., Section 13–1102 (2012), defines *negligent homicide* as follows: "A person commits negligent homicide if with criminal negligence the person causes the death of another person, including an unborn child."
[2] "Famous Faces," *Houston Chronicle* (1 December 2011), p. 2.

Misdemeanor or Negligent Manslaughter

In some jurisdictions, involuntary manslaughter is called *misdemeanor manslaughter*. Involuntary manslaughter may also include deaths that occur as the result of **negligent manslaughter**, which is a killing that is not lawful or justified but does not involve malice or any other form of intent, only negligence. In addition, misdemeanor or negligent manslaughter charges may be brought in cases in which a parent's negligence (such as in the failure to obtain necessary medical treatment) results in a child's death.

Vehicular and DUI Manslaughter

Another type of involuntary manslaughter is *vehicular manslaughter*, which usually encompasses numerous types of vehicular homicides, including those caused by gross negligence. Some states include within this category a killing that results from an accident while the driver is intoxicated (driving under the influence, or DUI; if death results, the act may be charged as a DUI manslaughter).

Deaths that result from vehicular accidents occurring while defendants are under the influence of alcohol or other drugs may also be prosecuted as involuntary manslaughter if the state does not have a vehicular homicide or DUI manslaughter statute. They may be prosecuted as murder if the prosecution has evidence that would take the case beyond that of manslaughter and shows evidence of intent, but a murder conviction for automobile accidents is very unusual.

In cases involving negligent drivers, it is important to recall earlier discussions of discretion in criminal justice systems. Prosecutors have wide discretion in deciding whether to prosecute these cases. They may, and frequently do, decline to prosecute drivers whose negligence causes death to others when the drivers were neither speeding excessively nor driving under the influence of alcohol or other drugs.

Failure-to-Act Manslaughter

Manslaughter charges may also be brought when *failure to act* is the crime, such as the failure to render aid or summon help when one has put another in circumstances that could reasonably be expected to cause bodily injury or death to that person. The charge may also apply when a person neglects to perform an act that he or she has a legal duty to perform.

SUMMARY

This chapter focused on the violent acts of murder and manslaughter, two types of homicide. Homicide occurs when a human being kills another human being by his or her own act, omission, or procurement. Thus homicide refers to killings that are justifiable or excusable (such as killings by police officers under some circumstances and killings by anyone when the use of deadly force is necessary for self-defense or the defense of others) as well as to killings that are not legally acceptable and thus may result in criminal responsibility.

Confusion over the differences among justifiable, excusable, and criminal homicides—the three common law categories—has led some jurisdictions to abandon those categories. Most divide homicides into two categories: murder and manslaughter, the approach taken in this chapter. Some states follow common law distinctions, while others have a mixture of both or yet another version individually drafted.

In some cases, confusion may arise over what is meant by *human being* and what is meant by *death*, for criminal homicide must involve a person who was alive at the time the criminal act occurred. These issues are particularly confusing with the advent of modern medicine that prolongs life, the desire of some to be able to terminate their own lives (or have assistance in doing so), and the legalization of abortion.

Causation is frequently a difficult problem in homicide cases, especially when two or more acts may contribute to the victim's death. Some courts look to the intent of the offender; evidence of a criminal intent may be sufficient to establish criminal culpability when actual causation is mixed. Some states require that the defendant's act must have been a substantial factor in the victim's death.

The difficulties of determining the cause (or causes) of death led common law to adopt the year-and-a-day rule. Modern science gives us greater accuracy and speed in determining the cause of death; thus some states have abandoned the rule, while others have retained the concept but extended the time period.

Distinguishing between murder and manslaughter may present problems in homicide prosecutions. Usually murder requires premeditation and malice aforethought, which may be expressed or implied from other facts. Manslaughter is an unlawful killing without malice. But the word *malice* is confusing, too, because it does not necessarily mean hatred or ill will, but rather, an evil motive. Some jurisdictions have abandoned this requirement, but even in those that no longer require the element of malice aforethought, the concept may be used to distinguish first-degree from lesser degrees of murder. In general, first-degree murder includes deliberate, premeditated, intent-to-kill murders as well as felony murders.

Second-degree murder may be defined in terms of murder that is not first-degree. Included might be deaths that occur while an offender is engaged in another criminal act that is not included in the felony murder category. Also included might be intent-to-kill murders that are not deliberate or premeditated, depraved heart murders, and intent-to-inflict-serious-bodily-harm murders. Acts that under other circumstances might be considered murder may not be classified as such if they involve mercy killing or physician assisted suicide (PAS). Mercy killing is not recognized in U.S. criminal justice systems. Oregon and Washington have adopted PAS legislatively, and by judicial interpretation, PAS may be used as a defense in some Montana murder cases.

Second-degree murder may be difficult to distinguish from manslaughter, which may be divided into two categories. *Voluntary manslaughter* is a killing that would be murder except that it is committed under circumstances of extreme mental or emotional disturbance (or in the heat of passion); *involuntary manslaughter* is a criminal killing that is committed recklessly but unintentionally, usually during the commission of an unlawful act, such as driving while intoxicated. In addition, acts that do not reach the level of voluntary manslaughter may be called *misdemeanor manslaughter, vehicular manslaughter,* or *failure-to-act-manslaughter.*

Chapter 6 continues the discussion of violent personal crimes.

STUDY QUESTIONS

1. Define *homicide,* and distinguish justifiable and excusable from criminal homicide.
2. What are the three types of criminal homicide?
3. What is infanticide, and how is it related to modern criminal law? What is the meaning of *born alive*? How has its meaning changed in recent years?
4. What is the meaning of *person* in homicide statutes?
5. Define *death* for legal purposes.
6. What causation problems does homicide present?
7. What is the year-and-a-day rule? Why have some states abandoned or revised it?
8. What is *corpus delicti*? How important is that concept today compared to the past?
9. Distinguish between murder and manslaughter.
10. List and define the elements of murder.
11. What is meant by *malice aforethought*?
12. Explain what is meant by these types of murder: intent to kill, intent to inflict great bodily harm, and depraved heart.
13. What is felony murder? Murder for hire?
14. Distinguish between first- and second-degree murder.
15. What is meant by *lesser included offenses*? How does that concept apply to murder?
16. Should mercy killing be considered murder?
17. What is the legal status of physician assisted suicide (PAS) in the United States?

18. Name and define the types of manslaughter.
19. Discuss the legal issues involved in the convictions of James Arthur Ray and Dr. Conrad Murray.

FOR DEBATE

As medical science improves our chances of living longer, some people are questioning whether they wish to do so if they are suffering from painful diseases. A few have chosen to take their own lives or have asked others, even physicians, to help them. The U.S. Supreme Court has upheld the right of a state to permit this form of death, but it has refused to recognize a constitutional right to physician assisted suicide. This debate issue is designed to assist students in exploring the legal, practical, moral, and ethical implications of physician assisted suicide (PAS).

RESOLVED: Physician assisted suicide should be considered a constitutionally protected right; in the alternative, states should enact statutes to permit it, but strict safeguards should be part of the provisions.

KEY TERMS

Baby Moses laws   95
corpus delicti   96
corroborating evidence   96
crime rate   92
crimes known to the police   92
excusable homicide   93
felony murder   99
fetal alcohol syndrome   94
homicide   93
infanticide   94
involuntary manslaughter   104

justifiable homicide   93
lesser included offense   101
malice aforethought   97
manslaughter   102
murder   97
negligent manslaughter   105
premeditation   101
Uniform Crime Reports (UCR)   91
violent crime   91
voluntary manslaughter   103

INTERNET ACTIVITY

1. Many jurisdictions recognize the unlawful killing of a fetus as murder. For a discussion and listing of state laws, consult the National Conference of State Legislatures Web page, http://www.ncsl.org/ (accessed 11 May 2012), and search fetal homicide. Is your state included in this group?
2. Shortly before this book had gone to press, a shooting rampage occurred in an Aurora, Colorado, theater on 20 July 2012. James E. Holmes was arrested and charged with murdering 12 people and wounding 58 others. The young man, who recently dropped out of graduate school, was dressed in commando-style clothing and carrying three weapons. Using your favorite search engine, search the Web for updates on this massacre. How does it compare to other

mass murders? How does he compare to other mass murderers? Think back to Chapter 4 of this text and consider what, if any, defenses might be appropriate in this case.

NOTES

1. Federal Bureau of Investigation, *Crime in the United States: Uniform Crime Reports, 2006; Crime in the United States: Uniform Crime Reports, 2010* (September 2011); "Preliminary Annual *Uniform Crime Report,* January–December, 2011," http://www.fbi.gov/ (accessed 18 July 2012).
2. Unborn Victims of Violence Act of 2004, USCS, Chapter 18, Section 90A (2012).
3. "Special Session Called on Nebraska Safe-Haven Law," *New York Times* (30 October 2008), p. 20.
4. See Tex. Family Code, Section 262.302 (2012).
5. "10 Years of Giving Mothers A Safe 'Out,'" *Chicago Tribune* (21 August 2011), p. 7.
6. Cal Pen Code, Section 194 (2012).
7. Federal Bureau of Investigation, *Crime in the United States, 2010,* http://www.fbi.gov/ (accessed 11 May 2012).
8. Federal Bureau of Investigation, *Crime in the United States, 2010*; Federal Bureau of Investigation, "Preliminary Annual *Uniform Crime Report,* January–December, 2011.
9. Cal Pen Code, Section 188 (2012).
10. *Keys v. State,* 766 P.2d 270, 271 (Nev. 1988), quoting *Moser v. State,* 544 P.2d 424, 426 (Nev. 1975).
11. *Washington v. Glucksberg,* 521 U.S. 702 (1997); *Vacco v. Quill,* 521 U.S. 793 (1997).
12. ORS, Section 127.880 *et seq.* (2011).
13. See Rev. Code Wash., Section 70.245.010 *et seq.* (2012).
14. *Baxter v. State,* 224 P.3d 1211 (Mont. 2009). The Montana statute is codified at Mont. Code Anno., Section 45-2-211 (2011).
15. See, for example, *Burger v. State,* 231 S.E.2d 769 (Ga. 1977).

Assault, Robbery, Rape, and Other Crimes Against the Person

CHAPTER OUTLINE
Introduction
Assault
  Simple Assault
  Aggravated Assault
  Reckless Assault
  Mayhem
Robbery
  The Elements of Robbery
  Home Invasion Robbery
Forcible Rape and Sodomy
  Definitional Issues
  The Elements of Forcible Rape and Sodomy
    Gender of the Actor and of the Victim
    The Requirement of Penetration
    Lack of Consent
Domestic Violence
  Intimate Partner Violence (IPV)
  Marital Rape
  Date Rape
  Child Abuse
    Statutory Rape
    Incest
  Elder Abuse
False Imprisonment and Kidnapping
Hate Crimes
Stalking
Cyberstalking
Bullying

INTRODUCTION

Discrete, easily differentiated definitions of crimes are impossible. Perhaps this is illustrated most clearly by some of the crimes discussed in this chapter, for there is overlap between such crimes as forcible rape and forcible sodomy and the crimes of assault and battery. More specifically, some crimes against the person, such as aggravated sexual assault, may be indistinguishable from others, such as aggravated assault, except that they focus on sex. Likewise, robbery, which is discussed in this chapter, is a violent personal crime, but it is also a property crime.

Some of the crimes against the person included in this chapter are violent; others are allegedly consensual but occur in situations in which the law does not permit consent, such as sex with minors. Sex crimes against adults and children have become issues of national concern in recent years. Crimes that previously were considered either improper for discussion (such as sex with children) or merely a domestic concern (such as date and marital rape) are now viewed as serious crimes against the person.

The chapter begins with assault and battery and continues with the violent personal crimes of robbery, forcible rape, and sodomy. The chapter then turns to an analysis of domestic violence, which includes some of the already discussed violent crimes but deserves special attention since those crimes occur in the domestic setting. The section on domestic violence also includes child abuse and crimes against the elderly. It is important to understand that the acts included within the domestic violence discussion are crimes, not just problems. A person who assaults and batters or rapes his or her date or spouse commits a violent crime. Parents or other adults who engage in sexual activities with children are committing crimes even if their acts are not violent. Elder abuse is a crime even though it often occurs within the home.

The crimes of false imprisonment and kidnapping, although they are not by definition violent, may become so; certainly they are crimes against the person. Hate crimes, a relatively newly named type of crime, may also involve violence. Stalking is a serious crime because it usually creates fear and threatens the safety of its targets; it may involve violence. Cyberstalking is a specific form of stalking and represents a new section in this text, as does the final topic: bullying.

ASSAULT

The terms *assault* and *battery* are used together or interchangeably, but technically they are different crimes; each can occur without the other. Generally, **assault** refers to the unlawful attempt or threat to inflict immediate harm or death, whereas **battery** refers to the unauthorized harmful or offensive touching of another. Under this approach, it is incorrect to say that A assaulted B when describing a physical attack by A on B. That is the battery, although it is quite possible that the battery was preceded by an assault, that is, A threatened to inflict an immediate battery on B.

Under common law, assault and battery were misdemeanors. In most modern statutes, these crimes may be categorized as misdemeanors or felonies and are further divided by degrees or types, depending on the nature of the acts. In some jurisdictions, assault and battery are merged into one crime and are referred to only as *assault*. This chapter refers to assault and battery as *assault,* and the discussion begins with an analysis of *simple* assault.

Simple Assault

Some jurisdictions require that for an act to be an assault there must be a threat of *immediate* or *imminent* harm; an intent to frighten in the future will not be sufficient. Most statutes require the present ability to succeed in carrying out the threat.

Simple assaults and batteries include acts that do not involve aggravation, which refers to conditions, such as the use of a weapon, that add to the seriousness of the act. The law recognizes that some unauthorized touchings are offensive even if they are not dangerous and, therefore, they constitute a crime as well as a tort. For example, it has long been considered a battery to spit in the face of another. Thus, a person who engages in this act might be prosecuted for the crime of simple assault and also sued by the victim in a civil action.

The law recognizes, however, that some unauthorized, even offensive, touchings will inevitably occur in a crowded society. People bump into each other in lines; domestic authorities restrain persons; and so on, but these acts are not included within assault statutes.

Aggravated Assault

A more serious assault is referred to as an **aggravated assault**, which, as Focus 5.1 noted, refers to an unlawful attack upon another "for the purpose of inflicting severe or aggravated bodily injury." These attacks may be performed with a "weapon or some other means likely to produce death or great bodily harm."

Aggravated assaults are the most frequently committed of the four serious violent crimes as categorized and reported by the FBI's *Uniform Crime Reports,* accounting for approximately 62.5 percent of those crimes in 2010. The estimated number of aggravated assaults that year declined 4.1 percent from 2009 and 14.3 percent from 2001.[1] In 2012, the FBI announced its preliminary data for 2011. Aggravated assaults declined 4.0 percent over that period in 2010.[2]

Aggravated assaults may involve acts performed with the intention of committing another crime or acts accompanied by particularly outrageous or atrocious circumstances. This may include assault with a dangerous weapon.

In some cases, aggravated assault charges are brought in conjunction with attempt crimes, such as aggravated assault with an attempt to commit rape, in which an assailant beats a victim brutally but does not complete the attempted rape. The degree of assault and the subsequent penalty may be greater when the accused is charged with an attempt to commit another felony. This is true particularly when a dangerous weapon is involved in the commission of an assault.

If the use of a deadly weapon defines an act as an aggravated assault, the court must define *deadly weapon* if the statute has not done so. Each case must be decided on its individual facts. Thus, the hands of a prizefighter might be considered a deadly weapon, while those of an average person would not be.

Some jurisdictions list other crimes that might be considered a type of aggravated assault. For example, a statute might refer to as *assault with intent to*... and then name specific crimes, such as the following:

- Kill
- Commit first-degree sexual abuse, second-degree sexual abuse, or child sexual abuse
- Commit robbery
- Mingle poison with food, drink, or medicine with intent to kill
- Willfully poison any well, spring, or cistern of water[3]

Reckless Assault

Another category of assault is an assault involving reckless behavior, defined by the Model Penal Code as follows:

> A person commits a misdemeanor if he recklessly engages in conduct which places or may place another person in danger of death or serious bodily injury. Recklessness and danger shall be presumed where a person knowingly points a firearm at or in the direction of another, whether or not the actor believed the firearm to be loaded.[4]

Some jurisdictions divide assault into degrees and include reckless acts within the lowest of those degrees.

Mayhem

The crime of **mayhem**, which refers to permanent injury inflicted on a victim with the intent to injure and which may disable or disfigure that person, may also be stated as a separate crime or may be included within assault statutes. Under common law, *mayhem* referred to rendering a person less able to fight. Mayhem could occur by disfigurement (which referred to a battery that changed the appearance of a person) or disablement. Later, mayhem was extended to include disfigurement that did not disable the victim.

Today, some jurisdictions retain the separate crime of mayhem without reference to the ability to fight but with reference to disfigurement. Some statutes require the prosecution to prove that the defendant accused of mayhem had the intent to injure, and some require an intent to disable or disfigure. Some statutes list the body parts that are included. Others do not specify mayhem in their criminal codes but do include the crime within another category, such as aggravated assault, based on the assumption that the crime falls within such phrases as *serious bodily injury.*

Under early common law, mayhem was a felony punishable by causing the perpetrator to lose the same body part that the victim lost. Under most modern statutes mayhem is a felony, but the punishment is not as severe as it was under common law.

ROBBERY

The FBI categorizes **robbery** as one of the four serious violent crimes. *Robbery* involves the taking or attempting to take anything of value from the care, custody, or control of a person or persons by force or threat of force or violence or by putting the victim in fear. Today the trend is to consider robbery as a violent crime against the person, but it is also a property crime. The element of fear makes robbery a crime against the person; the items taken make the crime similar to theft crimes. Although most robberies may not involve the actual use of violence, the threat is there—and some robberies are violent and result in death.

In 2010, robberies accounted for 29.5 percent of the four serious violent crimes as recorded by the FBI. The estimated number of robberies for that year was 10.5 percent lower than in 2009 and 18.1 percent down from 2006.[5] The FBI's preliminary data for the 2011 estimate was that robberies declined by 4.0 percent from that period in 2010.[6]

The Elements of Robbery

The elements of robbery are as follows:

1. A trespassory taking
2. A carrying away
3. Of the personal property
4. Of another
5. With the intent to steal

Historically, and in many modern statutes, the first element meant that the stolen property had to be taken from the person or presence of the victim by force or intimidation. The requirement of *from the person or presence of the victim* means that the possessor of the property must be close enough that he or she could exercise control over the property and prevent the robbery except for the presence of force or intimidation. Not all jurisdictions retain that requirement.

The second element of robbery, the process of carrying away, is known as **asportation**, which refers to moving things or people from one place to another.

The third element requires that items taken must constitute **personal property**, not real property. Technically, in the law, *property* refers to anything that belongs exclusively to an individual. Quite simply, for purposes of criminal law, property is divided into two types. *Real property* refers to immovable property, such as land. *Personal property* refers to property that can be moved, such as furniture, although the law may provide that some movable property (e.g., brackets inserted into walls for the purpose of hanging drapes) are part of the real property of the structure and thus may not be removed upon sale of the property unless the buyer agrees. The drapes, however, are personal property and thus could be the subject of a robbery if the other elements of that crime are met.

The fourth element of robbery means that the personal property that is carried away belongs to another person. Finally, the fifth element means that the perpetrator had the required intent to steal the property, that is, to deprive its owner of that property.

Some robbery statutes do not enumerate all of these elements; they may be covered, however, by reference to the jurisdiction's theft statutes.

The requirement of force or intimidation causes difficulty in distinguishing robbery from larceny-theft. Consider, for example, a quick purse snatching. Cases differ on whether that act constitutes robbery or larceny-theft, but generally it depends on how quickly the snatching occurs. If the purse is grabbed so quickly that the victim does not even miss it, the act may be interpreted as larceny-theft, not robbery. But if the victim is aware of the act, is in fear, and may even struggle to retain the purse, the act may be considered a robbery.

Pickpocketing is generally included in the category of larceny-theft crimes, although if the victim realizes what is happening and struggles to prevent the crime but is overcome by the actor, the offender may be charged with robbery. If the offender uses force to render the victim helpless and then steals, the act may be robbery or even aggravated robbery.

The use of intimidation to commit a larceny-theft may constitute robbery. Actual violence is not required; a threat will suffice. The threat need not be directed at the victim. It could be directed at the victim's family, but the threat must be of an *immediate* act.

Unlike larceny-theft statutes, most robbery statutes do not distinguish acts by the value of what is taken. In robbery, it is the threat or actual use of violence that is crucial. Robbery statutes, however, may grade the crime in terms of aggravating factors, such as the aid of an accomplice, actual injury, or the use of a dangerous weapon. *Simple robbery* may be distinguished from *aggravated robbery*, which requires an aggravating circumstance, such as the exhibition or use of a deadly weapon. Robbery statutes may also be classified by degrees, such as robbery in the first, second, or third degree.

Home Invasion Robbery

Special statutes have been enacted to cover the crime of robbery that occurs within a home. The crime is usually termed **home invasion robbery**. Home invasion robbery statutes generally refer to entering a dwelling with the intent to commit a robbery and then committing that robbery. In that sense, the crime is distinguished from *burglary* (discussed in Chapter 7), which does not require an actual theft. Home invasion robbery is usually a first-degree felony. Focus 6.1 discusses three cases of home invasion robbery and reproduces two state statutes. As noted in the Connecticut statute, the crime of home invasion need not involve a robbery or an attempted robbery.

Focus 6.1

Home Invasion and Bank Robbery: Unusual Cases

The text notes that the act of invading a home to commit a robbery (or in some cases, any other crime) is considered so serious that jurisdictions provide separate statutes for *home invasion robbery*. The following cases illustrate the combination of home invasions and bank robberies and other crimes. The first two occurred in Florida.

Three masked men confronted Diego Uscamayta, 25, and his father in their South Florida apartment shortly after midnight in September 2010 and held them captive for approximately seven hours until almost time for banks to open. One stayed with the father while the other two kidnapped Uscamayta and drove him in his own car to the Bank of America branch bank that he normally helped open in the mornings. He was told to get as much money from the vault as he could. The robbers warned their victim that if he did not follow their instructions, they could detonate the bomb they had strapped to him. Only one other person, the female branch manager, was in the bank at the time.

Uscamayta entered the bank and returned to the assailants with an undetermined amount of cash. They escaped in Uscamayta's car, which was later found a few blocks away. It was reported that the robbers got about $100,000 and that the bomb was a fake, although the FBI reported that it did contain materials used in making bombs.

Law enforcement officials noted the similarities between this bank robbery and one that occurred in Hollywood, Florida, three years earlier and that had not been solved. In that case, three masked men allegedly abducted Christopher Ferreira, 26, and his girlfriend, Cindy Wade, also 26, from their apartment after strapping a device on the man's chest and subsequently ordering him to go into the Wachovia bank, where he worked, and get money. The assailants remained in the car with a gun to Cindy's head. Police were concerned that neither Ferreira nor Wade could describe the masks worn by the alleged robbers and that they gave inconsistent statements.[1]

These two alleged crimes have not been solved. Florida's home invasion robbery statute defines the crime as "any robbery that occurs when the offender enters a dwelling with the intent to commit a robbery, and does commit a robbery of the occupants therein."[2]

What legal issues might be involved in applying the Florida statute to the facts mentioned in this focus? Of course, other crimes could be charged on the facts presented if any suspects are arrested.

A far more extensive set of facts were alleged in a Connecticut case. On 23 July 2007, two masked parolees broke into a Cheshire, Connecticut, home, bound the family, and held them hostage for hours while they ransacked the home for cash and other valuables. Joshua Komisarjevsky kidnapped Jennifer Hawke-Petit, the wife and mother, forced her into her car, ordered her to drive to her bank, and remained in the car while she went inside and withdrew money after being promised that her family would not be harmed if she followed the kidnapper's instructions. The second assailant, Steven Hayes, remained in the home and raped the younger daughter. Komisarjevsky raped and strangled Hawke-Petit after they returned from the bank. The husband and father, prominent physician Dr. William Petit Jr., was badly beaten but escaped. The assailants doused the house and the girls with gasoline and set the house on fire before they fled. Both men were convicted of multiple felonies, including capital murders. Both were sentenced to death in a state that came very close to abolishing the death sentence prior to their trials. On 9 June 2009, the governor vetoed the legislative bill to repeal the state's death penalty.[3]

During a special legislative session in January 2008, the Connecticut legislature passed a bill, which was signed by the governor, to become effective 1 March 2008. This bill created a new statute entitled *home invasion*, which provides as follows:

> (a) A person is guilty of home invasion when such person enters or remains unlawfully in a dwelling, while a person other than a participant in the crime is actually present in such dwelling, with intent to commit a crime therein, and, in the course of committing the offense: (1) Acting either alone or with one or more persons, such person or another participant in the crime commits or attempts to commit a felony against the person of another person other than a participant in the crime who is actually present in such dwelling, or (2) such person is armed with explosives or a deadly weapon or dangerous instrument.

> (b) An act shall be deemed "in the course of committing" the offense if it occurs in an attempt to commit the offense or flight after the attempt or commission.[4]

On 25 April 2012, the Connecticut governor signed the state's bill repealing the death penalty.

[1] "Gables Bank Heist Similar to 2007 Hollywood Case," *Sun-Sentinel* (Ft. Lauderdale, FL) (28 September 2010), p. 4B.
[2] Fla. Stat., Title 46, Section 812.135 (2012).
[3] "Home Invasion: Key Dates," *Hartford Courant* (Connecticut) (11 December 2011), p. 6; "No Mercy: After Five Days of Deliberations, Jury Votes for Death," *Hartford Courant* (Connecticut) (10 December 2011), p. 1.
[4] Conn. Gen. Stat., Section 53a-100aa (2012).

FORCIBLE RAPE AND SODOMY

Forcible **rape** and forcible **sodomy** could be included within the crime of assault, for each constitutes offensive, unauthorized applications of force to the person of another, usually preceded by a threat. But both crimes are considered so serious that traditionally they have been defined as separate crimes rather than included within assault statutes.

Definitional Issues

Under common law, rape was defined as the unlawful carnal knowledge of a female without her consent. The word *unlawful* meant that the act was not authorized by law. *Carnal knowledge* is synonymous with *sexual intercourse*; under common law the phrase was limited to acts involving the penis and the vagina. The crime required *penetration*, which was defined as the insertion of the penis into the vagina to any extent; emission was not required for the crime to be complete.

Another element of common law was that sexual intercourse occurred without the consent of the victim. Proving the lack of consent was a factual problem, which led to many interesting statutory and case law rules about evidence in rape cases. As a result, most jurisdictions now have a **rape shield statute** prohibiting the prosecution from presenting evidence of the alleged victim's prior sexual experiences (there are some exceptions to this policy). Further, frequently the media will not report the names of alleged sex crime victims, even when they are adults (generally the media will not report the names of any alleged juvenile offenders unless their trials are transferred to adult criminal courts).

For 80 years, the FBI, in its annual collection of crime data, defined *forcible rape* as "the carnal knowledge of a female forcibly and against her will." This definition essentially followed common law. The *UCR* includes assaults and attempts. The FBI's definition was more restricted than those of many state statutes, which include males as potential victims and women as potential perpetrators. The modern statutes also define penetration more broadly, including oral and anal as well as vaginal cavities. In addition, rape can be perpetrated by instrumentation as well as by a penis.

In 2011, the Obama administration announced that it would expand the FBI's definition of *rape*, and in early 2012, the following definition was official. Forcible rape is now defined as "the penetration, no matter how slight, of the vagina or anus with any body part or object, or oral penetration by a sex organ of another person, without the consent of the victim."[7]

Some jurisdictions do not use the term *rape* in their statutes; rather, they refer to such crimes as *sexual assault* or *criminal sexual assault*. This Illinois statute defines *criminal sexual assault* as follows:

(a) A person commits criminal sexual assault if that person commits an act of sexual penetration and:
  (1) uses force or threat of force;
  (2) knows that the victim is unable to understand the nature of the act or is unable to give knowing consent;
  (3) is a family member of the victim, and the victim is under 18 years of age; or
  (4) is 17 years of age or over and holds a position of trust, authority, or supervision in relation to the victim, and the victim is at least 13 years of age but under 18 years of age.[8]

Forcible rapes constituted approximately 6.8 percent of the four serious violent crimes reported to the FBI in 2010. Reported rapes have been decreasing, with the FBI reporting a 2 percent decline in 2010 over 2009 and a 10.6 percent decline from 2006.[9] The FBI's preliminary data show a 4.0 percent decrease in 2011 compared to that time frame in 2010.[10] Despite the problems with FBI data, they are the official crime data, although the Bureau of Justice Statistics (BJS) provides data on self-reports by alleged crime victims. The BJS reported in late 2011 that it had initiated several projects to improve tests for this reporting.[11] The latest BJS data on rape/sexual assault reported a decline of 24.1 percent between 2001 and 2010.[12]

Sodomy was not a common law crime in England, but it was later defined by statute. It was an American common law crime, later defined by statute, and generally included both the ancient and religious crimes (punishable by ecclesiastical courts) of bestiality (sex with an animal) and buggery (sexual intercourse *per anum,* or per anus), later defined to include sex *per os,* or oral sex. The sex acts involved in these offenses were considered to be unnatural.

A few current statutes retain the definition of sodomy in terms of "that abominable crime against nature," including both anal and oral sex within the crime. Some jurisdictions include oral stimulation of the penis either within sodomy statutes or within the interpretation of those or rape statutes. Oral sexual stimulation of a woman is included in some criminal statutes. However, it is doubtful that any of these statutes will be upheld since the 2003 U.S. Supreme Court decision striking a Texas statute that criminalized private consensual sexual behavior between adults of the same gender.[13]

Some statutes have introduced a term such as *deviant sexual behavior* to encompass oral and anal sex but have included that phrase within the criminal law only when persons use force, fraud, or duress or engage in acts with persons considered unable to give consent, such as minors or adults who are mentally or physically challenged. In effect, then, these statutes, like that of Illinois, eliminate from coverage in the criminal law all other sexual acts engaged in by consenting adults in private.

Another method of categorizing sexual offenses in recent criminal law revisions is to establish *degrees* of criminal sexual conduct, with declining seriousness and penalties. Examples might be first-degree sexual assault, second-degree sexual assault, and so on. Or they might include only the term *sexual assault,* with a second category of *aggravated sexual assault.* Some may retain the traditional term by adding degrees: *first-degree rape,* or *rape in the first degree,* and so on.

The Elements of Forcible Rape and Sodomy

Despite the problems of definition and of interpreting the elements of forced sexual acts, there are some general elements of these offenses, listed here and discussed individually.

1. Female gender (extended to males in an increasing number of jurisdictions)
2. Penetration
3. Lack of consent

Gender of the Actor and of the Victim

The common law limitation of rape to male perpetrators and female victims is retained in some modern statutes. As noted earlier, the Federal Bureau of

Investigation has changed its definition, but it will continue to break out the data by the old definition for the purposes of comparing new data with those of previous years. In recent years some states have adopted gender-neutral language for both perpetrators and victims, as illustrated by the Illinois statute cited earlier.

The Requirement of Penetration

Under common law, penetration was usually interpreted to mean *any* penetration of the vagina by a penis, and this approach was followed in most U.S. jurisdictions. More recently enacted statutes no longer require penetration of the vagina by a penis but include penetration of any body opening by a foreign object (often called *rape by instrumentation*) for the purpose of sexual gratification or humiliation. Returning again to the Illinois criminal code, *penetration* is defined as follows:

> "Sexual penetration" means any contact, however slight, between the sex organ or anus of one person by an object, the sex organ, mouth or anus of another person, or any intrusion, however slight, of any part of the body of one person or of any animal or object into the sex organ or anus of another person, including but not limited to cunnilingus, fellatio or anal penetration. Evidence of emission of semen is not required to prove sexual penetration.[14]

The penetration requirement has been one of the most difficult and frequently litigated elements of rape and sodomy. In a case in which the defendant who committed oral sex on his daughter was convicted of aggravated criminal sodomy (among other offenses), the appellate court reversed his conviction for sodomy (but upheld his conviction for indecent liberties with a child, a less serious crime, carrying a much shorter prison term than aggravated criminal sodomy) because there was no evidence of penetration or oral copulation. The state statute was revised subsequently, and today defines *sodomy* as "oral contact or oral penetration of the female genitalia or oral contact of the male genitalia; anal penetration, however slight, of a male or female by any body part or object; or oral or anal copulation or sexual intercourse between a person and an animal." The statute excludes anal penetration conducted for recognized health care practices.[15]

Lack of Consent

A conviction for forcible rape or forcible sodomy requires that the victim did not consent to the sexual act. Lack of consent is another element that is difficult to prove because in most cases there are no witnesses. Consent is not legal if obtained by duress, threats of harm if one refuses, or fraud or if it is given by a person who cannot consent legally (e.g., mentally incompetent or underage persons).

Because of the difficulty of proving consent or lack of consent, evidence of a struggle was a common requirement in rape cases in the past. Today in many jurisdictions it is not necessary to prove that the victim risked great bodily injury or death by struggling with the assailant, thus showing resistance. Generally, the requirement is that the resistance was reasonable in light of the victim's age and strength, the surrounding facts, and all attendant circumstances, or that no resistance need be shown. The issue is whether or not consent was given. The modern trend is that the victim's testimony is sufficient on the consent issue, although as with any witness, the jury can reject that testimony.

Two types of rape, date and marital, are discussed in the next section, which focuses on crimes that victimize family members or others close to the perpetrator.

DOMESTIC VIOLENCE

Chapter 4 discussed the battered person syndrome defense, which is permitted in some cases in which defendants, usually women, are tried for murdering an intimate partner, whom they claim had battered them for years. In recent years, greater attention has been paid to crimes of violence that occur in close personal relationships. In a special report on family violence, the Bureau of Justice Statistics (BJS) reported that 7 out of every 10 women who reported being raped were victimized by an intimate, a friend, or a relative. Data on such incidents are difficult to obtain, but the BJS reported that, in a study of 18 states and the District of Columbia, family violence accounted for 33 percent of all violent crimes. Two-thirds of all murders with victims under 13 were committed by family members. Fifteen percent of the nearly 500,000 inmates incarcerated for violent crimes committed crimes against members of their own families.[16]

In its 2010 annual report on victimization, the BJS reported that stranger violence had decreased but varied by the victim's gender. Male victims knew only 40 percent of their violent perpetrators, while female victims knew 64 percent of those who victimized them. The known perpetrators for both genders were most often acquaintances or friends. "Females were more likely to be victimized by someone they knew (a nonstranger) than by a stranger for all measured violent crimes except robbery."[17]

Today the concept of **domestic violence** is used to refer to the infliction of physical and other forms of harm, including death, on members of the family, including spouses, children, parents, and, in some cases, friends with whom the perpetrator has a close relationship. Some jurisdictions have special domestic violence statutes, while others attach the term *domestic violence* to murders, aggravated assaults, and so on, that occur within domestic situations. Focus 6.2 contains examples of state domestic violence statutes.

Family or domestic violence can be categorized into violence against spouses or other intimate partners, violence against children, and violence against the elderly.

Intimate Partner Violence (IPV)

We noted in Chapter 4 that, historically, little attention was paid to violence within marriage, and if the police did intervene, it was usually in the role of mediator, not law enforcement. In recent years criminal law, law enforcement officers, prosecutors, and judges have taken a different view, looking at such incidents as crimes. These changes, along with an emphasis on victimization, have led to studies of **intimate partner violence (IPV)**, which is defined in various terms

---

Focus 6.2

Domestic Violence Type Statutes: A Sample

New York: Executive Law, Article 21. New York State Office for the Prevention of Domestic Violence (2012)

Section 1. Legislative findings and declaration of intent

The legislature hereby finds domestic violence to be a problem of enormous magnitude and tragic consequence that scars the lives of its victims, destroys family integrity and leads to injury or death of many innocent people in our state.

The legislature declares that New York state is committed to helping families affected by violence to overcome the indignity and pain they suffer and is dedicated to preventing such violence from claiming new victims.

The legislature further declares that the office for the prevention of domestic violence created heretofore by executive order should be established within the executive department as a statutory office to respond to this statewide problem, to evaluate, improve and strengthen the service system, to coordinate the efforts of the public agencies which provide services or funding of services, and to provide centralized training, technical assistance, education and outreach.

The legislature hereby finds and declares that establishment of programs designed to help batterers and their violent behavior is essential in the effort to end domestic violence and that the establishment of such programs is in the public interest and to the benefit of all persons in this state.

The legislature further declares that batterers should be held accountable for their violent behavior, and that programs designed to stop the cycle of family violence and teach more appropriate behaviors should be viewed as a vital component of a community's response to domestic violence. [The act contains provisions for evaluating the established programs.]

Burns Ind. Code Ann., Section 35–41–1–6.3 (2012)

Crime of domestic violence

"Crime of domestic violence," for purposes of [other statutes], means an offense or the attempt to commit an offense that:

(1) has as an element the:

(A) use of physical force; or

(B) threatened use of a deadly weapon; and

(2) is committed against a:

(A) current or former spouse, parent, or guardian of the defendant;

(B) person with whom the defendant shared a child in common;

(C) person who was cohabiting with or had cohabited with the defendant as a spouse, parent, or guardian; or

(D) person who was or had been similarly situated to a spouse, parent, or guardian of the defendant.

Colorado's Legislative Declaration, C.R.S. 26–7.5–101 (2011)

The general assembly hereby finds that a significant number of homicides, aggravated assaults, assaults and batteries, and other types of abuse and coercive control occur within the home; that the reported incidence of domestic abuse represents only a portion of the total number of incidents of domestic abuse; that a large percentage of police officer deaths in the line of duty result from police intervention in domestic abuse situations; and that domestic abuse is a complex problem affecting families from all social and economic backgrounds. It is the purpose of this article to encourage the development of domestic abuse programs by units of local government and nongovernmental agencies.

Code of Ala., Section 13A-6-130 (2012)

Domestic violence in the first degree

[Alabama has three degrees of the crime of domestic violence]

(a) A person commits the crime of domestic violence in the first degree if the person commits the crime of assault in the first degree pursuant to [the statutes on assault in the first degree and aggravated stalking, with the latter added effective 1 September 2011], and the victim is a current or former spouse, parent, child, any person with whom the defendant has a child in common, a present or former household member, or a person who has or had a dating or engagement relationship with the defendant. Domestic violence in the first degree is a Class A felony, except that the defendant shall serve a minimum term of imprisonment of one year without consideration of probation, parole, good time credits, or any other reduction in time for any second or subsequent conviction under this subsection.

---

but, in general, refers to violence toward a current or former spouse, girlfriend, or boyfriend.

The National Center for Injury Prevention and Control of the Centers for Disease Control and Prevention (CDC) published a study in 2011, based on 2010 data. The survey indicated that 51.1 percent of women who reported having been raped were assaulted by an intimate partner; 40.8 percent were attacked by an acquaintance. Among men, 52.1 percent reported being raped by an acquaintance. Of the one in 21 men who said they were made to penetrate someone, 44.8 percent said that person was an intimate partner; 44.7 percent said the individual was an acquaintance.[18]

In the federal system, the Violence against Women Act of 1984 provides some protection for female victims of sexual assault and other forms of violence, as well as stalking. This statute also contains provision for police training in how to respond to such violence and for establishing departmental policies for mandatory arrests of those accused of engaging in domestic or intimate partner violence.[19]

These provisions and the emerging statutes covering domestic violence do not tell the entire story. Although it may not be a typical reaction, in October 2011, the Topeka, Kansas, City Council voted 7–3 to repeal that town's misdemeanor domestic violence ordinance. Disputes over the budget led the city to take this action after a county attorney refused to prosecute misdemeanors, leaving only the city to process misdemeanor domestic violence acts.[20]

The most violent acts that occur in families and other intimate personal situations often result in the deaths of victims, but personal injuries also occur from other violent acts, such as rape. The next two sections focus on marital and date rape.

Marital Rape

Under common law, a man could not be charged with raping his spouse unless he aided another man to have sexual intercourse with her. The law assumed that implicit in the marriage contract was a willingness on the part of the wife to participate in sexual intercourse at her husband's desire.

Today, many jurisdictions have statutes that define **marital rape** (forced sexual intercourse with a spouse) as a crime, usually a felony. In some jurisdictions in which such statutes do not exist, courts have construed traditional rape statutes to include spousal victims. For example, in 1985, the Georgia statute that defined *rape* as "carnal knowledge of a female forcibly and against her will" was interpreted by the Georgia Supreme Court to include marital rape. The court held that when a woman says "I do," she does not mean "I always will" as far as sexual intercourse is concerned. According to the court, "certainly no normal woman who falls in love and wishes to marry…would knowingly include an irrevocable term to her revocable marriage contract that would allow her husband to rape her." The defendant's convictions for the rape and sodomy of his wife were upheld.[21]

In some jurisdictions both husband and wife may be considered as spousal rape victims, although in either case, there have been few prosecutions, and most are not successful. Further, the statutes may place restrictions on prosecutions and on penalties. For example, in California, unless there is independent evidence that is admissible at trial, a marital rape prosecution may not proceed unless the alleged incident was reported to named authorities (such as medical personnel, attorneys, or the clergy).[22]

Date Rape

Sexual violence on college and university campuses as well as in other venues has led to increased attention to the crime of **date rape**, which refers to forced sexual acts that occur during a consensual social occasion. The victim may have agreed to some sexual intimacy, but not to the activities defined in that jurisdiction as constituting rape. But because of the consensual social interaction, prosecutions are difficult, as jurors may not believe the complainant. The issue, however, is not whether the two people knew each other but whether the complainant consented to sexual intercourse. There is no legal concept of *real rape* versus *date rape*. If the elements of forcible rape are present, the crime is rape, whether the parties are strangers, acquaintances, casual dates, steady lovers, or, in jurisdictions that provide, spouses.

Studies show that alcohol and other drugs play a major role in date rape crimes. Concern with the role of drugs in date rape led the Drug Enforcement

Administration to announce in 1996 that it was listing Rohypnol, the "date rape drug," as a Schedule I drug (those that have no accepted medical use in the United States and which have a high potential for abuse),[23] along with LSD and heroin. Rohypnol is a powerful hypnotic that causes short-term memory loss, a feeling of well-being, and prolonged sedation. It is not approved for sale or use in the United States, but in many other countries it is used legally for insomnia and as a preoperative anesthetic. It is called the *date rape drug* because it is dropped into drinks (in which it is odorless, tasteless, and colorless) and given to dates for the purpose of taking advantage of them sexually. After consuming what are popularly called "roofies," the victim shows little resistance to the pressures and actions of others and does not remember what happened during the period of the drug's influence.

Child Abuse

Another area of domestic violence is **child abuse**, which refers to the physical (including **sexual abuse**) or psychological abuse of a child by parents, other relatives, acquaintances, or strangers. Child abuse may also include involving children in pornography or showing them pornography. Any of the violent personal crimes discussed previously in this text may constitute child abuse. In recent years, however, the trend has been toward processing some forms of child abuse through special statutes designed to protect children. Some jurisdictions have also enacted legislation aimed at preventing the *continued* abuse of children, especially in the area of sexual abuse.

Although in some cases of child sexual abuse children are alleged to have consented, these acts are criminal because children are not legally capable of consenting.

Statutory Rape

Unlike forcible rape, statutory rape (sexual intercourse, and in some jurisdictions, other sexual acts with an underage person even though that person consented) was not an early common law crime, although in 1275 English common law criminalized it, setting the age at 12 and lowering that to 10 in 1576. In the 1700s and 1800s, statutory rape laws in the United States set the age of consent at 10 or 12, but between 1885 and 1900, those ages were raised to 16 or even higher in most states. The philosophy behind these statutes is that minors may be taken advantage of sexually and that they are not old enough to know how to avoid sexual predators. The age under which minors may not give legal consent to sexual relations varies among jurisdictions.

Historically, statutory rape included only sexual intercourse with an underage girl, but today some statutes are gender-neutral. In most jurisdictions statutory rape is a strict liability crime, meaning that the perpetrator does not have to be aware of the minor's age. However, a reasonable mistake of fact concerning the minor's age may constitute a defense in some jurisdictions.

Not all jurisdictions have statutory rape laws as such, but they may have statutes that cover the behavior, and they may have degrees of the crime. For example, the state of Washington defines *rape of a child in the first degree* as involving "sexual intercourse with another who is less than twelve years old and not married to the perpetrator and the perpetrator is at least twenty-four months older than the victim." *Rape of a child in the second degree* occurs when "the person has sexual intercourse with another who is at least twelve years old but less than fourteen years old and not married to the perpetrator and the perpetrator is at least thirty-six months older than the victim."[24]

Some statutory rape laws have been successfully challenged when they involve young persons as perpetrators. In 2011, the Ohio Supreme court declared unconstitutional that state's law prohibiting sexual activity with a child under 13 after it was applied to a 12-year-old boy accused of engaging in anal sex with an 11-year-old boy and a 12-year-old boy. The trial court found no evidence of force and the court ruled that to charge one participant with violating the statute and not charge the other participants was unconstitutional. The statute could be found constitutional in other circumstances but not in this case, in which the prosecutor chose to charge only one of the three underage boys. The U.S. Supreme Court declined to hear the case.[25] The facts of this case are, of course, quite unusual, but they do illustrate some of the problems that courts face with enforcing such strict liability statutes.

Incest

Sexual relations between children and family members or relatives who are legally too close to marry is called **incest** and may be classified as a separate crime by that name. Incest may also be prosecuted as, or along with, other sex crimes. Incest victims are not all children, but it is discussed here in that context, as most victims are under the legal age of consent. The New Mexico and Minnesota statutes illustrate two ways of defining the crime. The New Mexico statute provides as follows:

> Incest consists of knowingly intermarrying or having sexual intercourse with persons within the following degrees of consanguinity: parents and children including grandparents and grandchildren of every degree, brothers and sisters of the half as well as of the whole blood, uncles and nieces, aunts and nephews.[26]

The Minnesota statute takes a different approach while achieving the same result:

> Whoever has sexual intercourse with another nearer of kin to the actor than first cousin, computed by rules of the civil law, whether of the half or the whole blood, with knowledge of the relationship, is guilty of incest and may be sentenced to imprisonment for not more than ten years.[27]

Elder Abuse

As Americans live longer, due primarily to medical advances, the problem of abusing the elderly gains more attention. **Elder abuse** takes many forms, ranging from emotional abuse by family and caretakers to sexual and other forms of physical abuse and including financial scams.

Some jurisdictions have specific statutes aimed at preventing elder abuse. For example, Missouri has three degrees of elder abuse, with *elder abuse in the first degree* defined as follows:

A person commits the crime of elder abuse in the first degree if he attempts to kill, knowingly causes or attempts to cause serious physical injury,… to any person sixty years of age or older or an eligible adult as defined in [another statute].[28]

Another approach is to define elder abuse along with the abuse of other so-called protected categories of persons. The Alabama code provides an example, as follows:

It shall be unlawful for any person to abuse, neglect, exploit, or emotionally abuse any protected person. For purposes of this section, residence in a nursing home, mental institution, developmental center for people with an intellectual disability [changed in 2009 from the mentally retarded], or other convalescent care facility shall be prima facie [on its face sufficient to establish a fact] evidence that a person is a protected person.[29]

Elderly people are also the victims of sexual abuse, although this type of abuse is often hidden. But a research analysis of sexual abuse of the elderly in Virginia reported that the most common type of abuse involved women as victims of sexualized kissing and fondling (79 percent of the reported cases), followed by the abuse of an unwelcome sexual interest in the older person's body (43 percent of the reported cases). Many of the perpetrators were other residents of the care facilities, although there were also cases of abuse by caretakers.[30]

Some jurisdictions have specific statutes covering elder abuse, while others include elder abuse within other domestic violence statutes (see again Focus 6.2) or simply use traditional statutes, such as assault and battery.

Some family and other caretakers target the elderly for financial gain, for example, stealing their Social Security checks or cash. But the elderly are also easy targets for property scams entered into on their own. Some elderly are willing to invest their savings and other assets in order to make the promised "big bucks." Many become the victims of scam artists.

Elder abuse has captured the attention of Congress, and in March 2010, the Elder Justice Act became law as part of the Patient Protection and Affordable Care Act. Focus 6.3 contains some of the Congressional findings and provisions of the act.

FALSE IMPRISONMENT AND KIDNAPPING

Two other crimes against the person are false imprisonment and kidnapping. These are similar crimes in that both require restricting victims' freedom. They differ in the elements required to establish the crimes, the seriousness of the offenses, and the punishments.

Under common law, **kidnapping** (restricting the freedom of a victim against his or her will and removing the victim from one place to another) required the asportation (removal from one place to another) of a victim from his or her own country to another. **False imprisonment** (the unlawful and knowing restraint of a person against his or her wishes so as to deny freedom) did not require

Focus 6.3

U.S. Elder Justice Act

Section 2. Findings
Congress finds the following:

(1) The proportion of the United States population age 60 years or older will drastically increase in the next 30 years as more than 76,000,000 baby boomers approach retirement and old age.

(2) Each year, anywhere between 500,000 and 5,000,000 elders in the United States are abused, neglected, or exploited.

(3) Elder abuse, neglect, and exploitation have no boundaries, and cross all racial, social class, gender, and geographic lines.

(4) Victims of elder abuse, neglect, and exploitation are not only subject to injury from mistreatment and neglect, they are also 3.1 times more likely than elders who were not victims of elder abuse, neglect, and exploitation to die at an earlier age than expected.

(5) There is a general dearth of data as to the nature and scope of elder abuse, neglect, and exploitation....

(6) Despite the dearth of data in the field, experts agree that most cases of elder abuse, neglect, and exploitation are never reported and that abuse, neglect, and exploitation shorten a victim's life, often triggering a downward spiral of an otherwise productive, self-sufficient elder's life....

(9) No Federal law has been enacted that adequately and comprehensively addresses the issues of elder abuse, neglect, and exploitation and there are very limited resources available to those in the field that directly deal with the issues.

(10) Differences in State laws and practices in the areas of elder abuse, neglect, and exploitation lead to significant disparities in prevention, protective and social services, treatment systems, and law enforcement, and lead to other inequities.

(11) The Federal Government has played an important role in promoting research, training, public safety, and data collection, and the identification, development, and dissemination of promising health care, social, and protective services, and law enforcement practices, relating to child abuse and neglect, domestic violence, and violence against women. The Federal Government should promote similar efforts and protections relating to elder abuse, neglect, and exploitation....

(16) All elements of society in the United States have a shared responsibility in responding to a national problem of elder abuse, neglect, and exploitation.

SOURCE: Patient Protection and Affordable Care Act, P.L. 111–148 (2010).

asportation. Sometimes called *false arrest,* false imprisonment referred only to the unlawful confinement of another person. Thus, kidnapping was the same as false imprisonment with the added element of asportation. Some jurisdictions do not define a separate crime of false imprisonment; likewise, some states do not define kidnapping as a separate crime if it is committed incidental to another crime.[31]

Asportation remains a required element of kidnapping in most jurisdictions. It is important because courts are trying to avoid making the lesser crime of false imprisonment into the more serious crime of kidnapping by finding the asportation element when it has nothing to do with the crime of kidnapping or by creating two crimes (false imprisonment and kidnapping) when only one actually occurred.

Some kidnapping statutes require that the victim be isolated in a secret place; others require only proof that there was an intent to isolate the victim. Some statutes define more than one degree of kidnapping, requiring aggravating circumstances for the more serious offense of first-degree kidnapping. Kidnapping a child for purposes of prostitution or pornography is an example of an aggravating circumstance; kidnapping any person for ransom is another. Kidnapping may be accompanied by other crimes, such as extortion, sexual assault, terrorism, torture, and murder.

Some jurisdictions define a separate crime of child stealing or parental kidnapping. Congress passed the Parental Kidnapping Prevention Act of 1980, which permits federal authorities to issue warrants for parents who flee a state's jurisdiction to avoid prosecution for parental kidnapping. The statute also obligates states, under specified circumstances, to recognize child custody determinations of other states.[32]

A major problem with child kidnapping cases is that parents who take children illegally from a custodial parent may be difficult, if not impossible, to locate. Some move to other countries, while others begin a new life with successful disguises. Further, parental kidnapping cases are difficult to win, and lower courts have disagreed over whether a natural parent may be convicted of kidnapping his or her child under the various state statutes.

One final method of handling these types of cases within the criminal law is illustrated by an Ohio statute entitled *Interference with custody.* The statute includes children "under the age of eighteen, or a mentally or physically handicapped child under the age of twenty-one" as well as adults institutionalized for mental retardation or mental illness and children under the state's juvenile custody. It is a crime for anyone "knowing the person is without privilege to do so or being reckless in that regard" to "entice, take, or harbor" persons in the enumerated categories.[33]

HATE CRIMES

In 1990, Congress called for the collection of data on crimes involving bias against persons. The Hate Crimes Statistics Act, subsequently amended, refers to crimes, usually called **hate crimes**, which represent traditional crimes (such as battery, rape, and murder) that are motivated by a person's actions toward another based on certain characteristics, such as race, ethnicity, national origin, sexual orientation, disability, or a combination of these or other traits. Jurisdictions vary with regard to which of these or other bias targets are included within their statutes.

In 1994, Congress amended the federal statute to include physical and mental disabilities. In 2009, President Obama signed the Matthew Shepard and James Byrd Jr. Hate Crimes Prevention Act, named after two hate crime victims. This amendment added the categories of gender and gender identity and directed the collection of data by and directed against juveniles.[34] On 21 September 2011, Texas executed Lawrence Russell Brewer, one of the three convicted defendants in the killing of Byrd. Another awaits execution; the third is serving a life sentence.

The official data on hate crimes, collected by the Federal Bureau of Investigation for its *Uniform Crime Reports,* include all of these categories, as illustrated by the FBI's definition of hate crime:

> A hate crime is a traditional offense, like murder, arson, or vandalism with an added element of bias. For purposes of collecting statistics, Congress has defined a hate crime as "a criminal offense committed against a person or property motivated in whole or in part by the offender's bias against a race, religion, disability, ethnic origin, or sexual orientation." Hate itself is not a crime—and the FBI is mindful of protecting freedom of speech and other civil liberties.[35]

Some jurisdictions do not have hate crime statutes but prosecute hate crimes under other statutes, such as murder. Other jurisdictions have statutes similar to that of the federal code; some include gender. Hate crime statutes have been challenged in the courts. Some have been upheld, while others have been voided as violating the First Amendment right to free speech (see Appendix A).

The Oregon Supreme Court upheld a state statute that makes it a crime for two or more people to injure another "because of their perception of that person's race, color, religion, national origin or sexual orientation." The court held that this statute is directed against conduct rather than speech. The U.S. Supreme Court refused to hear the case, thus permitting the ruling to stand.[36]

The California hate crime statute was upheld against claims of vagueness and equal protection.[37] In 1995, the statute was upheld against First Amendment claims.[38] In June 1993, the U.S. Supreme Court upheld a state statute that provided for enhanced sentences for persons convicted of crimes motivated by racial or other bias.[39] In 2000, in *Apprendi v. New Jersey,* the U.S. Supreme Court upheld the enhanced sentencing provision of a New Jersey statute.[40]

An example of an ordinance that did not survive a constitutional challenge is seen in a case that illustrates the difference between conduct and speech. In *R.A.V. v. St. Paul,* the U.S. Supreme Court invalidated a St. Paul, Minnesota, ordinance that prohibited displaying on public or private property a symbol that a person knew or should have known would arouse alarm, anger, or resentment on the basis of race, color, creed, religion, or gender. In *R.A.V.,* a white teenager was accused of burning a cross in the yard of an African American family. The Court found that the ordinance could have a chilling effect on the right to free speech because it permitted the expression of only one side of an issue.[41]

In 2003, the U.S. Supreme Court upheld the Virginia Supreme Court in its ruling that the state's statute concerning cross burning was unconstitutional. *Virginia v. Black* involved three defendants, one of whom was convicted of violating the state statute that prohibited cross burning with the intent to intimidate. A second defendant entered a guilty plea to attempted cross burning and conspiracy to commit cross burning. The third defendant was convicted of attempted cross burning. The convictions were affirmed by the Virginia Court of Appeals but reversed by the state supreme court, which ruled that the statute violated the First Amendment because it punished individuals for engaging in symbolic speech, which may be infringed upon by the government only if the speech involves obscenity, defamation, and fighting words. When the case was before the U.S. Supreme Court, eight of the justices viewed cross burning under the facts of this case as constituting free speech and ruled that in order for the prosecution to prevail under the Virginia statute, it must prove beyond a reasonable doubt that the speech in question was intended to intimidate rather than to express an opinion. The lone dissenter, Justice Clarence Thomas, declared, "There is no other purpose to the cross, no communication, no particular message. . . . It was intended to cause fear and to terrorize a population."[42]

STALKING

Some forms of behavior that do not rise to the level of physical injury or fall within traditional crimes, but that may be frightening for the targeted person, may now be covered under statutes designed to deter **stalking**. These statutes are designed to punish people who engage in behavior such as the following, enumerated by the Bureau of Justice Statistics (BJS), which reported that an estimated 3.4 million persons age 18 or older were subjected to one or more of these acts during a 12-month period:

> "Making unwanted phone calls.
> Sending unsolicited or unwanted letters or e-mails.
> Following or spying on the victim.
> Showing up at places without a legitimate reason.
> Waiting at places for the victim.
> Leaving unwanted items, presents, or flowers.
> Posting information or spreading rumors about the victim on the internet,
>   in a public place, or by word of mouth."[43]

Some of the statutes are too broad and thus unconstitutional. Others are narrowly drawn and have been upheld.

Stalking statutes have been challenged in the courts with some success. For example, Florida provides that "any person who willfully, maliciously, and repeatedly follows or harasses another person" may be charged with *stalking*, which is a first-degree misdemeanor. If the actor makes credible threats under specified circumstances, the charge is *aggravated stalking*, which is a third-degree felony. The state's trial courts split over the issue of whether this law is constitutional, but a state appellate court upheld the statute and the state supreme court affirmed. The U.S. Supreme court refused to review the case.[44]

An Ohio court of appeals held that the state law prohibiting a person from engaging in a "pattern of conduct" that he or she knows will "cause another to believe that the offender will cause physical harm to the other person or cause mental distress to the other person" is not vague or too broad. A "pattern of conduct" is defined as "two or more incidents closely related in time."[45]

In contrast, the Kansas antistalking statute was invalidated. That statute defined stalking as follows: "an intentional and malicious following or course of conduct directed at a specific person when such following or course of conduct seriously alarms, annoys, or harasses the person, and which serves no legitimate purpose."[46]

The Kansas Supreme Court held that the statute was void for vagueness because *alarms* and *annoys* are subjective terms and thus open to many interpretations. The court noted that there were no guidelines to enlighten persons on the meaning of "alarming, annoying, or harassing" concerning following or other conduct. As defined, the crime of stalking, according to the court, "depends upon the sensitivity of the complainant." The court did hold, however, that the word *following* is not vague.[47]

The Kansas statute was changed to read as follows:

Stalking is an intentional, malicious and repeated following or harassment of another person and making a credible threat with the intent to place such person in reasonable fear for such person's safety.[48]

Effective 1 July 2011, the Kansas statute was changed to define *stalking* as the following:

(1) Intentionally or recklessly engaging in a course of conduct targeted at a specific person which would cause a reasonable person in the circumstances of the targeted person to fear for such person's safety, or the safety of a member of such person's immediate family and the targeted person is actually placed in such fear;

(2) intentionally engaging in a course of conduct targeted at a specific person which the individual knows will place the targeted person in fear for such person's safety or the safety of a member of such person's immediate family; or

(3) after being served with, or otherwise provided notice of, any protective order included in K.S.A. 21-3843, and amendments thereto, that prohibits contact with a targeted person, intentionally or recklessly engaging in at least one act listed in subsection (f)(1) that violates the provisions of the order and would cause a reasonable person to fear for such person's safety, or the safety of a member of such person's immediate family and the targeted person is actually placed in such fear.[49]

CYBERSTALKING

One type of stalking statute is new and does not yet exist in most jurisdictions: electronic stalking, or **cyberstalking**, which refers to stalking by use of a computer.

On 1 January 1999, California's *computer stalking statute* became effective. It constitutes an amendment to the state's stalking statute by adding that the term *credible threat* in the original statute means

> a verbal or written threat, including that performed through the use of an electronic communication device, or a threat implied by a pattern of conduct or a combination of verbal, written, or electronically communicated statements and conduct made with the intent to place the person that is the target of the threat in reasonable fear for his or her safety or the safety of his or her family and made with the apparent ability to carry out the threat so as to cause the person who is the target of the threat to reasonably fear for his or her safety or the safety of his or her family. It is not necessary to prove that the defendant had the intent to actually carry out the threat.[50]

The first charge under this new statute came just a few weeks after the statute became law, when Gary Steven Dellapenta, a 50-year-old security guard, was accused of sending out an advertisement, via electronic mail, in which he described the alleged victim and listed her name, address, and phone number, along with information on how to bypass her home security system. The alleged victim, who did not even own a computer, was not injured, but six men showed up at her house over a period of several months. The men stated that they were responding to her advertisement. Dellapenta, who had been rebuffed by the victim, was impersonating her in the advertisement, which stated that she fantasized about being raped.[51] Dellapenta pleaded guilty to three counts of solicitation for sexual assault and one count of stalking. He was sentenced to six years in prison.

The *South China Morning Post* in Hong Kong carried this warning when it reported the crime: "Anti-stalking laws may be a valuable weapon in preventing worse crimes, but terror on the Internet is predicted to become a serious and growing problem."[52]

In November 2011, Jovica "Joshua" Petrovic, 61, was convicted in a federal court in St. Louis, Missouri, of four counts of cyberstalking and two counts of extortion (discussed in a subsequent chapter of this text). Petrovic was acquitted of interstate stalking. His acts included mailing approximately 150 postcards to his ex-wife's friends and associates. These items contained embarrassing information, insults, and lies, along with addresses to websites on which he posted other information, such as nude pictures of the two of them having sex. He demanded $100,000, her engagement ring, and items he claimed she stole from a storage unit. In exchange, he claimed, he would close down the site. The prosecutor accused the defendant of launching a psychological attack designed to destroy the woman. The judge described the defendant's acts as "stupid, vile, ignorant criminal things," and went beyond the federal guidelines in sentencing him to 8 years in prison.[53]

The Internet is often used for the next and final crime discussed in this chapter.

BULLYING

Bullying is not a new act; it has been around for years if not centuries, but its impact has been enhanced by the extensive use of the Internet in recent years. And specific legislation against *bullying* is recent. Bullying has been connected to suicides and other personal tragedies. In 2010, Phoebe Prince's sister found Phoebe's dead body, hanging from the stairwell in her home. Phoebe's apparent suicide followed cyberbullying from six classmates; all were students at South Hadley High School in Northampton, Massachusetts. Phoebe was only 16 when she apparently decided that she could no longer live with the bullying, which consisted of months of verbal abuse and threats of physical violence.

According to prosecutors, the day that Phoebe's body was found, her classmates hounded her and threw a beverage can at her as she walked home from school. The defendants were charged with criminal harassment; two were charged with stalking. All were spared incarceration. The charge of statutory rape against Austin Renaud, 19, was dropped. Sharon Velazquez, 17, Flannery Mulolins, 18, and Ashley Longe, 18, were placed on probation for less than a year. Sean Mulvenyill, 18, entered a guilty plea to one count of criminal harassment; Kayla Narey, 18, admitted to sufficient facts on the same charge. They each received one year of probation. Some of the defendants were also sentenced to community service. The Massachusetts legislature enacted a stiff anti-bullying statute, which became effective 3 May 2010. The statute is lengthy and thus is not reprinted here, but it defines *bullying* as follows:

> "Bullying," the repeated use by one or more students of a written, verbal or electronic expression or a physical act or gesture or any combination thereof, directed at a victim that: (i) causes physical or emotional harm to the victim or damage to the victim's property; (ii) places the victim in reasonable fear of harm to himself or of damage to his property; (iii) creates a hostile environment at school for the victim; (iv) infringes on the rights of the victim at school; or (v) materially and substantially disrupts the education process or the orderly operation of a school. For the purposes of this section, bullying shall include cyber-bullying. [The statute contains a lengthy definition of cyber-bullying.][54]

Focus 6.4 contains additional information on bullying.

SUMMARY

This chapter continued Chapter 5's discussion of violent crimes. It began with assault crimes. Assault, battery, and mayhem are violent crimes that involve inflicting bodily injury on others in an unlawful manner. These crimes may be minor or very serious, such as dismemberment in the case of mayhem or serious beatings in the case of aggravated assault. A simple assault may not involve any real physical injury but is a crime because it involves an unauthorized, offensive touching.

Focus 6.4

Bullying and Cybercrime

Federal and state agencies have focused on criminalizing cybercrime as one way to deter bullying. National and international media focused on Lori Drew, who was indicted on one count of conspiracy and three counts of accessing protected computers without authorization for the purpose of inflicting emotional distress on a 13-year-old girl, Megan Meier, age 13, who hanged herself in a St. Louis suburb in October 2006. Drew posed as a 15-year-old boy who was romantically interested in the victim but later spurned her and told her, among other things, that the world would be better off without her.

There was no cyberbullying statute under which Drew could be charged. Federal authorities interpreted the Computer Fraud and Abuse Act[1] as applicable and charged her with conspiracy and unauthorized use of a computer. For the latter, they were in effect charging Drew with criminal trespass on a computer by using MySpace without proper authorization. If the jury found that Drew used MySpace to commit a criminal or tortious act (in this case, intentional infliction of emotional distress), they could convict her of a felony. But the jury did not find that intent; the only alternative was a misdemeanor conviction of unauthorized use of protected access to a computer. Drew was convicted of three misdemeanor counts of accessing a computer without proper authorization for violating the terms of service of MySpace; the jury deadlocked on the conspiracy charge. A federal court granted Drew's motion for judgment of acquittal on the grounds that the MySpace rules were unconstitutionally vague.[2]

The Drew case led to the enactment of a cyber harassment law in Missouri. That law took effect in August 2008. The first trial under the statute ended in an acquittal in February 2011. Elizabeth A. Thrasher, 41, was charged with a felony for placing personal information about a teen on Craigslist. The teen's mother was dating Thrasher's ex-husband, and Thrasher reportedly thought that she was not a good influence on her own daughters. The teen had exchanged angry messages with Thrasher on MySpace. When law enforcement officials investigated who put personal information about the teen online, they traced the act to Thrasher. The teen received phone calls and text messages from men she did not know and said she feared for her welfare; she quit her job after one stranger showed up at her place of work. The jury said the state failed to prove one element of the new crime: that the recipient had actually suffered emotional distress as a result of the posting.[3]

---

[1] Computer Fraud and Abuse Act, USCS Section, Title 18, Section 1030 (2012).
[2] *United States v. Drew*, 259 F.R.D. 449 (C.D. Cal. 2009).
[3] "Jury Found No Proof in Cyber-Harassment Case," *St. Louis Post Dispatch* (20 February 2011), p. 27. For a discussion of the Missouri statute, see Note: "High-Tech Words Do Hurt: A Modern Makeover Expands Missouri's Harassment Law to Include Electronic Communications," *Missouri Law Review* 74, no. 2 (Spring 2009): 379. The statute is codified at Mo. Rev. Stat., Section 565.090 (2012).

The chapter's treatment of robbery noted that this crime may be categorized as a violent or a property crime. Although robbery involves all of the elements of larceny-theft (discussed in Chapter 7), it has the added element of putting the victim in fear of imminent harm. It is that element that calls for the categorization of robbery as a violent crime. Robberies within homes are particularly frightening, and recently home invasion robbery statutes have been enacted in many states to cover this type of robbery.

Forcible rape, which under common law included only unlawful carnal knowledge of a female without her consent, has been changed by statute in many jurisdictions to include male victims and female offenders and to expand the definition of carnal knowledge beyond that of penile-vaginal intercourse. The chapter noted that in January 2012, the FBI changed its definition of forcible rape. In many recent statutory changes, forcible rape and forcible sodomy are combined into crimes with such names as *aggravated sexual assault* or *abuse*.

Forcible rape and sodomy, as well as assault, have been recognized recently in many jurisdictions as including acts that also occur within the domestic setting. Some states have repealed their marital rape and sodomy exemptions; others have interpreted their statutes to exclude the exemption in some cases, such as forced sexual relations with an estranged spouse. This chapter discussed these crimes, along with other crimes between intimate partners, in the context of a section on domestic violence. Included was a discussion on date rape, another violent crime that received little attention until recently. Today it is recognized that, in a criminal case of alleged sexual assault, the issue is not whether the victim knew the assailant but whether the victim agreed to the behavior.

Child abuse is yet another area of violent crime that is the focus of attention today; the concern is not limited to physical abuse but also includes sexual abuse, which may cause serious psychological and physical problems for children.

At the opposite end of the age spectrum from children are the elderly, who are the targets of physical as well as emotional and financial abuse. Some states and Congress have enacted special legislation in their attempts to prevent crimes against the elderly.

Kidnapping is another crime against the person that may become violent. In one sense, it is identical to false imprisonment but with the added element of asportation. Modern kidnapping statutes do not require that the victim be taken to another country, as under common law, but there is no general agreement on what is meant by the asportation element. Some jurisdictions have abandoned the asportation element but do require that the victim be held secretly.

The chapter also discussed several recently defined crimes: hate crimes, stalking, cyberstalking, and bullying. Statutes as well as recent examples were detailed.

The violent crimes discussed in this chapter, along with homicide, discussed in Chapter 5, may create more fear in potential victims, but the most extensive crimes are those of property, the focus of Chapter 7.

STUDY QUESTIONS

1. Discuss assault, battery, and mayhem. Distinguish between simple and aggravated battery.
2. What is meant by *reckless assault and battery?*
3. How would you define a dangerous weapon?
4. Why is robbery a violent crime against the person?
5. What is meant by *home invasion robbery?* Why do we need separate statutes for this crime?
6. How do modern statutes and common law differ in their definition of forcible rape? Of sodomy? What is the FBI's current definition, and how does it contrast with the agency's traditional one?
7. What is meant by *domestic violence,* and why do we have separate crimes for this category of offenses?
8. Should date rape and rape by strangers be processed in different ways? How about marital rape?
9. What is meant by *child abuse?*
10. What is statutory rape, and what are its elements? Should any changes be made in the traditional statutory rape statutes? Why or why not?
11. Define *incest.*
12. What is *elder abuse?* Do we need separate statutes to cover this crime?
13. Should parental child kidnapping be a separate crime, or should it be prosecuted as kidnapping, requiring the same elements and carrying the same penalties as those provided for any kidnapping?
14. Explain the importance of asportation in kidnapping cases.
15. List and discuss ways in which men, women, adults, and children can prevent becoming kidnap victims.
16. What are hate crimes? Why are statutes covering these crimes so recent? Do we need these statutes?
17. Define *stalking* and *cyberstalking,* and analyze efforts to deter these crimes by statute.
18. Discuss developments in the crime of bullying.

FOR DEBATE

In recent years, several kidnappings captured national attention, some featured nightly for days, weeks, or even months. A few kidnappings involve positive endings in the sense that the child is recovered alive although harmed by the trauma of the kidnappings and perhaps sexually abused. But most kidnapping victims are found dead; some are raped or tortured in other ways prior to their deaths. This debate topic is designed to encourage students to evaluate the role of the media in kidnappings and to consider that role along with the constitutional rights of free speech and privacy of the press and of alleged victims and their families.

RESOLVED: The media should be encouraged to reduce its coverage of missing children cases and to show more respect for the privacy rights of the alleged victims and their families.

KEY TERMS

aggravated assault   112
asportation   114
assault   111
battery   112
child abuse   125
cyberstalking   133
date rape   124
domestic violence   121
elder abuse   126

false imprisonment   127
hate crime   129
home invasion robbery   115
incest   126
intimate partner violence
   (IPV)   121
kidnapping   127
marital rape   124
mayhem   113

personal property   114
rape   117
rape shield statute   118
robbery   114
sexual abuse   125
sodomy   117
stalking   131

INTERNET ACTIVITY

1. Access the National Center for Victims of Crime, http://www.ncvc.org (accessed 11 May 2012), and click on Dating Violence Resource Center. What can you find out about violence among young people during courtship? Should these acts of violence be treated as criminal acts? If so, how serious should the penalties be?
2. Consult the above source for information on stalking. Click on Victim Assistance followed by Stalking Resource Center. What are the data? How prevalent is stalking on college campuses? What are the effects of being a stalking victim?

NOTES

1. Federal Bureau of Investigation, *Crime in the United States: Uniform Crime Reports, 2010* (September 2011), http://www.fbi.gov (accessed 11 May 2012).
2. Federal Bureau of Investigation, "Preliminary *Annual Uniform Crime Report*, January–December 2011," Table 3, http://www.fbi.gov (accessed 18 July 2012).
3. See D.C. Code, Title 22, Section 22-401 (2012).
4. Model Penal Code, Section 211.2.
5. Federal Bureau of Investigation, *Uniform Crime Reports, 2010.*
6. Federal Bureau of Investigation, "Preliminary *Annual Uniform Crime Report*."
7. Federal Bureau of Investigation, http//www.fbi.gov (accessed 11 May 2012).
8. ILCS, Chapter 720, Section 5/11-1.20 (2012).
9. Federal Bureau of Investigation, *Uniform Crime Reports, 2010.*
10. Federal Bureau of Investigation, "Preliminary *Annual Uniform Crime Report*."
11. Bureau of Justice Statistics (BJS), "BJS Activities on Measuring Rape and Sexual Assault," Press release (19 December 2011), http://www.bjs.gov (accessed 11 May 2012).
12. Jennifer L. Truman, Bureau of Justice Statistics, *Criminal Victimization, 2010* (September 2011), p. 2, http://www.bjs.gov/content/pub/pdf/cv10/pdf (accessed 11 May 2012).

13. *Lawrence v. Texas,* 539 U.S. 558 (2003).

14. ILCS, Chapter 720, Section 5/12-12 (2012).

15. *State v. Moppin,* 783 P.2d 878 (Kan. 1989), *superseded by statute as stated in Norton v. State,* 1991 Kan. App. LEXIS 796 (Kan.Ct.App. 1991). The new statute is K.S.A., Section 21-3501 (2011).

16. Matthew R. Durose *et al.,* Office of Justice Programs, Bureau of Justice Statistics, *Family Violence Statistics* (Washington, D.C.: U.S. Department of Justice, June 2005), pp. 1–8.

17. Jennifer L. Truman, Bureau of Justice Statistics, *Criminal Victimization, 2010* (September 2011), p. 9, http://www.bjs.gov (accessed 11 May 2012).

18. Michele E. Black *et al.,* Centers for Disease Control and Prevention (CDC), http://www.cdc.gov (accessed 11 May 2012).

19. Violence Against Women Act, USCS, Chapter 136, Section 1381 (2012).

20. "When Government Forsakes Its Duty To Protect: With Money Tight, A City in Kansas Decides It Won't Prosecute Wife Beaters," *Newsday* (New York) (21 October 2011), p. 42.

21. *Warren v. State,* 336 S.E.2d 221 (Ga. 1985). The Georgia rape statute is codified at O.C.G.A., Section 16-6-1; the sodomy statute is at sections 16-6-2 (2012).

22. Cal Pen Code, Title 9, Section 262 (2012).

23. Schedules of Controlled Substances, USCS, Title 21, Section 812 (2012). See Chapter 11 of this text for a more detailed discussion.

24. Rev. Code Wash. (ARCW), Section 9A.44.073 (first degree) and Section 9A.44.076 (second degree) (2012).

25. *In re D.B.,* 950 N.E. 2d 528 (Ohio 2011), *cert. denied, mot. granted, Ohio v. D.B.,* 132 S. Ct 846 (2011).

26. N.M. Stat. Ann., Section 30-10-3 (2012).

27. Minn. Stat., Section 609.365 (2012).

28. R.S.Mo., Title 38, Section 565.180 (2012).

29. Code of Ala., Section 38-9-7 (2012).

30. "When Elders Are Molested: Sexual Abuse of Nursing Home Residents Too Often Goes Unreported," *Legal Times* (27 June 2005), n.p.

31. See *Apodaca v. People,* 712 P.2d 467 (Colo. 1985).

32. USCS, Title 28, Section 1738A (2012).

33. ORC, Section 2919.23 (2012).

34. The federal hate crime act is codified at USCS, Title 28, Section 534 (2012).

35. Federal Bureau of Investigation, "Hate Crime: Overview," http://www.fbi.gov/about-us/investigate/civilrights/hate_crimes/overview (accessed 11 May 2012).

36. *State v. Plowman,* 838 P.2d 558 (Ore. 1992), *cert. denied,* 508 U.S. 974 (1993).

37. See *In re Joshua H.,* 13 Cal.App.4th 1734 (1993), *review denied,* 1993 Cal. LEXIS 3412 (Cal. 1993); and *People v. MacKenzie,* 34 Cal.App. 4th 1256 (6th Dist. 1995). The California hate crime statute is codified at Cal Pen Code, Section 422.6 (2012).

38. *In re M.S.,* 896 P.2d 1365 (Cal. 1995).

39. *State v. Mitchell,* 508 U.S. 476 (1993).

40. *Apprendi v. New Jersey,* 530 U.S. 466 (2000). The New Jersey enhanced sentencing statute is codified at N.J. Stat., Section 2C:44-3 (2012).

41. *R.A.V. v. St. Paul,* 505 U.S. 377 (1992).

42. *Virginia v. Black,* 538 U.S. 343 (2003).

43. Katrina Baum et al., Bureau of Justice Statistics, National Crime Victimization Survey, *Stalking Victimization in the United States* (January 2009), p. 1, http://www.ovw.usdoj.gov/docs/stalking-victimization.pdf (accessed 11 May 2012).

44. *Bouters v. State,* 659 So.2d 235 (Fla. 1995). *Cert. denied,* 516 U.S. 894 (1995). The Florida anti-stalking statute is codified at Fla. Stat. 784.048 (2012).

45. *State v. Dario,* 665 N.E.2d 759 (Ohio App. 1995). The statute is codified at ORC Ann. 2903.211 (2012).

46. Kan. Stat. Ann., Section 21-3438 (1994).

47. *State v. Bryan,* 910 P.2d 212 (Kan. 1996).

48. K.S.A., Section 21-3438 (2006).

49. K.S.A., Section 21-3438 (2011).

50. Cal Pen Code, Section 646.9(g) (2012).

51. "Computer Stalking Case a First for California," *New York Times* (25 January 1999).

52. "Movie Watch," *South China Morning Post* (Hong Kong) (16 September 2000), p. 7.

53. "Husband Is Convicted of Cyberstalking Wife," *St. Louis-Post-Dispatch* (Missouri) (19 November 2011), p. 2; "Law and Order Public Safety," *St. Louis Post-Dispatch* (16 February 2012), p. 3.

54. ALM GL Ch. 71, Section 370 (2011).

Property and Related Crimes

INTRODUCTION

Modern property law cannot be understood without looking at its history, particularly in English common law. Life was much simpler when property laws first emerged. That simplicity is important in understanding how and why certain rules developed concerning property crimes and why some acts included in criminal laws today were considered acceptable business practices under common law.

The influence of early English common law on the development of common law and statutory law in the United States was particularly strong in the area of property law. Although U.S. criminal laws have embraced some acts that historically were not considered crimes in England, they have retained many of the elements of English common law. Thus, some sections in this chapter look briefly at English common law definitions and interpretations before discussing modern property law. They also look at some generalities about each crime, as well as examples of current property crime statutes.

The first part of the chapter focuses on the four **property crimes** categorized by the Federal Bureau of Investigation (FBI) as serious crimes: larceny-theft, burglary, motor vehicle theft, and arson, for which the FBI publishes data on occurrences and arrests. For crimes categorized as less serious property offenses, the FBI reports only arrest data. Some of those crime categories are discussed in the second part of the chapter. Particular attention is given to several types of fraud, as some of those crimes are capturing considerable national attention today. The chapter also looks at various types of computer crimes, which can involve the theft of property as well as of identity and can even encompass stalking, which was discussed in Chapter 6. The chapter closes with a relatively newly defined crime, that of carjacking.

SERIOUS PROPERTY OFFENSES

The official FBI crime data, published in the agency's annual *Uniform Crime Reports (UCR)*, list four serious property offenses: larceny-theft, burglary, motor vehicle theft, and arson. The *UCR's* definitions of those crimes are reproduced in Focus 7.1. The latest data available for a full year are for 2010, and Figure 7.1 graphs the changes in property crimes between 2006 and 2010, revealing a decline in property offenses during that period. The estimated offenses fell 2.7 percent between 2009 and 2010. In 2012, the FBI published its preliminary data on property offenses for 2011, showing an estimated 0.8 percent decline over the previous year for that same period.[1]

Focus 7.1

Serious Property Crimes: *UCR* Definitions

Burglary: "the unlawful entry of a structure to commit a felony or theft."

Larceny-theft: "the unlawful taking, carrying, leading, or riding away of property from the possession or constructive possession of another."

Motor vehicle theft: "the theft or attempted theft of a motor vehicle."

Arson: "any willful or malicious burning or attempt to burn, with or without intent to defraud, a dwelling house, public building, motor vehicle or aircraft, personal property of another, etc."

SOURCE: Federal Bureau of Investigation, *Crime in the United States: Uniform Crime Reports, 2010* (September 2011), http://www.fbi.gov/ (accessed 12 May 2012).

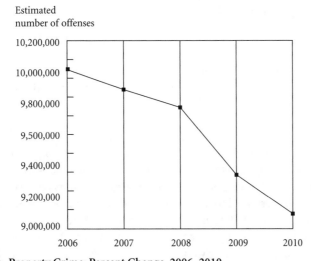

Estimated
number of offenses

FIGURE 7.1 Property Crime: Percent Change, 2006–2010
SOURCE: Federal Bureau of Investigation, *Crime in the Unites States: Uniform Crime Reports, 2010* (September 2011), http://www.fbi.gov (accessed 12 May 2012).

Larceny-Theft

The oldest common law theft crime is **larceny-theft**, which is the most frequently committed serious property crime, accounting for an estimated two-thirds of the four serious property crimes in the United States yearly.

Larceny-theft means stealing, but there are a variety of ways to steal. The contribution of common law to the evolution of modern theft crime statutes is important.

Common Law Larceny-Theft

Under early common law, larceny-theft (usually referred to only as *larceny*; today's FBI definition categorizes *theft* as *larceny-theft*) was the only type of theft punishable as a crime, and its elements were interpreted narrowly. The crime was defined as the unlawful taking, carrying, leading, or riding away of property from the possession of another with the intent to steal. Many actions that we consider theft today were not included under that definition and its interpretations through case law. As one early case noted, it was not a crime to "make a fool of another" by deliberately delivering fewer goods than the purchaser had ordered.[2]

Also under English common law, because of the seriousness of larceny-theft (which at times carried the death penalty), the elements of the crime were stated carefully. However, some judges were reluctant to convict because of the death penalty. Consequently, technicalities crept into the law, making some of the elements a disgrace and embarrassment. Attempts to erase these loopholes led one scholar to conclude that the "intricacies of this patchwork pattern are interesting as a matter of history but embarrassing as a matter of law enforcement."[3]

The elements of larceny-theft are as follows:

1. A trespassory taking
2. A carrying away (asportation)
3. Of the personal property
4. Of another
5. With the intent to steal.

Under common law, technically no act could be larceny-theft unless all of these elements were present. Modern statutes make some exceptions, however, at least in interpretations.

Trespassory Taking. The phrase *trespassory taking* was used in common law to refer to the unlawful taking away of goods from an owner's possession. The crime of larceny-theft was developed to deter people from committing thefts that might cause personal retaliation. It was assumed that if an owner saw someone taking away his (women were not permitted to own property at that time) property, he would react in a way that might lead to violence. If no trespassory taking occurred but someone outsmarted him and thereby misappropriated his personal property, the owner might be angry but the offender would not likely be available to take immediate retaliatory action. Thus, the peace of society was less likely to be challenged, and consequently, common law provided civil but not criminal remedies in this situation.

As society became more complex, especially in business transactions, judges thought it necessary to expand larceny-theft to cover thefts that did not involve trespassory takings. But instead of abolishing trespassory taking as a requirement of larceny, they developed fictions in which a taking was assumed. The judicial fiction might operate like this: When a master delivered property to his servant to be used for the benefit of the master, it was argued that the servant had *custody* of the property but that the master retained *possession,* which in this situation was called **constructive possession**. *Constructive possession* is a legal doctrine that refers to the condition of having the power to control an item along with the intent to do so. Other fictions developed, but a case decided in 1953 illustrates the problems created when judges began trying to expand the law of larceny-theft without developing new offense categories.

The defendant stopped at a service station and asked to have his car's gas tank filled. The attendant pumped 6½ gallons of gas, worth $1.94, which was below the requirement for **grand larceny**. The defendant drove off without paying for the gas. He was convicted of **petit larceny**, which refers to a smaller theft than that of grand larceny. The crimes are distinguished only by the amount stolen, and that amount is generally specified by statute. The defendant appealed, arguing that because the station attendant parted voluntarily with the possession and ownership of the gasoline, he was not guilty of petit larceny, one element of which is a trespass. In upholding the conviction, the court emphasized that the owner retained constructive possession because actual possession was obtained by trick. The court stated: "The obtaining of the property by the consent of the owner under such conditions will not necessarily prevent the taking from being larceny.... The trick or fraud vitiates the transaction, and it will be deemed that the owner still retained the constructive possession."[4]

Larceny in this manner is called **larceny by trick**, which refers to deceptively obtaining possession of goods from a victim who surrenders possession voluntarily and without knowledge of the deceit involved. In this case, the larceny by trick established the element of *taking* from the possession of the owner.

Another exception to the requirement of actual possession crept into the law as judges attempted to deal with the problem that occurred when a **bailee**, a person to whom goods are entrusted by a **bailor** (a person who entrusts goods to a bailee), converted those goods to his own use. Technically the bailee was not taking the goods from the possession of the owner; thus larceny-theft had not occurred.

New provisions were needed. The first solution was to rule that the bailee could be convicted of larceny-theft if he broke open a case of goods and took some of the contents. Some judges reasoned that once the bailee broke the bulk, possession returned to the owner, whereas others argued that the bailee never had possession of the contents, only of the container. The practical result was that a bailee who misappropriated the entire package could not be charged with larceny-theft because he had not taken the package unlawfully from the owner's possession. But if he broke open the package and took part of the contents, larceny-theft was an appropriate charge, provided the other elements of larceny-theft were present.[5]

146 CRIMINAL LAW: THE ESSENTIALS

These and other fictions led to changes in the law of larceny-theft. Today in the United States, when a bailee misappropriates property, some jurisdictions treat that act as larceny-theft if the package is broken but as embezzlement (discussed later in this chapter) if it is not broken. Other jurisdictions have a separate crime, *larceny by bailee,* to cover the misappropriation whether or not there was a breaking. Some have a general crime called *theft* that covers all of these and other fact patterns.

A Carrying Away. The second element of larceny-theft is that the goods must be taken away; this is called *asportation,* which means moving a thing (or a person) from one place to another. If the defendant attempts to take the article away and does not succeed, the asportation element is not complete and larceny-theft has not occurred. Thus a defendant who removes a coat from a store dummy and tries to take it away but cannot do so because it is attached by a chain has not committed larceny-theft.

Personal Property of Another. The third and fourth elements of common law larceny-theft are that the article must be the *personal property of another person.* This phrase means that real property, abandoned property, and wild animals are not included. Under common law, *personal property* referred only to tangible personal property. Trees, minerals, crops, and other items of real property could not be the subject matter of larceny-theft. If those items were severed, larceny-theft could be charged, but the severance and the theft had to be two separate acts.

Today, some statutes include trees and other items of real property within the definition of *theft* and therefore do not require separate actions to constitute the crime. In most cases, electricity and gas are considered property subject to larceny, but labor and services are not covered unless specified by statute, although they may be covered by other criminal statutes.

Some modern theft statutes cover services, such as boarding a chair lift at a ski resort without a lift ticket, or sneaking into a concert hall without paying.

With the Intent to Steal. The final element of common law larceny-theft is that the defendant must have had an intent to deprive the owner of the property.

In a very early case involving a 17-year-old who took another boy's bicycle, as he said, "to get even with the boy, and of course, I didn't intend to keep it," the California Supreme Court reversed the conviction and emphasized the common law position that the intent required for larceny-theft must be an intent to deprive the owner of the property permanently.[6]

Modern Theft Codes

The common law elements of larceny-theft are important because most of those elements are retained in modern theft statutes, and frequently common law is used to interpret those statutes. In recent years, many jurisdictions have enacted legislation more specific than common law larceny-theft, and usually the term used is *theft* rather than *larceny-theft,* with the exception of the FBI, as noted earlier. For example, common law excluded services from the personal property requirement of larceny-theft. Today, some jurisdictions include *theft of services* under a special statute, while others have expanded their existing statutes to include theft of services.

Another modern approach regarding theft crimes is to combine all, or at least most, theft-related crimes into one crime of *theft*, while some jurisdictions continue to have numerous theft statutes covering the various types of the crime. The following Texas statute is illustrative of some of these changes:

> Theft, as defined in Section 31.03 [which defines the elements of theft] constitutes a single offense superseding the separate offenses previously known as theft, theft by false pretext, conversion by a bailee, theft from the person, shoplifting, acquisition of property by threat, swindling, swindling by worthless check, embezzlement, extortion, receiving or concealing embezzled property, and receiving or concealing stolen property.[7]

The Texas penal code does contain some separate theft crimes, such as theft of services, theft of trade secrets, unauthorized use of a vehicle, and so on.[8]

Burglary

A major property crime similar to but distinct from larceny-theft is **burglary**, which refers to the breaking and entering of an enclosed structure without consent and with the intent to commit a felony therein. Unlike larceny-theft, burglary does not require an actual theft. Burglary is an offense against habitation and occupancy, and thus breaking and entering a structure to commit any felony is a crime in many jurisdictions; some specify the required intended crime.

Before examining the elements of common law burglary, it is necessary to distinguish burglary from robbery, discussed in Chapter 6. Although it is common for a victim of household (or other structures) burglary to say, "I was robbed," this statement is incorrect; burglary and robbery have some distinct elements. Robbery requires the taking of property from the person or presence of the victim by the use of force or threat of force, elements that are not required for burglary, although burglary may lead to robbery if the structure is occupied.

Common Law Burglary

Common law burglary was defined as breaking and entering the dwelling of another during the night with the intent to commit a felony. Thus, its elements were as follows:

1. A breaking and entering
2. Of the dwelling of another
3. During the nighttime
4. With the intent to commit a felony therein.

The requirement of *breaking and entering* did not require destruction of any part of the property in order to enter, but it did require a "breaking, removing, or putting aside of something material, which constitutes a part of the dwelling house, and is relied on as a security against intrusion."[9] The emphasis on security is important. If the door was already open, entering by that means did *not* constitute a breaking. If the door was closed but unlatched, opening the door constituted a breaking. In some cases, if the door was partially open and if it was necessary to open it further to enter, breaking was deemed to have occurred.

Under some circumstances, such as obtaining entry by fraud, by threatening to use force, by going through a chimney, or by having a servant or some other person within the structure open the door, it was argued that constructive force sufficient to constitute a breaking had occurred. The breaking had to involve a **trespass**, a crime referring to the entering or remaining unlawfully in or on the premises (including land, boats, or other vehicles) of another under certain circumstances as specified by statute. This crime is discussed in more detail later in this chapter. In addition to a trespass, the entry must have been accomplished by means of the breaking. Therefore, it would not be sufficient if the offender broke a window but then entered the dwelling through a door that had been left open by the owner.

Under common law burglary, the requirement of *entry* could be satisfied if any part of the person (e.g., a hand or foot) entered; it was not necessary that the person's whole body enter the dwelling. The entry requirement could also be accomplished by the use of a tool, provided that the tool was used for the purpose of committing the intended felony. Using an auger (a boring tool) to drill a hole through a floor to steal grain by letting the grain fall into a sack constituted an entry. It would not be an entry, however, if the offender inserted a tool into the dwelling to effect his or her own entry but did not actually enter.[10] Nor could entry be accomplished constructively by sending in someone who was not legally capable of committing a crime, such as a child, a mentally challenged person, or a trained monkey or other animal, to commit the felony.

The second element of common law burglary required that the *dwelling of another* be entered. Under common law, burglary was limited to acts that occurred within the home, referred to as the *dwelling* or the *dwelling place.* Usually a dwelling was a place where someone slept regularly; occasional sleeping was not sufficient. If the building was used regularly during one season (e.g., a summer home), that would suffice, provided the possessor intended to return another summer. The dwelling requirement was met if someone slept regularly in an office or other structure; it was the regular sleeping that was critical to this element of the offense.

Included within the definition of *dwelling* were pertinent buildings that were "within the **curtilage**," such as the enclosed ground, garage, barn, stable, cellar, or other buildings immediately surrounding the dwelling. If there was no fence, the buildings considered to be within the curtilage were required to be reasonably close to the dwelling to be fenced. One final requirement was that the dwelling place must be that of *another* person. Burglary did not encompass breaking and entering one's own property with the intent to commit a felony.

Common law burglary required that the crime occur during the night, usually defined as from sunset, or when the countenance of a person could not be discerned, until sunrise. Both the breaking *and* the entering had to occur at night, although they were not required to occur on the same night; a person could break on one night and enter on a subsequent night.

The final element of common law burglary was the *intent to commit a felony,* usually larceny-theft, but any felony would suffice. It was sufficient if a person entered the building to commit the felony but did not actually engage in the intended act. It was the unlawful breaking and entering with the intent to commit the felony that constituted burglary. If the felony (e.g., larceny-theft) was completed, the offender could be charged with and convicted of both larceny-theft and burglary.

Finally, if the individual entered the dwelling without an intent to commit a felony and once inside decided to commit a felony, he or she might be convicted of that felony but not of burglary. To constitute common law burglary, the intent to commit the felony must have been present at the time of the unlawful breaking and entering. The intent to commit a misdemeanor would not be sufficient; there must have been an intent to commit a felony.

Statutory Burglary

The crime of burglary is covered today by statute. Most, if not all, common law requirements are retained in modern burglary statutes, some with modification. Although they may require *unlawfully remaining,* most statutes no longer require a breaking: Any illegal entrance may be sufficient. Further, some statutes are specific with regard to the *structure* involved, perhaps listing numerous structures. Even if they are not specific in listing target structures, most modern burglary statutes expand the common law requirement of a *dwelling* to include *any* structure, although they may provide greater penalties for persons who burglarize a dwelling. The distinction between night and day is retained in some statutes; in others, it is eliminated or made relevant only to punishment.

Some statutes define *grades* of burglary, such as *aggravated burglary* or *burglary of the first* or *second degree.* Others classify certain types of burglary as a felony of the first, second, or third degree and provide differential sentences depending on the perceived seriousness of the type of burglary.

Not all jurisdictions permit the defendant to be charged with both the crime of burglary and the crime for which the defendant committed the illegal entry, for example, larceny-theft. Some statutes have restrictions concerning multiple convictions. Finally, in recent years some jurisdictions have enacted new statutes to cover the entry of a dwelling for the purpose of committing a robbery. This new approach to crimes against the person and the habitation, usually referred to as *home invasion robbery,* was discussed in Chapter 6.

Motor Vehicle Theft

Since motor vehicles did not exist, common law did not need a statute to cover stealing vehicles. Modern statutes differ in how they define motor vehicle theft, but the FBI distinguishes thefts *from* vehicles from theft *of* motor vehicles, with the latter defined as "the theft or attempted theft of a motor vehicle." This definition includes "automobiles, trucks, buses, motorcycles, motorscooters, snowmobiles, etc." but "excludes the taking of a motor vehicle for temporary use by those persons having lawful access."[11]

In most jurisdictions, motor vehicle theft is covered by general theft statutes and thus does not warrant a separate statute. Others retain specific auto theft statutes, while some statutes distinguish between *motor vehicle theft* and *joyriding,* the unauthorized use of a motor vehicle without the intent to steal it.

Arson

The fourth serious property crime, according to official FBI crime data, is **arson**, which, as noted in Focus 7.1, is defined as "any willful or malicious burning or attempt to burn, with or without intent to defraud, a dwelling house, public building, motor vehicle or aircraft, or personal property of another person." Some statutes include the burning of one's own property if done with the intent to defraud; others classify that act only as *fraud.*

Arson was first classified by the FBI as a serious property crime in 1978. Arson is indeed a serious crime, causing significant property damage and, in some cases, injury and death. But it is difficult to acquire sufficient evidence for arson convictions because much, if not all, of the evidence of the crime may be destroyed by the fire.

In recent years, increasing attention has been given to arson not only because of the high percentage of young people involved but also because of the serious injuries, deaths, and extensive property damage caused by this crime.

Common Law Arson

Common law arson, which at times carried the penalty of death by burning, had the following elements:

1. The malicious burning
2. Of the dwelling
3. Of another.

A *malicious burning* meant that the perpetrator must have a criminal intent. Negligence was not sufficient to establish arson, nor was there a felony arson crime analogous to felony murder, which was discussed in Chapter 5. A fire that resulted from the commission of another crime was not arson. Nor did an individual commit arson by burning his own dwelling. If in the process of burning his own dwelling, however, the owner created an unreasonable fire hazard for other dwellings—one or more of which burned—the property owner could be charged with arson for the burning of the other's dwelling.

The criminal intent element did not require malice toward the property owner or the property in question. It required either the intent to burn the dwelling, the knowledge that a fire would burn the dwelling, or the setting of a fire without excuse or justification that created an obvious hazard to the dwelling of another.

The requirement of *burning* did not mean that the dwelling had to be burned completely. Earlier cases established the requirement that there must be a burning, not just a smoking or a maliciously set fire that was put out before any of the dwelling was burned.

The common law requirement that arson be of a *dwelling* was identical to that of common law burglary, discussed earlier. The requirement *of another* referred to possession, not ownership. If a landlord burned a dwelling rented to a tenant, the element would be satisfied because the tenant had a legal right to possession of that dwelling at the time of the burning.

Statutory Arson

Although some jurisdictions retain the common law definition of arson, others have expanded the crime to include the burning of many structures other than dwellings and the burning of one's own structures. Some statutes eliminate the requirement of actual burning and permit an arson charge when damage is caused by an explosion that does not result in a fire or when a fire that is started purposely does not burn the structure in question. But it must be shown that the actor had the intent to damage or to destroy that structure. The statutes may also include the burning of trees, especially forests.

Some states have individual statutes aimed at specific types of structures, such as churches, houses, trailers, mobile homes, walls, stables, offices, warehouses, coach houses, outhouses, shops, mill, barns, and so on. For example, North Carolina has a statute covering the burning of a mobile home, a manufactured-type house, or a recreational trailer home. A person who maliciously burns any of these structures, occupied and serving as the dwelling house of another, may be charged with arson in the first degree.[12]

A second North Carolina statute covers the crime of *fraudulently setting fire to dwelling houses.* The act must be malicious or wanton or done for a fraudulent purpose and may include the dwelling of the perpetrator, who may be convicted of the crime even if he or she does not actually burn the structure. It is sufficient to "aid, counsel or procure the burning of such building." The statute also requires, however, that the actor be "the occupant of any building used as a dwelling house."[13]

A third North Carolina statute prohibits burning, aiding, counseling, or procuring the burning of numerous types of buildings (such as an uninhabited house or a stable, office, warehouse, coach house, outhouse, shop, mill, barn, and so on) "used or intended to be used in carrying on any trade or manufacture."[14]

North Carolina also has a statute that covers damage (exclusive of burning or attempting to burn) to houses, churches, fences, and walls.[15]

Statutes may also specify *degrees* of arson, such as first, second, third, fourth, and so on. New York has four degrees, ranging from the first degree (arson of a building occupied by another not involved in the crime when the offender knows that the circumstances are such that someone is likely to be in that building) to the fourth degree (reckless arson).[16]

LESS SERIOUS PROPERTY OFFENSES

In addition to requesting law enforcement agencies to collect data on the serious property crimes of larceny-theft, burglary, motor vehicle theft, and arson, the FBI compiles data on less serious property crimes, some of which are discussed in this section. It is important to understand that the term *less serious* does not mean that these offenses have a lesser economic impact on society or their immediate victims. But for the general public, the crimes may not arouse the fear and anger that occur with burglary and larceny-theft.

Embezzlement

Acts that are defined as **embezzlement** in today's statutes were not included in common law larceny-theft because a person already in lawful possession of property could not be charged with larceny-theft. Statutory requirements were necessary to bring under the criminal law the acquisition of another's property by misappropriation or misapplication when the actor already had legal control of the property.

Embezzlement refers to misappropriating or misapplying property or money that was already entrusted to the individual. Embezzlement requires **conversion**, which refers to the process of using the property or goods of another for one's own use and without permission. Thus, conversion is an interference with the owner's property, not merely a movement of that property.

Although some statutes define the property that may be subject to embezzlement in the same way as property subject to larceny-theft, others define the crime more broadly, some even including real property. Some statutes do not distinguish between larceny-theft and embezzlement. Consider the following Virginia statute:

> If any person wrongfully and fraudulently use, dispose of, conceal or embezzle any money, bill, note, check, order, draft, bond, receipt, bill of lading or any other personal property, tangible or intangible, which he shall have received for another or for his employer, principal or bailor, or by virtue of his office, trust, or employment, or which shall have been entrusted or delivered to him by another or by any court, corporation or company, he shall be deemed guilty of embezzlement. Proof of embezzlement shall be sufficient to sustain the charge of larceny.[17]

Some jurisdictions have a separate statute to cover embezzlement by public officials, making the penalty more severe for them than for others.

Fraud

The crime of **fraud** refers to falsely representing a fact, either by conduct or by words or writing, in order to induce a person to rely on the misrepresentation and surrender something of value. The crime has many types; thus, it is difficult to generalize, but one court has articulated the following as the general elements of fraud:

1. A representation
2. Its falsity
3. Its materiality
4. The speaker's knowledge of its falsity or ignorance of its truth
5. The speaker's intent that it should be acted upon by the person and in the manner reasonably contemplated

6. The hearer's ignorance of its falsity
7. The hearer's reliance upon its truth
8. The right of the hearer to rely upon it
9. The hearer's consequent and proximate injury or damage[18]

There are many types of fraud. A few are discussed. But first, attention is given to one of the frequent types of fraud victims.

Fraud Against the Elderly

According to the American Association of Retired Persons (AARP), over half of U.S. victims of telemarketing fraud (estimated by Congress to amount to at least $40 billion annually) are age 50 or older and thus qualify as "elderly" for purposes of the AARP.[19]

The elderly are often easy targets for fraud scams, and many jurisdictions are paying more attention to such scams. The *New York Times* ran this headline on a lead story: "Bilking the Elderly, With a Corporate Assist." Pictured was 92-year-old Richard Guthrie, who was duped into giving out his personal identifiers to telephone callers, who then sold the information to other criminals. Guthrie, like many elderly people, according to an attorney for the Federal Trade Commission, was afraid to ask for help for fear his children would take over his accounts. Also, some elderly do not understand what is happening when they attempt to withdraw money and there are insufficient funds. According to the article, names and personal information are sold for as little at 6.5 cents a name. In this case, the victim was quoted as saying, "I loved getting these calls. . . . Since my wife passed away, I don't have many people to talk with. I didn't even know they were stealing from me until everything was gone."[20]

According to a study by MetLife Mature Market Institute, about 50 percent of the fraud loss suffered by elderly persons is due to scams by strangers; the rest is at the hands of family members or businesses.[21]

Florida's legislature responded to fraud against the elderly. Among other legislative provisions is the following section from the state's White Collar Crime Victim Protection Act:

> Due to the frequency with which victims, particularly elderly victims, are deceived and cheated by criminals who commit nonviolent frauds and swindles, frequently through the use of the Internet and other electronic technology and frequently causing the loss of substantial amounts of property, it is the intent of the Legislature to enhance the sanctions imposed for nonviolent frauds and swindles, protect the public's property, and assist in prosecuting white collar criminals.[22]

Many types of fraud exist; this discussion focuses on mortgage fraud, mail and wire fraud, and securities fraud.

Mortgage Fraud

With the housing market in a downward tailspin in recent years, it is not surprising that the U.S. Department of Justice (DOJ) and the FBI are investigating mortgage fraud. According to U.S. Attorney General Eric Holder, "Mortgage fraud ruins lives, destroys families and devastates whole communities, so attacking the problem from every possible direction is vital."[23]

The FBI defines *mortgage fraud* as follows:

> Mortgage fraud is a material misstatement, misrepresentation, or omission relied on by an underwriter or lender to fund, purchase, or insure a loan. This type of fraud is usually defined as loan origination fraud. Mortgage fraud also includes schemes targeting consumers, such as foreclosure rescue, short sale, and loan modification.[24]

The FBI states that the amount of money lost through mortgage fraud is unknown, but various estimates run over $10 billion in loan originations in 2010.[25]

It is not uncommon for one or more defendants in a mortgage fraud scheme to be convicted of multiple charges, including various crimes, and to serve long terms. For example, in 30 June 2011, Lee Bentley Farkas was sentenced to 30 years in federal prison. Farkas, the former chair and owner of Taylor, Bean & Whitaker (TBW), was also required to forfeit $38.5 million. He was convicted of 14 counts of securities fraud, bank fraud, wire fraud, and conspiracy to commit all of those crimes in a $2.9 billion fraud scheme that resulted in the failure of TBW, once one of the "largest privately held mortgage lending companies in the United States," and Colonial Bank, "one of the 25 largest banks in the United States." Farkas and others involved in this fraud scheme sold fake mortgage assets and double- and triple-sold mortgage loans. According to the FBI, the "scheme affected those at the heart of the financial crisis, including major financial institutions, government agencies, taxpayers, and employees and investors."[26]

Mail and Wire Fraud

Historically, most frauds were prosecuted in state courts by state prosecutors, but federal statutes are necessary to cover fraud across state lines. The mail fraud statute was passed in 1872 and is the oldest of the federal statutes that cover crimes traditionally considered to be state problems. It provides a $1,000 fine or imprisonment for not more than five years, or both, for anyone convicted of using the post office or any other authorized depository for mail matter for the purpose of defrauding people of their money or other property rights. The penalty may increase to a $1 million fine or 30 years in prison, or both, if the violation involves a financial institution.[27]

The development and use of modern technological devices that transport information across state lines have created an even greater need for federal laws. The wire fraud statute, enacted in 1952, provides the same penalties as the mail fraud statute for persons convicted of using "wire, radio, or television communications in interstate or foreign commerce" for the purpose of fraud.[28]

Mail and wire fraud statutes constitute an important tool in the government's efforts to combat white-collar crime, for the statutes are broad and flexible. In

1984, Congress added a section on *bank fraud* to the federal statute. It provides for sanctions against writing checks with insufficient funds as well as crimes associated with the failure of banks and other financial institutions.[29]

A successful mail or wire fraud case requires that the government prove three elements:

1. A scheme or artifice formed with the intent to defraud
2. Using or causing the mails or wire to be used
3. In furtherance of the scheme

The prosecution is not required to show that the scheme was successful or even that victims suffered losses; it has to show only that the defendant had the specific intent to defraud.[30]

To satisfy the *use* requirement, the second element, the defendant need not have been directly involved in using the mail or wire; nor must the victim have received the information through either means. But there must be evidence that either the mail or the wire actually was used and that its use was a reasonably foreseeable result of the defendant's actions.

The final element does not require that the mail or wire be essential to the scheme but only that either or both are useful to the defendant or closely related to the scheme.[31]

Health Care Fraud

One of the high-priority areas for federal prosecutors in recent years has been health care fraud, which includes defrauding Medicare, Medicaid, and the Department of Veterans Affairs or other government and health care insurers as well as individuals. The alleged fraud may be related to double billing, the quality of care provided, billing for unnecessary care, or billing for services that were not provided. Cases are typically brought against health care professionals, hospitals, pharmacies, medical supply companies, nursing homes, and persons associated with any of these. The cases may involve large sums of money and many victims, with the estimated cost of health care fraud nationally to be around $100 billion annually.[32]

Health care fraud may occur at all levels, but it is easier to commit at the federal level because of the size of the programs and the amount of time and effort required for management to respond. Making price adjustments, for example, can take months of paperwork in the federal system.

Concern with fraud in the area of health care led Congress in 1996 to enact a bill that created a new crime of *health care fraud,* which carries a maximum penalty of 10 years in prison for knowingly defrauding any federal health care benefit program. If a person is injured as a result of the violation, the perpetrator may be sentenced to life in prison. A final provision is that a person who commits theft or embezzlement in connection with health care may be incarcerated for up to 10 years in prison.[33]

Recent examples of health care fraud cases are featured in Focus 7.2.

Focus 7.2

Health Care Fraud: Recent Convictions

Health care fraud arrests, indictments, and convictions dominate FBI news releases; here are only a few of the more recent ones.

In December 2011, the U.S. Department of Justice (DOJ) announced that three operators of a Miami health care agency entered guilty pleas involving $60 million in a Medicare fraud scheme. In making this announcement, the DOJ stated that since March 2007, when it began its work, the Medicare Fraud Strike Force had charged over 1,140 defendants with combined false Medicare billings of $2.9 billion.[1]

In May 2011, two corporations based in Miami, Florida, entered guilty pleas to submitting more that $200 million in fraudulent Medicare claims. American Therapeutic Corporation (ATC) and Medlink Professional Management Group Inc. "were charged with conspiracy to defraud the United States and to pay and receive illegal health care kickbacks." According to an FBI press release,

> The fraud scheme was staggering in scope, and those who concocted the scheme exhibited a complete disregard for the elderly, infirm, and disabled victims who were used to commit it.…
>
> The defendants altered patient files, diagnoses, and medication types and levels to make it appear that patients being treated qualified for PHP treatments [a type of intensive treatment for severe mental illness]….This was done so that the defendants could fraudulently bill Medicare for more than $200 million in medically unnecessary services.[2]

For three years the FBI and other agencies collected millions of documents, along with electronic evidence, and in September 2010, Allergan, a pharmaceutical company, agreed to pay $600 million in criminal and civil penalties "for aggressively promoting its flagship drug Botox for uses not approved by the Food and Drug Administration (FDA), for paying kickbacks to doctors, and for other violations of the False Claims Act." This Act prohibits knowingly submitting false claims to obtain money from the federal government.[3]

In September 2010, in Houston, Texas, three individuals entered guilty pleas to conspiracy to commit health care fraud. Melvin Jean Barnes, Johnnie Lee Andrews, and Monica Renee Perry admitted that they received kickbacks for submitting false claims to a durable medical equipment company for medically unnecessary devices, in particular, power wheelchairs, wheelchair accessories, and motorized scooters. That company, Luant & Odera Inc., submitted approximately $3 million in false Medicare claims.[4]

In September 2010, the El Centro Medical Center in Imperial County, California, agreed to pay the U.S. government $2.2 million to settle Medicare fraud allegations. Federal prosecutors had alleged that the Center fraudulently inflated its charges to Medicare patients.[5]

[1]U.S. Department of Justice, Office of Public Affairs, press release, "Three Operators of Miami Home Health Company Plead Guilty in $60 Million Health Care Fraud Scheme" (20 December 2011), http://www.justice.gov (accessed 20 December 2011).

[2]Federal Bureau of Investigation Miami, press release, "Two Miami-Area Corporations Plead Guilty to More than $200 Million Medicare Fraud," (3 May 2011), http://miami.fbi. gov/dojpressrel/pressrel11/mm050311.htm (accessed 6 May 2011).

[3]Federal Bureau of Investigation, "Headline Archives: Health Care Fraud, $600 Million Settlement in Botox Case," Press release (1 September 2010), http://www.fbi.gov/page2/september10/ botox_090110.html (accessed 2 September 2010). The False Claims Act is codified at USCS, Chapter 31, Section 3729 *et seq.* (2012).

[4]U.S. Department of Justice, Office of Public Affairs, "Three Individuals Plead Guilty for Their Roles in a Houston Medicare Fraud Scheme Involving Claims of Hurricane Damage to Power Wheelchairs," Press release (23 September 2010), http://www.justice.gov/opa/pr/2010/ September/10-crm-1073.html (accessed 24 September 2010).

[5]U.S. Department of Justice, Office of Public Affairs, "Southern California Medical Center to Pay U.S. $2.2 Million to Resolve Fraud Allegations" (20 September 2010), http://www.justice.gov/ opa/pr/2010/September/10-civ-1054.html (accessed 21 September 2010).

States may also have health care fraud statutes. Some are in state criminal codes, while others are in state public welfare codes.

Securities Fraud

The exchange of securities is a highly regulated business in the United States. **Securities** include stocks, bonds, notes, and other documents that are representative of a share in a company or a debt of the company. Of the several federal statutes covering the exchange of securities, two are used most frequently for prosecution of securities violations.

The Securities Act of 1933 requires the registration of securities that are to be sold to the public. Complete information must be given concerning the stock offering and the issuer. The Securities and Exchange Act of 1934 regulates the operation of over-the-counter trading and the buying and selling of stock. It specifies the information that must be published concerning stocks listed on the national securities exchanges. These statutes and others are administered by the Securities and Exchange Commission (SEC).[34]

The securities statutes prohibit the following:

- The use of any device, scheme, or artifice to defraud
- The making of an untrue statement of facts material to the buying and selling of securities
- The omission of information that would result in a misleading statement
- Acts that operate to defraud or deceive the stock purchaser

Intent is a material element of the crimes under these statutes. In addition, the defendant must use interstate commerce through the mail or other methods, and closely related crimes—such as mail and wire fraud, conspiracy, aiding and abetting, and the making of false statements—may also be prosecuted under these acts. Finally, the object of the transaction in question must be a security as defined by the statutes.

Administrative, civil, and criminal actions and remedies are provided by the securities acts. Initial investigations into possible violations of the statutes (or the rules promulgated by the SEC in accordance with the administrative powers delegated to that agency by Congress) are conducted by the SEC. The U.S. DOJ has sole jurisdiction to prosecute criminal violations under these statutes.

In response to the economic recession of recent years, Congress passed the Dodd-Frank Wall Street Reform and Consumer Protection Act (the Dodd-Frank Act, named for the two major proponents of the bill). President Obama signed the Act in July 2010. This legislation constitutes the greatest overhaul in the regulation of U.S. financial institutions since the Great Depression. It requires the SEC to make numerous changes in its oversight of the regulation of financial institutions. The stated purpose of the Act is:

> To promote the financial stability of the United States by improving accountability and transparency in the financial system, to end "too big to fail," to protect the American taxpayer by ending bailouts, to protect consumers from abusive financial services practices, and for other purposes.[35]

The penalties for many corporate crimes, such as securities fraud, were increased by the Sarbanes-Oxley Act (SOX) of 2002. This statute contains new laws concerning **obstruction of justice** (interference with the orderly processes of courts) by destroying documents, increases penalties for fraud and conspiracy, and requires the chief officers of corporations to certify that the company's financial statements comply with the requirements of the Securities and Exchange Act of 1934 and fairly represent the company's actual financial condition. Corporate executives who knowingly falsify such certification may be fined up to $5 million and may be imprisoned for up to 20 years. Penalties for mail and wire fraud are increased significantly. SOX is the first and only federal statute to provide for **whistle-blower claims** (claims that expose a person, group, or business for engaging in illegal acts, such as fraud), giving protection to an employee who is fired for reporting a company's financial improprieties. The statute requires the chief executive officer, the chief financial officer, and the auditors to certify the accuracy of the company's financial reports.

Under most circumstances, companies are not permitted to extend credit or loans to the company's executive officer or to any director. The company's general counsel is also under reporting requirements if he or she suspects any wrongdoing. A conviction for violating any of these requirements can result in a heavy fine, or even a prison sentence. Finally, the SOX directed the U.S. Sentencing Commission (discussed in Chapter 11) to revise the federal sentencing guidelines in accordance with the act and to reconsider the guidelines for all white-collar crimes. In January 2003, the U.S. Sentencing Commission approved an emergency plan that lengthens prison sentences for white-collar crimes. By April 2003, the commission was to have a permanent recommendation concerning the sentences to submit to Congress. That was done, and penalties were increased in 2003.[36]

In 2010, in *Free Enterprise Fund v. Public Company Accounting Oversight Board,* the U.S. Supreme Court unanimously upheld the constitutionality of the

SOX but split 5–4 on the issue of how the members of the oversight board, who are appointed by the SEC, can be removed.[37]

False Pretense

Similar to fraud is the crime of **false pretense**, which refers to obtaining title to property by falsely representing facts to the owner with the intent to defraud. The crime was necessary to cover a loophole in common law larceny-theft. For example, under common law a person who obtained title to property by false pretense but did not get possession of that property had not met the elements of larceny-theft and thus had not committed a crime. The English Parliament created the crime of false pretense to cover this act, and most U.S. jurisdictions followed that English precedent, although the crime may be called by other names, such as *theft by deception* or *deceptive practices.*

The general elements of false pretense are as follows:

1. A false representation of a past or present fact
2. That causes the victim
3. To pass the title of the property
4. To the wrongdoer
5. Who
   (a) knows the representation to be false and
   (b) thereby intends to defraud the victim.

The requirement that the statement be false means that the representation must be false at the same time the property is obtained; if the representation is false when made but later becomes true, it does not meet the requirement. The false representation must be made about a material fact (one that is essential to the case). It may be communicated orally or in writing.

Traditionally, the false representation had to relate to a past or present but not to a future fact; thus, promises did not count. The reason for not including false promises in the crime of false pretense was the concern that the crime would be used against someone who meant to keep a promise but, because of changes in circumstances, could not live up to the bargain. An example would be a person who could not pay a bill and thus became a debtor, but who, at the time the financial transaction was made, intended to pay that bill in the future. The current trend is to consider false promises or other false statements of future intentions to meet the requirement for false representations of a fact.

The second, third, and fourth elements of false pretense are that the false representation causes the victim to pass to the wrongdoer the title to the property— that is, the victim's act is done in reliance on the actor's misrepresentation. Title must be passed to the wrongdoer; simple possession is not sufficient in this case, although it would be sufficient for the crime of larceny by trick. As noted previously, under common law, the term *property* included only tangible personal property and money. The modern trend is to include all items that may be the subject of larceny-theft.

The final element of false pretense is the mental state of the actor. Generally, false pretense statutes require that the misrepresentation must be made knowingly or with the intent to defraud and that this mental element must occur at the same time as the transfer of title, even if it did not occur at the time the misrepresentation was made.

Forgery

Another crime that may be included within a general theft statute or defined separately is **forgery**, which refers to falsely making or altering, with the intent to defraud, a negotiable and legally enforceable instrument, such as a check. Forgery is similar to false pretense in that both require an intent to defraud. They are dissimilar because forgery is complete even when the potential victim is not defrauded of money or property. Thus, one may forge a document but not have the opportunity to pass it on to another. In most cases, forgery is associated with money or securities.

Some statutes provide that writing a false or bogus check is a felony. Among these statutes, some require that the check must be more than a specified amount and others require that more than one check must be involved.

Stolen Property: Buying, Receiving, Possessing

Some thieves, particularly professional thieves, do not intend to use the property they steal. They depend on a **fence**, a person who receives stolen property from a thief and in turn disposes of it in a profitable manner. Other thieves, particularly those who steal for the purpose of obtaining money to support a habit, such as drugs, may sell their stolen items to dealers.

In early common law, the person who received stolen property from the thief could not be convicted of a crime, but the importance of controlling the fence led to statutes making the receipt of stolen property a crime. Generally these statutes are interpreted to mean that, in addition to knowing the property is stolen, the actor must receive the property with the intent to deprive the owner of it.

The crime of receiving stolen property has four elements:

1. Receiving
2. Stolen property
3. Knowing it to be stolen
4. With the intent to deprive the owner of the property.

To sustain a conviction for this crime, the prosecution must prove (1) each of these elements and (2) that the knowledge, conduct, and criminal intent concurred in time. The element of receiving may be used or interpreted broadly.

Some jurisdictions specify types of receivers, such as junk dealers, and provide greater penalties for them than for people who are not usually in the business of receiving stolen property. Some provide greater penalties for larger amounts (grand receiving) as compared to smaller amounts (petit receiving), analogous to penalties for grand and petit theft.

Some states divide criminal possession of stolen property into degrees. Finally, the receipt and possession of stolen property may be covered by a comprehensive theft statute.

Malicious Mischief

The malicious destruction or infliction of damage to the property of another constitutes **malicious mischief** or *criminal mischief.* Malicious mischief is similar to larceny-theft in that it involves a crime against the property of another person but dissimilar in that it does not require taking the property away or intending to deprive the owner of possession. Unlike larceny, malicious mischief may target real property. Another difference is that, in some jurisdictions, malicious mischief requires destruction of the property. Malicious mischief is similar to arson, too; both involve damage to property. Unlike arson, however, malicious mischief does not require burning.

In modern codes, malicious mischief may be defined broadly. One approach is to consolidate this common law crime with other statutes related to the destruction of property. This consolidated crime may include damaging or destroying tangible property; causing substantial loss or inconvenience to the owner of the property; and marking, drawing on, or otherwise defacing the property. These and other crimes may be graded by degrees or in terms of the monetary loss caused by the acts in question. The crime may be further classified in terms of whether it was committed intentionally, knowingly, or recklessly. In addition, states may have separate statutes covering graffiti, which includes painting with aerosol paint or using other methods of defacing property without the consent of the owner.

Finally, some states distinguish *criminal mischief* from the crime of *aggravated criminal mischief,* with the latter designated by the type or value of the property damaged.

Trespass

Some jurisdictions provide for punishment of people who trespass but whose actions are not sufficient to sustain convictions for malicious mischief or burglary. This crime involves entering or remaining unlawfully in or on the premises of another (this could include land, houses, offices, garages, boats, or other vehicles), knowing that one is not licensed or privileged to do so, under certain circumstances that may be specified by statute. It does not require the destruction of property (as in malicious mischief) or the intent to commit a crime, which is an element of burglary.

Extortion or Blackmail

Common law robbery, which carried the death penalty, was restricted to threats of *immediate* harm. This left threats of future actions uncovered. Under common law and in most of the early statutes, **extortion** or **blackmail** was limited to the unlawful taking of money by public officials who did so within the scope of their employment. Congress and many states have extended this definition to include acts by private individuals. Today, *extortion* may be defined as obtaining property from another by wrongful use of actual or threatened force, fear, or violence, or the corrupt taking of a fee by a public officer, under color of his or her office, when that fee is not due. *Blackmail* is similar and is usually included in extortion statutes, but often this crime is associated with the unlawful demand of money or something else of value by threats to expose some embarrassing or disgraceful allegation or fact about the victim, to accuse that person of a crime, to do bodily harm to him or her, or to damage property.

Extortion statutes may be part of general theft statutes.

COMPUTER CRIME

Computers play an increasingly important role in our business lives, but when the computer is not functioning, many transactions stop, creating frustrating waiting periods and, in some cases, crippling websites, electronic communications, and daily business.

Computers have also made our daily lives more convenient. Money may be obtained from machines as well as from bank tellers, and products may be ordered online. Communications with friends and business associates are easier through electronic mail, text messaging, and cell phones. But with these and other conveniences have come problems. Privacy is more likely to be invaded now that extensive personal data are kept in computer files. Although computers have been used to process valuable data leading to the apprehension of criminals, they also have created serious problems and a new field of crime for individuals and businesses to combat.

Computer crime refers to crime committed by the use of a computer. Computer criminals have developed programs that access, scramble, or erase computer files and that aid in theft, as well as the invasion of privacy and stealing of a person's identity. **Cybercrime** refers to the use of the computer to commit a crime through the Internet.

Types of Computer Crime

In addition to viruses and other forms of hacking, *Internet fraud* is committed by use of a computer. Much of that fraud involves *identity theft,* in which the hacker steals the personal identity (usually by accessing a person's accounts through his or her social security number). Identity theft is discussed in more detail later in this chapter.

In addition, computers are used to distribute sexually explicit material, including child pornography (which is illegal), but detection and successful prosecution of these distributions are difficult because of the widespread use of computer bulletin boards and the lack of legislation dealing explicitly with computer pornography.

However, efforts have been made to control the unwanted receipt of sexually explicit material. Congress enacted the **CAN-SPAM Act**, a federal antispam law that became effective in January 2004. The act directs the Federal Trade Commission (FTC) to adopt a rule requiring a mark or notice on spam that contains sexually explicit material. Effective 19 May 2004, all such spam must include the warning "SEXUALLY-EXPLICIT" in the subject line. Violation of this requirement may result in civil lawsuits as well as criminal prosecutions that could lead to a prison sentence and fines as high as $250,000 for individuals and $500,000 for organizations.[38]

Computer crimes may involve the same kinds of crimes discussed elsewhere in this chapter, as well as those discussed in other chapters, except that a computer is used in the perpetration of the crime. According to a white-collar-crime expert, "Computer crime may also take the form of threats of force directed against the computer itself. These crimes are usually 'sabotage' or 'ransom' cases. Computer crime cases have one commonality: the computer is either the tool or the target of the felon."[39]

Computers and cell phones and other handheld devices are also used for sending sexually explicit messages and texting at inappropriate times (such as when driving) or to inappropriate persons (such as minors). Focus 7.3 discusses some of these new areas of activity considered to be violations, infractions, or crimes.

Focus 7.3

Texting and Sexting as Violations and Crimes

In 2010, 19-year-old Daniel Schatz was texting while driving and caused an accident that resulted in two deaths, including his own. The teen at the other end of the text messages said he thought his friend was at work and did not know he was driving. The accident involved Schatz' pickup, a semi cab, and two school buses, which were transporting high school band students. The National Transportation Safety Board (NTSB) and the state highway patrol in Missouri, where the accident occurred, determined that Schatz caused the accident. The NTSB was using that fatal pileup of vehicles to support the federal recommendation that all cell phones, even hands-free ones, should be banned while driving.[1] Some jurisdictions have already enacted ordinances or statutes banning cell phoning while driving, but most do not.

Texting while driving has been cited in numerous accidents in recent years, and some jurisdictions have made the practice illegal as a violation or as a crime. Consider, for example, the following section from the California Vehicle Code, "Use of electronic wireless communications device to write, send, or read text-based communication; Infraction":

(a) A person shall not drive a motor vehicle while using an electronic wireless communications device to write, send, or read a text-based communication.

(b) As used in this section "write, send, or read a text-based communication" means using an electronic wireless communications device to manually communicate with any person using a text-based communication, including, but not limited to, communications referred to as a text message, instant message, or electronic mail....[Section (c) excludes cell phoning]

(d) A violation of this section is an infraction punishable by a base fine of twenty dollars ($20) for a first offense and fifty dollars ($50) for each subsequent offense.[2]

One particular use of cell phones and other electronic devices that is a focus of ordinances and statutes is called sexting. This act involves sending lewd pictures (often of oneself) or requesting such from others. Sexting is

(Continued)

Focus 7.3 (*Continued*)

prosecuted under other statutes when it involves the use of child pornography or targeting persons who are not legally capable of consenting. To illustrate, a Pennsylvania teacher entered a guilty plea to sexting students after
she was apprehended and charged for sending inappropriate text messages
to students. Jennifer Lynn Sowa Smith, age 30, pleaded guilty to corruption of
minors, solicitation of sex acts, solicitation of child pornography, endangering
the welfare of children, and unlawful contact with a minor. Smith used her cell
phone to send students pictures of herself in a black bra, one of her breasts,
and another of her genitalia. She also sent sexual text messages to several of
her students. She was sentenced to five years' probation and must register as
a sex offender and avoid any contact with persons under the age of 18. She
lost her teaching license.[3]

[1]"Texting Is No Debate for Teens in '10 Crash," *Dallas Morning News* (18 December 2011), p. 10.
[2]Cal Veh Code, Section 23123.5 (2012).
[3]"Former Steel Valley Teacher Pleads Guilty to Sexting Students," *Pittsburgh Post-Gazette* (4
January 2012), p. 8B.

Computers may also be instrumental in the commission of violent crimes in
that the computer is used to gain access to persons who are then victimized by
violence, even death.

Controlling Computer Crime

One way to control computer crimes is to prevent them by educating computer
users, all of whom should be careful about making financial transactions and
meeting personally with strangers encountered over the Internet. In particular,
children and teens should be taught that agreeing to meet in person with strangers
with whom they have had only Internet contact may be dangerous, even fatal.

Another way of controlling computer crimes is through legislation. Such
legislation is relatively recent and reflects the varying definitions of this type of
crime. In 1978, Florida and Arizona became the first states to enact computer crime
statutes, and most states followed suit. Despite several attempts, Congress did not
pass a computer crime statute until 1984. Prior to that time, federal computer
crimes were prosecuted under about 40 federal statutes, such as those covering
wire and mail fraud, theft and embezzlement, and the transportation of stolen
property. Because these statutes were written for other purposes, many problems
arose when they were applied to computer crimes. The federal Computer Crime
Control Act is part of the general revision of the federal criminal code, known as
the Comprehensive Crime Control Act of 1984.[40]

In 2002, the U.S. Congress enacted legislation (as part of the Homeland Security
Act, discussed in Chapter 9) to increase the penalties for computer crimes. The
Cyber Security Enhancement Act of 2002 also contains provisions for research on

cybersecurity. The U.S. Sentencing Commission was directed to study the penalties for computer crimes and to consider a variety of sentencing factors, such as the perpetrator's purpose in committing the crime, whether a government computer was involved in the crime, and whether the offense "was intended to or had the effect of significantly interfering with or disrupting a critical infrastructure." The commission was required to report its recommendations concerning any proposed revision of federal sentencing guidelines to Congress by 1 May 2003.[41] That was done, and the USA Patriot Act (also discussed in Chapter 9), among other provisions, amended existing laws concerning computers, increased penalties, and redefined the word *terrorism* to include crimes such as computer hacking and cyberterrorism.[42]

Legislation to control computer crimes has also occurred at the state level. In 1995, Connecticut became one of the first states to criminalize harassment or stalking by means of a computer. Other jurisdictions followed, but it is possible that the enactment of statutes designed to prevent computer crimes will not be as effective as some would like to think. First, many establishments might not want the public to know that their employees committed crimes with the company's computers and thus may not press charges.

Second, in addition to a lack of reporting or willingness to prosecute and the difficulties of apprehension and prosecution, law enforcement officials may not have the technical expertise to solve computer crimes, and most cases that go to trial are highly technical, costly, and extremely time-consuming.

Third, federal and state computer crime statutes, like all statutes, are subject to interpretation, and we can expect considerable litigation in this area.

Legislation, however, is not always a solution to a crime, and that is particularly the case in computer crimes. As quickly as officials learn how to protect computers and detect those who violate them, offenders learn new ways to commit computer crimes. One technique developed by hackers, spoofing, is used to trick a computer into thinking that it is being accessed by a friendly computer. According to a government-funded group called the Computer Emergency Response Team, spoofing can lead to high-level computer hijacking. By spoofing, a cyberthief can elude firewalls (electronic gates that keep out all but friendly users); enter computers; and alter, copy, or delete data.[43]

One final issue with regard to computers is that they have made it possible for persons to invade the privacy of individuals in a way not contemplated prior to their use. Computer hackers may commit various crimes against individuals and companies, one of which is to steal identities. Identity theft may also be committed in other ways, such as taking identification numbers from credit card and other documents. Identity theft is growing and deserves special attention.

IDENTITY THEFT

Fraud on the Internet is a serious and growing problem. One form that it takes is **identity theft**. This crime involves the stealing of a person's Social Security number or another personal identifier, such as a bank account number, and using that information to steal from the person.

Characteristics of Identity Theft

Some of the methods of committing identity theft are as follows:

- Opening a new credit card account in the victim's name
- Forging checks from the victim's bank accounts
- Opening a bank account in the victim's name and writing checks
- Using the victim's birth date or Social Security number for personal gain

In November 2011, the Bureau of Justice Statistics (BJS) reported the following highlights about its 2010 analysis of identity theft:

- 7.0% of households in the United States, or about 8.6 million households, had at least one member age 12 or older who experienced one or more types of identity theft victimization.
- Among households in which at least one member experienced one or more types of identity theft, 64.1% experienced the misuse or attempted misuse of an existing credit card account in 2010.
- From 2005 to 2010, the percentage of all households with one or more type of identity theft that suffered no direct financial loss increased from 18.5% to 23.7%.[44]

The increase in financial losses due to identity theft during the reported period was primarily due to the misuse of existing credit cards. Other identity theft losses are due to stolen identities such as financial loans. On 21 December 2011, the U.S. Department of Justice (DOJ) issued a press release on the 94-month sentencing of Janika Fernae Bates of Alabama, who was convicted of identity theft, wire fraud, aggravated identity theft, and conspiracy to make false claims for tax refunds. Bates obtained the Social Security and loan numbers of individuals who had borrowed money for student loans. She got the information from her employer and, with a co-conspirator, used the account numbers to steal money from a bank and the government. Bates was also ordered to pay restitution: $30,211 to the Internal Revenue Service and $246,664 to HSBC Taxpayer Financial Services.[45]

State and Federal Statutes

Most states have identity theft statutes, although they vary significantly in their coverage. The federal system also has an identity theft statute, which is entitled *Fraud and Related Activity in Connection with Identification Documents and Information.* This statute is lengthy; under some circumstances, violation of the statute carries a penalty of a fine and imprisonment for not more than 15 years.[46]

The final section of this chapter focuses on a crime that is a property crime involving car theft, but it is also a violent crime, as it involves confronting the operator of that car. In many cases, it may result in serious injuries or death.

CARJACKING

The crime is an old one, but it has a new name. **Carjacking** refers to the theft of a motor vehicle by use of force or the threat of force, especially force involving a deadly weapon. The stealing or attempted stealing of a motor vehicle is classified by the FBI as a property crime, as the discussion earlier in this chapter noted. However, as the discussion of robbery in Chapter 6 emphasized, stealing from a person with the use of a threat of force or the actual use of force, is a violent crime. Carjacking has some of the aspects of larceny-theft and some of robbery. The FBI does not solicit data on carjacking, and in some jurisdictions it is reported as motor vehicle theft. The escalation of carjackings in recent years, along with their frequent brutality, has led many states and the federal government to enact special statutes to cover carjacking.

The federal system has enacted a carjacking statute, which applies to the theft of a motor vehicle "that has been transported, shipped or received in interstate or foreign commerce" and is taken "from the person or presence of another by force and violence or by intimidation." Attempts are included within this crime.[47]

An example of a state carjacking statute is that of New Jersey, which refers to *carjacking* as "a specific type of robbery" that involves "the unlawful taking of a motor vehicle in the course of which the perpetrator":

(1) inflicts bodily injury or uses force upon an occupant or person in possession or control of a motor vehicle;
(2) threatens an occupant or person in control with, or purposely or knowingly puts an occupant or person in control of the motor vehicle in fear of, immediate bodily injury;
(3) commits or threatens immediately to commit any crime of the first or second degree; or
(4) operates or causes said vehicle to be operated with the person who was in possession or control or was an occupant of the motor vehicle at the time of the taking remaining in the vehicle.[48]

SUMMARY

Although the fear of being victimized by violent crimes is greater than that associated with property crimes, property crimes claim the largest number of victims. It is not easy to separate the two kinds of crimes, for many property crimes—such as robbery, extortion, burglary, and arson—may involve personal violence or even death. Nevertheless, for purposes of analysis, crimes are divided into categories. This chapter discussed those crimes generally considered to be crimes against property or crimes that involve both violence against a person and damage to property.

Property rights were extremely important in common law. The emergence and development of laws to protect property have been closely related to those rights. Some of the restrictions on the elements or requirements for property crimes do not make much sense in modern times. Some of those have changed; others remain. Thus it is important to understand the common law of property crimes.

One of the most complicated and fascinating crimes, larceny-theft, illustrates the importance of common law. Although all the common law elements of this crime are no longer required, some remain. Others are important in interpreting modern statutes, many of which refer to the crime as *theft*. Likewise, the common law division of larceny-theft into grand and petit larceny is retained in some jurisdictions.

Common law larceny-theft required a trespassory taking and a carrying away of the personal property of another with the intent to steal. The requirement of trespassory taking prevented the inclusion of some crimes that evolved over the years. To cover these "new" crimes, judges invented fictions, such as constructive possession, to refer to the property a master had delivered to his servant to be used for the benefit of the master. If that servant misappropriated the property, his act could be included within common law larceny-theft.

The common law requirement of asportation, or taking away, generally has been replaced today with a requirement that the offender exercise unlawful control over property even if it is not carried away, provided he or she does so with the intent and purpose of depriving the owner of that property. Under common law, the property stolen had to be the personal property of another, meaning tangible personal property. Modern statutes have extended larceny-theft to some real property, services, admissions to exhibitions, and many other areas.

The common law interpretation of *intent to steal* as requiring an intent to permanently deprive the owner of his property has been retained in some jurisdictions but abolished in others to permit inclusion of crimes such as joyriding. Another way of handling this element has been to create separate offenses for acts such as joyriding.

Burglary is another property offense in which common law definitions and interpretations are important to an understanding of modern statutes. Today the common law requirement of breaking and entering may be met in some statutes by the act of remaining on the property illegally. The breaking requirement may also be met by entering illegally. The requirement that the structure be the dwelling of another has been extended to include all dwellings as well as other buildings. The common law required nighttime for burglary; most modern statutes omit that requirement. Today the common law requirement of an intent to commit a felony may be extended to include an intent to commit a misdemeanor. Even when modern statutes have abandoned or changed some of the common law elements of burglary, the influence of these older crimes is seen in the differentiation of the crime by degrees. Although it may not be required that the burglar enter a home for the crime to be complete, entering a home may result in a higher degree of burglary and a harsher sentence.

Although larceny-theft includes the theft of parts from motor vehicles, the theft of motor vehicles themselves constitutes a separate category of serious property crimes in the FBI's *Uniform Crime Reports*. The chapter included a brief discussion of motor vehicle theft. The final serious property crime, arson, was discussed in terms of its common law background as well as modern statutory approaches.

The second major section of the chapter covered less serious property offenses. These crimes are labeled *less serious* by the FBI, but they may create a significant problem for their immediate victims as well as for society in general. For example, embezzlement and fraud-related crimes may involve millions of dollars, compared to far smaller losses from larceny-theft. A number of lesser property crimes were discussed individually. Although the modern trend is toward consolidating theft-type offenses into fewer categories, some jurisdictions retain the common law larceny-theft category, which excluded such offenses as larceny by trick, fraud, false pretense, forgery, and embezzlement. These jurisdictions have separate statutes for such offenses. Other jurisdictions have abandoned the use of the term *larceny-theft* and refer only to *theft* crimes, which may be subdivided into many categories.

The chapter also discussed such property-related crimes as false pretense, forgery, crimes associated with stolen property, malicious mischief, trespass, and extortion or blackmail. The chapter contained sections on computer crime, identity theft, and carjacking, all relatively newly recognized crimes that are gaining more attention today and all of which have had a significant financial and personal impact. Attention was given to the emerging violations and criminal statutes associated with sexting and texting.

STUDY QUESTIONS

1. Generally, what is meant by common law *larceny-theft?*
2. Distinguish common law petit larceny from common law grand larceny.
3. Should the amount paid or the market value of a stolen item have any effect on the sentence of a convicted offender? Why or why not?
4. Under common law, what was meant by (a) *a trespassory taking,* (b) *asportation,* and (c) *with the intent to steal?*
5. What is the difference between actual possession and constructive possession?
6. What is meant by *larceny by trick?*
7. How does the larceny element of taking apply to shoplifting?
8. How have modern statutes changed the common law definition of *larceny-theft?*
9. How does burglary differ from larceny-theft? What are some of the ways in which modern burglary statutes differ from common law burglary?
10. What are the elements of arson? Why is the crime considered a serious one?
11. Why would embezzlement and fraud not fit in the common law category of larceny-theft?
12. Describe what is meant by *mail* and *wire fraud.* How should these crimes be handled?
13. What is the importance of health care fraud? Give some examples of this category of crimes. Do you have any suggestions for improving our attempts to combat it?
14. Describe the nature and impact of securities fraud.

15. Explain what is meant by the following element of false pretense: a false representation of a past or present fact. How do the common law and modern law differ regarding this element?
16. How does forgery differ from false pretense?
17. What is malicious mischief?
18. Define *criminal trespass*.
19. Why are the crimes of extortion and blackmail important?
20. What is computer crime? Discuss the legislative efforts to combat this crime. Can you suggest improvements in the way this crime is handled?
21. What is meant by *cybercrime*?
22. Discuss texting and sexting. Should these acts be covered by criminal law?
23. What is identity theft, and how can it be prevented?
24. What is carjacking, and why is it a recently defined crime?

FOR DEBATE

The chapter's discussion of property and related crimes covers numerous acts, some traditional, some relatively new. Of the latter, the crime of identity theft is often featured in the media. Consider the nature and impact of this crime by debating the following two resolutions.

RESOLVED: Identity theft crimes should be prosecuted as felonies and carry a sentence of 25 years to life.

RESOLVED: Personal privacy should be less important than solving computer crimes; thus greater power should be given to law enforcement officials regarding investigations of computer crimes, particularly those involving identity theft.

KEY TERMS

arson 150	fence 160
bailee 145	forgery 160
bailor 145	fraud 152
blackmail 161	grand larceny 145
burglary 147	identity theft 165
CAN-SPAM Act 162	larceny by trick 145
carjacking 166	larceny-theft 144
computer crime 162	malicious mischief 161
constructive possession 145	obstruction of justice 158
conversion 152	petit larceny 145
curtilage 148	property crimes 142
cybercrime 162	securities 157
embezzlement 152	trespass 148
extortion 161	whistle-blower claims 158
false pretense 159	

INTERNET ACTIVITY

1. Various government agencies have created websites concerning identity theft. Review the information provided by the government at these two sites (both accessed 12 May 2012): http://www.ftc.gov, and http://www.justice.gov/olp (search for identity theft).

   Based on their descriptions of identity theft, risky behaviors associated with this crime, and various methods of preventing the crime, how would you assess your risk of becoming a victim of identity theft or identity fraud? What can you find out about Internet and telemarketing fraud?

2. Check the Federal Bureau of Investigation's website for the latest official crime data, which, as of this writing, incorporates all of the 2010 data and preliminary data for 2011, http://www.fbi.gov/ (accessed 12 May 2012), and analyze the data for the four serious property crimes: larceny-theft, burglary, motor vehicle theft, and arson.

NOTES

1. Federal Bureau of Investigation, *Crime in the United States: Uniform Crime Reports, 2010* (September 2011), http://www.fbi.gov/ucr/ (accessed 12 May 2012); "Preliminary *Annual Uniform Crime Report*, January–December 2011," Table 3, http://www.fbi.gov (accessed 20 July 2012).
2. *Rex v. Wheatly,* 97 E.R. 746 (1761).
3. Rollin M. Perkins, *Criminal Law,* 3d ed. (Mineola, N.Y.: Foundation Press, 1982), p. 291.
4. *Hufstetler v. State,* 63 S0.2d 730 (Ala.Ct.App. 1953).
5. *The Carrier's Case,* Y.B. 13 Edw. IV, f.9, p.5 (Star Chamber 1473).
6. *People v. Brown,* 38 P.518, 519 (Cal. 1894).
7. Tex. Penal Code, Section 31.02 (2012).
8. Tex. Penal Code, Section 31.04 *et seq.* (2012).
9. *State v. Boon,* 35 N.C. 244, 246 (1852).
10. See *Walker v. State,* 63 Ala. 49 (1879).
11. Federal Bureau of Investigation, *Uniform Crime Reports,* 2010.
12. N.C. Gen. Stat., Section 14-58.2 (2012).
13. N.C. Gen. Stat., Section 14-65 (2012).
14. N.C. Gen. Stat., Section 14-62 (2012).
15. N.C. Gen. Stat., Section 14-144 (2012).
16. NY CLS Penal, Title 1, Section 150.05 *et seq.* (2012).
17. Va. Code Ann., Section 18.2-111 (2012).
18. *Avco Financial Services v. Foreman-Donovan,* 772 P.2d 862, 864 (Mont. 1989).
19. Reported on the webpage of The Elder Fraud Project, http://www.fraud.org/elderfraud/eldproj.htm (accessed 12 May 2012).
20. "Bilking the Elderly, With A Corporate Assist," *New York Times* (20 May 2007), p. 1.

21. Cited in "More Financial Scams Targeting Florida's Elderly," *Orlando Sentinel* (Florida) (24 November 2011), p. 29.

22. Fla. Stat., Section 775.0844(2) (2012).

23. Federal Bureau of Investigation, "Financial Fraud Enforcement Task Force Announces Results of Broadest Mortgage Fraud Sweep in History," Press release (17 June 2010), http://www.fbi.gov/pressrel/pressre110/financial-fraud_061710.htm (accessed 12 May 2012).

24. Federal Bureau of Investigation, *Mortgage Fraud Report 2010*, p. 1, http://www.fbi.gov (accessed 12 May 2012).

25. Ibid., p. 2.

26. Federal Bureau of Investigation, "Former Chairman of Taylor, Bean & Whitaker Sentenced to 30 Years in Prison and Ordered to Forfeit $38.5 Million," Press release, Washington Field Office (WFO) (30 June 2011), http://www.fbi.gov/washingtondc/press-releases/2011 (accessed 12 May 2012).

27. See USCS, Title 18, Section 1341 (2012).

28. See USCS, Title 18, Section 1343 (2012).

29. USCS, Title 18, Section 1344 (2012).

30. See USCS, Title 18, Section 1341 *et seq.* (2012).

31. See, for example, *Schmuck v. United States,* 489 U.S. 705 (1989).

32. CNNMoney.com, "Health Care: A 'Goldmine' for Fraudsters," (13 January 2010), p. 1, http://money.cnn.com/2010/01/13/economy/news/health_care_fraud/ (accessed 12 May 2012).

33. The health care fraud statute is Public Law 104-191, amending USCS, Section 1347 (2012). The theft or embezzlement provision amends USCS, Title 18, Section 669 (2012).

34. USCS, Title 15, Section 77a *et seq.* (2012).

35. The Dodd-Frank Wall Street Reform and Consumer Protection Act, Pub. L 111-203 (2011).

36. "Panel Clears Harsher Terms in Corporate Crime Cases," *New York Times* (9 January 2003), p. 1C. The Sarbanes-Oxley Act of 2002, Public Law 107-204, is codified, as amended, in various sections of the federal securities statutes in Titles 15 and 28 of the USCS (2012).

37. *Free Enterprise Fund v. Public Company Accounting Oversight Board,* 130 S.Ct. 3138, *on remand, remanded,* 2010 U.S. App. LEXIS 20200 (D.C. Cir. 2010).

38. "FTC Rule Requires Warning on Sexually Explicit Spam," *Computer & Internet Lawyer* 21, no. 8 (August 2004): 26. The CAN-SPAM Act of 2003, Public Law 108-187, is codified at USCS, Title 15, Section 7701 (2012).

39. August Bequai, *Computer Crime* (Lexington, Mass.: D. C. Heath, 1978), p. 4.

40. Federal Computer Crime Control Act, USCS, Title 18, Section 1030 (2012).

41. Section 225 (b)(2)(B)iii-vii of the Homeland Security Act of 2002, Public Law 107-296 (H.R. 50051) (25 November 2002).

42. The original USA Patriot Act was Public Law No. 107-56, 115 Stat. 272 (26 October 2001). The 2005 revision is referred to as the USA Patriot Improvement and Reauthorization Act of 2005, Public Law No. 109-177, 120 Stat.192

(9 March 2006). The USA Patriot Act, revised and codified, is located at USCS, Title 42, Section 5332 *et seq.* (2012).

43. "New Breed of Hacker Breaking and Entering on Internet," *Miami Herald* (24 January 1995), p. 1.

44. Lynn Langton, Bureau of Justice Statistics, "Identity Theft Reported by Households, 2005–2010," (30 November 2011), p. 1, http://www.bjs.gov/ (accessed 12 May 2012).

45. U.S. Department of Justice, "Alabama Woman Sentences to 94 Months in Prison for Stealing Identities of Student Loan Borrowers," (21 December 2011), http://www.justice.gov (accessed 12 May 2012).

46. USCS, Title 18, Section 1028 (2012),

47. The federal statute is codified at USCS, Title 18, Section 2219 (2012).

48. N.J. Stat., Section 2C:15-2(a) (2012).

Crimes Against Public Order and Public Decency

CHAPTER OUTLINE

Internet Activity
Notes

INTRODUCTION

This chapter covers crimes that are often omitted from criminal law casebooks written for law schools, as well as most criminal law texts written for the college and university audience. Perhaps the primary reason is that little attention is given to a discussion of misdemeanors, and many of the crimes in this chapter fall into that category. Even though by definition misdemeanors are less serious offenses than felonies, some are extremely important in terms of the frequency with which they occur and the societal values which they threaten. Likewise, although there are few prosecutions for some of the crimes covered in this chapter, statutes regulating the offenses may infringe on basic constitutional rights. Some of the covered offenses represent areas in which there is no agreement concerning whether the criminal law should be used to regulate the activity.

Although space does not permit an extensive discussion of constitutional law, it is important to keep the subject in mind while reading this chapter. Chapter 1 briefly discussed the relationship of the U.S. Constitution to criminal law and examined the void-for-vagueness and overbreadth doctrines. These doctrines require that statutes must be written so that reasonable people know what they mean, and they must be specific regarding the conduct prohibited. Statutes must not reach beyond conduct that may be prohibited constitutionally and include conduct that is protected by the Constitution. Frequently these issues arise in cases involving free speech. Although the First Amendment (see Appendix A) states that Congress shall pass no law inhibiting free speech, the interpretation has been that some speech and some actions that convey speech may be regulated, although the rules for doing so are strict.

Chapter 1 also introduced another constitutional doctrine important to this chapter, the right of privacy. That discussion provided a backdrop for this chapter's analysis of sexual acts that are still defined as criminal in some jurisdictions. This chapter discusses offenses that go to the heart of a free society, offenses that force us to consider under what circumstances individual rights should prevail over society's right to protect its members. For example, some people argue that the rights of free speech and expression require that the law should not limit access to pornography, while others take the position that the availability of pornography is harmful and leads to sex crimes. And the courts have held that free speech rights do not entitle individuals to engage children in pornography or, for that matter, to possess child pornography.

CRIMES AGAINST PUBLIC ORDER

Early common law was concerned with preserving peace and order to the extent that in England, most statutes concluded with the phrase "to preserve the peace of the King" or "against the peace of the King." In the United States, many early statutes contained the phrase "against the peace and dignity of the state." These phrases emphasized the need to preserve the peace and tranquillity of society. To do that, it was thought necessary to criminalize behaviors that might incite people to fight or retaliate in other ways.

All crimes might be considered offenses against the peace of the king or of the state, but common law and modern statutes use "offenses against the public peace and order" to refer to those offenses that are punishable primarily because they invade society's peace and tranquillity.[1]

Breach of the Peace

A willful act that disturbs the public tranquillity or order and for which there is no legal justification may constitute the crime of **breach of the peace**. Under common law, this crime covered numerous actions, but the main thrust of it was to include acts that were not otherwise defined as criminal but that tended to disturb peace and tranquillity.

Breach of the peace statutes are frequently held unconstitutional as they may infringe on the right to assemble or the right to free speech. The statutes also tend to be vague or too broad.

Fighting Words

Breach of the peace is similar to the crime of **fighting words**, which have a tendency to incite violence by the person to whom they are directed. Fighting words are not protected by the First Amendment. They are viewed as words designed to inflict harm rather than to communicate ideas. As such, fighting words are more analogous to a punch in the mouth than to the communication of ideas. They are designed to elicit immediate violent reaction (unprotected speech), not to arouse thought and debate (protected speech).

The key cases that the U.S. Supreme Court has decided on the fighting words doctrine are old, and the facts must be considered carefully. Essentially, the cases convey that the police may not suppress words because they (or others) do not agree with them; something more must be present. It is clear that even words that might offend the average person may be considered free speech rather than fighting words.

Some insight comes from *Cohen v. California*, decided by the U.S. Supreme Court in 1971. The Court reversed the conviction of Robert Cohen, who, in protest of the draft, walked into a Los Angeles courthouse wearing a jacket imprinted with the words "Fuck the Draft." The Court concluded that in the context in which the behavior occurred, there was not a substantial invasion of privacy "in an intolerable manner" (people in public must expect to see and hear some words and signs of which they may not approve). The words were not a "direct personal insult" aimed specifically at the hearer. Nor were the police, in arresting Cohen, as in a precedent case, attempting "to prevent a speaker from intentionally provoking a given group to a hostile reaction."[2]

Cohen was cited with approval by a federal circuit court of appeals in a 1997 case, which held that an individual who used the gesture known as "giving the finger" while shouting "fuck you" as he rode in a car past a group of antiabortion picketers was exercising his right to free speech and thus should not have been arrested. According to the court, these actions "were not likely to inflict injury or to incite an immediate breach of the peace." The words were not "fighting words" as the U.S. Supreme Court has interpreted that concept, and, finally, referring to *Cohen,* "the use of the 'f-word' in and of itself is not criminal conduct."[3]

However, as Matthew Bartlett, a 28-year-old observer, found when he flipped his middle finger during a court session in the Casey Anthony trial in July 2011 in Orlando, Florida, and was held in criminal contempt of court, the well-known gesture can still result in criminal issues. Bartlett was sentenced to six days in jail, along with a $400 fine and court costs of $223. Trial judge Belvin Perry denied a motion that Bartlett be released on bail.[4]

A case decided by the Ohio Supreme Court in 2002 illustrates the changing nature of the fighting words doctrine, along with the crime of solicitation, which was discussed in Chapter 3. In *State v. Thompson,* Ohio's highest court reversed the conviction of an appellant who was found guilty of violating the state's statute prohibiting soliciting sex from a member of the same gender. After he offered to perform a sex act on another jogger, the appellant was charged with violating the statute providing that "no person shall solicit a person of the same sex to engage in sexual activity with the offender, when the offender knows such solicitation is offensive to the other person, or is reckless in that regard." In 1979, the Ohio Supreme Court had upheld that statute, stating that the acts prohibited were the equivalent of fighting words. In 2002, however, the court ruled that the statute violated the equal protection clause of the Fourteenth Amendment (see Appendix A) because the state did not prohibit such behavior when the target was a member of the opposite gender.[5]

These and other cases suggest that although the U.S. Supreme Court and lower courts have not rejected the fighting words doctrine, any conviction under it will be examined closely and may be reversed.

Disorderly Conduct, Vagrancy, and Loitering

Common law did not include **disorderly conduct**, which refers to minor offenses, such as drunkenness or fighting, that disturb the peace or behavior standards of a community or shock the morality of its population. But some acts that were included in common law breach of the peace are typical of acts covered by modern disorderly conduct statutes. Today, most jurisdictions have a statute providing for the criminal punishment of certain minor acts, sometimes enumerated, and in many jurisdictions these offenses are called *disorderly conduct.* The statutes vary considerably from one jurisdiction to another, and they may be confused with vagrancy statutes (discussed next). On the one hand, a disorderly conduct statute may specify that being vagrant is an example of the proscribed conduct. On the other hand, vagrancy statutes may refer to people behaving in a disorderly manner.

A crime often associated with disorderly conduct, **vagrancy**, dates back centuries, focusing on idle persons. Common law vagrancy referred to people who wandered about from place to place without any visible means of support, refusing to work even though able to do so, and living off the charity of others.

Early English statutes required able-bodied people to work and made it a crime for them to wander about the country looking for higher wages or avoiding work. Idleness continued to be a major problem, however, particularly in England.

Most vagrancy laws are broader than disorderly conduct laws, and many of them have been declared unconstitutional. They have been attacked as permitting police to exercise too much discretion, which has led to unconstitutional discrimination against racial and ethnic minorities as well as the homeless. Vagrancy and disorderly conduct statutes may be unconstitutional because they are vague or overbroad.

Some modern statutes use the term *loitering* rather than *vagrancy*. Again, such statutes may be found unconstitutional if they are vague or overbroad; they may be upheld if they are clear. For example, a municipal loitering ordinance was upheld against charges of vagueness and overbreadth. The ordinance makes it an offense to loiter "in a place, at a time, or in a manner not usual for law-abiding individuals under circumstances that warrant alarm for the safety of persons or property in the vicinity."[6] Likewise, an ordinance that prohibits loitering "in or about any toilet open to the public for the purpose of engaging in or soliciting any lewd or lascivious or any unlawful act" was upheld against charges of vagueness.[7]

In contrast, an ordinance that prohibited loitering "in a manner and under circumstances manifesting the purpose" to solicit prostitution was declared unconstitutional. Some of the reasons given were that the ordinance was vague, overly broad, too harsh compared to similar statutes, and violative of substantive due process. The ordinance could be interpreted to prohibit known prostitutes from hailing a cab, waving to a friend, or engaging in other protected behavior.[8]

In recent years, many cities and states have enacted ordinances or statutes preventing begging, camping, sitting, or lying down in specified public places. Some of these regulations have been upheld; others have not. In 1999, the U.S. Supreme Court struck down a Chicago antiloitering ordinance that had been used to arrest over 42,000 persons while it was in effect from 1992 until the state court ruled on it in 1995. This ordinance had served as a model for many other cities that, like Chicago, were trying to bring gangs under control.[9]

The Chicago ordinance made it a crime to "remain in any one place with no apparent purpose" in the presence of a gang member if requested by a police officer to leave. The U.S. Supreme Court held that the ordinance was vague and thus unconstitutional. It left too much discretion to the subjective judgment of the police officer. Thus it made no difference whether a gang member and his father might loiter at the baseball field waiting to rob someone or to "get a glimpse of Sammy Sosa leaving the ball park."[10]

Chicago tried again, and in 2002, its revised ordinance was upheld against a constitutional challenge. This ordinance is designed to inconvenience gangs by disbursing them frequently to prevent their getting a hold on any area of the city. The judge who upheld the ordinance stated that the previous case provided a road map for a constitutional ordinance and "the Chicago framers of the revised ordinance knew how to read the map."[11]

It can be expected that local ordinances and state and federal statutes designed to regulate behavior in public places will continue to be challenged in the courts.

But for those determined to free the streets and parks of persons they consider undesirable, an easier way is to ban public intoxication.

Alcohol- and Drug-Related Offenses

Many offenses related to substance abuse are covered in criminal statutes. Chapter 10 is devoted to a thorough discussion of drug abuse and drug trafficking; the next section considers several offenses, often categorized as misdemeanors, that are related to the use of alcohol and other drugs.

Public Intoxication and Drug Incapacitation

Statutes that criminalize substance abuse in public are based on the assumption that the abusers disturb public order or morality and that they may be a threat to themselves or to others. Whether designated as a separate crime or one falling under the general category of disorderly conduct, vagrancy, or disturbing the peace, the public abuse of alcohol and other drugs is another category of criminal activity that raises serious debate on constitutional issues.

The U.S. Supreme Court has upheld a defendant's conviction based on its conclusion that his being drunk in public was an *act*, not a condition.[12] As long as the Court embraces that position, most public drunkenness statutes will be upheld. However, some jurisdictions have enacted statutes that emphasize treatment and rehabilitation instead of the prosecution of public drunkenness, as illustrated in Focus 8.1.

Focus 8.1

Treatment Rather Than Punishment of Substance Abuse

Today, some jurisdictions are emphasizing treatment rather than punishment for substance abusers. Idaho's Alcoholism and Intoxication Treatment Act is an example.

> It is the policy of this state that alcoholics, intoxicated persons or drug addicts may not be subjected to criminal prosecution or incarceration solely because of their consumption of alcoholic beverages or addiction to drugs but rather should be afforded treatment in order that they may lead normal lives as productive members of society.
>
> The legislature hereby finds and declares that it is essential to the health and welfare of the people of this state that action be taken by state government to effectively and economically utilize federal and state funds for alcoholism and drug addiction research, and the prevention and for the treatment and rehabilitation of alcoholics or drug addicts. To achieve this, it is necessary that existing fragmented, uncoordinated and duplicative alcoholism and drug treatment programs be merged into a comprehensive and integrated system for the prevention, treatment and rehabilitation of alcoholics.
>
> The legislature continues to recognize the need for criminal sanctions for those who violate the provisions of the uniform controlled substances act.[1]

[1]Idaho Code, Section 39–301 (2012).

Despite the fact that most states have enacted legislation to decriminalize public drunkenness, many people are held in jail for this offense, mainly because so many jurisdictions have no other facilities for detaining and treating people who are apprehended for public drunkenness or related offenses and do not have anyone to drive them home.

Driving Under the Influence (DUI)

It is illegal to operate motor vehicles while under the influence of alcohol or other drugs, although states and counties vary with regard to how they define the offenses as well as what those offenses are called. Such terms as *driving under the influence (DUI), operating under the influence of liquor (OUIL), driving while intoxicated (DWI),* and *unlawful blood alcohol level (UBAL)* are examples. Focus 8.2 presents the Michigan statute, which illustrates one way to define offenses related to the operation of motor vehicles while under the influence.

With regard to both public drunkenness and driving under the influence, some jurisdictions now emphasize treatment and rehabilitation. For example, Michigan provides as follows:

> Before imposing sentence for a violation of [the state statute] or a local ordinance substantially corresponding to [the state statute] the court shall order the person to undergo screening and assessment by a person or agency designated by the office of substance abuse services to determine whether the

=== Focus 8.2 ===

Prohibitions Against Driving While Impaired

The following is an example of the Michigan statute that prohibits driving a motor vehicle while under the influence of alcohol or other drugs.

(1) A person, whether licensed or not, shall not operate a vehicle upon a highway or other place open to the general public or generally accessible to motor vehicles, including an area designated for the parking of vehicles, within this state if the person is operating while intoxicated. As used in this section, "operating while intoxicated" means either of the following applies:
   (a) The person is under the influence of alcoholic liquor, a controlled substance, or a combination of alcoholic liquor and a controlled substance.
   (b) The person has an alcohol content of 0.08 grams or more per 100 milliliters of blood, per 210 liters of breath, or per 67 milliliters of urine, or, beginning October 1, 2013, the person has an alcohol content of 0.10 grams or more per 100 milliliters of blood, per 210 liters of breath, or per 67 milliliters of urine.[1]

[1]MCLS, Section 257.625 (2012).

CHAPTER 8 • Crimes Against Public Order and Public Decency   181

person is likely to benefit from rehabilitative services, including alcohol or drug education and alcohol or drug treatment programs. Except as otherwise provided in this subsection, the court may order the person to participate in and successfully complete 1 or more appropriate rehabilitative programs as part of the sentence. If the person has 1 or more prior convictions, the court shall order the person to participate in and successfully complete 1 or more appropriate rehabilitative programs as part of the sentence. The person shall pay for the costs of the screening, assessment, and rehabilitative services.[13]

It is also illegal for licensees to sell to a person who is obviously intoxicated, which, according to the Arizona Code, "means inebriated to such an extent that a person's physical faculties are substantially impaired and the impairment is shown by significantly uncoordinated physical action or significant physical dysfunction that would have been obvious to a reasonable person."[14]

Alcohol Offenses and Minors

Although some substance-related offenses, such as the possession and sale of specific drugs, are prohibited for all, others are prohibited only for persons under a specified age.

Sale of Alcohol to Minors. The legal drinking age in the United States is 21, and all jurisdictions have statutes regulating the sale, giving, or furnishing alcohol to persons under that age. For example, Arizona provides that it is unlawful:

Except as provided in...[other sections of this statute] for a licensee or other person to sell, furnish, dispose of or give, or cause to be sold, furnished, disposed of or given, to a person under the legal drinking age or for a person under the legal drinking age to buy, receive, have in the person's possession or consume spirituous liquor.[15]

Minors in Possession. Some readers of this text will no doubt be familiar with the criminal offense known as *minors in possession,* or *MIP.* As the Arizona statute prohibiting the illegal sale of alcohol to minors makes clear, it is also illegal for minors to be in possession of alcohol. MIP refers to a broad array of situations, such as being in an automobile in which others have placed alcohol, even though the minor did not know that. MIP does not require that the minor drink the alcohol, only that the minor is actually or constructively in possession of the illegal substance. The offense of MIP may also apply to other acts, such as a minor in possession of weapons, although the legal age of majority may be lower in those cases.[16]

Unlawful Assembly, Rout, and Riot

Under common law, **unlawful assembly**, a misdemeanor, referred to the meeting of three or more persons to disturb the public peace, with the intention of participating in a forcible and violent execution of an unlawful enterprise or of a lawful enterprise in an unauthorized manner. To constitute unlawful assembly, the individuals were not required to carry out its purpose, but if they took steps to carry out the plan, they committed a **rout**. If they carried out the plan, they committed a **riot**.

Riot and *rout* come from the same word; *rout* is used to communicate that those who have assembled unlawfully are on their way. *Riot* may be defined as "a tumultuous disturbance of the peace by three or more persons assembled and acting with a common intent; either in executing a lawful private enterprise in a violent and turbulent manner, to the terror of the people, or in executing an unlawful enterprise in a violent and turbulent manner."[17]

The English Riot Act of 1714 made it a capital felony for 12 or more persons to continue together for an hour after an official proclamation that people should disperse because of an existing riot. The official command to disperse was known as *reading the riot act.*[18]

Some modern statutes retain the crimes of unlawful assembly and riot; fewer retain rout. California statutes include all three, although the definitions differ somewhat from common law crimes. For example, California defines *riot* and *rout* as requiring two or more persons, whereas common law required three or more. Texas requires seven or more and specifies that the act must be done *knowingly.*[19]

Most statutes classify riots as misdemeanors, although some jurisdictions provide that aggravated riots are felonies. Statutes may provide for additional penalties if defendants commit other crimes, such as carrying weapons, during the riots. Some riot statutes include related crimes.

Some statutes divide riots into categories according to seriousness, such as first-degree and second-degree riot. New York has two degrees of riots. Riot in the second degree is a Class A misdemeanor, but riot in the first degree is a Class E felony. The crimes are similar but involve a different number of actors. "A person is guilty of riot in the second degree when, simultaneously with four or more other persons, he engages in tumultuous and violent conduct and thereby intentionally or recklessly causes a grave risk of causing public alarm." Riot in the first degree occurs when a person engages in such behavior with 10 or more other people and when someone other than those involved in the riot is injured or when property damage occurs as a result of the riot.[20]

Weapons Offenses

Under common law, because of the danger of breaching the peace if weapons were carried, it was a misdemeanor to "terrify the good people of the land by riding or going armed with dangerous or unusual weapons." The emphasis was on terrifying the king's citizens.[21]

Today, most U.S. jurisdictions have statutes regulating the sale, possession, and carrying of weapons, but the statutes differ so much that it is not possible to generalize. Many of the statutes have been tested in the courts.[22]

Obstructing a Highway or Public Passage

Public authorities have the right to regulate the flow of traffic and people on public streets, highways, and sidewalks, and individuals do not have the right to block the access of law enforcement or of others to those public areas. Problems arise, however, when the statutes are vague or so broad that they permit law enforcement too much discretion in their enforcement efforts. Most problems arise when authorities attempt to suppress demonstrations they consider unpopular, thus infringing on free speech without justifiable reasons.

Animal Abuse

An act that was usually ignored in the past but that is now being treated as criminal is animal abuse. Professional journals, law school case books, and law school courses now include this crime. Animal abuse arises in the context of the use of animals for research as well as the ways in which people treat or neglect their pets or other animals. Animal abuse is attracting more attention now due to research showing that it is often committed by persons who also engage in violence against humans. In some jurisdictions, animal abuse may be treated as a felony, especially if the offender has committed other crimes.

In 2007, a shocking and extensive case of animal abuse dominated the papers for weeks, culminating in the guilty plea of Michael Vick, Atlanta Falcons quarterback. Vick, who protested for weeks that he had not violated the law, entered a plea to the federal crime of conspiracy with regard to dog fighting allegations. Under the federal criminal code, it is "unlawful for any person to knowingly sell, buy, possess, train, transport, deliver, or receive any animal for purposes of having the animal participate in an animal fighting venture."[23] Vick was sentenced to 23 months in prison and was incarcerated in a minimum security federal facility in Leavenworth, Kansas. He served 21 months in prison, returned to professional football and, in 2010, was voted comeback player of the year as he set several career records. Nike, which had dropped him from advertising their products after his guilty plea, signed him to do so in 2011.[24]

In addition to the federal statute, animal abuse statutes exist in all states, with many of the statutes enacted years ago. In fact, New York, the first state to enact legislation in this area, passed its first statute in 1828. But, according to the American Bar Association (ABA), in the 43 states with statutes providing that animal abuse is a felony, 29 were enacted in the decade ending in 2007.[25]

In recent years, awareness of the need to enforce animal abuse statutes has increased, as has the coverage and penalties of those laws. For example, Texas revised its statute on nonlivestock animals, to become effective in 2007. The new law was influenced by the mistrial in the case of James M. Stevenson, when the jury deadlocked on the animal cruelty charges based on his shooting a cat because it was killing birds. The statute at the time prohibited killing a cat "belonging to another," and the defense argued that the cat in that case was feral and thus was excluded from the reach of the statute. The prosecution presented pictures of food, bedding, and toys under the bridge where the cat lived and argued that the cat was cared for by the toll bridge operator and thus "belonged to another." The jury did not agree; the legislature took action for future cases.[26]

In recent years, several states have toughened their legal protection of animals, although not all changes are in criminal codes. California now prohibits leaving a pet unattended in a car in very hot and very cold weather or without adequate

184 CRIMINAL LAW: THE ESSENTIALS

food, water, and ventilation.[27] And, as part of its health and safety code, that state was one of the first to establish a limit (three hours) on how long a pet can be tethered while its custodian runs errands.[28]

An interesting twist on laws protecting pets is that in 2006, Maine became the first state in the nation to provide for the inclusion of pets in protective orders in domestic violence cases. That state's statutes covering domestic relations and protection from abuse now include threats to harm pets. Maine officials estimated that in 70 percent of domestic violence cases, pets as well as humans are threatened.[29]

A related issue with regard to animal abuse involves depicting animal cruelty in videos. In 2010, the U.S. Supreme Court held that the federal statute prohibiting such depictions was unconstitutionally broad. The statute prohibited knowingly creating, selling, or possessing "a depiction of animal cruelty with the intention of placing that depiction in interstate or foreign commerce for commercial gain." Conviction could result in a sentence of up to five years in prison, a fine, or both. The statute permitted exceptions of "any depiction that has serious religious, political, scientific, educational, journalistic, historical, or artistic value." The conduct specifically prohibited was

> conduct in which a living animal is intentionally maimed, mutilated, tortured, wounded, or killed, if such conduct is illegal under Federal law or the law of the State in which the creation, sale, or possession takes place, regardless of whether the... wounding... or killing took place in [that] state.[30]

The statute was enacted to focus on "crush videos" that feature the torture and killing of animals and are thought to appeal to people with a sexual fetish. The appellant was convicted for selling videos that depicted dog fighting. His conviction was vacated by the lower appellant court, which held that the statute violated free speech because it regulated content-based speech. The U.S. Supreme Court, by an 8–1 vote in *United States v. Stevens,* agreed. According to the majority's opinion, written by Chief Justice John Roberts,

> From 1791 to the present... the First Amendment has "permitted restrictions upon the content of speech in a few limited areas" and has never "include[d] a freedom to disregard these traditional limitations." [Justice Roberts listed those areas: obscenity, defamation, fraud, incitement, and speech integral to criminal conduct that are] "well-defined and narrowly limited classes of speech, the prevention and punishment of which have never been thought to raise any Constitutional problem." [The court declined to increase that list.]

According to the Supreme Court, the statute is overbroad because its definition of "depiction of animal cruelty" does not even require that the depicted conduct be cruel. For example, the words *wounded* and *killed* do not necessarily convey cruelty. Nor do some state and federal laws that are enacted for the protection of endangered species prohibit cruelty—they prohibit any killing or wounding of the protected animals. Furthermore, views of cruelty to animals differ from jurisdiction to jurisdiction, leaving people who seek to comply with the law facing "a bewildering maze of regulations." For example, some statutes restrict hunting with crossbows, while others permit it. "The sharp-tailed grouse may be hunted in Idaho, but not in Washington."[31]

In short, it would be impossible for people to know when they were in danger of violating the law because of the wide coverage of this federal statute. Thus, the statute puts a chilling effect on Free Speech, which includes videos as well as actual speech and violates the First Amendment's provision that "Congress shall make no law...abridging the freedom of speech" (see Appendix A).

Harassment

One final example of a crime against the public order that has received considerable attention in recent years is *harassment*. Some jurisdictions criminalize various harassment techniques, such as insults, challenges, phone calls, or other means of inciting an individual to violence; subjecting another to offensive touching; engaging in alarming conduct; or making repeated communications anonymously or at times or in places that are inconvenient to the recipient. Some of these acts may constitute sexual harassment, hate crimes, or other offenses, and may be included under other statutes.

Harassment statutes may be categorized by degrees (e.g., aggravated harassment in the first degree, second degree, and so on) and may specify types, such as harassment against persons because of the following characteristics:

Ancestry
Gender
Religious practices
Age
Disability
Sexual orientation
Race or ethnicity

Harassment statutes may also include language qualifying the characteristics, noting that it is the *perception* of the actor concerning those characteristics that is critical. Thus, if the actor perceives the proposed victim to be gay and harasses him or her, it makes no difference that the target is not gay. Finally, acts of harassment may be defined as felonies or as misdemeanors.

OFFENSES AGAINST PUBLIC DECENCY

Chapter 1's discussion of the purposes of criminal law looked briefly at the arguments for and against including morality within criminal law. Certainly criminal law should encompass forced sexual behavior, but there is disagreement over whether it should include private, consensual sexual behavior between adults and, if so, to what extent.

Historically, many of the acts discussed in this section were considered within the area of morality and to be governed by the church rather than by the state (for example, through its criminal statutes).

The early criminal statutes of the American colonies and subsequently the United States were patterned after biblical laws. In the Massachusetts Code of 1648, the death penalty was provided for rape and adultery, as well as for many other acts. The Puritans equated sin and crime, and frequently they prosecuted offenders for sexual crimes. Within the past two decades, some jurisdictions have decriminalized some of the behaviors, such as private consensual sexual behavior between unmarried adults. But the debate remains over who should control morality—the church, the state, or, neither—and which acts should be included within criminal law. The following sections discuss some behaviors that are still covered by criminal law.

Prostitution

Historically, **prostitution** was accepted as inevitable, even essential, and in some societies the practice was not only accepted but also esteemed. Critics of prostitution claim that it exploits women (and, in some cases, children) and contributes to the spread of sexually transmitted diseases. In the United States, prostitution is illegal in all but some rural Nevada counties.

Statutes regulating prostitution vary. So do definitions of the term *prostitution,* although basically it refers to indiscriminate sexual intercourse for hire. Some statutes specify women as the offenders, but others also include men or use a neutral term, such as *gender,* in describing who may commit the offense. The criminal offense may include not only the prostitute but also any persons who solicit or promote prostitution or who live off a prostitute's earnings. Special terms may be used to criminalize those persons. For example, **pandering** refers to procuring or securing a person, usually a female, to satisfy the lust of another, usually a male, or catering to the lust of another person. Pandering is also called *pimping.*

Despite some attempts to legalize prostitution in the United States (as it is in some other countries), most would agree that the use of children in the crime should be covered by criminal law. Some states have enacted statutes under which adults who hire juvenile prostitutes will be treated as sex offenders, sentenced to prison if convicted, and required to register as sex offenders upon release.

Human Trafficking

Trafficking women and children into prostitution is not the only manifestation of human trafficking; in fact, not all trafficking is for purposes of sex. In its 2000 Trafficking Victims Protection Act, Congress included numerous findings about national and international trafficking. In its 2003 reauthorization of that act, it listed additional findings, which are included in part in Focus 8.3.

In 2012, the FBI emphasized that eradicating human trafficking is a priority in its civil rights program but noted that trafficking occurs also in the criminal arena. "Human trafficking generates billions of dollars of profit each year, making it one of the world's fastest growing criminal activities."[32]

Other acts that fall under statutes aimed at protecting public morality are obscenity, lewdness, and indecency.

===== **Focus 8.3** =====

Human Trafficking

Following is a selection of the Congressional findings in its 2003 reauthorization of the Trafficking Victims Protection Act, which was originally enacted in 2000, P.L. 106–386. The Purpose and Findings are located at USCS, Title 22, Section 7101 (2012).

(1) ...Trafficking in persons is a modern form of slavery, and it is the largest manifestation of slavery today. At least 700,000 persons annually, primarily women and children, are trafficked within or across international borders. Approximately 50,000 women and children are trafficked into the United States each year.

(2) Many of these persons are trafficked into the international sex trade, often by force, fraud, or coercion....

(3) Trafficking in persons is not limited to the sex industry. This growing transnational crime also includes forced labor and involves significant violations of labor, public health, and human rights standards worldwide.

(4) Traffickers primarily target women and girls, who are disproportionately affected by poverty, the lack of access to education, chronic unemployment, discrimination, and the lack of economic opportunities in countries of origin. Traffickers lure women and girls into their networks through false promises of decent working conditions at relatively good pay as nannies, maids, dancers, factory workers, restaurant workers, sales clerks, or models. Traffickers also buy children from poor families and sell them into prostitution or into various types of forced or bonded labor....

(7) Traffickers often make representations to their victims that physical harm may occur to them or others should the victim escape or attempt to escape. Such representations can have the same coercive effects on victims as direct threat to inflict such harm....

(11) Trafficking exposes victims to serious health risks. Women and children trafficked in the sex industry are exposed to deadly diseases, including HIV and AIDS. Trafficking victims are sometimes worked or physically brutalized to death....

(17) Existing laws often fail to protect victims of trafficking, and because victims are often illegal immigrants in the destination country, they are repeatedly punished more harshly than the traffickers themselves.

(18) Additionally, adequate services and facilities do not exist to meet victims' needs regarding health care, housing, education, and legal assistance, which safely reintegrate trafficking victims into their home countries....

(23) The United States and the international community agree that trafficking in persons involves grave violations of human rights and is a matter of pressing international concern.

Obscenity, Lewdness, and Indecency

Words such as *obscene, lewd, lascivious, lecherous,* and *indecent* have been used to describe a variety of behaviors that some people find offensive to the extent that the criminal law is invoked to try to curb them. These words may be used to describe acts such as appearing nude in public or living openly and notoriously with a member of the opposite gender without being married (also called *illicit* or *lewd cohabitation*). Generally, these acts are defined as misdemeanors and carry only slight penalties. Most of the statutes are rarely, if ever, enforced.

Some statutes that prohibit lewdness are brief and general. Pennsylvania, for example, has a statute entitled "open lewdness," defined as follows: "A person commits a misdemeanor of the third degree if he does any lewd act which he knows is likely to be observed by others who would be affronted or alarmed."[33]

Other statutes prohibiting lewd and lascivious acts mention specific sexual acts. These statutes may describe any sexual acts between members of the same gender even when they occur in private, or they may refer only to sexual acts considered serious whether they involve the same or opposite genders. They may also refer to sexual acts with minors when force is not used. The Idaho Criminal Code, for example, prohibits *lewd conduct with a minor child under 16.* This conduct is described as including but not limited to "genital-genital contact, oral-genital contact, anal-genital contact, oral-anal contact, manual-anal contact, or manual-genital contact, whether between persons of the same or opposite sex," or involving minor children in any of these acts when they are done "with the intent of arousing, appealing to, or gratifying the lust or passions or sexual desires of such person, such minor child, or a third party." The penalty for conviction of this felony is a prison term of not more than life.[34]

Some lewdness statutes are difficult to interpret, particularly when intent is an element of the crime. For example, a Florida court held that the state's statute that prohibits public nudity does not prohibit all public nudity. Rather, a charge based on this statute requires that the public exposure of sexual organs must relate to "a lascivious exhibition of those private parts."[35]

Statutes prohibiting lewdness and indecency may encompass speech as well as conduct, and in so doing, they may be unconstitutional. This is particularly the case with statutes that regulate **obscenity**, a term that the U.S. Supreme Court has difficulty defining. In *Stanley v. Georgia,* the U.S. Supreme Court held that "mere private possession of obscene matter" in one's own home is not a crime, but the Court emphasized the right of states to regulate obscenity. The Court had problems defining *obscenity,* but in 1973, in *Miller v. California,* the Court articulated three conditions, all of which must be met for information to be considered *obscene:*

1. "The average person, applying contemporary community standards, would find that the work, taken as a whole, appeals to the prurient interest [in sex]; and
2. the work depicts or describes, in a patently offensive way, sexual conduct specifically defined by the applicable state [or federal] law; and
3. the work, taken as a whole, lacks serious literary, artistic, political, or scientific value."[36]

In its 2011–2012 term, in *FCC et al. v. Fox Television Stations, Inc. et al.*, the U.S. Supreme Court considered the issue of whether the Federal Communications Commission (FCC)'s indecency policy is unconstitutional. Indecent speech is fully protected by the U.S. Constitution; obscene speech is not protected. Any infringement on speech must be analyzed by strict scrutiny, and the policy may not be vague, meaning that it must give the person of ordinary intelligence reasonable notice of what speech is prohibited. Broadcasters are entitled to the same notice as individual persons. On 21 June 2012, the U.S. Supreme Court vacated and remanded the lower federal court's decision in this case, which involved alleged obscene words uttered during two live broadcasts aired by Fox television stations. The Court also considered a second case, which involved an ABC television network broadcast that revealed the nude buttocks and the side breast of an adult female. The FCC had ruled that the fleeting expletives and the momentary nudity of these cases violated its recently enacted standards of decency. The U.S. Supreme Court held that it did not need to reach the constitutional free speech issue in these cases because the FCC's standards did not provide adequate and clear notice and thus were void for vagueness. The Court remanded the cases to the lower federal court for resolution of the constitutional issue regarding free speech.[37]

Sodomy

Chapter 6 discussed forced sodomy as a serious (and violent) crime, but some jurisdictions also define *consensual sodomy* as a crime. The Idaho statute is illustrative. It prohibits "the infamous crimes against nature, committed with mankind or with any animal."[38]

To avoid the problem of vagueness that this language creates, some jurisdictions have revised their statutes to include specific acts. For example, California changed its sodomy statute from one referring to "the infamous crime against nature, committed with mankind or with any animal" to "sexual conduct consisting of contact between the penis of one person and the anus of another person." The current California statute does not define sodomy as a punishable offense unless it is committed under any one of numerous specified circumstances, such as those involving force, violence, or duress; or involves acts committed with an underage person, a mentally challenged person, or a person known by the actor to be unconscious or asleep.[39]

Other jurisdictions do not use the term *sodomy* in their statutes. If they criminalize the acts traditionally included within this term, they may do so by using words such as *deviate sexual intercourse* or *deviant sexual acts*. The debate over the use of the criminal law to regulate private, consensual sexual behavior between adults escalated after the U.S. Supreme Court decision in *Bowers v. Hardwick*, decided in 1986. In that case, the Court upheld the Georgia statute prohibiting sodomy, defined as "any sexual act involving the sex organs of one person and the mouth or anus of another." The Court held that the statute did not violate the fundamental rights of gay males.[40]

In 1996, the Georgia Supreme Court upheld a conviction for solicitation of sodomy, a misdemeanor, and a probation sentence of 12 months against a challenge that the statute violated the defendant's privacy rights under the Georgia constitution. The U.S. Supreme Court refused to review the case, thus permitting the Georgia Supreme Court decision to stand.[41]

In 1998, the Georgia Supreme Court held that the statute on which *Bowers v. Hardwick* was based violated the right to privacy as provided in the Georgia Constitution. The case, *Powell v. State,* involved a man and his wife's 17-year-old niece. The defendant was acquitted of rape and aggravated sodomy but was convicted of sodomy. Although force was charged, it was not proved, and the state supreme court dealt with the same sodomy statute as that of *Bowers,* although involving members of opposite genders. The sodomy conviction was reversed and the statute declared unconstitutional by the Georgia court that stated:

> We conclude that [the statute], insofar as it criminalizes the performance of private, non-commercial acts of sexual intimacy between persons legally able to consent, "manifestly infringes upon a constitutional provision" which guarantees to the citizens of Georgia the sexual intimacy with one legally capable of consenting thereto in the privacy of his home.[42]

Some jurisdictions in which sodomy has been redefined have enacted a separate statute covering sexual intercourse or sexual contact with same-gender persons. Texas, for example, defined the crime of *homosexual conduct* as engaging "in deviate sexual intercourse with another individual of the same sex."[43] In 2003, in *Lawrence v. Texas,* the U.S. Supreme Court declared that statute unconstitutional and overruled *Bowers v. Hardwick.*[44]

Seduction and Fornication

Under common law, **seduction** was not a criminal offense, but many U.S. jurisdictions established the crime by statute. Historically, *seduction* referred to the act by a man who used solicitation, persuasion, promises, bribes, or other methods to entice a woman to have unlawful sexual intercourse with him. Seduction was a felony, although some statutes provided that a subsequent marriage between the two parties negated the crime. The modern trend has been to repeal seduction statutes, but those that remain generally categorize the crime as a misdemeanor and may provide that women can also be considered perpetrators and that males may be victims.

Even when seduction statutes are repealed, laws may criminalize the act of inducing consent to a sexual act by the use of fraud or fear. And seduction statutes may limit the ages of victims, such as to persons under the age of 18.

Another sex act considered a crime against public morals in some jurisdictions is **fornication**, which comes from *fornix,* a Latin word for *brothel.* Usually the term refers to unlawful sexual intercourse between two unmarried persons of opposite genders. Some jurisdictions do not limit the act to the opposite sex.

Adultery

In some jurisdictions, fornication also applies to a single person involved in unlawful sexual intercourse with a person who is married to someone else. Other states define the acts of both parties as **adultery**, consensual sexual intercourse between a married person and someone other than his or her spouse. Like fornication, adultery was not a common law crime, although it was an ecclesiastical (pertaining to or belong to the church) offense. Like most other sex crimes, adultery has various definitions. Some jurisdictions define it as sexual intercourse between two people, one of whom is married to someone else, while others hold only the married party in that relationship to the crime of adultery. In earlier laws, only the married woman was committing adultery; sexual behavior by married men with women other than their wives was not considered criminal.

Some statutes distinguish between *single adultery,* in which only one party is married, and *double adultery,* in which both parties are married to other persons. Some states criminalize adultery only when the act is "open and notorious," but the current trend is toward decriminalizing adultery. The adultery statutes that remain in effect are rarely enforced by prosecutors, although they may come into play in divorce proceedings.

Bigamy

Like adultery, **bigamy** is considered a crime against the family; it may be defined as an individual's knowingly and willingly contracting a second marriage when he or she is aware that another marriage is undissolved. Some jurisdictions consider the crime one of strict liability; thus, *knowledge* of a prior marriage is not required.

Bigamy was not a common law crime. Historically, bigamy has been criminalized in the United States, although few prosecutions have occurred. Despite the infrequent prosecutions for bigamy even when the crime is known to have been committed, most states still criminalize the act. The New York statute is typical of bigamy statutes that designate the offense as a felony: "A person is guilty of bigamy when he contracts or purports to contract a marriage with another person at a time when he has a living spouse, or the other person has a living spouse." In New York, bigamy is a felony; adultery is a misdemeanor.[45]

Pornography

It is not illegal for adults to possess pornographic materials, although it is illegal to possess materials that depict child pornography, which is considered sexual exploitation of those children. To combat such exploitation, Congress and many states have enacted statutes aimed solely at child pornography. The federal statute is an example of legislation in this area. Referred to as the Protection of Children Against Sexual Exploitation Act of 1977, the statute has subsequently been amended. It was based on the Congressional findings reported in Focus 8.4.

The federal statute is a lengthy one. It imposes liability on parents and guardians as well as on coercers, producers, and distributors of child pornography. The statute provides that, through a process called **forfeiture**, the government may take any property involved in the crime. It includes the dissemination of pornographic depictions of children by use of a computer.[46]

The U.S. Supreme Court has, however, upheld *virtual child pornography,* which involves images that are created by computer simulations that make adults

192 CRIMINAL LAW: THE ESSENTIALS

Focus 8.4

Congressional Findings on Child Pornography

1. Child pornography has developed into a highly organized, multimillion dollar industry which operates on a nationwide scale;
2. Thousands of children including large numbers of runaway and homeless youth are exploited in the production and distribution of pornographic materials; and
3. The use of children as subjects of pornographic materials is harmful to the physiological, emotional, and mental health of the individual child and to society.[1]

[1]The Child Protection Act of 1984, USCS, Title 18, Section 2251 *et seq.* (2012).

---

look like children.[47] In reaction to this U.S. Supreme Court case, Congress passed and President George W. Bush signed the Prosecutorial Remedies and Other Tools to End the Exploitation of Children Today Act of 2003 (the PROTECT Act). The lengthy statute contains provisions aimed at protecting children from sexual assaults, pornography, kidnapping, and other crimes.[48]

In 2008, the U.S. Supreme court upheld the constitutionality of the PROTECT Act in the case of *United States v. Williams.* Michael Williams, who used a sexually explicit screen name, posted this message on the Internet: "Dad of toddler has 'good' pics of her an [*sic*] me for swap of your toddler pics, or live cam." Williams and an undercover agent exchanged nonpornographic pictures, which led to a hyperlink that showed children between approximately 5 and 15 years old engaging in sexually explicit conduct. Officers got a search warrant, searched Williams's home, and found pictures of real children engaging in sexually explicit behavior. Some of the pictures were sadomasochistic.[49]

In upholding the constitutionality of the PROTECT Act, the majority of the U.S. Supreme Court, in an opinion written by Justice Antonin Scalia, stated that its First Amendment concerns in the previous statute were eliminated by the fact that the current statute limits the crime to the pandering of child pornography and the requirement that the panderer believes and states that the depictions are of real children or that he or she communicates in a way designed to make others so believe. Justice Scalia concluded as follows:

> Child pornography harms and debases the most defenseless of our citizens. Both the State and Federal Governments have sought to suppress it for many years, only to find it proliferating through the new medium of the Internet. This Court held unconstitutional Congress's previous attempt to meet this new threat, and Congress responded with a carefully crafted attempt to eliminate the First Amendment problems we identified. As far as the provision at issue in this case is concerned, that effect was successful.[50]

The U.S. Congress has enacted additional statutes designed to protect children from viewing or becoming actors in pornography.[51]

SUMMARY

This chapter discussed a wide range of offenses, many of which are misdemeanors. But some of those offenses, such as public intoxication, may consume enormous amounts of law enforcement time and other resources. For example, incarcerating public drunks may contribute to jail overcrowding.

Many of the offenses discussed in this chapter are important in that their regulation may and often does infringe on basic constitutional rights, such as free speech, due process, equal protection, and privacy. However, it is argued that these offenses threaten public order, the sanctity of the family, and general morality, and therefore the regulations are necessary. But enforcement is lax in many areas, and discretionary enforcement is extensive, leaving room for illegal discrimination.

The first substantive crime discussed, breach of the peace, illustrates the philosophy behind the common law crimes included in this chapter. The crime was designed to cover acts not otherwise criminalized that might disrupt society's peace and tranquillity. Breach of the peace has been retained as a crime by most jurisdictions, although the definitions vary. Like many of the other crimes included in this chapter, breach of the peace statutes may be vague or too broad, in which case they should be declared unconstitutional.

The preservation of peace and order may be threatened by language as well as by actions. The criminal law attempts to avoid these problems by criminalizing fighting words, a situation that comes dangerously close to violating the First Amendment right to free speech.

Historically, it has not been uncommon for societies to attempt to suppress unpopular views and keep certain types of people out of sight. Statutes covering disorderly conduct, vagrancy, loitering, public intoxication, and drug incapacitation are used for this purpose. Many of these statutes are vague or too broad, leaving police with wide discretion in deciding whether or not to make an arrest. In recent years, some of these statutes have been declared unconstitutional but, if properly worded, the statutes may be used effectively to control order and will be upheld by the courts.

The desire to protect society from physical dangers to people and property that may result from some gatherings has led to statutes encompassing unlawful assembly, rout, and riot. Once again, however, these statutes must be examined carefully to ensure that they do not conflict with the constitutional rights to assemble and to communicate ideas.

Criminal laws that cover weapons offenses are a topic of controversy today. Countering the argument by many that individuals have a right to have weapons to protect themselves is the argument that society has an interest in protecting the health and welfare of its citizens and should be able to restrict the use of weapons under certain circumstances.

A wide variety of other offenses are thought to threaten the public, including obstructing public highways or public passages, exhibiting cruelty to animals, and harassment. Recent developments in these areas were examined.

Another major category of offenses covered in this chapter includes acts that some people think should be criminalized to protect public decency. Despite one's beliefs about whether consensual sexual activities between adults should be covered by the criminal law, it is important to understand the full implications of criminalizing these acts. The effects of the acts may reach far beyond their impact on immediate victims or society; some or all of them may be the source of other crimes, such as extortion and blackmail. This is particularly the case with prostitution and consensual same-gender sodomy. Both involve human sexual behavior that may be engaged in by consenting adults in private with no financial arrangements, but both may also involve commercialized sex. The U.S. Supreme Court decision concerning the regulation of same-gender sexual behavior may, however, render most, if not all, of these statutes unenforceable.

It is difficult to draft and interpret indecency and lewdness statutes to achieve the desired goal of protecting people from being forced to view sexual behavior they choose to avoid. These statutes risk becoming so broad as to prohibit behavior, such as cohabitation, of which many approve today.

Some of the crimes discussed in this chapter are aimed primarily at preserving the family structure. Seduction, fornication, adultery, and bigamy are examples. Although most jurisdictions have abolished statutes criminalizing seduction and fornication and some have abolished adultery statutes, others have retained statutes prohibiting these acts, although the statutes are rarely enforced.

In addition, pornography statutes pose the question of what should be allowed as private behavior and what should be regulated by criminal law. Over the years, courts have disagreed in their interpretations of what is and is not permissible in this area. This chapter noted the emphasis that Congress and courts have placed on protecting children from the potentially harmful effects of pornography.

This chapter focused on some of the most controversial areas of criminal law. By their nature, some of the offenses are delicate and sensitive. But the discussion is important, for it touches on some of our most valued rights—the right to privacy and the right to procreation, which involves the right to sexual expression. Others involve the right to free speech. Although these and other constitutional rights may be regulated by the state or federal government under some circumstances, they may not violate basic constitutional protections. Finally, it is important to ensure that statutes such as those discussed in this chapter, most of which are not enforced rigorously, are not used for the purpose of harassing persons because of their gender, their sexual orientations, their homeless status, their disability, or their racial or ethnic status.

STUDY QUESTIONS

1. Discuss the origin of statutes prohibiting breach of the peace and the circumstances under which these and related statutes may be unconstitutional.
2. Explain the fighting words doctrine.
3. Why do we have disorderly conduct, vagrancy, and loitering statutes? What are the potential problems with statutes prohibiting these acts?
4. To what extent should public intoxication and drug incapacitation be regulated by criminal law? Discuss the application of such laws to minors.

5. Distinguish rout, riot, and inciting to riot.
6. What is unlawful assembly?
7. What type of criminal statutes should we have concerning weapons offenses?
8. How is the right to free speech affected by statutes prohibiting obstructing a highway or other public passage?
9. Although it may be offensive to some people if others are cruel to animals, would the law's deterrent effect be greater if these acts were part of the civil law only, giving animal custodians a right to compensation from those who injure or kill their animals? What does the criminal law add?
10. List all of the behaviors you think should be covered by criminal harassment statutes.
11. Discuss some of the problems of enforcing statutes that prohibit prostitution.
12. What is human trafficking? How extensive is it? What can be done to combat this offense?
13. Should obscenity, lewdness, and indecency statutes be abolished?
14. Discuss the U.S. Supreme Court's 1986 holding and rationale concerning consensual sodomy involving gay males. What are the implications of the Texas sodomy case, decided by the U.S. Supreme Court in 2003?
15. Which, if any, of the following behaviors—seduction, fornication, adultery, bigamy—should remain within the criminal law?
16. Should criminal law distinguish between pornography involving adults and that involving children?
17. Discuss the legal implications of attempts to control pornography through the criminal law.

FOR DEBATE

Many of the crimes discussed in this chapter are classified as misdemeanors or less than the highest category of felonies in jurisdictions in which felonies are graded. Given these classifications, debate the following topic.

RESOLVED: The law should not be utilized to criminalize acts that are private and do not interfere with or threaten the public directly—acts such as the use of drugs, private sexual behavior between consenting adults, and the possession of dangerous weapons or pornography.

KEY TERMS

adultery   191
bigamy   192
breach of the peace   176
disorderly conduct   177
fighting words   176
forfeiture   191
fornication   190
obscenity   188
pandering   186
prostitution   186
riot   182
rout   182
seduction   190
unlawful assembly   181
vagrancy   177

INTERNET ACTIVITY

1. In recent years, many jurisdictions have enacted laws to protect animals against abuse. Check the website of The Humane Society of the United States, http://www.humanesociety.org (accessed 13 May 2012), to read about these laws. What can you find out about legislation at the national level? What can you discover about animal abuse?

2. There is controversy over whether private, consensual, sexual behavior between adults should be included within the criminal law. Go on line to the following website: http://www.findlaw.com (accessed 23 July 2012). Click on Criminal Law, then Criminal Charges and then Sex Crimes. Check the definitions of prostitution and indecent exposure and assess their inclusion within criminal law. Also consider the crime of disorderly conduct. How broadly is the law stated?

NOTES

1. For a discussion, see Rollin M. Perkins and Ronald N. Boyce, *Criminal Law*, 3d ed. (Mineola, N.Y.: Foundation Press, 1982), pp. 477–497. This source is the basis of the discussion in this section.
2. *Cohen v. California*, 403 U.S. 15, 20 (1971).
3. *Sandul v. Larion*, 119 F.3d 1250 (6th. Cir. 1997), *cert. dismissed*, 522 U.S. 979 (1997).
4. "Judge Keeps Spectator in Jail: Contempt Order Appealed," *Orlando Sentinel* (Florida) (2 July 2011), p. 9B.
5. *State v. Thompson*, 767 N.E.2d 251 (Ohio 2002).
6. *Milwaukee v. Nelson*, 439 N.W.2d 562 (Wis. 1989), *cert. denied*, 493 U.S. 858 (1989).
7. *People v. Superior Court (Oswell)*, 758 P.2d 1046 (Cal. 1988).
8. *Wyche v. State*, 619 S0.2d 231 (Fla. 1993); and *Holliday v. City of Tampa, Florida*, 619 S0.2d 244 (Fla. 1993).
9. "Loitering Law Aimed at Gangs Is Struck Down by High Court," *New York Times* (11 June 1999), p. 1.
10. *Chicago v. Morales*, 527 U.S. 41 (1999).
11. "Anti-Loiter Ordinance: Does It Have a Leg to Stand On?" *South Bend Tribune* (Indiana) (1 April 2002), p. 1C.
12. *Powell v. Texas*, 392 U.S. 514 (1968).
13. MCLS, Section 257.625b(5) (2012).
14. A.R.S., Section 4-244.14 (2012).
15. A.R.S., Section 4-244.9 (2012).
16. See A.R.S., Section 13-3111 (2012).
17. *State v. Abbadini*, 192 A. 550, 551–552 (Del. 1937).
18. Sir James Stephen, *A History of the Criminal Law of England* (London: MacMillan, 1883), p. 203.

19. Cal Pen Code, Section 404 *et seq* (2012); Tex. Penal Code, Section 42.02 (2012).
20. NY CLS Penal, Sections 240.05 and 240.06 (2012).
21. Perkins and Boyce, *Criminal Law*, p. 492.
22. See, for example, *District of Columbia v. Heller*, 554 U.S. 570 (2008); and *McDonald v. Chicago*, 130 S.Ct. 3020 (2010), involving the use of hand guns. For a discussion, see Sue Titus Reid, *Criminal Law*, 9th ed. (New York: Oxford University Press, 2012), pp. 249–52.
23. USCS, Chapter 7, Chapter 54, Section 2156(b) (2012).
24. "Vick, Nike Join Forces Again," *Chicago Tribune* (3 July 2011), p. 5C.
25. Terry Carter, "Beast Practices," *American Bar Association Journal* 93 (November 2007): 39.
26. "Judge Declares a Mistrial in Texas Cat Killing Case," *New York Times* (17 November 2007), p. 11. The statute is Tex. Penal Code, Section 42.092 (2012). The statute covering abuse of livestock is Section 42.09 (2012).
27. Cal Pen Code, Part I, Title 14, Section 597.7 (2012).
28. Cal Health & Safety Code, Section 122335 (2012).
29. M.R.S., Title 19-A, Section 4006 (2011); Arin Greenwood, "Saving Fido: New State Law Allows Pets to Be Included in Protective Orders," *American Bar Association Journal* (4 August 2006), p. 1.
30. Depiction of Animal Cruelty, USCS, Title 18, Section 48 (2012).
31. *United States v. Stevens*, 130 S.Ct. 1577 (2010), cases and citations omitted.
32. Federal Bureau of Investigation, "Human Trafficking Prevention," press release (20 January 2012), http://www.fbi.gov (accessed 20 January 2012).
33. Pa.C.S., Title 18, Section 5901 (2012).
34. Idaho Code, Section 18-1508 (2012).
35. *United States v. A Naked Person Issued Notice of Violation No. P419490*, 841 F.Supp. 1153 (M.D.Fla. 1993).
36. *Stanley v. Georgia, 394 U.S. 557 (1969); Miller v. California*, 413 U.S. 15, 24 (1973).
37. *FCC v. Fox TV Stations, Inc.*, 556 U.S. 502 (2009), *on remand, remanded, Fox TV Stations, Inc. v. FCC*, 613 F.3d 317 (2d Cir. 2010), *vacated and remanded*, 132 S.Ct. 2307 (2012). The companion case is *Federal Communications Commission v. ABC, Inc., et al*, 404 Fed. Appx. 520 (2d Cir. 2011).
38. Idaho Code, Section 18-6605 (2012).
39. Cal Pen Code, Section 286 (2012).
40. *Bowers v. Hardwick*, 478 U.S. 186 (1986); *and overruled by Lawrence v. Texas*, 539 U.S. 558 (2003). The statute is codified at O.C.G.A., Section 16-6-2 (2011).
41. *Christensen v. State*, 468 S.E.2d 188 (Ga. 1996), *cert. denied sub nom.*, 522 U.S. 1128 (1998), citations omitted. The statute at issue is O.C.G.A., Section 16-6-15(a) (2011).
42. *Powell v. State*, 510 S.E.2d 18 (Ga. 1998).
43. Tex. Penal Code, Section 21.06 (2012).

44. *Lawrence v. Texas*, 539 U.S. 558 (2003).
45. NY CLS Penal, Section 255.15 (2012). The adultery statute is NY CLS Penal, Section 255.17 (2012).
46. The federal statute is codified at USCS, Title 18, Section 2251 *et seq.* (2012).
47. See *Ashcroft v. Free Speech Coalition*, 535 U.S. 234 (2002).
48. The Prosecutorial Remedies and Other Tools to End the Exploitation of Children Today Act of 2003 (the PROTECT Act), Public Law 108-21 (2008).
49. *United States v. Williams*, 553 U.S. 285 (2008).
50. *United States v. Williams*, 553 U.S. 285 (2008).
51. See, for example, the Communications Decency Act of 1996, USCS, Title 47, Section 2236(a) to (h) (2012); and The Children's Internet Protection Act (CIPA), 114 Stat. 2763A.335 (2012).

CHAPTER 9

Crimes Against the Government and Terrorism

CHAPTER OUTLINE

INTRODUCTION

This chapter covers two important areas that are often omitted from criminal law texts despite their importance in today's world: crimes against the government and terrorism. Crimes against the government have been on the statute books for years but were infrequently enforced until recently. Acts of terrorism are relatively new in statutory form but in recent years have, unfortunately, become far-reaching in their impact.

At a time in which the United States and other countries are experiencing problems with ethics and morality within the governmental as well as the private sector, it is imperative that students gain some knowledge of major crimes against the administration of government. This chapter examines six types of crime that fall into this category: perjury and related crimes, bribery, official misconduct in office, obstruction of justice, contempt of court, and treason.

Terrorism, the focus of the second major section of this chapter, has been a research interest of criminology and criminal law scholars for years; many colleges and universities offer seminars or regular courses on the topic. It has not, however, generally been a topic covered extensively in undergraduate criminal law texts. Hopefully this will change as a result of the need to combat terrorist attacks in the United States and throughout the world, which have captured international attention and have probably increased the fear that most, if not all, people have of such acts.

In a real sense, many crimes are similar to terrorism. Rapists strike fear in the minds of their victims; fear is a crucial element of robbery; assault contains an element of fear; murder may involve torture and fear; domestic violence, especially when it occurs over a period of time, creates fear. Those topics have already been discussed in this text; this chapter focuses specifically on those acts included within discussions of terrorism.

CRIMES AGAINST THE GOVERNMENT

In ancient times, most problems within societies were handled informally; the emphasis was on protecting the population from outsiders. As societies became more complex and developed formal laws and governments, they faced the necessity of dealing with their own people who tried to disrupt legal and governmental structures. Additionally, there was the possibility that government and government officials might mistreat citizens; eventually, the crimes discussed in this section emerged.

There are many crimes against the administration of government; this section covers perjury, bribery, official misconduct in office, obstruction of justice, contempt of court, and treason.

Perjury

Under common law, **perjury** covered false statements willfully made under oath in a judicial proceeding. In early common law, the punishment for perjury was death. Later, when the punishment was lessened, the convicted perjurer was not permitted to give sworn testimony in court again.

Today, the elements of perjury vary from jurisdiction to jurisdiction, but the following are generally required:

1. The accused has taken an oath to tell the truth.
2. The oath was administered by legal authority.
3. The oath was taken in a judicial proceeding (or a statutory affidavit).
4. The accused has testified in that proceeding.
5. The testimony is material to the proceeding.
6. The testimony was false.
7. The testimony was given willingly, with the knowledge that it was false and with the intention that it be believed.

Focus 9.1 summarizes recent perjury and related cases that have gained publicity in the media.

Focus 9.1

Perjury and Related Cases in the News

False declarations in judicial and other proceedings are frequently in the news. Here are some recent examples. Roger Clemens, major league baseball pitcher, was indicted in 2010, accused of lying to Congress when he said that he had never used performance enhancing drugs. His first trial ended after two days, when the prosecution introduced evidence that should have been excluded. His second trial began in April 2012, and he was acquitted.

In 2008, Olympic star sprinter Marion Jones was sentenced to six months in prison for perjury after she lied to federal authorities during their investigations of her on two occasions. She was stripped of her records and Olympic titles.

Martha Stewart, who founded the billion-dollar business empire Martha Stewart Omnimedia, was convicted of two counts of lying to federal agents about the sale of her 4,000 shares of ImClone stock shortly before the announcement that ImClone's attempts to market a controversial cancer drug had not been approved. The announcement resulted in a significant decline in the price of the stock; Stewart saved $45,000. Apparently the prosecutors decided they did not have sufficient evidence to convict Stewart of insider trading, as they could not prove that she had advance knowledge of the pertinent events. They did charge her with securities fraud, but the judge dismissed those charges for lack of evidence. Lying to federal authorities, however, along with convictions for obstruction of justice and conspiracy, resulted in a prison sentence for Stewart, who entered prison in the fall of 2004. She was released in March of 2005 and was driven to a private jet to return to her home to begin serving a term of house arrest.

(Continued)

Focus 9.1 (*Continued*)

High-profile athletes and successful businesspersons are not the only ones in the news concerning false statements and the consequences, often expensive to society as well as to the participants. Remember the balloon boy? Richard and Mayumi Heene reported that their five-year-old son, Falcon, had apparently gotten into a balloon before it became airborne and floated for hours as the nation watched. The parents were accused of engaging in this project for attention for a reality show and allegedly knowing that Falcon was hiding in an upstairs area of their home. Even before the balloon landed and the boy was not inside, authorities became suspicious. Richard Heene subsequently pleaded guilty to a felony charge of knowingly and falsely influencing the sheriff. He served 28 days in jail. Mayumi Heene pleaded guilty to a misdemeanor charge of knowingly filing a false report concerning the event and was sentenced to community service. In 2011, Richard Heene offered the balloon for sale on auction to benefit Japan's earthquake and tsunami victims. His lawyer handled the auction; Heene is not permitted to profit from his actions in the balloon incident. The balloon was sold for $2,502.[1]

Such false reports may cost law enforcement (and thus the public) thousands of dollars in rescue efforts. The issue was raised in July 2011, after Casey Anthony was acquitted of the murder of her little daughter in Florida. During the trial, Anthony's defense included a claim that the child drowned in the family's backyard pool; yet she lied to law enforcement and others, claiming that the child was kidnapped by a nanny. The state filed charges to recover the cost of its rescue efforts. The trial judge awarded the state $97,676 of the requested $500,000 for investigating the reported missing child. The judge ruled that the costs should cover only the period when detectives were investigating a missing person and not the homicide investigation.[2]

These and many other cases in the news raise the issue of whether lying to law enforcement, Congress, or anyone else, is becoming more prevalent. Pulitzer Prize–winning author James B. Stewart's new book, *Tangled Webs: How False Statements Are Undermining America: From Martha Stewart to Bernie Madoff*, claims that America is characterized by an epidemic of perjury that has "infected nearly every aspect of society." The book focuses on four criminal cases that received national and international media attention (Martha Stewart and Barry Bonds, both discussed in this focus; Bernie Madoff, discussed earlier in this text; and Lewis "Scooter" Libby, advisor to former Vice President Dick Cheney and convicted of perjury in connection with leaking the name of CIA operative Valerie Plame). Stewart raises the issue of why these individuals would risk their freedom and their careers by lying under oath. His conclusion: "They thought they could get away with it."[3]

---

[1]"Spring Hill Man Sells 'Balloon Boy' Dirigible," *Tampa Tribune* (1 July 2011), p. 6.
[2]"Casey Anthony Must Pay State $97,676," *Dallas Morning News* (16 September 2011), p. 9.
[3]James B. Stewart, *Tangled Webs: How False Statements Are Undermining America: From Martha Stewart to Bernie Madoff* (New York: Penguin, 2011), discussed in "When 'Nothing but the Truth' Is a Lie," *Washington Post* (22 May 2011), p. 1B.

A crime related to perjury is **subornation of perjury**, also a common law crime, which involved obtaining another to commit perjury. It carried the same penalties as perjury. Although the original common law crimes of perjury and subornation of perjury were limited to statements made under official oath in judicial proceedings, as other kinds of sworn statements gained recognition, the English courts developed additional crimes to cover the offenses, but they did not carry the term *perjury*. Many of these false statements were covered by the offense of **false swearing**, which included false statements that would have been perjury but for the fact that they were not made in a judicial proceeding.

Today, both perjury and subornation of perjury are crimes under the federal code, along with the crime of false declarations before a grand jury or court.[1]

In addition to statutes on perjury, subornation of perjury, and false swearing, many jurisdictions have statutes prohibiting offenses such as unsworn falsification to authorities, false alarms to agencies of public safety, false reports to law enforcement authorities, tampering with witnesses and informants or retaliating against them, tampering with or fabricating physical evidence, tampering with public records or information, and impersonating a public servant.

An important point with regard to perjury and related crimes is that these crimes are not frequently prosecuted. For example, in the 2011 Florida trial of Casey Anthony for the capital murder of her child allegedly by using chloroform to sedate her, the prosecution introduced evidence of searches for chloroform on the family computer to which Casey had access. Casey's mother, Cindy Anthony, testified that she personally made those searches. Despite the fact that the evidence revealed that she was at work at the time the searches were made, the prosecution chose not to charge Cindy with perjury.

Bribery

Another offense involving the administration of government is **bribery**. As a common law misdemeanor, bribery was limited to actions concerning judicial officials (a judge or another person performing judicial functions) and applied only to the official who *took* the bribe. By legislation in England, bribery was extended to the bribe giver, as well as to the bribe taker. In addition, the offense was extended to include other public officials, and attempted bribery also became an offense.

Early U.S. common law defined *bribery* to include the giver as well as the taker. Bribery included public officers and anyone else who performed a public function or duty when the gift involved a corrupt intention to influence the discharging of that duty. By statute in many jurisdictions, bribery was broadened so that today the offense also includes quasi-official and occupational bribery.

Current bribery statutes define who may be bribed and require a criminal intent, which is the most important element of the crime, for if it cannot be shown that the giver gave to the official for the purpose of influencing a decision, there is no bribery. If the recipient is the defendant, it must be shown that he or she received the gift with the intent of being influenced in making a decision affecting the one who offered the gift. It is possible, of course, that one party has the requisite criminal intent and the other does not. In that case, only the party with the required intent may be convicted of bribery. Recent bribery cases are discussed in Focus 9.2.

Finally, in cases involving the alleged bribery of a public official, a conviction requires that the money be given to the official to influence action over which that person has *some official* control.

Focus 9.2

High-Profile Bribery Cases

William J. Jefferson, 62, who was defeated for reelection to the U.S. Congress in 2008, was convicted in 2009 of 11 of 16 counts of bribery and other charges. Jefferson was accused of using his office to benefit himself and his family financially. The former Congressman was sentenced to 13 years in prison, but he was free on electronic monitoring pending the resolution of his appeal. All but one charge was affirmed on appeal, and Jefferson was ordered to report to prison. Jefferson was given the longest sentence to date ever assessed for a corruption case involving a member of the U.S. Congress.[1]

In 2011, Mark Ciavarella Jr., 59, a former Pennsylvania juvenile court judge, was sentenced to 28 years in prison, and former county judge Michael T. Conahan was sentenced to 17½ years as a result of their participation in a "kids for hire" scheme. The two men accepted $2.6 million in bribes from the builder of two juvenile detention centers and extorted money from the co-owner of the facilities. As a result of these crimes, the state's supreme court reversed about 4,000 convictions of juveniles on the grounds that Judge Ciavarella violated their constitutional rights in an effort to send them to the two for-profit institutions. After initial guilty pleas by the two defendants, a federal judge accepted the plea bargains in which the defendants faced only 7½ years in prison. That term is below the federal sentencing guidelines. Subsequently, however, the judge rejected the plea agreements, stating that both men had made statements and had taken actions that indicated they were not taking full responsibility for their crimes. In 2011, Conahan was sentenced to 17½ years and Ciavarella to 28 years in prison.[2]

One final example of recent bribery convictions is that of Monica Conyers, former Detroit City Council president, who pleaded guilty to bribery and is serving 37 months in a federal prison camp in West Virginia. In April 2011, a federal judge denied Conyers' request to serve the remainder of her sentence on house arrest. Conyers is the wife of U.S. Representative John Conyers, and her crime involved accepting bribes for her vote in a $1.2 billion sludge disposal deal.

[1]"Jefferson Could Shed 4 Guilty Counts," *Times-Picayune* (New Orleans) (14 December 2011), p. 1.
[2]"Ex-Judge in 'Kids for Cash' Case Gets 17 Years," *Dallas Morning News* (24 September 2011), p. 11; "Justice Ahead: The Supreme Court Responds to Mishandled Youths," *Pittsburgh Post-Gazette* (Pennsylvania) (31 March 2009), p. 4B; "Ex-Judges' Plea Deal Is Rejected," *Philadelphia Inquirer* (1 August 2009), p. 1A.

Bribery may merge with other crimes such as misconduct in office, accepting unlawful gratuities, compounding a crime, conspiracy, obstruction of justice, and extortion. In some cases, the offense in question may be prosecuted as one of these crimes, as bribery, or as both.

A common law crime related to bribery was **embracery**, a misdemeanor referring to a corrupt attempt to influence a juror by means of promises, money, persuasions, or similar techniques. Today a few jurisdictions include embracery as a crime, while others have a separate statute for jury tampering or include the crime within the definition of bribery.

Official Misconduct in Office

Any willful, unlawful behavior by public officials in the course of their official duties may constitute the crime of **official misconduct in office**. This may include the failure to act (*nonfeasance*); engaging in a wrongful act that the official has no right to do (*malfeasance*); or improperly performing an act that the official has a right to do (*misfeasance*).

Official misconduct in office was a common law crime punishable by imprisonment, fine, or, in some circumstances, removal from office. Some offenses, such as bribery, are designated as separate crimes. They are not covered by the crime of official misconduct, although an official may be convicted of both if, after accepting a bribe (the crime of bribery, assuming all the elements are met), the official carries out the bribe, at which point misconduct in office has been committed.

The first requirement for official misconduct in office is that the offender must be a public official or one acting in that capacity. Second, the offender must have an evil intent. An act performed because of ignorance or in good faith will not qualify. The act itself must be an unlawful act of corruption or one of depravity, perversion, or taint—that is, an act requiring an evil intent or motive.[2] Finally, the misconduct must occur during the course of the offender's *official* duties, which, in law, is referred to as **under color of law**, as illustrated by the following federal statute:

> Whoever, under color of any law, statute, ordinance, regulation, or custom, willfully subjects any person of any State, Territory, Commonwealth, Possession, or District to the deprivation of any rights, privileges, or immunities secured or protected by the Constitution or Laws of the United States, or to different punishments, pains, or penalties, on account of such person being an alien, or by reason of his color, or race, than are prescribed for the punishment of citizens, shall be [the statute continues with the penalties.][3]

Corruption in office may take many forms, and the FBI lists public corruption as one of its top priorities, alleging that it "undermines our country's national security, our overall safety, the public trust, and confidence in the U.S. government, wasting billions of dollars along the way."[4]

Public corruption also occurs at state and local levels. The latter is illustrated by the 2010 arrest of six city council members, the mayor, and the former city manager of Bell, California. All of these officials were charged with public corruption, voter fraud, and misuse of public funds in defrauding the residents of that city. Most of the charges related to the high salaries that these public officials appropriated for themselves. All claimed to believe they were operating within the law. In December 2011, the judge, who refused defense motions to drop the corruption charges, declared that ignorance of the law is not a defense and that the defendants "should have known that their conduct was illegal." In February 2012, some felony charges were dismissed. No trial date had been set, and all defendants remained free on bond pending trial.[5]

Obstruction of Justice

In early common law, interference with the orderly processes of the civil and criminal courts was a misdemeanor known as *obstruction of justice*. The crime could take many forms, including tampering with a jury; interfering with an officer who was attempting to perform official duties; suppressing or refusing to produce evidence; intimidating witnesses; and bribing judges, witnesses, or jurors.

These acts and others are recognized today by criminal statutes in most jurisdictions. They may be prosecuted as obstruction of justice crimes or as related crimes such as contempt, conspiracy, perjury, embracery, bribery, or extortion. The crime may be committed by judicial and other officials and might constitute official misconduct in office.

A recent illustration of obstruction of justice was in the news when in December 2011, baseball giant Barry Bonds, who set a home run record, was given a light sentence for his conviction on one charge of obstructing justice. Bonds had been charged with perjury during his testimony before Congress regarding allegations of the use of illegal steroid drugs. Jurors could not agree on the three perjury charges; the judge declared a mistrial and dismissed the charges without prejudice, which meant that the prosecution could refile, but they chose not to do so. Bonds was sentenced to two years of probation, 250 hours of community service, 30 days of home confinement, and a $4,000 fine. Imposition of the sentence was delayed pending Bond's appeal of the conviction.[6]

Contempt of Court

Courts and other institutions have the power to enforce their internal orders and maintain decorum. Persons who refuse to follow these legitimate orders may be cited for **contempt**, which refers to willfully disregarding or disobeying a public official's orders. Florida statutes define *contempt* as, "A refusal to obey any legal order, mandate, or decree, made or given by any judge...relative to any of the business of said court, after due notice thereof."[7] Courts may issue civil or criminal contempt citations, referred to as *contempt of court*.

The U.S. Congress also has contempt powers, referred to as *contempt of Congress*, which can be used against persons who deliberately interfere with Congressional powers and duties as for example, refusing to testify when ordered to do so.

Focus 9.3 presents several examples of contempt citations.

Focus 9.3

Criminal Contempt of Court: Recent Examples

The highly publicized 2011 Florida trial of Casey Anthony for capital murder cap-tured media attention from across the United States and throughout the world. Judge Belvin Perry made it clear from the beginning that he would be in strict control of the trial. A spectator at the trial experienced the reality of the judge's proclamation. Matthew Bartlett, 28, was photographed flipping his middle fin-ger at the prosecutor during a court session. Judge Perry called Bartlett before the bench, asked him what that meant and why he did it; showed him a notice of unpermitted behaviors and asked whether that was posted on the doors into the court room. The judge noted that announcements were also made in court concerning appropriate behavior. Judge Perry held Bartlett in contempt of court and sentenced him to six days in the Orange County Jail, a $400 fine, and $223 in court costs. Bartlett was handcuffed and led away to be held for an hour or so until the judge could process the appropriate paperwork, after which he was taken to jail. Bartlett appealed the order; his appeal was denied.[1]

Later in July 2011, Judge Perry sentenced Mark Schmidter to jail for 141 days and 151 days respectively, for violating two of the judge's orders. One order involved handling out pamphlets outside the courthouse to influence jurors, while the other prohibited First Amendment activities outside the designated "free-speech zones." Media attention had been given to Schmidter's acts of hand-ing out pamphlets earlier in the year, but when he did so during the Casey Anthony trial, Judge Perry cited him for contempt. A trial was held in July, and Schmidter, a local roofing contractor, was convicted of indirect criminal contempt. In addition to the jail term, the defendant was fined $250 for each violation.[2]

In 2009, Clifton Williams, 33, was held in contempt of an Illinois court and was sentenced to six months in jail after he yawned loudly during a sentenc-ing hearing. Judge Daniel Rozak freed Williams, who was brought to court in shackles, after three weeks. The judge told the defendant that he was jailed not only for the yawning but also for a sound "that was offensive to the court." Williams was in court attending his cousin's sentencing on a drug felony charge. The cousin was sentenced to two years' probation.[3]

In 2009, tax attorney Francis X. Moore was sentenced to 20 days in jail when he failed to return to a court hearing after the recess. He was also given a concurrent sentence of 20 days for failure to post $80,000 bond with regard to an attorney fee award. Clayton County (Georgia) Superior Court Chief Judge Matthew Simmons also sentenced Loletha Denise Hale to up to 10 days in jail and removed her from the case after she purposely came to court unprepared because her client had not paid her in full.[4]

---

[1]"Judge Keeps Spectator in Jail: Contempt Order Appealed," *Orlando Sentinel* (Florida) (2 July 2011), p. 9B.
[2]"Man Sentenced in Free-Speech Issue at Court," *Orlando Sentinel* (Florida) (27 July 2011), p. 1B.
[3]"No Babies, No Yawning, No Bears," *Chicago Tribune* (16 August 2009), p. 3C.
[4]American Bar Association, "Judge Jails 2 Attorneys for Contempt in 4 Days," *American Bar Association Journal* (18 November 2009), n.p., http://www.abajournal.com/weekly/judge_jails_2_attorneys_for_contempt_within_4_Days (accessed 20 November 2009).

Treason

Historically, it has been considered that the most serious crimes against the administration of government and its people are those that attempt to overthrow the government. These acts consist of **treason** and related offenses. *Treason,* which means attempting to overthrow the government of which one is a citizen or betraying that government to a foreign power, was thought to be such a serious offense that it was included in the U.S. Constitution, the only crime defined in that document. Article III, Section 3, provides, "Treason against the United States, shall consist only in levying War against them, or in adhering to their Enemies, giving them Aid and Comfort." Congress has the power to define and legislate punishment for treason.[8]

Fewer than 50 cases of treason have been prosecuted in the United States, although some cases involving treasonous acts have been brought under other statutes. For example, Julius and Ethel Rosenberg, who were accused of providing protected information to the Soviet Union during World War II, were convicted of conspiracy to violate the federal espionage act. **Espionage**, or spying, is defined by the federal code as "gathering, transmitting or losing" national defense information with the intent or reasonable belief that the information will be used against the United States. The Rosenbergs were executed in 1953.[9]

Elements of Treason

Treason consists of three elements:

1. An allegiance owed to the government (which may be state or federal)
2. An act that violates the offender's allegiance
3. A criminal intent

A person who is not a U.S. citizen cannot commit treason against the United States because, by definition, treason requires an allegiance to the government. This allegiance requirement applies even if the person has had U.S. citizenship and either lost or renounced it. The owed allegiance must be breached by an overt act. As the Constitution specifies, the allegiance may be breached by levying war against the country or by aiding and comforting the enemy, which may consist of acts such as providing arms and other supplies for the enemy to use against the United States or delivering deserters and prisoners to the enemy.

The criminal intent required for treason may be shown by proving that the accused was aware that the actions in question would assist the enemy in its efforts against the United States. One final constitutional requirement for conviction of treason is a confession in open court or the testimony of two witnesses.

Most states have treason statutes that apply to offenses against their governments. These statutes may not violate the U.S. Constitution's provisions; otherwise, states have discretion in framing their statutes or constitutional provisions regarding treason.

Treason-Related Crimes

The concealment of the known treason of another, called **misprision of treason**, is punishable under federal and most state statutes. Several other offenses are also related to treason. The federal code includes inciting a rebellion against the United States, seditious conspiracy, advocating the overthrow of the government, willfully interfering with the armed forces, recruiting for service against the United States, and enlistment to serve against the United States.[10] State statutes also include related offenses, though some have been held unconstitutionally broad or vague.

Another crime related to treason is **sedition**, which is a communication or agreement aimed at stirring up treason or defaming the government. Generally sedition takes the form of written expression and as such is called *seditious libel,* but some codes also prohibit *seditious conspiracy.*

This brief look at treason and related crimes sets the stage for a more detailed discussion of terrorism.

TERRORISM

According to a noted criminologist, the "very word *terrorism* holds us at attention. To be terrified is a dreadful experience.... [Terror] is an alarming emotion, and to provoke it is to invite alarm." But invoking terror is not always a limited, focused attempt; rather, it may be, and often is, used as a means for social change, and when that occurs, "it invites among us a kind of social alarm, a disturbance of the basic sense of social order."[11]

The Problem of Definition

There is little agreement on a definition of **terrorism**, although most people have a concept of what it means. A broad legal definition is found in the American Law Institute's Model Penal Code (MPC), which defines *terrorist threats* as follows:

> A person is guilty of a felony if he threatens to commit any crime of violence with purpose to terrorize another or to cause evacuation of a building, place of assembly, or facility of public transportation, or otherwise to cause serious public inconvenience, or in reckless disregard of the risk of causing such terror or inconvenience.[12]

Applied to the political arena, terrorism has been defined simply as "motivated violence for political ends."[13] The Task Force on Disorders and Terrorism of the National Advisory Committee on Criminal Justice Standards and Goals (hereafter referred to as The Task Force) defined *terrorism* as "a tactic or technique by means of which a violent act or the threat thereof is used for the prime purpose of creating overwhelming fear for coercive purposes." Terrorism is a political crime, but it may also be a violent personal crime. Terrorist acts are planned in advance, and, to be effective, terrorists must manipulate the community to which the message is addressed. The inculcation of fear is paramount and deliberate; it is the real purpose of the activity, and an audience is important. In this respect, the terror involved in an individual robbery differs from terrorism. In the latter, the immediate victim is not the important focus; the emphasis is on the larger audience.[14]

One final definition of terrorism is relevant. H. H. A. Cooper, an international authority on terrorism, published an article in 2001 in which he referred to his definition of terrorism that had evolved during his 25-year law school teaching career. According to Cooper, "Terrorism is the intentional generation of massive fear by human beings for the purpose of securing or maintaining control over other human beings." He continued, "Terrorism is not a struggle for the hearts and minds of the victims nor for their immortal souls. Rather, it is…about who is to be master, that is all." It is a "naked struggle for power, who shall wield it, and to what ends." Cooper admitted that the definition of terrorism is "as needful and as illusory as ever." But, he said, as with pornography, "we know it well enough when we see it."[15]

Because there is no consensus on the definition of terrorism, it is not possible to recite a particular history of the acts that constitute terrorism. Nor is there agreement on the history of terrorism or who are terrorists.

The Federal Criminal Code

Traditional criminal statutes, such as murder, robbery, or conspiracy, may be used to prosecute terrorist acts. But the federal criminal code and individual state criminal codes contain statutes expressly prohibiting terrorism, along with definitions of the term and related ones.

Title 18, Section 2331, of the federal criminal code contains a section that defines two types of terrorism: international and domestic. Those definitions are as follows:

> (1) the term "international terrorism " means activities that—
>   (A) involve violent acts or acts dangerous to human life that are a violation of the criminal laws of the United States or of any State, or that would be a criminal violation if committed within the jurisdiction of the United States or of any State;
>   (B) appear to be intended—
>   (i) to intimidate or coerce a civilian population;
>   (ii) to influence the policy of a government by intimidation or coercion; or
>   (iii) to affect the conduct of a government by mass destruction, assassination or kidnapping; and
>   (C) occur primarily outside the territorial jurisdiction of the United States, or transcend national boundaries in terms of the means by which they are accomplished, the persons they appear intended to intimidate or coerce, or the locale in which their perpetrators operate or seek asylum;…
> (5) the term "domestic terrorism" means activities that—
>   (A) involve acts dangerous to human life that are a violation of the criminal laws of the United States or of any State;
>   (B) appear to be intended—
>   (i) to intimidate or coerce a civilian population;
>   (ii) to influence the policy of a government by intimidation or coercion; or
>   (iii) to affect the conduct of a government by mass destruction, assassination, or kidnapping; and
>   (C) occur primarily within the territorial jurisdiction of the United States.[16]

State Terrorism Statutes

The California Penal Code, in a section that covers hanging a noose or placing signs on property designed to terrorize individuals, defines the word *terrorize* as "to cause a person of ordinary emotion and sensibilities to fear for personal safety."[17]

California's Penal Code also contains several provisions relating to terrorist acts. Title 7 is called the "Street Terrorism Enforcement and Prevention Act." These statutes are aimed at preventing the terrorism caused by street gangs. The statutes state that, although it is not the intention of the legislature to infringe on the civil rights of anyone in California, the state is under siege with street gangs and all persons in the state are entitled to protection against the terrorist acts of such gangs.[18]

Title 1 of the California Penal Code contains several sections pertaining to permitting the use of weapons of mass destruction, citing these findings:

> The Legislature hereby finds and declares that the threat of terrorism involving weapons of mass destruction, including, but not limited to, chemical, biological, nuclear, or radiological agents, is a significant public safety concern. The Legislature also recognizes that terrorism involving weapons of mass destruction could result in an intentional disaster placing residents of California in great peril. The Legislature also finds it necessary to sanction the possession, manufacture, use, or threatened use of chemical, biological, nuclear, or radiological weapons, as well as the intentional use or threatened use of industrial or commercial chemicals as weapons against persons or animals.[19]

Some states do not include in their statutes specific acts defined as terrorism but, rather, define *terrorism* in general and then indicate that the commission of specific acts under the enumerated conditions constitutes terrorism. Some state statutes specify acts such as the following:

- Hindering prosecution of terrorism in the first degree
- Criminal possession of a chemical weapon or biological weapon in the first degree
- Criminal use of a chemical weapon or biological weapon in the first degree
- Soliciting or providing support for an act of terrorism in the first degree

Some state terrorism and terrorism-related statutes are in direct response to the terrorist acts of 9/11. For example, the Vermont criminal code contains a chapter on Weapons of Mass Destruction in which it declares that state's need for a counterterrorism statute as being required by the events of 9/11. That chapter also states that the purpose of the statute is to protect the state's citizens, not to deny them their civil rights and liberties.[20]

All of these and other statutes must deal with the fact that terrorism may consist of acts or threats, or both, and they must be drafted to account for the fact that modern terrorism may be distinguished from classical terrorism in its original form. First, as the result of our technological vulnerability, the potential for harm is greater today than in the past. This development, which includes improved intercontinental travel and mass communication, has increased the bargaining power of the modern terrorist.

Second, television has carried the activities of terrorists to the entire world, giving modern terrorists more power than classical terrorists. Finally, modern terrorists believe that through violence they can maintain or increase hope for their causes, and they are relentless in their desire to do so.

One tool of modern terrorism is that of the computer. Although much of the potentially dangerous information disseminated through computers can also be located in books or television, the use of the Internet allows more information to be dispersed to more people in a much shorter time and with less risk of detection. Chapter 7 discussed the impact of computers on life in general and on crime in particular. This next section focuses on the use of the computer to commit terrorist threats and acts.

Cyberterrorism

The use of the Internet for terrorist threats is called **cyberterrorism**, which may involve disseminating viruses or even destroying an entire information infrastructure. It does not carry the threats of immediate injury, property destruction, or even death that may result from the other methods of mass destruction, but its harmful effects can be far-reaching and thus frightening.

Chapter 7 covered *identity theft*, which is often committed by use of a computer. This crime can result in severe economic losses to victims, who must spend extensive time and money to repair the damage. Other harmful uses of the computer are:

- Dissemination of information on how to build bombs and other destructive devices
- Information on how to infiltrate or destroy telecommunication networks
- Posting of terrorist propaganda urging action
- Computer viruses
- "Logic bombs, set to detonate at a certain time and destroy or rewrite data"
- "High-energy radio frequency guns that disable electronic targets through high-power radio signals"[21]

FBI Director Robert Mueller referred to a "cyber arms race," in which cyber thieves and law enforcement compete with each other to stay ahead in the race. Mueller emphasized that what might start as a criminal investigation into cyber crime might eventually become a national security threat. "At the start of a cyber investigation, we do not know whether we are dealing with a spy, a company insider, or an organized group."[22]

In fighting cyber crime, the FBI relies not only on local and state law enforcement, but on universities, businesses, intelligence communities, international law enforcement, and others. The agency established the National Cyber Investigative Joint Task Force, which, according to Mueller, brings together law enforcement, intelligence, and defense agencies to focus on high-priority cyber threats. Within the private sector we run InfraGard, where we exchange information with 32,000 partners from private industry.... [But despite these efforts] we are still outnumbered by cyber criminals.... We all have a responsibility to protect the infrastructure that protects the world.[23]

Data on the extent of cybercrimes are difficult to collect, but the President's National Strategy to Secure Cyberspace directs the U.S. Department of Justice (DOJ) to improve data collecting on cybercrimes. Among other initiatives, the DOJ developed the National Computer Security Survey (NCSS) to develop ways to measure the effect of cybercrimes on businesses. In a 2008 report, based on 2005 data, the agency reported that at least 67 percent of its respondents reported some form of cybercrime. The NCSS estimated that U.S. businesses suffered $867 million losses in 2005, with cyber theft accounting for approximately one-half of that loss. "Computer viruses accounted for 193,000 hours and other computer security incidents resulted in more than 100,000 hours of system downtime."[24]

One of the latest developments in cybercrime is that hackers are hacking other hackers, as reported by the *New York Times* in 2011. And in late 2011, hackers who call themselves Anonymous stole credit card numbers, passwords, and home and email addresses and used the personal information to "contribute" to charities. The hacking target was a U.S. think tank, Stratfor Global Intelligence, with alleged clients such as the United Nations, the Miami Police Department, the Bank of America, Doctors Without Borders, and The U.S. Department of Defense.[25]

The Control of Terrorism

After terrorist attacks on U.S. planes skyjacked in large numbers in the 1970s, security measures were required in all U.S. airports, and skyjacking decreased. But terrorists are adaptable, as demonstrated by their planting of bombs *outside* the secure areas of airports. It was obvious on 11 September 2001 that, although efforts to secure airports and aircraft had increased, they were not sufficient to prevent such attacks. The hijackers boarded airplanes carrying box cutters, which were apparently used to subdue and murder flight attendants to get into the cockpits. And even with the increased security that followed those attacks, passengers have boarded planes with knives, guns, and even explosives.

Legislation is a major approach to controlling terrorism. This section considers legislative efforts at the national level and then at state levels.

The National Level

Some of the legislation enacted after 9/11 is based on the recommendations of a national commission that was appointed after those terrorist attacks.

The 9/11 Commission. After the 9/11 terrorist attacks, the U.S. Congress and President George W. Bush created the National Commission on Terrorist Attacks upon the United States, known as the 9/11 Commission. The Commission interviewed more than 1,200 people in 10 countries, held 10 days of hearings, took testimony from over 160 witnesses, and reviewed more than 2.5 million pages of documents. In the summer of 2004, the Commission presented its 567 pages of findings and recommendations to the Congress, the president, and the public, stating:

> We learned about an enemy who is sophisticated, patient, disciplined, and lethal. The enemy rallies broad support in the Arab and Muslim world by demanding redress of political grievances, but its hostility toward us and our values is limitless. Its purpose is to rid the world of religious and political pluralism, the plebiscite, and equal rights for women. It makes no distinction between military and civilian targets. *Collateral damage* is not in its lexicon.[26]

The commission made the following five major recommendations for reorganizing the government:

- "unifying strategic intelligence and operational planning against Islamist terrorists across the foreign-domestic divide with a National Counterterrorism Center;
- unifying the intelligence community with a new National Intelligence Director;
- unifying the many participants in the counterterrorism effort and their knowledge in a network-based information-sharing system that transcends traditional governmental boundaries;
- unifying and strengthening congressional oversight to improve quality and accountability;
- and strengthening the FBI and homeland defenders."[27]

The commission issued its report on 22 July 2004, but it was highly controversial, and many questions remained, not only about the 9/11 Commission report but also about the possibility of additional terrorist acts. Public debate centered on how to secure peace and safety in U.S. airports and other places in which large numbers of people gather. The terrorist acts of 9/11 targeted the United States, but the nation's allies were aware that other countries could be next, and they were correct.

Legislation at the national level also followed the April 1995 terrorist bombing of the federal building in Oklahoma City, Oklahoma. After considerable negotiation, the House and Senate passed a bill, and President Clinton signed it shortly before the first anniversary of the Oklahoma City bombing. It is discussed in the following section.

The Antiterrorism and Effective Death Penalty Act. The Antiterrorism and Effective Death Penalty Act of 1996 is an extensive piece of legislation. It restricts the legal opportunities for death row and other inmates to appeal their sentences. It makes it more difficult for foreign terrorist groups to raise money in the United States and provides for easier deportation of alien terrorists. It authorizes funds for fighting terrorism in the United States. It contains provisions for terrorism victims, such as mandatory restitution, and a provision for victims to have access to closed-circuit television to view a trial that has been moved more than 350 miles from the venue in which they were victimized by a terrorist act.[28]

Additional legislation was also enacted at the federal level as a result of 9/11.

The USA Patriot Act. In the fall of 2001, President George W. Bush signed legislation that expanded the powers of law enforcement to deal with terrorism threats. The **USA Patriot Act** (Uniting and Strengthening America by Providing Appropriate Tools Required to Intercept and Obstruct Terrorism Act of 2001) includes, among others, the following general powers:

- Expansion of wiretaps on terrorist suspects' email, use of the Internet, and telephone conversations
- Tighter controls on immigration
- Tighter control on **money laundering**[29]

The USA Patriot Act was enacted quickly and has been very controversial, but has been renewed.[30]

The Department of Homeland Security (DHS). One of the major federal reactions to 9/11 was President Bush's establishment of the **Department of Homeland Security (DHS)**. Subsequently, the passage of The National Homeland Security and Combating Terrorism Act of 2002 converted DHS into a cabinet-level position, merging 22 agencies into one agency, the most sweeping overhaul of federal government in 50 years.

Among other responsibilities, the DHS coordinates the federal agencies involved in domestic preparedness and emergency planning. It has direct control over the Federal Emergency Management Agency (FEMA), the U.S. Customs Service, the U.S. Border Patrol, and the Coast Guard. The Federal Bureau of Investigation (FBI) and the Central Intelligence Agency (CIA), both keys in the fight against terrorism, were not included. The new agency does, however, have its own intelligence-gathering functions. The legislation also provides for the creation of a White House Office of Combating Terrorism, which is empowered to oversee government-wide antiterrorism policies and coordinate threats, to be in charge of a national strategy to combat terrorism, and to exercise control over the budget for counterterrorism.[31]

To the flying public, perhaps the most important department reporting to the DHS is the one in charge of airport security. Certainly it is one of the most controversial federal agencies.

The Transportation Security Administration (TSA). The **Transportation Security Administration (TSA)** was created by the Aviation and Transportation Security Act (ATSA), enacted in November 2001. It was created to assume the screening functions for all commercial flights, a responsibility that previously had been under the Federal Aviation Administration (FAA), which was restructured by the statute.[32] After initially long waits at most airports, the TSA system has reduced the security time significantly, and most passengers appear to have become accustomed to removing their shoes, coats, and sweaters; taking cell phones, change, and metal out of their pockets; and following the 3-1-1 rule, which limits each passenger's carry-on liquids and gels (excluding prescribed medications and provisions for babies) to those that can be contained easily within a single one-quart see-through zip-lock plastic bag that does not contain any containers of more than three ounces capacity. And although passengers may not bring water through security, they may purchase water inside the secure area of the airport and carry it onto planes. TSA has reduced some of these restrictions for frequent flyers at a few airports. The agency continues to tweak its requirements, but some, such as body scans, remain controversial.

Numerous other counterterrorism acts have been enacted at the federal level, and most states have also enacted counterterrorism measures.

The State Level

An example of a state counterterrorism measure is that of New Jersey, which was passed by both houses of the legislature without a dissenting vote or an abstention. It became effective on 18 June 2003. The legislation has been described as "one of the most sweeping measures passed by a state since the 9/11 attacks, being aimed at terrorists, those who aid them and those whose acts play on public fears of terrorism." The law is viewed as a backup if the federal statutes are deemed invalid or federal prosecutors decline to prosecute.[33] Some of the provisions are as follows:

- The law creates a crime of first-degree terrorism.
- The law criminalizes aiding or harboring terrorists, hindering their apprehension or prosecution, and raising money to support their activities.
- The law establishes a first-degree offense for developing, possessing, using, or threatening to use biological, chemical, or nuclear devices. A person who has legitimate use for these devices can be punished for a second-degree crime for negligent behavior in allowing access to them by an unauthorized person.
- Other provisions of the criminal code, such as aggravated manslaughter, vehicular homicide, producing or possessing chemical weapons, damaging a nuclear plant, carjacking, and disarming a law enforcement officer, are considered terrorist acts if they are committed "with the intent to incite an act of terror, terrorize five or more people; influence government policy or conduct; or interfere with public transportation, public communications, public or private buildings or public services."[34]

The statute includes many other changes to the existing criminal code, all of which are designed to deter terrorism threats.

SUMMARY

This chapter represented a major revision from the previous edition's chapter, as it began with the topics under administration of government, removed from Chapter 8 of the previous edition. This included perjury, bribery, official misconduct in office, obstruction of justice, contempt of court (new to this edition), and treason. All of these crimes make it difficult for governments, including courts, to work effectively and efficiently. New examples were used to illustrate the various crimes, ranging from the bribery convictions of former U.S. Congressman William Jefferson of New Orleans to the contempt of court citation resulting in the jailing of a spectator in the infamous Florida trial and acquittal of Casey Anthony, charged with capital murder in the death of her toddler.

The administration of government is seriously hindered by such crimes as perjury and subornation of perjury. These crimes were originally limited to false statements under oath in a judicial proceeding but have been expanded by statutes to cover other proceedings, such as grand jury and Congressional hearings. Some jurisdictions accomplish the same purpose by enacting separate statutes, such as false swearing or false declaration before a grand jury.

Another offense against the administration of government is bribery. Common law bribery referred to offering, receiving, giving, or soliciting anything of value for the purpose of influencing action by public officials. It referred only to the judge who took the bribe. Modern statutes have extended bribery to include the one who makes or offers the bribe. Some have extended statutes to include people other than public officials. In many cases, bribery is combined with other crimes, such as official misconduct in office or obstructing justice.

This edition of the text included a section on contempt of court, which was illustrated by several recent examples in which judges imposed jail terms on court observers who exhibited behavior unacceptable to their respective judges. The chapter then proceeded to discuss the ancient crime of treason, the highest crime against a government. To be convicted of treason against the U.S. government, a defendant must owe an allegiance to the federal government, an act must be committed that violates that allegiance, and there must be a criminal intent. Two witnesses must testify to the crime unless the defendant confesses. The chapter then turned to an analysis of terrorism.

The 9/11 terrorist attacks on the United States forever changed not only its landscapes but also the lives of people all over the world. No longer can anyone feel safe and secure despite all of the efforts and assurances of politicians and law enforcement officials.

In a real sense, all violent crimes are crimes of terrorism, but this chapter focused on the acts that are most frequently associated with the word *terrorism* today. The section began with a look at the various ways of defining terrorism and then looked at federal and state statutes. It continued with an in-depth analysis of cyberterrorism.

The final section focused on controlling terrorism, looking first at the federal level and the 9/11 Commission. The discussion then turned to the Antiterrorism and Effective Death Penalty Act of 1996, followed by a brief look at the USA Patriot Act. Attention to new federal laws included those that established the Department of Homeland Security (DHS) and the Transportation Security Administration (TSA). The discussion of controlling terrorism closed with a look at one state's approach, that of New Jersey.

STUDY QUESTIONS

1. What is meant by crimes against the government?
2. Distinguish perjury and subornation of perjury.
3. Explain how modern bribery statutes differ from the English common law definition.
4. What is meant by official conduct in office? How does the phrase *under color of law* affect the crime?
5. Explain what is meant by *obstruction of justice.*
6. What is *contempt of* court? Give examples and explain.
7. Explain the elements of treason, and contrast the crime with misprision of treason.
8. What is sedition? What are the First Amendment problems with prosecuting defendants for this crime? Define *espionage.*
9. What does the Antiterrorism and Effective Death Penalty Act of 1996 have to do with terrorism?
10. Why is the USA Patriot Act so controversial?
11. What is the purpose of the Department of Homeland Security (DHS)?
12. What is the purpose of the Transportation Security Administration (TSA)?
13. Analyze the New Jersey approach to controlling terrorism.

FOR DEBATE

This chapter discussed several crimes, all of which create fear in the targeted victims and usually in others. All have potentially enormous impacts on individuals and on the entire society. Yet attempts to deter any or all of these crimes may infringe on individual liberties. With these issues in mind, debate the following resolution.

RESOLVED: Given the significant impact that terrorism and related crimes have on individuals and on society, local, state, and the federal governments should be given extensive powers in their efforts to combat these crimes, even if that means curbing the individual constitutional rights of the accused.

KEY TERMS

bribery   203
contempt   206
cyberterrorism   212
Department of Homeland
   Security (DHS)   215
embracery   205
espionage   208
false swearing   203
misprision of treason   208
money laundering   215

official misconduct in office   205
perjury   200
sedition   209
subornation of perjury   203
terrorism   209
Transportation Security
   Administration (TSA)   215
treason   208
under color of law   205
USA Patriot Act   215

INTERNET ACTIVITY

1. Check the Internet for recent examples of contempt of court citations.
2. The USA Patriot Act is a set of laws passed to give federal agencies new tools to fight terrorism and other crimes. Critics claim that the Act allows the government to invade the privacy of all Americans. Visit http://www.justice.gov (accessed 14 May 2012), to see what you can find out about the U.S. government's position on the Act. In contrast, visit http://www.aclu.org (accessed 14 May 2012), to see what the American Civil Liberties Union states about the controversial Act.

NOTES

1. USCS, Title 18, Sections 1621-1623 (2012).
2. *State v. Seitz,* 14 A.2d 710, 711 (Del. 1940).
3. USCS, Title 18, Section 242 (2012).
4. Federal Bureau of Investigation, "Headline Archives: Public Corruption: Why It's Our #1 Criminal Priority," (26 March 2010), http://www.fbi.gov/page2/mar10/corruption_032610.html (accessed 3 March 2010).
5. "Judge Refuses to Throw Out Bell Charges," *Los Angeles Times* (2 December 2011), p. 3AA; "Some Charges Dismissed Against 2 Ex-Bell Officials," *Los Angeles Times* (29 February 2012), p. 3.
6. "Bonds Bypassing Prison...Cooperstown?" *Arkansas Democrat-Gazette* (Little Rock) (20 December 2011), n.p.
7. Florida Stats., Section 38.23 (2012).
8. The federal treason statute is codified at USCS, Title 18, Section 2381 (2012).
9. *Rosenberg v. United States,* 346 U.S. 273 (1952). The federal espionage act is codified at USCS, Title 18, Section 793 *et seq.* (2012).
10. USCS, Title 18, Section 2383 *et seq.* (2012).
11. Todd R. Clear, "Foreword," in Jonathan R. White, *Terrorism: An Introduction,* 3d ed. (Belmont, Calif.: Wadsworth Thompson Learning, 2001), p. xi.
12. American Law Institute, Model Penal Code, Section 211.3.
13. Brian Crozier, *Terroristic Activity, International Terrorism, Part 4: Hearings Before the Subcommittee to Investigate the Administration of the Internal Security Laws of the Senate Committee on the Judiciary,* 94th Cong., 1st Sess. 180 (1975); quoted in H. H. A. Cooper, "Terrorism: New Dimensions of Violent Criminality," *Cumberland Law Review* 9 (1978): 370.
14. National Advisory Committee on Criminal Justice Standards and Goals, *Disorders and Terrorism* (Washington, D.C.: U.S. Government Printing Office, 1976), p. 3.
15. H. H. A. Cooper, "Terrorism: The Problem of Definition Revisited," *American Behavioral Scientist* 44 (February 2001): 881–893; quotations are on pp. 883, 890, 891, 892.
16. USCS, Title 18, Section 2331 (2012).
17. Cal Pen Code, Title 1, Section 11411 (e) (2012).
18. Cal Pen Code, Title 7, Section 186.21 (2012).

19. Cal Pen Code, Title 1, Section 11416 (2012).
20. V.S.A., Title 13, Section 3501 (2012).
21. Walter Laqueur, *The New Terrorism: Fanaticism and the Arms of Mass Destruction* (New York: Oxford, 1999), pp. 74–75.
22. Federal Bureau of Investigation, Headline Archives, "Operation Phish Phry: Major Cyber Fraud Takedown," http://www.fbi.gov (accessed 10 October 2009).
23. Ibid, p. 2.
24. Ramona R. Rantala, Bureau of Justice Statistics, *Cybercrime Against Businesses, 2005* (September 2008), http://www.bjs.ojp.usdoj.gov (accessed 15 May 2012).
25. "Hackers Hit Security Firm and Donate Stolen Funds," *Boston Globe* (26 December 2011), p. 1.
26. The Commission was established by Public Law 107-306 (27 November 2002). The report is entitled *The 9/11 Commission Report: Final Report of the National Commission on Terrorist Attacks upon the United States,* Authorized Edition (New York: Norton, 2004), p. xvi.
27. *9/11: Commission Report,* pp. 399–400. The Intelligence Reform and Terrorism Prevention Act of 2004 is codified as Public Law 108-458 (2006).
28. Antiterrorism and Effective Death Penalty Act of 1996, 104th Cong., 2d Session, No. 104-518 (1996), codified at USCS, Title 18, Section 2254 (2012).
29. The original USA Patriot Act was Public Law No. 107-56, 115 Stat. 272 (26 October 2001).
30. The revision Reauthorization Act of 2005, Public Law No. 109-177, 120 Stat. 192 (9 March 2006), is referred to as the USA Patriot Improvement and Reauthorization Act of 2005. Some provisions of the Act were reauthorized in 2011. The revised USA Patriot Act is codified at USCS, Title 42, Section 5332 *et seq.* (2012).
31. The Homeland Security Act of 2002 is codified as Public Law 107-296 (25 November 2008).
32. "TSA Meets Deadline; Deploys More Than 44,000 Feds to Airports," *Federal Human Resources Week* 9, no. 32 (5 December 2002): 1.
33. "Sweeping Criminal Law Puts State at Front Line of the War on Terror," *New Jersey Law Journal* (28 June 2002), n.p.
34. The September 11th, 2001 Anti-Terrorism Act is codified at N.J. Stat., 2C:38-1 (2012).

CHAPTER 10

Substance Abuse Crimes

CHAPTER OUTLINE

INTRODUCTION

As emphasized throughout this text, crime is widely recognized as a significant problem in the United States, but there is little agreement over how to cope with it. From time to time, federal, state, and local governments, along with law enforcement agencies, focus on one or more target areas of criminality. Tougher legislation is enacted; police increase their surveillance and arrests; prosecutions are increased; longer sentences are imposed; treatment programs are eliminated; punishment is the key. But, at times, there is a swing back to treatment rather than punishment. This has been the story of the country's reaction to alcohol and other drugs, the focus of this chapter.

One of the issues that Chapter 8 covered was that of public order, which included a discussion on public intoxication and drug incapacitation. This chapter enlarges the discussion of alcohol and other drugs, beginning with a brief look at the prohibition and regulation of alcoholic beverages before turning to the main focus of the chapter: controlled substances. That discussion wrestles with the problem of definitions before turning to an analysis of the prohibitions that criminal law places on controlled substances as well as drug paraphernalia. It considers the manufacture and sale of controlled substances, paying particular attention to the dynamics of drug trafficking. Special attention is given to the abuse of prescription drugs and to fetal abuse caused by drug abuse. A section on the economic cost of drug abuse analyzes data and the lack thereof in this important area.

All elements of criminal justice systems are impacted by drug violations, but in particular, this chapter looks at the relationship of drug offenses to other crimes, the impact of illegal drugs on campus crimes, and the effect that drug violations have on criminal justice systems. The next focus of the chapter is the control of illegal drugs. It looks briefly at forfeiture before analyzing control efforts at the federal and state levels. These discussions include the war on drugs at the federal level; the stringent laws of some states that mandate long sentences for drug possession, such as a small amount of marijuana; and the recent turn toward treatment rather than punishment of drug offenders in a few jurisdictions. In particular, drug courts are featured. Finally, the current efforts to legalize the production, sale, and possession of marijuana for medicinal purposes are highlighted.

The individual criminal law violations that are discussed in this chapter may be, and often are, combined with crimes that the text has already discussed, such as attempt crimes, conspiracy, aiding and abetting, and obstruction of justice. Thus, for example, one might be charged with conspiracy to distribute a controlled substance, for example, cocaine. This chapter's coverage, however, is limited to particular drug-related crimes. Finally, many of the statutes that define drug offenses include the words *with the intent to*, for example, *possession of cocaine with the intent to distribute.*

ALCOHOL PROHIBITION AND REGULATION

Although alcohol is generally recognized as a drug, many discussions of this and other drugs do not include a definition of the terms *drug* or *alcohol*. First, it is important to consider what is meant by the term **drug**. Dictionaries contain several definitions, of which the following is applicable to this text:

> An article intended for use in the diagnosis, cure, mitigation, treatment, or prevention of disease in man or other animals and any article other than food intended to affect the structure or any function of the body of man or other animals.[1]

The first part of this definition refers to the use of drugs for positive reasons—to improve the condition of humans and of other animals. The second part of the definition suggests a negative meaning, and it is that portion that concerns criminal law. Drugs may be used to alter the structure and function of the body, and that may be done in illegal or legal ways but to excess or abuse. It is the *abuse* of drugs that is at issue where society is concerned, but defining **drug abuse** is also difficult. This term may be defined as a "state of chronic or periodic intoxication detrimental to the individual and to society, produced by the repeated consumption of a drug, natural or synthetic."[2]

There is general agreement that alcohol is a drug and that it is the most frequently used of all drugs. *Alcohol* is "a liquid obtained by fermentation of carbohydrates by yeast or by distillation."[3] Alcohol comes in many forms, and it is even considered medicinal by some authorities, who suggest limiting consumption to two drinks per day for men and one for women. However, when used to excess, alcohol, a depressant, may lead to various mental and physical health issues. Nevertheless, in most U.S. jurisdictions, it is legal for adults to possess and to drink alcoholic beverages, although this has not always been the case.

The Eighteenth Amendment to the U.S. Constitution (see Appendix A), which was ratified by the states in 1919 (to become effective one year later), prohibited the "manufacture, sale, or transportation of intoxicating liquors" within the country, along with the importation or exportation of alcohol. The prohibitions of this amendment were widely ignored, and in 1933, the states ratified the Twenty-first Amendment (see again Appendix A), which repealed prohibition.

Alcohol is still regulated today. Its sale is prohibited in some areas; it may not be sold or given to persons considered to be underage, usually under 21; and it may not be consumed under some circumstances (e.g., within so many feet of a place that has a license to sell). The regulations are not always criminal; in fact, many of the regulations concerning alcoholic beverages appear in a special code section, such as *alcohol beverage control law*, rather than in the jurisdiction's criminal code. For example, New York has a statute within its alcohol beverage control law section, entitled *Unlawful Possession of an Alcoholic Beverage with the Intent to Consume by Persons Under the Age of Twenty-one Years*. A person who violates this statute may be required to appear before a court and fined up to $50, ordered to perform community service of up to 30 hours, and required to complete an alcohol awareness program. This particular statute, however, does not give arrest powers to law enforcement authorities. New York, like some other jurisdictions, also includes exceptions, such as excluding minors who are attending a licensed or registered course that requires tasting, along with those whose parents or guardians give them the beverage.[4]

The statutes regulating the possession of alcohol by minors (called *minors in possession,* or MIP) and the methods by which minors obtain alcohol also include such acts as providing false identification to minors or, if a minor, using false identification for the purpose of buying alcoholic beverages. Statutes and ordinances govern which institutions may serve alcohol and under what circumstances. They provide penalties for persons who drive under the influence (DUI) of alcohol or other drugs or who drive with an open container of an alcoholic beverage in the vehicle.

For regulations pertaining to alcoholic beverages that are contained in a section of law other than the criminal code, statutes may provide that under specified circumstances, violation of these regulations could lead to criminal charges, even felonies. Thus, a DUI might be categorized as a traffic violation or offense for the first occurrence, but as a crime for repeat offenses or for an offense that results in the death of another. The latter could also be classified as vehicular or DUI manslaughter, discussed in Chapter 5.

Jurisdictions also regulate drugs other than alcohol.

CONTROLLED SUBSTANCES

The federal government and the various states have the power to regulate the possession and the sale, distribution, and classification of **controlled substances**, which refers to any drug that the statute in question has designated as such. The best known of the controlled substances acts is that of the federal government, the Uniform Controlled Substances Act, which establishes five categories of controlled substances. These categories are listed and explained in the portion of the statute that is reproduced in Focus 10.1. References are made to the information in Focus 10.1 where pertinent throughout the chapter, but it should be noted here that the federal government categorizes controlled substances primarily in terms of their perceived potential for abuse. States are free to devise their own controlled substances acts as long as they do not conflict with the federal statute. The discussion of controlled substances begins with the issue of *possession.*

Possession of Controlled Substances

Governments have the power to regulate the possession of controlled substances. Possession may be actual or constructive. *Actual possession* means that a person has actual physical control over the drug in question. *Constructive possession* occurs when a person who may not have actual possession has the power to possess. Students are probably most familiar with the term *minor in possession (MIP),* which refers to a minor in actual possession of alcohol (or other drugs) but may also encompass all minors in a car (or other designated areas) in which law enforcement authorities find alcoholic beverages, even if not all of those minors know about the illegal beverages. For example, New York has a statute covering *criminal possession of a controlled substance; presumption.* That statute, with a few exceptions, permits a presumption that all persons in an automobile (other than a public omnibus) are presumed to know about the existence of a controlled substance in that vehicle. [5]

Schedule of Drugs in the U.S. Federal System

[The U.S. Congress has categorized drugs into five groups, ranging from the most serious (Schedule I) to the least serious. Included in this focus is the statute defining those five groups. Following this portion of the statute is a very long list of drugs by category. That list is not reproduced because of its length and the fact that this chapter does not consider most of those drugs, but the statute stating the characteristics of each schedule number is reproduced.]

Schedules of Controlled Substances, USCS, Title 21, Section 812 (2012)

    (a) Establishment. There are established five schedules of controlled substances, to be known as schedules I, II, III, IV, and V. Such schedules shall initially consist of the substances listed in this section. The schedules established by this section shall be updated and republished on a semiannual basis during the two-year period beginning one year after the date of enactment of this title [enacted October 27, 1970] and shall be updated and republished on an annual basis thereafter.

    (b) Placement on schedules; findings required. Except where control is required by United States obligations under an international treaty, convention, or protocol, in effect on the effective date of this part, and except in the case of an immediate precursor, a drug or other substance may not be placed in any schedule unless the findings required for such schedule are made with respect to such drug or other substance. The findings required for each of the schedules are as follows:

     (1) SCHEDULE I.

      (A) The drug or other substance has a high potential for abuse.
      (B) The drug or other substance has no currently accepted medical use in treatment in the United States.
      (C) There is a lack of accepted safety for use of the drug or other substance under medical supervision.

     (2) SCHEDULE II.

      (A) The drug or other substance has a high potential for abuse.
      (B) The drug or other substance has a currently accepted medical use in treatment in the United States or a currently accepted medical use with severe restrictions.
      (C) Abuse of the drug or other substances may lead to severe psychological or physical dependence.

     (3) SCHEDULE III.

      (A) The drug or other substance has a potential for abuse less than the drugs or other substances in schedules I and II.
      (B) The drug or other substance has a currently accepted medical use in treatment in the United States.
      (C) Abuse of the drug or other substance may lead to moderate or low physical dependence or high psychological dependence.

(Continued)

Focus 10.1 (*Continued*)

(4) SCHEDULE IV.

(A) The drug or other substance has a low potential for abuse relative to the drugs or other substances in schedule III.

(B) The drug or other substance has a currently accepted medical use in treatment in the United States.

(C) Abuse of the drug or other substance may lead to limited physical dependence or psychological dependence relative to the drugs or other substances in schedule III.

(5) SCHEDULE V.

(A) The drug or other substance has a low potential for abuse relative to the drugs or other substances in schedule IV.

(B) The drug or other substance has a currently accepted medical use in treatment in the United States.

(C) Abuse of the drug or other substance may lead to limited physical dependence or psychological dependence relative to the drugs or other substances in schedule IV.

Statutes prohibiting the possession of controlled substances may be categorized as *felonies* or *misdemeanors,* and they vary in terms of which category they use and the extent of the fines or other sanctions imposed. Marijuana is the most frequently used illicit drug, and a few state statutory penalties, along with the amount of the drug required for those penalties, are noted here. The National Organization for the Reform of Marijuana Laws (NORML) website contains a map of the United States, and you can click on your state and find the penalties for possession of marijuana. The citation is contained in the endnote to the following, which lists a few of the states and their respective categories of the violation, jail or prison time, and amount of fine:

1. California; all possession offenses over 28.5 g are misdemeanors; the highest penalty is for possessing more than 28.5 grams on school grounds by an adult while school is open, a misdemeanor, punishable by incarceration of 6 months and a $500 fine.

2. Texas, 2 to 4 oz., misdemeanor, one year of incarceration, $4,000 fine; 5 to 50 pounds, felony; 2–10 years in prison, $10,000 fine.

3. Vermont, less than 2 oz., first offense, misdemeanor, 6 month sentence, $500 fine; second offense, felony, 2 year sentence, $2,000 fine.

4. New York, 25 g or less (first offense), civil citation; no incarceration; $100 fine.

5. New Hampshire, any amount, misdemeanor, 1 year, $2,000.

6. Idaho, 3 oz. or less, misdemeanor, 1 year, $1,000; more than 3 oz., felony, 5 years, $10,000.[6]

Possession statutes may specify varying degrees of offenses. Offenses may also be classified in terms of intent—for example, *possession with the intent to sell or distribute.*

Possession of Drug Paraphernalia

Criminal laws against possession of a controlled substance may also prohibit the possession of **drug paraphernalia,** which refers to any item, product, or material that could be used to violate the controlled substance statutes of that particular jurisdiction. The statute may require that the accused be in possession of the items *with the intent* to violate a statute designed to regulate controlled substances.

Statutes may also specify that it is illegal to "own, possess, keep or store...any implement or paraphernalia for the manufacture, sale, distribution, bottling, rectifying, blending, treating, fortifying, mixing, processing, warehousing or transportation of alcoholic beverages with intent to use the same" in any one of several illegal ways.[7] Iowa, for example, specifically includes as a felony the act of using drug paraphernalia to transmit HIV.[8]

Finally, the possession of drug paraphernalia may be divided into degrees of seriousness.

The Manufacture, Prescription, and Sale of Drugs

Governments may permit the manufacture, prescription, and sale of drugs, including controlled substances. Thus licensed manufacturers are permitted to manufacture drugs, pharmacists and others are permitted to sell them, and specified medical persons are permitted to prescribe them. Persons under the care of those licensed medical personnel may possess controlled substances without fear of criminal sanctions, provided they follow the rules pertaining to those drugs, which prohibit, among other acts, giving or selling the drugs to others.

Governments may also establish restrictions on the manufacturing, prescription, sale, and possession of alcohol and controlled substances. These restrictions may govern the locations and conditions under which alcohol may be manufactured, how the beverages are packaged and shipped, who may legally transport and accept, the hours of sales, the ages of those permitted to sell, advertising, the size of containers in which beverages may be served, package sales deals, free drinks, sales to intoxicated persons, and many other requirements. With regard to controlled substances, government may regulate many aspects of manufacturing and selling, including, but not limited to, the following:

- Which substances are included within the controlled substances act
- Transportation
- Possession of drug paraphernalia
- Licensing
- Sales by manufacturers and others (such as pharmacies)
- Disposal of drugs
- Record keeping
- Drug prescriptions

- Labeling of drugs
- Drug testing of products and of individuals
- Counterfeit drugs

Governments may also designate persons (such as medical personnel and pharmacists) who are exempt from these restrictions; even then, laws regulate the conditions under which those persons may possess, prescribe, or sell controlled substances. Likewise, individuals are permitted to possess controlled substances when those are prescribed by licensed persons, but if these patients violate the rules regarding that possession, they may be charged, for example, with a crime such as *illegal possession of a prescribed controlled substance.*

Drug Trafficking

Those who violate criminal law statutes regulating the manufacture and sale of controlled substances may also be charged with **drug trafficking**, which is one of the most widespread criminal problems in the world. *Drug trafficking* refers to the illegal sale of controlled substances. Statutes covering drug trafficking may be simple, stating that, for example, a person is guilty of the criminal sale of a controlled substance if he or she knowingly and unlawfully sells a narcotic drug. But such a phrase usually will be followed by a long list of conditions. It may specify the types of drug, and there are many (see Focus 10.2 for a sample). It may specify the amount of the drug that is required for the offense in question; and so on. Often these statutes are written in terms of degrees and may involve the sale of drug paraphernalia as well as of the actual drugs. Other crimes, such as aiding and abetting, attempt

---

Focus 10.2

Drugs: A Sample of Definitions and Facts

Cocaine
"A white crystaline narcotic alkaloid extracted from coca leaves. Used as a local anesthetic. A 'controlled substance' as included in narcotic laws."[1]

Heroin
"Narcotic drug which is a derivative of opium and whose technical name is diacetyl-morphine. It is classified as a Class A substance for criminal purposes and the penalty for its possession is severe."[2]

Marijuana
"An annual herb, cannabis sativa, having angular rough stem and deeply lobed leaves. . . . Marijuana is also commonly referred to as 'pot,' 'grass,' 'tea,' 'weed,' or 'Mary Jane'; and in cigarette form as a 'joint' or 'reefer.' "[3]

Club Drugs
The so-called "Club Drugs," which have become popular in recent years at dances and "raves," are described by the office of National Drug Control Policy as follows:

In recent years, certain drugs have emerged and become popular among teens and young adults at dance clubs and "raves." These drugs, collectively termed "club drugs," include MDMA/Ecstasy (methylenedioxymethamphet-amine), Rohypnol (flunitrazepam), GHB (gamma hydroxybutyrate), and ke-tamine (ketamine hydrochloride).

MDMA is a synthetic, psychoactive drug chemically similar to the stimu-lant methamphetamine and the hallucinogen mescaline.

The tasteless and odorless depressants Ropypnol and GHB are often used in the commission of sexual assaults due to their ability to sedate and intoxicate unsuspecting victims. Ropypnol, a sedative/tranquilizer, is legally available for prescription in over 50 countries outside the U.S. and is widely available in Mexico, Colombia, and Europe. . . .

GHB, available in an odorless, colorless liquid form or as a white powder material, is taken orally, and is frequently combined with alcohol. In addi-tion to being used to incapacitate individuals for the commission of sexual assault/rape, GHB is also sometimes used by body builders for its alleged anabolic effects.

The abuse of ketamine, a tranquilizer most often used on animals, be-came popular in the 1980s, when it was realized that large doses cause re-actions similar to those associated with the use of PCP, such as dream-like states and hallucinations.[4]

[1]*Black's Law Dictionary*, special deluxe 5th ed. (St. Paul, Minn.: West Publishing Co., 1979), p. 233.
[2]Ibid., p. 654.
[3]Ibid, p. 871.
[4]Office of National Drug Control Policy, *Drug Facts*, http:// www.whitehousedrugpolicy.gov/ drugfact/club/index.html (accessed 30 January, 2008), footnotes omitted.

crimes, and conspiracy, may be involved. As these various elements are added, the statutes and the prosecution of violating them become even more complex.

The illegal sale of drugs may be committed by small-time offenders, and they are most frequently the ones who are apprehended and prosecuted, but it is the large sales, often connected to organized crime, that governments target. The statutes designed to control illegal drug trafficking present law enforcement officials with challenges.

Although some illegal drugs are produced in the United States, significant quantities of illegal drugs are smuggled into the country. These illegal drugs are difficult to detect, as they may be concealed in many ways. Drugs are brought into the country by couriers, who have been found with drugs surgically implanted under the skin of their thighs, stuffed in teddy bears, sewn into undergarments, in shoes, or even inside swallowed balloons. Drugs have been shipped inside concrete fencing posts, in packages with bananas or other fruits on top, inside fake bottles or boxes, in plastic packets within fruit, in fruit cans, in asparagus cans, inside dead fish, and by many other means.

Drugs may be airdropped from planes so that the pilot need not land the aircraft to get the drugs to the intended location. Drugs have been hidden in the fuel tanks of cabin cruisers and in van compartments that could only be opened electronically. Suitcases filled with drugs have been found hidden behind interior panels within commercial airplanes, sewn into the interior roof of a station wagon driven by a family pretending to be on vacation, and buried under eight tons of onions in a truck. Further problems arise because of the many points of entry by air, sea, and land and because of the millions of people who cross U.S. borders daily, some of them illegally.

Some drugs are smuggled into the United States (or any other country) in small amounts, which are valuable because of the high price they command. Drugs are also smuggled in large shipments and then are divided and sold to dealers. The purity of the drugs may be diluted. There may be several stages in the processes of receiving, distributing, and selling drugs, and the processes may cover a large geographic area, be highly organized, and involve many people.

Violence is also common in drug trafficking. It is used to reduce or eliminate competition, expand markets, and intimidate anyone who interferes with the trafficking. That includes witnesses, law enforcement officers, and other personnel. Drug informers and anyone who cheats, steals from, or lies to a drug dealer may be killed. Another important characteristic of illegal drug trafficking is that, although a few drug dealers make millions, most are not wealthy. Many of the lower-level dealers are drug addicts whose habits consume their profits; these persons may spend years in jails or prisons while the big drug dealers are not apprehended or, if apprehended, not convicted and incarcerated. Even the small-time sellers, however, create significant problems.

Prescription Drug Abuse

The Office of National Drug Control Policy (ONDCP) classifies prescription drug abuse as the fastest-growing drug problem in the United States. The Centers for Disease Control and Prevention (CDCP) describe prescription drug abuse as an epidemic. National surveys on drug abuse reveal that prescription drug abuse is the second most frequent type of substance abuse (after marijuana) and that over 70 percent of people who abuse prescription drugs got their supply from family or friends for whom the drugs are legally prescribed. Drug-induced deaths are second only to motor vehicle fatalities.[9]

The seriousness of prescription drug abuse has led the ONDCP to develop a prescription drug abuse prevention plan, which is outlined in Focus 10.3.

Fetal Abuse

One of the many problems resulting from prescription drug abuse is that pregnant women give birth to deformed babies, leading some jurisdictions to enact legislation to criminalize **fetal abuse**, which may lead to stillborn babies or babies with serious birth defects.

Focus 10.3

Prescription Drug Abuse Prevention Plan

The Office of National Drug Control Policy (ONDCP) has issued the following prescription drug abuse prevention plan:

- "**Education**. A crucial first step in tackling the problem of prescription drug abuse is to educate parents, youth, and patients about the dangers of abusing prescription drugs, while requiring prescribers to receive education on the appropriate and safe use, and proper storage and disposal of prescription drugs.

- **Monitoring**. Implement prescription drug monitoring programs (PDMPs) in every state to reduce "doctor shopping" and diversion, and enhance PDMPs to make sure they can share data across states and are used by healthcare providers.

- **Proper Medication Disposal**. Develop convenient and environmentally responsible prescription drug disposal programs to help decrease the supply of unused prescription drugs in the home.

- **Enforcement**. Provide law enforcement with the tools necessary to eliminate improper prescribing practices and stop pill mills."

SOURCE: Office of National Drug Control Policy, http://www.whitehouse.gov/ondcp/prescription-drug-abuse (accessed 15 May 2012).

It is estimated that approximately one-half of babies who are born HIV positive or with AIDS "result from injection drug use or sex with injection drug users by the child's mother."[10] Even without being HIV positive or with AIDS, pregnant women who use tobacco, alcohol, or illegal drugs may endanger or even kill their children as a result.

Some jurisdictions have considered prosecuting pregnant women who abuse drugs, but most of these cases have not resulted in convictions. A few examples illustrate. In Illinois, a grand jury refused to indict a young mother whose infant died shortly after birth and whose death was linked to the mother's use of cocaine. The prosecutor's earlier announcement of his intention to bring charges brought serious criticism on the grounds that such action might deter pregnant drug users from seeking prenatal care. The practice was objected to on the privacy issue as well. One attorney questioned, "If the state can create prenatal patrols for cocaine use, then where would they draw the line?"[11]

The Florida Supreme Court held that the state's statute prohibiting delivering drugs to minors was not applicable to the case of a woman who ingested illegal drugs while pregnant and gave birth to a drug-addicted baby.[12]

The Connecticut Supreme Court ruled that a pregnant woman's cocaine injections shortly before she gave birth did not constitute child neglect in the case of her child, who was born suffering from cocaine withdrawal. The court held that the statute did not cover a pregnant woman's prenatal conduct.[13]

Different results occurred in South Carolina, which has the toughest laws on drug use during pregnancy and is the only state in which a woman can be charged with murder for using drugs while pregnant. Regina McKnight, 24, was convicted of homicide by child abuse and sentenced to 12 years in prison after a second trial (the first ended in a mistrial). McKnight used crack cocaine during her pregnancy and gave birth to a stillborn fetus. In 2003, the South Carolina Supreme Court upheld the conviction. The U.S. Supreme Court refused to review the case. McKnight petitioned the trial court for post-conviction relief on the grounds that she had ineffective assistance of counsel. Her motion was denied by that court, but in 2008, the South Carolina Supreme Court reversed that decision.[14]

Prior to the McKnight case, another South Carolina woman, Brenda Kay Peppers, was charged with child abuse after her stillborn baby was found to have cocaine in its bloodstream. Peppers accepted a plea bargain under which she was placed on probation for two years, but she appealed the case to the state supreme court, which vacated her conviction and sentence on technical grounds, thus not reaching other issues.[15]

The U.S. Supreme Court has ruled that pregnant women suspected of drug abuse may not be tested for drugs without their permission if the purpose of the test is to alert police to their substance abuse. According to the Court's ruling in *Ferguson v. Charleston,* even with the possibility that the substance abuse could endanger the fetus, if the woman does not consent or the officials do not have a warrant, a drug test is an unconstitutional search and seizure.[16]

Babies born to women who used prescription drugs, especially pain killers, have difficulty breathing, are extremely sensitive to light and sound, engage in incessant, shrill cries, are underweight, have skin problems, and are more at risk than healthy babies to sudden infant death syndrome. They suffer drug withdrawal symptoms, and doctors use drugs such as morphine or methadone to assist the infants in withdrawal from the drugs they ingested while in utero. The medical effects on the infants may last for years and may even lead to behavioral problems, but the issues with regard to prescription drugs are so new that the long-term impacts are not yet known.

The State of Florida proposed to attack this problem immediately and to establish model legislation and solutions for the nation. The state is focusing directly on the abuse of prescription drugs by pregnant women. The state's attorney general proposed a task force to study the extent of the problem and recommend solutions for what some are calling an epidemic in that state. On 19 April 2012, the state's governor signed legislation establishing the Statewide Task Force on Prescription Drug Abuse and Newborns.[17]

THE ECONOMIC COST OF DRUG ABUSE

The economic cost of drug abuse to individuals and to society is impossible to measure accurately, but there are many facets, the cost of which may be estimated but vary greatly. The federal estimates alone are staggering. The White House National Drug Control Strategy Budget request for 2013 included a total of $25.6 billion, which was an increase of $415.3 million (1.6 percent) over the 2012 budget.[18]

The National Institute on Drug Abuse (NIDA) estimates that the annual cost of substance abuse in the United States is over $484 billion.[19]

The National Council on Alcoholism and Drug Dependence Inc. (NCADD) estimates that each year, more teens enter drug abuse treatment for marijuana than for all other illegal drugs combined, resulting in approximately $190 billion yearly costs to society, including the following:

- "$130 billion in lost productivity
- $20 billion in healthcare costs
- $40 billion in legal costs including efforts to stem the flow of drugs."[20]

THE IMPACT OF ILLEGAL DRUGS

The illegal use of controlled substances has harmful effects on users, their families and friends, and society. Of the many harmful effects of illegal drugs, this section discusses its effect on other crimes, on college and university campuses, and on criminal justice systems.

Relationship to Other Crimes

One of the stated reasons for criminalizing the manufacture, sale, and possession of controlled substances is that substance abuse and drug trafficking have been associated with other criminal acts. Some drug users commit crimes to finance their drug habits. The use of drugs per se may not *cause* these crimes, but the association between drug use and crime must be given serious attention. Table 10.1 contains a summary of the relationship between illegal drugs and other crime.

Social scientists have conducted research on the relationship between drugs and crime, such as between crack cocaine use and crime. Researchers have emphasized that the evidence does not show that drug use *causes* crime—or enslaves drug abusers into crime—for many of the abusers had already engaged in criminal activity before they turned to drugs. But it is argued that "drugs are driving crime. That is, although drug use does not necessarily initiate criminal careers among users it freezes users into patterns of criminality that are more intense and unremitting than they would have been without drugs."[21]

Club Drugs, Alcohol, and Campus Crime

The illegal use of alcohol and other drugs on college and university campuses is extensive, as Focus 10.4 notes. The National Institute on Alcohol Abuse and Alcoholism (NIAAA) posts on its website information about the risks of drinking by college and university students between the ages of 18 and 24. Focus 10.4 contains the most recent data.

Table 10.1   Drugs and Crime: A Summary of Their Relationship

Drugs/Crime Relationship	Definition	Examples
Drug-defined offenses	Violations of laws prohibiting or regulating the possession, use, distribution, or manufacture of illegal drugs.	Drug possession or use. Marijuana cultivation. Methamphetamine production. Cocaine, heroin, or marijuana sales.
Drug-related offenses	Offenses to which a drug's pharmacologic effects contribute; offenses motivated by the user's need for money to support continued use; and offenses connected to drug distribution itself.	Violent behavior resulting from drug effects. Stealing to get money to buy drugs. Violence against rival drug dealers.
Drug-using lifestyle	A lifestyle in which the likelihood and frequency of involvement in illegal activity are increased because drug users may not participate in the legitimate economy and are exposed to situations that encourage crime.	A life orientation with an emphasis on short-term goals supported by illegal activities. Opportunities to offend resulting from contacts with offenders and illegal markets. Criminal skills learned from other offenders.

SOURCE: Office of National Drug Control Policy, *Drug-Related Crime* (Washington, D.C.: U.S. Government Printing Office, March 2000), p. 1.

One of the results on college campuses, when alcohol and other drugs are involved, is that date rape may occur. Date rape is often associated with the use of club drugs. Focus 10.5 notes the use of the club drug *Ecstasy* in date rape. A second club drug, GHB (gamma hydroxybutyrate), is even more closely associated with date rape. In fact, GHB is often called the *date rape drug* because it is odorless and colorless and, when slipped into a drink, can cause the victim to lose consciousness within 20 minutes and usually have no memory of subsequent acts, such as rape. The impact of GHB has led to legislation against it.

In 2000, President Bill Clinton signed into law a bill that toughened the penalties for possessing and distributing GHB. This statute places GHB in the category of drugs that receive the highest regulation by the federal Controlled Substances Act, Schedule I (see again Focus 10.1) and provides for a prison term of up to 20 years for anyone convicted of manufacturing, distributing, or possessing GHB.[22]

The Reducing Americans' Vulnerability to Ecstasy (RAVE) Act of 2002 was passed and signed into law by President George W. Bush in April 2003. RAVE cracks down on persons who put teenagers at risk of using Ecstasy or other club drugs by prohibiting renting, leasing, or profiting from any place in which the drugs are used. RAVE provides both civil and criminal penalties.[23]

Over 20 states have also enacted legislation to regulate club drugs, but one of the problems with some of the new statutes that prohibit the possession and sale

---

Focus 10.4

Substance Abuse and the College Campus

The National Institute on Alcohol Abuse and Alcoholism (NIAAA) posts on its website the following information concerning college students between the ages of 18 and 24 and drinking.

- **Death**: 1,825 die from alcohol-related unintentional injuries, including motor vehicle crashes.
- **Injury:** 599,000 are unintentionally injured under the influence of alcohol.
- **Assault:** 696,000 are assaulted by another student who has been drinking.
- **Sexual Abuse**: 97,000 are victims of alcohol-related sexual assault or date rape.
- **Unsafe Sex:** 400,000 had unprotected sex and more than 100,000 report having been too intoxicated to know if they consented to having sex.
- **Academic Problems**: About 25 percent report academic consequences of their drinking including missing classes, falling behind, doing poorly on exams or papers, and receiving lower grades overall.
- **Health Problems/Suicide Attempts:** More than 150,000 develop an alcohol-related health problem, and between 1.2 and 1.5 percent indicate that they tried to commit suicide within the past year due to drinking or drug use.
- **Drunk Driving**: 3,360,000 drive under the influence of alcohol.
- **Vandalism:** About 11 percent report that they have damaged property while under the influence of alcohol. . . .
- **Police Involvement:** About 5 percent are involved with the police or campus security as a result of their drinking, and 110,000 are arrested for an alcohol-related violation such as public drunkenness or driving under the influence.
- **Alcohol Abuse and Dependence:** 31 percent met criteria for a diagnosis of alcohol abuse and 6 percent for a diagnosis of alcohol dependence in the past 12 months, according to questionnaire-based self-reports about their drinking."

SOURCE: National Institute on Alcohol Abuse and Alcoholism (NIAAA), citations and "college students between the ages of 18 and 24" omitted, http://www.collegedrinkingprevention.gov/StatsSummaries/snapshot.aspx (accessed 15 May 2012).

---

of club drugs is that substitute drugs have been developed to avoid the reach of the statutes. To combat this problem, some statutes include chemicals that have "substantially similar structures or substantially similar effects" to the named club drugs. Statutes may also prohibit specific sexual acts with someone placed under

========== **Focus 10.5** ==========

Ecstasy, the Club Drug

On 24 March 2011, Gil Kerlikowske, Director of the National Drug Control Policy, issued a press release emphasizing that there had been a significant increase in recent years in the number of people admitted to U.S. emergency rooms after using the illegal drug Ecstasy.[1]

Ecstasy (also referred to as MDMA)[2] is a synthetic drug that was used by some doctors to facilitate psychotherapy; however, in 1988, the U.S. Congress designated the drug as a Schedule I (see again Focus 10.1) substance under the federal substance control laws. In recent years Ecstasy, also referred to as a club drug, has been used primarily at all-night dance parties (called raves), but it has recently moved to such venues as private homes, shopping malls, high schools, and college dorms. The drug, which is usually taken orally in pill form, produces a psychedelic effect that can last for several hours. The drug is also a stimulant.

Ecstasy may produce psychological effects such as confusion, depression, anxiety, sleeplessness, drug craving, and paranoia. The drugs may also produce physical reactions, such as muscle tension, involuntary teeth clenching, nausea, blurred vision, faintness, tremors, rapid eye movement, and sweating or chills. Persons who use Ecstasy at raves are at a higher risk of the side effects that may occur when the drug is used in hot, crowded situations, combined with the long hours of dancing users have the capability of doing. Possible side effects are dehydration, hyperthermia, heart, and kidney failure. The drug may cause damage to the parts of the brain that are associated with thought and memory. Death may also occur.

The effects of using Ecstasy may linger for a long time. Repeated use of the drug may cause long-term neuropsychiatric problems and major physical health problems. Some of the side effects of the drug, such as problems with sleep or mood, anxiety disturbances, and even memory deterioration, "may persist for up to two years after the user ceases taking the drug."[3]

Men who use the drug in combination with Viagra to enhance their sexual abilities may face a greater risk of stroke and heart attack. This combined use is also associated with a higher risk of contracting diseases, such as HIV.[4]

The Ecstasy Anti-Proliferation Act of 2000 instructed the U.S. Sentencing Commission to recommend increased penalties for trafficking in MDMA. The new penalties, which became effective 1 November 2001, increased by 300 percent the penalty for trafficking 800 MDMA pills from 15 months to 5 years. The penalty for selling 8,000 MDMA pills was increased nearly 20 percent, from 41 months to 10 years.[5]

[1] Office of the White House Drug Policy, "Statement from White House Drug Policy Director Gil Kerlikowske Regarding Dramatic Rise in Ecstasy-Related Emergency Room Visits," http://www.whitehousedrugpolicy.gov/mobile/032411.html (accessed 11 July 2011).

[2] Unless otherwise noted, the information in this focus is summarized or quoted from Office of National Drug Control Policy, Drug Policy Information Clearinghouse, Fact Sheet: MDMA (Ecstasy), February 2004, http://www.streetdrugs.org/pdf/MDMA2004.pdf (accessed 25 November 2008).

[3]"Chronic Ecstasy Use May Promote Long-Term Neuropsychiatric Damage," *Alcoholism & Drug Abuse Weekly* 14, no. 30 (5 August 2002): 6.

[4]"Men Combining Viagra, Illicit Drugs, to Heighten Sexual Experience," Alcoholism & Drug Abuse Weekly 13, no. 33 (3 September 2001): 8.

[5]The Ecstasy Anti-Proliferation Act of 2000 is codified as Section 3663 of Pub. Law 106-310 (2006).

the influence of the date rape or a similar drug as the felony of aggravated indecent assault (or some other offense).

Effect on Criminal Justice Systems

Every aspect of criminal justice systems is impacted by drug abuse and efforts to control it. Courts are crowded, creating a backlog of cases in the civil division as the courts try to process those in the criminal division. More defense lawyers, prosecutors, judges, and court staff are needed, along with courtrooms and other facilities.

Illegal drugs also present all criminal justice system personnel with some of their most frustrating problems. The escalation of drug trafficking results in corruption, violence, enormous expense, and a crushing blow to all elements of criminal justice systems.

Drug cases in criminal justice systems have an impact on the courts. A significant number of cases before trial and appellate courts, including the U.S. Supreme Court, involve drug-related issues. In sheer numbers, the drug cases coming before courts are staggering, and many penal facilities are overcrowded in part because of the number of drug offenders sentenced to serve time or awaiting trial for drug abuse offenses. Although overall prison population growth has slowed in recent years, federal populations increased 3.4 percent between 2008 and 2009, and although the number of drug offenders in state prisons decreased by 12,400 (7.8 percent) between 2000 and 2008, the total number of inmates in state prisons who were serving terms for drug offenses in 2008 was almost as high as the combined number of serious property offenders. The 2011 BJS report on 2010 U.S. inmates revealed that 51 percent in the federal system were incarcerated for drug offenses.[24]

The U.S. Sentencing Commission (see Chapter 11) issued this statement with regard to overcrowded prisons and jails:

> Changes in sentencing law and policy, not increases in crime rates, explain most of the six-fold increase in the national prison population. These changes have significantly impacted racial disparities in sentencing, as well as increased the use of "one size fits all" mandatory minimum sentences that allow little consideration for individual characteristics.[25]

The Sentencing Commission emphasized that in 2010, over 60 percent of the inmates in U.S. prisons were racial and ethnic minorities. On any given day, one out of every eight U.S. black males in their twenties was in prison or jail, and three-fourths of all persons incarcerated for drug offenses were persons of color. The Sentencing Commission, citing two studies, attributed these disproportionate numbers to the U.S. war on drugs, especially the crack/cocaine sentence disparity.[26] Chapter 11 discusses the role of that commission in changing this disparity.

Illegal drugs also have a negative impact on law enforcement officials, who face the problem of fighting illegal drugs with inadequate resources while being tempted by drug offenders.

THE CONTROL OF ILLEGAL DRUGS

Various approaches are used in the national effort to control illegal drugs, one of which is to confiscate money and property through a procedure known as *forfeiture,* which permits the government to order that the personal or real property acquired from money derived through the illegal acts be turned over to the government. Approximately 100 federal statutes permit forfeitures even though the accused may never be formally charged with a crime. Forfeitures are also permitted under many state statutes. Forfeitures may occur without prior notice, and the individual who wants the property back usually has the burden of proving that it should not have been confiscated. Under some statutes, before a hearing will be held on that issue, the owner of the forfeited property must post a bond for a specified percent of the value of the property.

The U.S. Supreme Court has shown some concern with the potential unfairness of forfeitures. The Court has ruled that the value of seized property must not be excessive when compared to the seriousness of the crimes in question. The Court views the forfeiture of property as punishment and applies the cruel and unusual punishment clause of the Eighth Amendment (see Appendix A) to the analysis of forfeitures.[27] However, the Court has also upheld the forfeiture of property belonging to an innocent owner who was not aware that the property would be used in a crime. The case involved a woman who was co-owner of a car in which her husband was apprehended while having sex with a prostitute. The state forfeited the wife's interest as well as her husband's interest in the car even though she did not know of her husband's illegal acts.[28]

In recent years, however, efforts to control drug-related crimes in the United States have focused primarily on long prison sentences. For example, several sections of the Violent Crime Control and Law Enforcement Act of 1994 involved enhanced penalties for drug offenses, including drug trafficking within prisons.[29]

Long sentences for drug offenses must be considered in terms of their total impact on criminal justice systems. It is expensive to investigate and prosecute drug trafficking cases because of the sophisticated techniques required for intelligence gathering. Trials are long and complicated. Drug traffickers are known to intimidate or kill witnesses. Potential danger to witnesses requires the government to protect them. Expensive monetary rewards are used to entice witnesses to give information that will lead to the indictment and arrest of high-level drug traffickers. Nevertheless, prison sentencing remains the primary approach in the drug control strategy.

The Federal Level

The major attempt to control high-level drug trafficking is at the federal level, and the efforts are relatively recent. In the latter half of the 1800s and the early part of the 1900s, drugs could be purchased in the United States by anyone without penalty. In 1914, the Harrison Act was enacted for the purpose of recording the sale of drugs and as a tax measure. It did not prohibit the prescribing of drugs by a physician. However, early court cases ruling against physicians who prescribed drugs for addicts apparently frightened physicians from the practice, although the cases involved an *abuse* of discretion by the participating physicians. The result was that drugs became increasingly difficult to get from physicians and the supply was driven underground. In 1951, the Boggs Act was passed, providing stiff mandatory minimum sentences for drug offenses. In 1956, the passage of the Narcotic Drug Control Act provided even stiffer penalties. In 1970, the Comprehensive Drug Abuse Prevention and Control Act was passed. This act, generally referred to as the Controlled Substances Act, among other provisions, established the five categories, called *schedules,* of controlled substances, as described earlier (see again Focus 10.1). Other federal statutes have been enacted in recent years, but the overall approach of the federal government's efforts to control drugs is generally referred to as the *war on drugs.*

The U.S. War on Drugs: A Brief History

President Richard M. Nixon initiated the war on drugs in the early 1970s, and it was continued by President Ronald Reagan and his administration. In June 1982, President Reagan appointed a 19-member special group of government agency heads and instructed them to report back to him with suggestions on how to fight illegal drugs. Four years later, the President signed the Anti-Drug Abuse Act of 1986, which increased penalties for federal drug-related offenses and provided funding for alcohol and drug abuse treatment, prevention, and rehabilitation programs. This legislation has withstood some constitutional challenges.[30]

As another part of the war on drugs, Congress passed the Anti-Drug Abuse Act of 1988. This act directed the president to examine the extent and nature of the drug problem and to propose policies for dealing with it. The Office of National Drug Control Policy (ONDCP) was established within the executive office of the president. The federal drug-control strategy also contained provisions for federal grants to state and local agencies for law enforcement purposes, along with numerous provisions for attempts at drug enforcement. It was praised strongly by some and criticized bitterly by others, but no significant effects were seen in the fight against illegal drugs. In an effort at greater control over drug violations, Congress increased penalties for drug offenses in its comprehensive crime act, the Violent Crime Control and Law Enforcement Act of 1994.[31]

The war on drugs has been hotly debated. Critics argue that the war denies to some sick people the drugs needed for treatment, noting that drugs such as marijuana and heroin are helpful in the treatment of cancer pain, nausea due to radiation and chemotherapy, and glaucoma (an eye disease that results in the loss of vision and can cause blindness). The legalization of marijuana for medicinal purposes is discussed later in this chapter.

The war on drugs is also expensive, costing billions of dollars while showing little success. Illegal drugs are still readily available, drug addiction remains a serious problem, and the association between drug abuse and violent and property crimes remains. Further, illegal drug trafficking associated with organized crime in general and drug gangs in particular continues to be a cause of great concern both inside and outside U.S. prisons.

Another issue that should be considered in the war on drugs is whether the government's approach has a differential impact on persons of color and the poor. Three scholars who analyzed National Institute of Justice publications concerning drug control concluded that the war on drugs perpetuates the image of the poor and minorities as a criminal class. The scholars concluded that "minorities and the poor are affected disproportionately by drug control campaigns, which lead to their overrepresentation in arrests, prosecutions, convictions, and incarcerations." They alleged that the studied reports "not only ignore the scholarly literature on race, class, and drugs but also fail to include research by other government agencies…that document such biases in drug control." The scholars proposed that this is a form of government propaganda—"the distortion of information for the purpose of influencing social action."[32]

Other areas of racial discrimination with regard to the drug war have been suggested. In particular, the 100:1 ratio for penalties of crack compared to powder cocaine, a ratio that impacts negatively on African Americans, is suggested. In May 2007, the U.S. Sentencing Commission recommended to Congress that the sentence guidelines for crack cocaine be lowered. Congress did not reject those recommendations and, as provided by law, they became effective in November 2007, reducing the average sentence from 10 years and 1 month to 8 years and 10 months. In December 2007, the Sentencing Commission voted unanimously to apply the new guidelines retroactively. As a result, 19,500 crack cocaine offenders who were sentenced under the original and harsher guidelines may petition to have their sentences lowered. Chapter 11 discusses the most recent changes in cocaine sentencing policies at the federal level.

In addition to differential penalties, African Americans have argued that they are more often selected for drug prosecutions. In 1996, the U.S. Supreme Court faced the issue but ruled that a defendant who alleges racial bias regarding prosecutorial discretion must show that similarly situated persons of other races were not prosecuted. This case involved crack cocaine, and the Supreme Court held that the appellants did not show *actual* racial bias in the prosecutions of that crime.[33]

Subsequent presidents tried different drug policies, but drug trafficking and substance abuse remained serious problems. Brief attention is given to the presidential approach in effect at the time of this writing.

Recent White House Drug Control Policies

In May 2009, President Barack Obama's choice for national drug czar, R. Gil Kerlikowske, police chief of Seattle, Washington, was confirmed and announced that he would focus the U.S. drug policy on reducing the demand for illegal drugs. In May 2010, Kerlikowske released President Obama's first *National Drug Control Strategy*; in July 2011 he released the update of that strategy; and in April 2012 he published the latest drug strategy. Kerlikowske emphasized that the administration was building on the previous two strategies and continuing to focus on the following areas:

- "preventing illicit drug use and addiction before their onset;
- bringing more Americans in need of treatment into contact with the appropriate level of care;
- protecting public safety while also ensuring that drug-involved offenders have the opportunity to end their drug use and rebuild their lives;
- countering drug production and trafficking within the United States;
- implementing new strategies to secure our borders against illicit drug flows;
- working with our international partners to reduce drug production and trafficking and strengthen rule of law, democratic institutions, transparency in government, alternative livelihoods, and respect for human rights around the world."[34]

The 2012 *Strategy* built on the 2010 and 2011 foundations and noted the progress the Obama administration believes it has made as it emphasized law enforcement, drug prevention, and a public health approach, among other goals. The Obama drug strategies focus on populations that are disproportionately affected by drug abuse: college and university students, women and their families, active-duty military and veterans, and individuals already in criminal justice systems. A primary focus is early intervention, along with diversion of nonviolent drug offenders and the expansion of drug treatment programs and facilities. The proposed budget for 2013 is $9.2 billion, which is an increase of 4.6 percent over the 2012 enacted federal level.[35]

The recent significant changes in federal drug sentencing are discussed in Chapter 11, as they involve the U.S. Sentencing Commission, which is covered in that chapter. Recent state changes in drug sentences, however, are discussed in the following section.

The State Level

Although many drug offenses are handled at the federal level, state and local control are also important. Jurisdictions vary significantly in the offenses included, as well as in the sentences that may be (and in some *cases must* be) imposed. For years, New York has had the harshest drug laws and is the focal point in this discussion.

Mandatory Sentencing

Mandatory sentencing statutes were typical of the harsh sentencing efforts to control drug trafficking as well as the use of illegal drugs. New York's efforts are illustrative.

Statutes that went into effect in 1973 in New York increased the penalties for drug possession and the sale of drugs. Called the Rockefeller laws, after Governor

Nelson Rockefeller (a popular governor who believed in the deterrence nature of stiff laws), these statutes were passed with two purposes in mind: (1) to frighten drug users and drug dealers into quitting, and (2) to curb drug-related crimes. A report of the results, published in 1977, concluded that neither goal had been met. The study by the state bar association and a drug abuse council concluded that, in addition, "it is implausible that social problems as basic as these [that cause drug use and sales] can be effectively solved by the criminal law."[36]

The study of the effects of tough drug laws in New York also revealed a significant increase in court congestion, increased costs of all criminal justice court-related matters, and overcrowding of jails and prisons. Crimes related to drug use did not go down; rather, some crimes (such as theft, robbery, and burglary)—often associated with heroin users—increased faster in New York than in some neighboring states.[37]

New York state judges openly criticized the stiff laws. In imposing a mandatory minimum sentence of 15 years to life on a defendant convicted of possessing four ounces of a controlled substance, one trial judge said, "I am obliged to enforce the law, however stupid and irrational and barbarous it be." A report of judicial reaction to New York's drug laws cited other judges making similar comments. Among other problems, they noted, the long mandatory sentences discouraged defendants from exercising their constitutional right to a trial, for if they were convicted, the sentence had to be imposed. Some of the sentences were longer than those for murder. Because of the harshness of the sentences upon conviction, many defendants would plead guilty to a lesser offense (some even if they were not guilty) to avoid taking the risk of being convicted and being assessed the long mandatory sentence.[38]

In December 2004, the New York legislature passed a bill to reform portions of the Rockefeller laws, and Governor George Pataki signed the bill into law, to become effective 13 January 2005. In addition to expanding drug treatment in prisons, the statute reduced sentences for most nonviolent first offenders and for some nonviolent repeat offenders, eliminated life terms for certain offenses and permitted residential treatment after a portion of a sentence is served, and permitted resentencing for inmates who are serving terms of 15 years to life.[39]

In subsequent years, other changes were made to the Rockefeller laws, but in 2008, one editorial proclaimed, "The Rockefeller Drug Laws Still Need Fixing."[40] Specifically, it was argued that the legislature should return some sentencing discretion to judges and remove the long mandatory sentences. According to one group that monitors New York prison conditions, in 2008 it was costing the state over $500 million a year to incarcerate its drug offenders, 4 out of 10 of whom were convicted for possession, not selling drugs. Many of those persons were drug addicts who might benefit from treatment rather than incarceration, but under the harsh mandatory sentencing policies, that is not possible.[41] The New York legislature did make some of those changes in 2009, giving judges greater discretion in sentencing drug offenders, shortening the sentences of some nonviolent drug offenders, expanding drug treatment and alternatives to incarceration, and permitting the resentencing of approximately 1,500 inmates who were sentenced under the original Rockefeller laws. The revisions increased sentences for selling drugs to a child.[42]

Other states also have long mandatory minimum sentences for drug offenses, and although these sentences may have been designed to incarcerate the hard-core traffickers for years, that has not been the result. An analysis of the 58,000 drug convictions won by local prosecutors in the Houston, Texas, area revealed that 77 percent involved defendants who had less than a gram of a drug in their possession. Of these "small-time offenders," 35,000 were sent to jail or prison. According to the local paper, "The numbers suggest that these men and women are collateral damage in the war on drugs, arrested because they were easy targets rather than objects of a grand strategy."[43]

Such results have been confirmed on a national basis by the Sentencing Project, which stated on its website that over one-half of inmates serving prison time for drug offenses have no history of "high-level" drug acts (importing drugs and distributing them to dealers) and no history of violence. Furthermore, three-fourths of all inmates serving time for drug offenses are persons of color.[44] The Sentencing Project posted an analysis of sentencing changes, noting, among others, that three states had reduced the use of mandatory minimum sentences for drug offenses.[45]

Mandatory minimum drug sentences, especially long ones for minor, nonviolent offenders, are under fire in many jurisdictions. Such laws were repealed in Michigan in December 2002. A newswire from that state announced:

> Public Acts 665, 666 and 670 of 2002 eliminate most of the state's Draconian mandatory minimum sentences for drug offenses. Judges can now use sentencing guidelines to impose sentences based on a range of factors in each case, rather than solely drug weight, and lifetime probation for the lowest-level offenders has been replaced with a five-year probationary period. Earlier parole is now possible for some prisoners, at the discretion of the parole board.[46]

The result of such changes is a greater emphasis on drug treatment.

Substance Abuse and Treatment
One approach to controlling drug abuse is to reduce or discontinue punishment and focus on treatment. The treatment approach is seen in the reactions of some jurisdictions, which are moving toward providing treatment and rehabilitation rather than prosecuting substance-abuse violations under the criminal law.

The treatment approach is illustrated by the following Idaho statute:

> It is the policy of this state that alcoholics, intoxicated persons or drug addicts may not be subjected to criminal prosecution or incarceration solely because of their consumption of alcoholic beverages or addiction to drugs but rather should be afforded treatment in order that they may lead normal lives as productive members of society.[47]

The statute continues with the declaration that the government should utilize state and federal resources to facilitate research of and treatment for alcoholism and drug addiction.

Perhaps the boldest example of a return to treatment of drug offenders is that of California. California's Proposition 36, providing for treatment for first or second minor drug offenses, took effect in 2001. The new proposition does not apply to persons who sell or manufacture, but it does apply to minor drug offenders who violate their parole. Funds provided for treatment may not be used for drug testing, and once an offender has completed his or her treatment program, the conviction is dismissed.[48]

Although California continues to face severe budget problems and funding treatment for drug offenders is an issue, the estimates are that, according to a state-sponsored study mandated by the legislation and conducted by the Drug Policy Alliance (DPA), California saved $1.4 billion in the first five years of Proposition 36. The director of DPA's Sacramento office declared,

> This study proves that treatment is the most humane and cost-effective approach to addiction. Now the pressure is on the legislature and the governor to continue this program to help California save more lives and more money.[49]

By far the most promising nationwide move toward treatment of substance abusers is the use of drug courts.

Drug Courts

Drug courts, which are based on a diversion and treatment approach to substance abusers, were begun in 1989 in Miami, Florida. These courts constitute an alternative to traditional prosecution in criminal courts, and most nonviolent defendants arrested on drug possession charges are funneled into these courts where they exist. The drug court has been described as follows: "Supervised by a sitting judge, a drug court is an intensive, community-based treatment, rehabilitation, and supervision program for drug defendants."[50]

In the 1994 federal criminal code revision, Congress included a provision for federal drug courts and for grants to states to develop drug courts.[51] By 2001, drug courts were in operation in all states, the District of Columbia, Puerto Rico, Guam, and two federal districts.[52] In May 2011, President Barack Obama issued a statement in observance of National Drug Court Commencement Week in which he emphasized that drug courts play a critical role in his administration's efforts to "break the cycle" of drug use and crime.[53]

Drug court programs vary in size and type, with some focusing on the addiction problems of offenders and others concentrating on those problems as well as on reintegrating those offenders back into their families. In California, for example, some drug courts specialize in reintegrating children back into their families after the children have been removed because of the abusive behavior of their addicted parents. Family drug courts also exist in other jurisdictions.[54]

This renewed emphasis on treatment, both at the state and the national level, especially of substance abusers, is enhanced by the changes in the way some people today view marijuana—at least for medicinal purposes.

LEGALIZING MARIJUANA FOR MEDICINAL PURPOSES

Many people agree that some aspects of substance abuse should be included in the criminal law. The production and sale of dangerous narcotics are examples. There is not much agreement, however, on the criminalization of the possession of small amounts of drugs such as marijuana, the use of which is considered by many people to be a private matter. Others say the drug is dangerous.

As of 30 July 2012, 17 states and Washington, D.C., had legalized the use of marijuana for medicinal purposes.[55] The movement to legalize the medicinal use of marijuana was led by California. In 1996, that state's voters passed Proposition 215, which legalized the use of marijuana by seriously ill persons, with a physician's prescription. It is argued that patients suffering from AIDS, glaucoma, cancer, and other illnesses can benefit from the use of marijuana, and that some of these patients cannot find any other pain reliever. In reaction to Proposition 215, the Oakland Cannabis Buyers' Cooperative was organized to provide for the distribution of marijuana to such people. But, in the federal system, marijuana is a Schedule I drug (see again Focus 10.1); thus, there are no legal reasons for its sale or use other than approved research. Subsequently, the district court enjoined (told it to stop) the cooperative, but the group refused and was held in contempt of court. The Ninth Circuit Court of Appeals ruled that the necessity defense (see again Chapter 4) applies in such cases. Thus, a medical need would constitute a defense to prosecution of the federal controlled substances statute.

In 2001, the U.S. Supreme Court reversed the Ninth Circuit and held that the necessity defense is not applicable to the use of marijuana for medicinal reasons. The Court emphasized that when Congress enacted the federal Controlled Substances Act, it allowed only one exception to the use of marijuana: It is permitted for government-approved research projects. The avoidance of an exception for medical necessity, ruled a unanimous Supreme Court, means that Congress did not intend that exception. The issue was not resolved, however. Government prosecutors did not want to pursue violators in criminal courts because the penalties for drug violations were so severe. They petitioned the court in California to issue an **injunction** prohibiting providing marijuana for medical reasons. The court issued first a temporary and then a permanent injunction.[56]

The injunction permitted the government to process any violators (i.e., those who grow, sell, or use marijuana for medicinal purposes) through the civil courts and thus avoid the potential of a harsh prison term as is required by the federal statute. The challenge now for those who believe that marijuana should be permitted for medicinal reasons is to convince Congress to amend the Controlled Substances Act. That will not be an easy job.

In 2005, the U.S. Supreme Court, by a 6–3 vote, ruled that Congress has the authority to enact legislation to regulate the growth of marijuana by persons who use it for medicinal reasons.[57]

Significant changes in 2011 are noted in ending this discussion on legalizing marijuana for medicinal purposes. By the end of 2011, federal agents were cracking down on those who make considerable profits by growing and distributing marijuana for medicinal purposes in California. The U.S. Department of Justice (DOJ) had indicated in 2009 that although the medical use of the drug is illegal under federal law, federal prosecutors would not generally pursue those who provided marijuana for ill patients with prescriptions. But in late 2011, federal agents began conducting raids of some dispensaries.[58]

On 1 November 2011, two state governors petitioned the federal government to reclassify marijuana from its current position as a Schedule I drug (see again Focus 10.1). Governor Christine Gregoire of Washington and Governor Lincoln Chafee of Rhode Island argued that this action is needed to enable their respective states to regulate the use of marijuana for medicinal purposes without fear of federal intervention and prosecutions. According to these two governors, "The divergence in state and federal law creates a situation where there is no regulated and safe system to supply legitimate patients who may need medical cannabis."[59]

Finally, in July 2011, researchers were seeking approval from the federal government to use marijuana in a study of its effects on veterans who suffer from chronic posttraumatic stress disorder (PTSD). According to one of the researchers, "These are people whom we put in harm's way, and we have a moral obligation to help them."[60]

SUMMARY

Drug abuse and drug trafficking have been serious problems in the world for years, and this chapter explored many of the issues associated with drugs. It began with a discussion of the historical prohibition and regulation of alcohol and looked at today's legal processing of alcohol-related offenses, including regulating the sale of alcohol to minors.

The chapter's main focus was on the regulation of controlled substances, beginning with an analysis of the crime of *possession*. The regulation of drug paraphernalia was also included in the chapter, along with an analysis of statutes that regulate the manufacture, prescription, and sale of drugs, with special attention given to drug trafficking, prescription drug abuse, and fetal abuse.

Although the exact relationship between drugs and crime is not and may never be known, and it is reasonable to assume that in some cases drug abuse does not involve criminal activity, it is obvious that drugs and crimes are associated. In particular, the chapter presented information on the relationship between illegal drugs and problems on college and university campuses. The use of club drugs was noted, followed by an examination of federal and state laws concerning such drugs. The effect of illegal drugs on criminal justice systems was also featured. Courts are crowded with the trials of persons accused of drug violations, creating backlogs among civil trials, which must wait for the criminal trials. Drug case appeals, usually involving procedural issues, are a growing problem, resulting in additional burdens on courts. Law enforcement officers face daily temptations from drug abusers, especially those who traffick in drugs; most officers refuse to become involved, but a few succumb.

It is, however, the *control* of illegal drugs that is a major focus today. The discussion began with the efforts at the federal level, analyzing the U.S. war on drugs historically and looking closely at the national drug policies of the administration of President Barack Obama. Likewise, the efforts of states to control drug trafficking and illegal possession were noted, especially the harsh sentencing laws that were, and to some extent still are, part of New York's drug control efforts.

Recently, a return to treatment efforts has evolved. Some people are realizing that long prison sentences have not reduced the drug problem but have created other problems for social institutions. The current emphasis in some jurisdictions on treatment rather than punishment of substance abusers, at least at some levels, was discussed. Special attention was given to the developments in California, where statutes now provide for treatment rather than punishment for nonviolent first and second drug offenses. The treatment approach is often combined with the use of drug courts (rather than the usual adult criminal courts) for processing drug offenders. Financing, however, remains an issue.

The final section of the chapter looked at recent efforts to legalize the use of marijuana for medicinal purposes, an effort that has led to a battle between states (especially California) and the federal government. The U.S. Supreme Court has ruled that the fact that California voters passed an initiative permitting the restricted use of marijuana for medicinal purposes does not provide a defense against prosecution for violating the federal statutes prohibiting such use. The government secured an injunction against the providing of marijuana for medicinal purposes, and this approach permits prosecutors to file civil actions against those who violate the federal statute, thus avoiding the more severe criminal penalties. The U.S. Supreme Court refused to review the case. In 2005, the U.S. Supreme Court ruled that Congress has the right to enact legislation to regulate the growth of marijuana, refusing to permit it for persons who wish to use it, even for medicinal purposes. At the end of 2011, two governors petitioned the federal government to reclassify marijuana from its current position as a Schedule I drug, as this is chilling state efforts to regulate the drug's use for medicinal purposes.

The war on drugs will continue at the federal level; states will also explore ways to combat drugs at their levels; drug education will be a priority. The success of any of these measures, however, is not so obvious. Reducing drug abuse and drug trafficking will take enormous work on the part of local and state governments as well as the federal government, but it will also take a massive effort on the part of private institutions as well as the family. Those efforts have been hindered to some extent by harsh sentencing policies, which are explored more thoroughly in the next chapter.

STUDY QUESTIONS

1. Why is alcohol considered a drug, and what is the history of regulating it?
2. Define the terms *drug, drug abuse, drug trafficking,* and *drug paraphernalia.*
3. Describe current issues with prescription drug abuse.
4. Define *fetal abuse* and discuss legal efforts to combat it.
5. What is the economic cost of drug abuse in the United States?
6. What is the relationship between illegal drug offenses and other crimes?
7. What are the issues surrounding the use of alcohol and other drugs on college and university campuses?
8. What is Ecstasy, and why is this drug dangerous? What changes have been made in legislation concerning this drug?

9. What is meant by *club drugs,* and what can be done to negate their impact on young people?
10. What is the relationship between drug offenses and criminal justice systems? In particular, how do drug offenses affect jail and prison overcrowding?
11. What is meant by *forfeiture?*
12. Assess the success or failure of the U.S. war on drugs, and make recommendations for the future.
13. Discuss the current White House approach to drug abuse and trafficking.
14. What are the arguments that the war on drugs discriminates against minorities?
15. Based on your reading of the material in this chapter, what do you think Congress and state legislatures should do about drug laws?
16. What should be the role of treatment in the war against drugs?
17. Discuss the nature of drug courts.
18. Should the use of marijuana be permitted for medicinal purposes? For any other reasons? Why or why not? What are the recent legal developments regarding these issues?

FOR DEBATE

The use of marijuana for medicinal purposes is permitted by statute in 16 states and the District of Columbia, but federal prosecutors have succeeded in nullifying those statutes, in effect, by obtaining an injunction in California, along with a U.S. Supreme Court ruling concerning the use of marijuana for medicinal purposes. In view of these developments, debate the following resolution, and in your debate consider the implications of your position on other social and/or legal issues.

RESOLVED: The federal government should reclassify marijuana from its current position as a Schedule I drug and thus remove the chilling effect that statute has on states that have legalized the use of marijuana for medicinal purposes.

KEY TERMS

controlled substances 224
drug 223
drug abuse 223
drug paraphernalia 227

drug trafficking 228
fetal abuse 230
injunction 245

INTERNET ACTIVITY

1. Since 1975, the University of Michigan, with the aid of federal funding, has conducted annual surveys of alcohol and drug use among teens (8th, 10th, and 12th graders). Check out the Monitoring the Future website at http://www.monitoringthefuture.org/ (accessed 15 May 2012), and find out the latest data on substance abuse. Is substance abuse down in any areas?

What are the trends in cigarette use among teens? How do the results reported by this survey compare to your recollection of the situation in your high school? What do you think the future holds for substance abuse among teens?

2. Assess the website of the U.S. Office of National Drug Control Policy (ONDCP), http://www.whitehousedrugpolicy.gov, and contrast its position on the legalization of marijuana to that of the National Organization for the Reform of Marijuana Laws (NORML), http://norml.org/ (both accessed 16 May 2012).

NOTES

1. *Black's Law Dictionary*, special deluxe 5th ed. (St. Paul, Minn.: West Publishing, 1979), p. 446.

2. *Black's Law Dictionary*, p. 446.

3. *Street Drugs: A Drug Identification Guide* (Plymouth, Minn: Publishers Group, 2004), p. 76.

4. NY CLS Al Bev, Section 65-c (2012).

5. NY CLS Penal, Section 220.25 (2012).

6. The National Organization for the Reform of Marijuana Laws (NORML), http://www.norml.org/ (accessed 28 July 2012).

7. See N.J. Stat., Section 33:1-50 (2012), Manufacture, sale, possession, etc., in violation of chapter; misdemeanor.

8. Iowa Code, Section 709C.1 (2012).

9. Office of National Drug Control Policy, "Epidemic: Responding to America's Prescription Drug Abuse Crisis" (April 2011), p. 1, citations omitted, http://www.whitehouse.gov/ (accessed 15 May 2012).

10. National Institute on Drug Abuse (NIDA), "Magnitude: Drug Abuse Is Costly," citation omitted, http://archives.drugabuse.gov/about/welcome/aboutdrugabuse/magnitude/ (accessed 15 May 2012).

11. "Here Come the Pregnancy Police," *Time* (22 May 1989), p. 104.

12. *Johnson v. State,* 602 S0.2d 1288 (Fla. 1992).

13. *In re Valerie D.*, 613 A.2d 748 (Conn. 1992).

14. "Woman Is Convicted of Killing Her Fetus by Smoking Cocaine," *New York Times* (18 May 2001), p. 12; *State v. McKnight,* 576 S.E.2d 168 (S.C. 2003), *cert. denied,* 540 U.S. 819 (2003), *and post-conviction relief granted, McKnight v. State,* 661 S.E.2d 354 (2008).

15. *State v. Peppers,* 552 S.E.2d 288 (S.C. 2001).

16. *Ferguson v. Charleston,* 532 U.S. 67 (2001).

17. "More Newborns Hooked on Drugs," *Tampa Tribune* (Florida) (31 July 2011), p. 1 Metro. See H.B. 227 (2012).

18. Office of White House Drug Policy, *National Drug Control Strategy: FY 2013 Budget and Performance Summary,* (April 2012), p. 1, http://www.whitehouse.gov/sites/default/files/ondcp/fy2013_drug_control_budget_and_performance_summary.pdf (accessed 28 July 2012).

19. National Institute on Drug Abuse, "Magnitude."

20. National Council on Alcoholism and Drug Dependence, Inc., "FAQs/Facts," http://www.ncadd.org/index.php/learn-about-drugs/faqsfacts (accessed 15 July 2012).

21. James A. Inciardi and Anne E. Pottieger, "Drug Use and Street Crime in Miami: An (Almost) Twenty-Year Retrospective," in *The American Drug Scene,* 3d ed., ed. Inciardi and Karen McElrath (Los Angeles: Roxbury Publishing, 2001), pp. 319–342; quotation is on pp. 337–338.

22. The Controlled Substances Act is codified at USCS, Title 21, Section 812 (2012).

23. Comprehensive Drug Abuse and Prevention Act of 1970, USCS, Title 21, Sections 801-966 (2012).

24. William J. Sabol et al., Bureau of Justice Statistics Bulletin, *Prisoners in 2006* (Washington, D.C.: U.S. Department of Justice, Office of Justice Programs, December 2007), pp. 5–6, 9; Heather C. West and William J. Sabol, Department of Justice, Bureau of Justice Statistics, *Prisoners in 2007* (December 2008), p. 1; http://bjs.ojp.usdoj.gov/content/pub/pdf/p07.pdf (accessed 12 July 2011); Department of Justice Press release (11 December 2008), http://ojp.usdoj/gov/bjs/pub/press/p07ppuspr.htm (accessed 11 March 2009); Heather C. West *et al.,* Bureau of Justice Statistics, *Prisoners in 2009* (December 2010), p. 1, http://bjs.ojp.usdoj.gov/content/pub/pdf/p09.pdf (accessed 11 July 2011); Paul Guerino *et al.,* Bureau of Justice Statistics Bulletin, *Prisoners in 2010* (December 2011), http://bjs.gov/content/pub/pdf/p10.pdf (accessed 15 May 2012).

25. The Sentencing Project, "Sentencing Policy, http://www.sentencingproject .org/ (accessed 15 May 2012).

26. The Sentencing Project, "Racial Disparity," http://www.sentencingproject .org/ (accessed 15 May 2012). The studies are The Human Rights Watch report, *Targeting Blacks: Drug Law Enforcement and Race in the United States,* http//www.hrw.org/sites/default/files/reports/US0508_1.pdf (accessed 15 May 2008); and Ryan S. King, The Sentencing Project report, *Disparity by Geography: The War on Drugs in America's Cities* (May 2008), http://www .sentencingproject.org (accessed 15 May 2012).

27. See *Austin v. United States,* 509 U.S. 602 (1993); and *Alexander v. United States,* 509 U.S. 544 (1993).

28. *Bennis v. Michigan,* 516 U.S. 442 (1996).

29. Violent Crime Control and Law Enforcement Act of 1994, Public Law 103-222 (13 September 1994). See Title IX, Drug Control.

30. Anti-Drug Abuse Act of 1986, Section 1 *et seq.,* 100 Stat. 3207; USCS, Title 21, Section 801 (2012). See *United States v. Jackson,* 863 F.2d 1168 (4th Cir. 1989).

31. Violent Crime Control and Law Enforcement Act of 1994, Public Law 103-222 (2012). See Title IX, Drug Control.

32. Michael Welch *et al.,* "Decontextualizing the War on Drugs: A Content Analysis of NIJ Publications and Their Neglect of Race and Class," *Justice Quarterly* 15 (December 1998): 719–742; quotations are on p. 734.

33. *United States v. Armstrong*, 517 U.S. 456 (1996).
34. Office of White House Drug Policy, *National Drug Control Strategy: FY 2013 Budget and Performance Summary* (April 2012), p. 1, http://www.whitehouse.gov/sites/default/files/ondcp/fy2013_drug_control_budget_and_performance_summary.pdf (accessed 28 July 2012).
35. Ibid, p. 2.
36. National Institute of Law Enforcement and Criminal Justice, *The Nation's Toughest Drug Law: Evaluating the New York Experience: Final Report of the Joint Committee on New York Drug Law Evaluation* (Washington, D.C.: U.S. Government Printing Office, 1977). The statutes are codified at New York Penal Code, Section 220.00 *et seq.* (2011).
37. Association of the Bar of the City of New York, News Release (21 June 1977).
38. "Many New York Judges Oppose Strict Drug Laws, Report Says," *Criminal Justice Newsletter* 31, no. 23 (24 December 2001): 4.
39. Thomas Adcock, "New Effort Is Vowed to Ease Drug Laws," *New York Law Journal* (7 January 2005), p. 16.
40. "Trying to Slide out of Town," *New York Times* (7 June 2008), p. 16.
41. "Thirty-Five Years of Rockefeller 'Justice,'" *New York Times* (27 May 2008), p. 22.
42. See N. Y. Law, Section AB 156/SB56 (2012).
43. "War on Drugs Nets Small-Time Offenders," *Houston Chronicle* (15 December 2002), p. 1.
44. The Sentencing Project, "Racial Disparity."
45. Nicole D. Porter, The Sentencing Project, *The State of Sentencing 2009: Developments in Policy and Practice* (March 2010), p. 1, http://www.sentencingproject.org/doc/publications/s_ssr2009Update.pdf (accessed 28 July 2012).
46. "Mandatory Minimum Drug Sentences Toppled in Michigan," *U.S. Newswire* (27 December 2002), n.p.
47. Idaho Code, Section 39-301 (2012).
48. The California Statute for First and Second-Time Drug Offenders, Cal Pen Code, Section 1210.1 (2012).
49. Drug Policy Alliance, "Prop. 36 Saved California $1.4 Billion in First Five Years," (6 August 2008), http://www.drugpolicy.org (accessed 15 May 2012).
50. Office of National Drug Control Policy, *Drug Treatment in the Criminal Justice System* (March 2001), http://www.whitehousedrugpolicy.gov/publications/pdf/94406.pdf, p. 4. (accessed 30 January 2008).
51. See Sections 50001-50002 of the Violent Crime Control and Law Enforcement Act of 1994, Public Law 103-322 (2012).
52. Office of National Drug Control Policy, *Drug Treatment in the Criminal Justice System*, p. 4.
53. Office of National Drug Control Policy, "President Obama: Drug Courts Are Smart Investments," (16 May 2011), http://ofsubstance.gov/ (accessed 11 July 2011).
54. "Innovative Drug Court Program Offers Early Intervention, Reunites Families," *Alcoholism & Drug Abuse Weekly* 14, no. 27 (15 July 2002): 1.

55. The National Organization for the Reform of Marijuana Laws (NORML), http://norml.org/marijuana/medical (accessed 28 July 2012).

56. *United States v. Oakland Cannabis Buyers' Cooperative,* 532 U.S. 483 (2001), *injunction granted sub nom.,* 2002 U.S. Dist. LEXIS 10660 (N.D.Cal. 10 June 2002).

57. *Gonzales v. Raich,* 545 U.S. 1 (2005).

58. "Medical Marijuana Trade Shaken by Crackdown," *New York Times* (24 November 2011), p.1.

59. "2 Governors Asking U.S. to Ease Rules on Marijuana to Allow for Its Medical Use," *New York Times* (1 December 2011), p. 19.

60. "Marijuana May Be Studied for Combat Disorder," *New York Times* (19 July 2011), p. 15.

CHAPTER 11

Sentencing

Internet Activity
Notes

INTRODUCTION

The first chapter of this text contained a brief discussion of the historical reasons for punishment: revenge, retribution, deterrence, incapacitation, and rehabilitation, noting that rehabilitation lost its position of prominence during the latter part of the twentieth century (although there are some signs of interest in this philosophy today). In its place are retribution (or just deserts), deterrence, and incapacitation. These are philosophies of sentencing or punishment, and all have had a place of importance at some period in history. Their positions change as other social, economic, and political conditions change. The philosophy in vogue at any given time is reflected in the nature and types of sentences that society uses for convicted offenders.

In recent years, however, we have seen some changes. Considerable attention has been given to criminal justice reform but especially to sentencing. In many jurisdictions, the emphasis on punishment rather than rehabilitation, along with the concern that sentencing should be more uniform, has led to significant changes in the type and nature of punishment, with punishment now a stated goal, as illustrated in Focus 11.1. That focus features an excerpt from the Washington Penal Code, which states several purposes of punishment. Although Washington enacted that revised code in 1981, the last purpose of punishment, to reduce the risk of reoffending, was not added until 1999.

Focus 11.1

Legislative Statement of the Purpose of Sentencing

Until recently, many state statutes did not include the purposes of sentencing. The movement away from the rehabilitative ideal and the indeterminate sentence toward a sentencing philosophy based on just deserts and deterrence, however, has been reflected in some of the revised codes.

In 1981, Washington enacted a comprehensive revision of its criminal code, the Sentencing Reform Act of 1981, in which the legislature for the first time stated the purpose of sentencing. The emphasis is on retribution, or just deserts. Specifically, the legislature made the six declarations in the first section of the sentencing act (the seventh statement was added in 1999):

> The purpose of this chapter is to make the criminal justice system accountable to the public by developing a system for the sentencing of felony offenders which structures, but does not eliminate, discretionary decisions affecting sentences designed to:
>
> (1) Ensure that the punishment for a criminal offense is proportionate to the seriousness of the offense and the offender's criminal history;

(2) Promote respect for the law by providing punishment which is just;

(3) Be commensurate with the punishment imposed on others committing similar offenses;

(4) Protect the public;

(5) Offer the offender an opportunity to improve himself or herself;

(6) Make frugal use of the state's and local governments' resources; and

(7) Reduce the risk of reoffending by offenders in the community.[1]

---

[1] Rev. Code Wash., Section 9.94A.010 (2012).

Many procedures and issues regarding sentencing could be discussed, but space and the purpose of an undergraduate text impose limitations. This chapter focuses on several of the more recent trends in sentencing and sentencing reform as well as some of the legal issues posed by these measures. But first, the chapter contains a brief overview of how sentences are determined.

DETERMINING SENTENCES

A **sentence** is the judgment pronounced formally by the court and imposed on a defendant who pleads guilty or who is found guilty after a trial. The type and length of the sentence may be determined legislatively, judicially, or administratively. The models discussed in the next section are important to an understanding of sentencing. Today it is popular to criticize judicial sentences when, in some cases, the traditional judicial discretion has been removed and judges are applying the law as they must. In other cases, judges do have discretion concerning sentence length, but they have that discretion because it is provided by law.

Sentencing Models

Most sentencing involves a combination of sentencing models, but for analytical purposes, each model must be defined.

In the *legislative model*, the type and length of sentence for each crime are determined by the legislature and specified in the criminal statute(s). In the purest form of this model, no discretion is permitted in sentencing. For example, a statute may provide that upon conviction of first-degree burglary, a defendant must be sentenced to 10 years in the state prison. That term cannot be reduced. Such a sentence established by the legislature is called a **determinate sentence**, in contrast to an **indeterminate sentence**, in which the legislature either does not set a term, leaves the decision to judicial discretion, or sets minimum and maximum terms and permits judges to set the actual sentence in each case. In either case, the legislature may establish sentences for categories of crimes (e.g., Class A felonies, Class B felonies) or for individual crimes (e.g., first degree-murder, second-degree murder, etc.).

Legislative and Congressional sentences vary widely, but some general comments are applicable. The text has already noted that crimes are usually defined as *misdemeanors* or *felonies*. Some jurisdictions also add the term *violations,* referring, for example, to driving infractions, but those generally are not crimes, although they might become so with multiple violations or with aggravating circumstances, such as driving while impaired. Categories may also be used for designating punishment. Texas offers an example of one approach, designating a range of penalties for each of its misdemeanor and felony categories. Texas has three misdemeanor categories, designated as Class A, Class B, and Class C. Penalties for Classes A and B involve a jail or prison term or a fine, or both. The penalties range from a fine not to exceed $4,000 and a jail term not to exceed one year for a Class A misdemeanor to a fine not to exceed $500 for a Class C misdemeanor. Felonies are classified, along with their respective penalties, as follows:

- Capital felony, life in prison or execution
- First-degree felony, 5 to 99 years or life imprisonment
- Second-degree felony, 2 to 20 years imprisonment
- Third-degree felony, 2 to 10 years imprisonment
- State jail felony, 180 days to 2 years in a state jail

For all of these, with the exception of capital felony, the state also provides for a fine of up to $10,000. Additionally, the Texas Penal Code provides exceptions. Specifically, there are punishment provisions for repeat and habitual offenders, for reducing a state jail felony to a misdemeanor punishment, and for increasing a penalty if a judge or a jury finds evidence of bias or prejudice.[1]

Penalties for criminal acts may also be specified for each crime, for example, 10 years in prison for anyone convicted of armed robbery. Or the legislature could specify a range of penalties for this or any other crime.

The second type of sentence model is the *judicial model.* In its purest form, judges are the only determiners of sentences. In reality, the pure forms of legislative and judicial sentencing rarely occur. Even during the push for determinate sentencing, most legislatures established ranges of possible sentences, as, for example, the Texas Penal Code cited earlier, and left some discretionary sentencing power with judges. Some retained at least part of the third model, the *administrative model,* in which parole boards may grant early releases or prison administrators may reduce time served for inmates who do not violate prison rules. The administrative model was prominent during the period in which the philosophy of rehabilitation was popular. It was based on the belief that the best way to determine when inmates were rehabilitated and thus should be released was to place that decision in the hands of the professionals who were most familiar with the inmates' progress (or the lack thereof) during incarceration.

Under any sentencing model, the power to determine the length of sentences may be altered by other factors. Power may be given to the governor (or the president, in the case of federal crimes) to reduce a sentence, to commute a life sentence to a term of years, or to commute a death sentence to life, a process called **clemency**. The governor (or president) may also have the power to grant a **pardon**, an act of grace that exempts the offender from punishment (or further punishment, if some time has already been served). Some legislatures also give governors authority to order the release of inmates when prisons reach their court-imposed maximum populations. This permits the system to incarcerate new (and presumably more dangerous) inmates.

Presumptive Sentencing

In **presumptive sentencing** the legislature specifies the normal sentence for each crime, and judges are permitted to deviate only under specified types of circumstances, by giving written reasons, or both. Presumptive sentencing is based on the assumption that once a person is found guilty of a particular crime, it is reasonable to impose a specified sentence unless significant reasons are found for not doing so. Presumptive sentencing enables the legislature to "retain the power to make those broad policy decisions that can be wisely and justly made about crime and do not involve the particulars of specific crimes and criminals." At the same time, it allows the sentencing judge "some degree of guided discretion to consider and weigh those pertinent factors that cannot be wisely evaluated in the absence of the particular crime and criminal."[2]

Sentencing Guidelines

Presumptive sentencing may be accomplished through the use of **sentencing guidelines**. These guidelines may be viewed as a way to control judicial discretion without abolishing it and as a means of correcting the disparity that can result from individualized sentencing. Basically, here is what happens. A judge has an offender to sentence. Without sentencing guidelines, the judge may consider the individual's background, the nature of the offense, or other accepted variables. When sentencing guidelines are used, the relevance of the variables considered may have been researched and quantified. In addition, the judge has a benchmark of an appropriate penalty in each case. The judge may decide that it is reasonable to deviate from the guidelines in some cases; in those situations, reasons should be given.

Guidelines need not be based on previous sentences. They may be developed on the basis of any reasons deemed appropriate. Some jurisdictions have experimented with appointing advisory committees, usually consisting of judges, to develop voluntary sentencing guidelines. They may also have sentencing guidelines established by the legislature, while providing for appellate judicial review of the application of those guidelines. Judicial review would be available to the prosecution as well as to the defense. This approach is illustrated by recent reforms at both the state and the federal levels.

State Sentencing Guidelines

State sentencing guidelines differ from state to state, and any attempt to summarize them could be misleading. The Washington state sentencing guidelines are used to illustrate state approaches.

After much controversy and a five-year study, the Washington state legislature enacted its Sentencing Reform Act of 1981, described by one scholar as "the most comprehensive—and in many respects the most thoughtful—sentencing reform measure enacted in the United States in the last half-century."[3]

The Washington legislature rejected the underlying assumptions of the indeterminate sentencing approach, which permits tailoring sentences to the individual needs of a particular defendant. But the legislature recognized that it is impossible (and undesirable) to attempt to eliminate all judicial discretion. (See again Focus 11.1, where the purpose of the 1981 Washington sentencing reform is reprinted in part.)

The result in Washington was legislative formulation of presumptive sentences that retain judicial discretion but are within the framework of legislative standards. The judge's sentencing decision is final (and in that sense, the sentence is a determinate, not an indeterminate, one), but if it deviates from the legislative standards, reasons must be given for the deviation, and the decision is subject to review by a higher court.[4]

Under Washington state's guidelines, a trial judge may sentence outside the range appropriate for a particular defendant, thereby departing from the sentencing guidelines, if **mitigating circumstances** or **aggravating circumstances** exist. *Mitigating circumstances* are those that do not justify or excuse a crime but that, because of justice and fairness, make the crime less reprehensible. They may be used to reduce a charge to a lesser offense, such as to reduce murder to manslaughter. *Aggravating circumstances* are those that are above or beyond the elements required for the crime but that make the crime more serious, such as robbery by use of a dangerous weapon. They may be used with reference to many crimes, but both aggravating and mitigating circumstances must be considered before capital punishment may be imposed.

Under specified conditions, the exceptional sentence would be subject to judicial review. The Washington statute enumerates some circumstances that may be considered by judges imposing an exceptional sentence, although the list, reproduced in part in Focus 11.2, is not meant to be exhaustive.

Federal Sentencing Guidelines

The federal sentencing guidelines were authorized by the Sentencing Reform Act of 1984, a part of the federal criminal code revision that was passed after years of discussion and multiple drafts.[5] One of the most important provisions was the establishment of the U.S. Sentencing Commission to develop sentencing guidelines, which must be adopted by Congress to become law. By 1 May of each year, the commission must submit proposed amendments to those guidelines. Those amendments become law if Congress does not enact legislation to the contrary prior to 1 November of the year in which the commission makes the proposals.

The goal of sentence reform at the federal level was to eliminate **sentence disparity**. Part of the problem, however, is to define the meaning of that concept. Generally, *sentence disparity* is used to describe the variations and inequities that result when defendants convicted of the same crime receive different sentences,

Focus 11.2

Aggravating and Mitigating Circumstances in Sentencing

[The Washington Sentencing Reform Act of 1981 provides that judges may impose sentences outside the sentencing guidelines after considering aggravating or mitigating circumstances such as provided by statute.
Some of the illustrations are as follows:]

(1) Mitigating Circumstances . . .

  (a) To a significant degree, the victim was an initiator, willing participant, aggressor, or provoker of the incident.

  (b) Before detection, the defendant compensated, or made a good faith effort to compensate, the victim of the criminal conduct for any damage or injury sustained.

  (c) The defendant committed the crime under duress, coercion, threat, or compulsion insufficient to constitute a complete defense but which significantly affected his or her conduct.

  (d) The defendant, with no apparent predisposition to do so, was induced by others to participate in the crime.

  (e) The defendant's capacity to appreciate the wrongfulness of his or her conduct, or to conform his or her conduct to the requirements of the law, was significantly impaired. Voluntary use of drugs or alcohol is excluded.

  (f) The offense was principally accomplished by another person and the defendant manifested extreme caution or sincere concern for the safety or well-being of the victim. . . .

  (h) The defendant or the defendant's children suffered a continuing pattern of physical or sexual abuse by the victim of the offense and the offense is a response to that abuse.

(2) Aggravating Circumstances—Considered and Imposed by the Court . . .

(3) Aggravating Circumstances—Considered by a Jury—Imposed by the Court . . .

  (a) The defendant's conduct during the commission of the current offense manifested deliberate cruelty to the victim.

  (b) The defendant knew or should have known that the victim of the current offense was particularly vulnerable or incapable of resistance.

  (c) The current offense was a violent offense, and the defendant knew that the victim of the current offense was pregnant.

  (d) The current offense was a major economic offense or series of offenses, so identified by a consideration of any of the following factors:

    (i) The current offense involved multiple victims or multiple incidents per victim;

    (ii) The current offense involved attempted or actual monetary loss substantially greater than typical for the offense;

(Continued)

Focus 11.2 (*Continued*)

      (iii) The current offense involved a high degree of sophistication or planning or occurred over a lengthy period of time; or

      (iv) The defendant used his or her position of trust, confidence, or fiduciary responsibility to facilitate the commission of the current offense.[1]

[1] Rev. Code Wash., Section 9.94A.535 (2012).

---

but it may also refer to varying legislative sentences among the states. The federal sentencing guidelines could do nothing about sentence disparity among states.

The federal sentencing guidelines were implemented to reduce disparity at the federal level. Of primary importance was the establishment of a sentencing structure that would "enhance the ability of the criminal justice system to reduce crime through an effective, fair sentencing system."[6]

The commission recognized that it might be impossible to achieve two of the goals established by Congress: uniformity and proportionality. To achieve *uniformity*, Congress intended for the sentencing structure to result in a narrowing of the wide disparity in sentences received by defendants committing the same offenses in different federal jurisdictions. *Proportionality* means that the sentence imposed should be commensurate with the severity of the offense; thus, an armed robbery might not be like an unarmed robbery because of the differences in circumstances.

The federal sentencing guidelines were controversial from the beginning and were quickly challenged in the courts. The U.S. Supreme Court upheld the constitutionality of the federal sentencing guidelines in 1989.[7]

Other challenges and decisions followed, and in 2005, the U.S. Supreme Court ruled that the federal sentencing guidelines are advisory, not mandatory, but the Court did not give guidelines regarding what *advisory* means and how much discretion federal judges retain.[8]

During its 2006–2007 term, the U.S. Supreme Court heard two cases that involved some of the questions often raised after its 2005 decision. One appeal raised the issue of whether a sentence set by the guidelines is *presumed* to be reasonable, which would effectively limit or eliminate an appeal should that sentence be imposed. The issue arose in the case of a defendant who was convicted of offenses related to providing false testimony before a grand jury. The defendant argued before the trial court that the guidelines were unreasonable in his case and that he should be given a lighter sentence due to his health, his fear of being abused in prison, and his distinguished military service. The U.S. Supreme Court upheld the lower court's ruling that the imposed sentence was reasonable because it was within the federal sentencing guidelines. The Court's reasons for denying a sentence below the guidelines were sufficient, even though brief.[9]

The second issue that the U.S. Supreme Court considered during its 2006–2007 term concerned what a federal judge is required to do to justify imposing a sentence that is significantly shorter than that of the federal sentencing guidelines. Specifically, prosecutors challenged a 15-month prison sentence imposed on a defendant who was convicted of possession with intent to distribute crack cocaine. The federal sentencing guidelines provided for a three-year minimum sentence for this offense. Unfortunately, the 23-year-old defendant in this case was murdered shortly before the Court's decision was announced, and the Court vacated the case.[10]

In 2007, the U.S. Supreme Court decided two cases involving the federal sentencing guidelines and the sentencing of drug offenders. Those cases are discussed in Focus 11.3.[11]

Focus 11.3

Federal Sentencing Guidelines in Drug Cases

In December 2007, the U.S. Supreme Court decided two cases regarding federal sentencing guidelines. In both, the appellants had been convicted of drug offenses. Brian Michael Gall was put on probation for 36 months after he pleaded guilty to conspiracy to distribute MDMA (also referred to as *Ecstasy*). The federal sentencing guidelines include a prison term for this offense, which is a class C felony. The length of the prison term depends upon the circumstances of the offense. Gall, a college student with no prior criminal record, who cooperated with authorities, filed a motion for a downward departure from the sentencing guidelines. That was granted by the trial court but reversed by the federal court of appeals, which held that such a departure requires "extraordinary circumstances." In *Gall v. United States,* the U.S. Supreme Court reversed and remanded, holding that extraordinary circumstances are not required.[1]

Kimbrough v. United States, decided on the same day, involved a 15-year prison sentence imposed on Derrick Kimbrough, an Iraq War veteran, who entered guilty pleas to four offenses:
- conspiracy to distribute crack and powder cocaine;
- possession with intent to distribute more than 50 grams of crack cocaine;
- possession with intent to distribute powder cocaine; and
- possession of a firearm in furtherance of a drug-trafficking offense.

The federal sentencing guidelines called for an aggregate sentence of 15 years to life in prison, but the trial court sentenced Kimbrough to 15 years in prison plus 5 years of supervised release. The Fourth Circuit Court of Appeals vacated the sentence, finding that a sentence imposed outside the federal guidelines was per se unreasonable. The U.S. Supreme Court reversed and remanded. In analyzing the facts of this case, the U.S. Supreme Court discussed the differential sentences for crack and for powder cocaine, along with the history and purpose of the federal sentencing guidelines and the U.S. Sentencing Commission empowered with making recommended guidelines. Noting that in prior decisions it had determined that the federal sentencing guidelines are *advisory,* not mandatory, the U.S. Supreme Court ruled in *Kimbrough* that the

(Continued)

Focus 11.3 (*Continued*)

lower federal court "erred in holding the crack/powder disparity [of the federal sentencing guidelines] effectively mandatory." The Court continued:

> A district judge must include the Guidelines range in the array of factors warranting consideration. The judge may determine, however, that, in the particular case, a within-Guidelines sentence is "greater than necessary" to serve the objectives of sentencing. In making that determination, the judge may consider the disparity between the Guidelines' treatment of crack and powder cocaine offenses.[2]

[1] *Gall v. United States*, 552 U.S. 38 (2007).
[2] *Kimbrough v. United States*, 552 U.S. 85 (2007).

Evaluation of Sentencing Guidelines

Sentencing guidelines are aimed at controlling judicial discretion, but discretion goes beyond the judge. Most of the sentencing reforms will have little or no effect on prosecutorial discretion. Prosecutors may refuse to prosecute a particular case or may control the nature and number of charges that will be filed. Prosecutors also have wide discretion in plea bargaining with defendants, and they may use that ability to avoid mandatory minimum sentences for offenders who cooperate with them. In addition, juries have considerable discretion. If they think a determinate sentence that would be imposed after a guilty verdict is unreasonable, they may decline to convict.

Another problem is that most reforms using sentencing guidelines provide that the guidelines apply only to prison or jail terms, with wide discretion permitted in the imposition of alternative sentences, such as probation or community service, leaving open the possibility of disparity.

Other results may also occur. When sentencing reform results in longer sentences, as has often been the case, it exacerbates the already overcrowded conditions of many prisons. Furthermore, mathematical approaches to sentencing give the appearance of being precise and more scientific than other methods, but arbitrariness and discrimination may creep into the system when guidelines contain ambiguous words that must be interpreted in the context of a specific case.

Sentencing guidelines may be so complicated that judges, prosecutors, and defense attorneys do not understand the system or must spend considerable time learning it. Further, although sentencing reform in some manner has occurred in most jurisdictions and in the federal system, the systems vary, which means that sentence disparity may continue when the various jurisdictions are compared. Finally, as long as the time served by an inmate may be reduced by good behavior or by a parole board (or some other administrative agency) acting on those or other factors, disparity may result.

RECENT SENTENCING REFORM MEASURES

Reforms other than sentencing guidelines have been implemented both at the state and the federal levels. Three of the most significant changes are discussed.

Three Strikes and You're Out Legislation

A recent movement of an old philosophy that embodies enhanced penalties for repeat offenders is **three strikes and you're out**. Generally, three strikes legislation provides for long mandatory or life sentences for persons who are convicted of a third offense, which usually must be a felony. Some jurisdictions state that the third strike felony must be serious, violent, or one of a specified number of felonies. Others state only that it must be a felony. For example, the California three strikes statute provides for the mandatory sentence for persons convicted of a third felony, which may be any felony, although the first two must be serious or violent ones. California also mandates harsher penalties for conviction of a second strike.[12]

In 2003, the U.S. Supreme Court decided two California three strikes cases, which are summarized in Focus 11.4. California has the most severe three strikes legislative package, as a third strike in that state may be a nonviolent offense, such as shoplifting. Of the 7,000 inmates who were serving life sentences under California's three strikes legislation at the time of the U.S. Supreme Court decision, 331 were in prison because their third strikes were for petty theft. The third strike for 603 additional inmates was for drug possession.[13]

A study of California three strikes legislation conducted by the Sentencing Project, a nonprofit research and advocacy group referred to earlier, concluded that California was targeting nonviolent criminals, who accounted for 58 percent of the sentences under this legislation. Under the state's companion two strikes legislation, 69 percent of those sentenced were convicted of nonviolent crimes. California had sentenced more than 50,000 persons under its three strikes law since it was approved in 1994. This number was far in excess of other states. The report emphasized that most criminals peak early in life and thus do not need long periods of incarceration. Further, such long sentences increase the state's costs for medical and other types of care. Finally, the researchers found no evidence that the three strikes legislation was responsible for the crime reduction in California, pointing out that crime decreased across the country, including in states such as New York and Massachusetts that did not have three strikes legislation.[14]

In the 2004 election, 53 percent of Californians rejected Proposition 66, which, among other provisions, would have resulted in the release of many nonviolent offenders from the budget-strapped state penal system. Proposition 66 also provided that the third strike must be a violent or serious felony in order to trigger a life sentence. Early polls showed that a majority of voters were in favor of Proposition 66, but the governor, Arnold Schwarzenegger, pushed an extensive and aggressive advertising campaign to defeat the measure. It is expected that efforts to reduce the prison population will continue, however, as the state, like many others, battles fiscal issues. In fact, California is under a federal mandate to

Focus 11.4

The U.S. Supreme Court Upholds Three Strikes Laws

The two California three strikes cases that the U.S. Supreme Court decided during its 2002–2003 term were those of Gary A. Ewing and Leandro Andrade. Both cases challenged the constitutionality of the state's three strikes legislation. The specific legal issue was whether cruel and unusual punishment had been imposed on either (or both) with the sentences in their respective cases. Both appellants were sentenced under state law, and to reverse those sentences, the U.S. Supreme Court had to find the violation of a *federal* constitutional right, such as the Eighth Amendment (see Appendix A) prohibition against cruel and unusual punishment.

Ewing was sentenced to 25 years to life in prison for a third strike involving the theft of golf clubs totaling $1,200. Ewing's previous strikes were for burglary and robbery. Andrade's third strike was for stealing $153.54 worth of videotapes from two KMart stores, for which he received two sentences of 25 years to life. His first strike was for burglarizing three homes, but because the videotapes were stolen from two stores, the trial judge counted those thefts as two strikes, thus giving Andrade three strikes for purposes of sentencing. Both Andrade and Ewing were sentenced for what California calls "petty theft with a prior," with the priors permitting the courts to treat the current misdemeanors as felonies. The sentence for petty theft without a prior in California is six months or less in jail. Andrade will be eligible for parole in 50 years, Ewing in 25. One of the prosecutors described Andrade as "a hopeless heroin addict" and concluded, "There comes a point at which the state has a right to say, 'Enough is enough.'"[1]

These two cases were decided in March 2003, with a bitterly divided U.S. Supreme Court ruling 5-to-4 that the sentences did not violate the Eighth Amendment prohibition against cruel and unusual punishment. Justice Sandra Day O'Connor, writing for the majority in the *Ewing* case, emphasized that the California legislature had a right to enact three strikes penalties in order to protect the public from criminals already convicted of at least one serious violent crime, noting that precedent cases have established that "States have a valid interest in deterring and segregating habitual criminals." O'Connor reviewed the history of three strikes legislation in California and concluded, "Ewing's sentence is justified by the State's public-safety interest in incapacitating and deterring recidivist felons, and amply supported by his own long, serious criminal record."[2]

Justice David H. Souter wrote the dissenting opinion in the *Andrade* case. In discussing the issue of proportionality, Justice Souter concluded, "If Andrade's sentence is not grossly disproportionate, the principle has no meaning."[3]

[1] "California's 3-Strikes Law Tested Again," *New York Times* (6 November 2002), p. 19.
[2] *Ewing v. California*, 538 U.S. 11 (2003).
[3] *Lockyer v. Andrade*, 538 U.S. 63 (2003).

cut its prison populations and improve prison conditions, particularly in the areas of medical and mental health care.[15]

Truth in Sentencing Legislation

The second major development in sentencing reform in recent years is the concept of **truth in sentencing**, which means that actual time served by offenders should be closer to the time allocated for the sentence. Many jurisdictions are establishing 85 percent as their goal, meaning that offenders must serve 85 percent of their prison sentences before they are eligible for early release.

The federal government offers incentives to encourage states to establish truth in sentencing measures. The federal Violent Offender Incarceration and Truth in Sentencing Incentive Grants Act provides money to states for prison construction and operation but requires that violent offenders serve 85 percent of their time for the state to be eligible. Most states have enacted such legislation, and prison populations have soared, in large part as a result of inmates' serving longer portions of their sentences.[16]

The Fair Sentencing Act of 2010

Chapter 10 mentioned the 100:1 differential for federal sentences for violating crack cocaine compared to powder cocaine statutes and the allegations that this represented discrimination against minorities. On 3 August 2010, President Barack Obama signed into law the Fair Sentencing Act of 2010, which was passed by Congress on 28 July 2010. The act became effective on 1 November 2010.[17]

U.S. Attorney General Eric Holder issued a press release on 28 July 2010. He congratulated the Congress on passing the new bill and stated that the bill "will go a long way toward ensuring that our sentencing laws are tough, consistent, and fair."[18]

The main purpose of this new sentencing law was to replace the 100:1 ratio disparity between sentences for convictions of crack cocaine compared to those for powder cocaine with a ratio of 18:1. The statute also eliminated the five-year mandatory minimum prison sentence for simple possession of crack cocaine. It increased some penalties, such as those for drug offenses that involve certain vulnerable victims, violence, and other specified aggravating factors. The statute contains provisions regarding drug courts (e.g., requiring collecting data on them) and many other programs.

The 2010 law came after years of consideration by the U.S. Congress, U.S. presidents, sentencing commissions, and the public. The U.S. Sentencing Commission had proposed to replace the 100:1 sentencing ratio, and Congress had made some changes, but in 1995, President Bill Clinton signed a bill that retained the differential. However, in March 2008, Clinton said that he wished he had worked harder to change the differential during his presidency, adding that he was "prepared to spend a significant portion of whatever life I've got left on the earth trying to fix this because I think it's a cancer."[19]

The U.S. Sentencing Commission recommended that the Fair Sentencing Act of 2010 be applied to cases that were decided before it was enacted, but Congress did not agree to that. In late November 2011, the U.S. Supreme Court agreed to review two cases appealed on this issue. The lower federal courts ruled that a general federal statute prohibits applying a new law retroactively unless Congress made it clear that was its intention. According to the majority opinion of the lower federal court in one of the appealed cases, the Fair Sentencing Act of 2010 should have been named the "Not Quite as Fair as it could be Sentencing Act of 2010 (NQFSA)." The court stated that only Congress could do anything about that and that the act "applies only to defendants who are sentenced based on conduct that took place after August 3, 2010." The U.S. Supreme Court disagreed and stated in its decision, "Congress intended the Fair Sentencing Act's new, lower mandatory minimums to apply to the post-Act sentencing of pre-Act offenders."[20]

Although space limitations of this text do not permit a discussion of all types of sentences, the chapter does take a close look at capital punishment, as that punishment sets the stage for the subsequent discussion of the constitutional issues of sentencing.

CAPITAL PUNISHMENT

The most severe of all sentences the government imposes is **capital punishment**. The U.S. Supreme Court has interpreted the Constitution as placing some restrictions on this punishment, but in 1972, the Court held that capital punishment is not per se unconstitutional, although it was found to be so in the provisions of the Georgia statute at issue. According to the Court, capital punishment under the Georgia statute was imposed in an arbitrary, capricious, and discriminatory manner. The Supreme Court left open the possibility that statutes could be drafted to survive constitutional scrutiny.[21]

In 1976, the U.S. Supreme Court upheld the constitutionality of the revised Georgia statute, which requires a consideration of aggravating and mitigating circumstances before imposition of the death penalty. That same year the Supreme Court had invalidated a statute that provided for the *mandatory* imposition of capital punishment.[22] In the intervening years, the U.S. Supreme Court has decided numerous capital punishment cases, some of which are discussed in the following section, along with other sentencing issues.

CONSTITUTIONAL ISSUES IN SENTENCING

Appellate courts are hesitant to interfere with legislative or judicial sentencing powers, but they do hear and decide sentences on appeal if it appears that those sentences violate defendants' constitutional rights. The U.S. Supreme Court hears cases in which it is alleged that sentences violate *federal* constitutional rights. The basis for reversing most sentences is the Eighth Amendment's prohibition against the infliction of cruel and unusual punishment (see Appendix A), but the definition of that concept is not clear. A few areas are illustrative.

Execution of the Mentally Challenged

In 1986, the U.S. Supreme Court held that it is cruel and unusual punishment to execute the insane or "someone who is unaware of the punishment they are about to suffer and why they are to suffer it."[23] Subsequently, the Court held that a mildly retarded person could be executed.[24]

In a 6–3 decision in 2002, the U.S. Supreme Court, stating that a national consensus rejects the execution of mentally retarded offenders, held that it is unconstitutional to do so. The Court left it to the states to determine the meaning of *mentally retarded* and provided little guidance for them in doing so.[25]

In 2007, in *Panetti v. Quarterman,* the U.S. Supreme Court ruled by a 5–4 vote that a mentally ill murderer who did not have a rational understanding of why the state planned to execute him could not be executed.[26]

The Right to a Trial by Jury

The Sixth Amendment to the U.S. Constitution (see Appendix A) guarantees the right to a trial by jury in criminal cases. That right cannot be infringed through any phase of the sentencing process, including the enhancement of sentences. In 2000, in *United States v. Apprendi,* the U.S. Supreme Court held that, "Other than the fact of a prior conviction, any fact that increases the penalty for a crime beyond the prescribed statutory maximum must be submitted to a jury, and proved beyond a reasonable doubt." Thus the finding of a fact that elevates a criminal conviction for an ordinary crime to the level of a hate crime, must be determined by a jury.[27]

Two years later, the U.S. Supreme Court held that an aggravating factor supporting a death sentence must be determined by a jury rather than a judge.[28] Also in 2002, the Court held that the additional fact upon which a mandatory minimum sentence imposed by the judge was based should have been determined by a jury rather than by a judge.[29] And in 2004, the Court again held that defendants have a right to have a jury determine *all* facts that might lead to sentence enhancement. The Court invalidated a Washington state statute that permitted judges to find facts about the defendant's conduct and thus sentence beyond the sentencing guidelines.[30]

In March 2005, the U.S. Supreme Court decided *Shepard v. United States.* This case reexamined the role of judges in sentencing. In the *Apprendi* case, the Court had ruled that any fact, other than a prior conviction, that is used in sentence enhancement must be determined by a jury. *Shepard* involved a defendant who had previously entered guilty pleas to four burglaries, but the necessary details of those crimes were not contained in the plea agreement. The appeals court had ruled that the trial court should have inquired into police reports to determine whether any of those prior felonies met the requirements of the federal statute under which Shepard was convicted. In *Shepard,* the U.S. Supreme Court stated that *Apprendi* and other recent precedent cases limit trial judges to official court documents when they investigate the nature of prior felonies for purposes of sentence enhancement. Thus, in Shepard's case, the trial judge should not have gone beyond the official transcript of the plea bargaining process to determine whether

Shepard's prior burglaries met the requirements for sentence enhancement under the Armed Career Criminal Act.[31]

In January 2007, the U.S. Supreme Court invalidated California's criminal sentencing law in a case involving a defendant who was convicted of continuous sexual abuse of a child. Under California law, this offense is punishable by a lower term sentence of 6 years, a middle term of 12 years, or an upper term of 16 years. California law required the trial court to impose the middle term unless there was evidence of mitigating or aggravating circumstances. In the 2007 case, the trial judge had imposed the upper term of 16 years after finding, by a preponderance of the evidence, six aggravating circumstances. The U.S. Supreme Court reversed, holding that the aggravating circumstances must be determined by a jury, which is required to find facts by the higher evidence standard of beyond a reasonable doubt. According to the majority opinion, "Factfinding to elevate a sentence from 12 to 16 years, our decisions make plain, falls within the province of the jury."[32]

Another issue with regard to sentencing and a defendant's right to trial by jury involves jury selection. In 2003, the U.S. Supreme Court considered the issue of alleged racial bias in jury selection in the case of death row inmate Thomas Miller-El, an African American. At Miller-El's jury selection, the prosecution eliminated 10 of the 11 African Americans in the jury pool. The prosecution argued that its actions did not constitute bias but, rather, represented the prejudice of those potential jurors, who stated that they would be hesitant to impose the death penalty. Miller-El presented evidence of racial bias in jury selection in the Texas county in which he was tried. His request to have the jury struck was denied. He was convicted and sentenced to death. His appeal was rejected by the federal Fifth Circuit. He appealed to the U.S. Supreme Court, which heard the case and sent it back with instructions that Miller-El was entitled to present evidence to the Fifth Circuit.

The U.S. Supreme Court chastised that court and urged the judges to rethink their "dismissive and strained interpretation of the proof in the case and to give more serious consideration to the significant evidence pointing to unconstitutional discrimination against black jurors during the jury selection process." The Fifth Circuit did not follow the U.S. Supreme Court's instructions and quoted extensively from that Court's dissenting justice, Clarence Thomas. Miller-El again appealed to the U.S. Supreme Court, which, by a vote of 6–3, ruled in his favor. Justice David H. Souter, who wrote for the majority, discussed the various tactics (which he called "trickery") used by the prosecution to avoid selecting African Americans for the jury. One tactic was to ask different questions of African Americans, as compared to whites, in an attempt to make it appear that they were disqualified because they opposed the death penalty, a position described by Justice Souter as one that "reeks of afterthought." Justice Clarence Thomas, the only African American on the U.S. Supreme Court, dissented, stating that he found the prosecution's explanation "eminently reasonable." On remand, the Fifth Circuit held that Miller-El did not state with clear and convincing evidence that the state had committed error in its decision. The U.S. Supreme Court again reversed and remanded the case to the Fifth Circuit, which remanded it to the district court, instructing that court to enter an order:

(1) granting the petition for writ of habeas corpus; (2) setting aside Petitioner's conviction and sentence for capital murder; (3) ordering the release of Petitioner from custody unless the State grants Petitioner a new trial within 120
days from the date of the entry of the district court's order; and (4) entering
final judgment for Petitioner.[33]

In 2008, Miller-El pleaded guilty in exchange for a life sentence.

Equal Protection

The sentencing process may not violate a defendant's right to the constitutional
guarantee of equal protection under the law. The issue arises in many cases,
particularly with regard to race and gender. First, it is necessary to understand
that by requiring equal protection in sentencing, the U.S. Constitution does not
require that *all* defendants be treated identically. The U.S. Supreme Court has held,
"The belief no longer prevails that every offense in a like legal category calls for
an identical punishment without regard to the past life and habits of a particular
offender."[34] Equal protection in sentencing means that, when there are differences,
the bases for sentencing must be legitimate factors (such as the nature of the
crime), rather than illegal ones, such as race or ethnicity.

Allegations of equal protection violations occur most frequently in the
sentencing of minorities, particularly when capital punishment is involved and
the defendant is African American. In 1996, the U.S. Supreme Court held that
selective prosecutions in cases involving crack cocaine do not alone support a
claim of racial discrimination. The Court ruled that the African American men in
Los Angeles who appealed their convictions did not meet the burden of proving
unfair racial discrimination.[35]

The Sentencing Project has repeatedly emphasized the need to reduce racial
disparity within criminal justice systems. One of its publications focused on
disparities in *state* sentencing, noting the following data concerning race and
incarceration and emphasizing that on any given day, one out of every eight black
males in their twenties is in prison:

- "African Americans are incarcerated at nearly six (5.6) times the rate of
  whites;
- Hispanics are incarcerated at nearly double (1.8) the rate of whites;
- States exhibit substantial variation in the ratio of black-to-white incarceration, ranging from a high of 13.6-to-1 in Iowa to a low of 1.9-to-1 in Hawaii;
- States with the highest black-to-white ratio are disproportionately located
  in the Northeast and Midwest.... This geographic concentration is true as
  well for the Hispanic-to-white ratio."[36]

The sentencing of female defendants also raises allegations of equal protection
violations. In general, it is illegal to discriminate against defendants solely because
of their gender. Some distinctions are permissible, but the state (or the federal
government) must show a rational reason for making those distinctions. Consider
the following example: A man in Illinois claimed that the state violated the equal

protection clause of the U.S. Constitution in providing for a greater penalty for a man convicted of incest with his stepdaughter than for a woman convicted of incest with her stepson. The appellate court affirmed the lower court ruling that the state had a rational reason for the distinction—the prevention of pregnancy in the case of a female victim. The U.S. Supreme Court refused to hear the case, thus allowing the ruling to stand.[37]

Other sentencing differences have also been questioned. The Sentencing Project noted that, with respect to drug offenses, women are sentenced differently when compared to men. Although women represent a much smaller percentage of the inmate population, their percentages have been growing faster than those of men, and that is due primarily to sentencing for drug offenses. One-third of all female inmates were sentenced for drug offenses. Further, the women who are sentenced to prison for drug offenses are disproportionately minority women.[38]

Proportionality

The Eighth Amendment prohibition against cruel and unusual punishment (see Appendix A) has been interpreted to mean that a sentence must be proportionate to the offense for which it is imposed. Proportionality may involve type or length of offense. This issue arises most often with respect to the death penalty. The major case in which the U.S. Supreme Court held that the death penalty is disproportionate for the crime of rape involved the rape but not killing of an adult female.[39]

In 2008, the U.S. Supreme Court held that capital punishment for the rape but not murder of a child also constitutes cruel and unusual punishment. In *Kennedy v. Louisiana,* the Court stated that punishment may be justified by one of three rationales: rehabilitation, deterrence, and retribution. According to the Court,

> It is the last of these, retribution, that most often can contradict the law's own ends. This is of particular concern when the Court interprets the meaning of the Eighth Amendment in capital cases. When the law punishes by death, it risks its own sudden descent into brutality, transgressing the constitutional commitment to decency and restraint.[40]

The Court cited its decisions with regard to the death penalty for mentally challenged persons and for juveniles and concluded that, despite the long-term effects that rape may have on a child, the penalty of death for the rapist is excessive when that child is not killed. We cannot compare such crimes, "in terms of moral depravity and of the injury to the person and to the public" to murder in their "severity and irrevocability."[41]

The proportionality issue also arises with respect to sentence length. Although most appellate courts defer to trial judges on this issue, some sentencing decisions are reversed on appeal. For example, a lower federal court reversed the sentence of a defendant who received a 10-year sentence (the maximum allowed by law) for conviction of illegal drug possession. When arrested, the defendant possessed only half of his daily dosage of drugs, a clear indication, said the court, that he was not intending to sell the drugs. Although possession was illegal, the court said the sentence was disproportionate in that it was at least twice as long as the *maximum* federal sentence for such major felonies as extortion, blackmail, perjury, assault with a dangerous weapon or by beating, arson (not endangering a human life), threatening the life of the President, and selling a man into slavery. It is severe both in its length and in its callous disregard for appellant's obvious need for treatment.[42]

The proportionality issue also arises in habitual offender or recidivism statutes (see the discussion of three strikes statutes earlier in this chapter), which provide for an increased penalty once a defendant has been convicted of multiple offenses. Recall, however, our earlier discussion that the U.S. Supreme Court has upheld the lengthy sentences under California's three strikes and you're out legislation (see again Focus 11.4).

The Sentencing of Juveniles

In 1988, the U.S. Supreme Court held that imposing capital punishment on a person who was 15 at the time he committed murder constituted cruel and unusual punishment, but the Court did not answer the question of where the line was to be drawn in deciding whether capital punishment is cruel and unusual in light of a defendant's age.[43]

In 2002, the U.S. Supreme Court refused to reconsider whether it is constitutional to execute persons who were 16 or 17 when they committed capital offenses. Justice David H. Souter wrote a dissenting opinion for himself and three colleagues, stating that executing juvenile offenders is "a relic of the past that is inconsistent with evolving standards of decency in a civilized society." The dissenters proclaimed, "We should put an end to this shameful practice." In 1985, the Supreme Court had upheld the death sentence of a defendant who was 18 at the time he committed his atrocious capital crime.[44]

In 2005, in *Roper v. Simmons,* involving a juvenile who was 17 when he committed murder, the U.S. Supreme Court ruled that the execution of a person who committed a capital crime at that age is unconstitutional.[45] The reasons for the Court's decision in that case are cited with the Court's approval in its 2010 case holding that the imposition of life without parole (LWOP) on a juvenile who commits a nonhomicide crime constitutes cruel and unusual punishment. This latter case is excerpted in Focus 11.5, which also features a 2012 case on juvenile sentencing.

SEX OFFENDER LAWS

This final topic in the chapter does not involve sentencing per se, but it is related to one philosophy of why criminal justice systems sentence offenders: to keep them from engaging in additional crimes.

State Registration Laws

Protection of society is a primary goal of punishment, and since 1994, when seven-year-old Megan Kanka was murdered by her New Jersey neighbor, Jesse Timmendequas, a released sex offender, all states, the District of Columbia, and

=== **Focus 11.5** ===

Juveniles and Cruel and Unusual Punishment

In 2005, the U.S. Supreme Court held that capital punishment of persons who were juveniles when they committed murder constitutes cruel and unusual punishment, which violates the Eighth Amendment (see Appendix A). That case, *Roper v. Simmons,* is noted in the text.

In 2010, the Court held that sentencing a juvenile to life without parole for a nonhomicide crime constitutes cruel and unusual punishment. The following excerpt from *Graham v. Florida* presents the facts and part of the Court's rationale for its decision. The Court had originally agreed to hear a second Florida case, *Sullivan v. Florida,* but dismissed that one as "improvidently granted."[1]

Justice Anthony M. Kennedy wrote the opinion for the Court in *Graham,*[2] in which Justices John Paul Stevens, Ruth Bader Ginsberg, Stephen G. Breyer, and Sonia Sotomeyer joined. Justice Stevens wrote a concurring opinion, in which Justices Ginsberg and Sotomeyer joined. Chief Justice John Roberts wrote an opinion concurring in the judgment. Justices Clarence Thomas, Antonin Scalia, and Samuel Alito dissented, with Justices Thomas and Alito writing opinions. The excerpt is followed by a 2012 decision on juvenile sentencing.

Graham v. Florida

The issue before the Court is whether the Constitution permits a juvenile offender to be sentenced to life in prison without parole for a nonhomicide crime. . . .

Petitioner is Terrance Jamar Graham. . . . Graham's parents were addicted to crack cocaine, and their drug use persisted in his early years. Graham was diagnosed with attention deficit hyperactivity disorder in elementary school. He began drinking alcohol and using tobacco at age 9 and smoked marijuana at age 13. . . . [When he was 16] he and three other school-age youths attempted to rob a barbeque restaurant. . . . [He was arrested for attempted robbery].

Under Florida law, it is within a prosecutor's discretion whether to charge 16- and 17 year olds as adults or juveniles for most felony crimes. Graham's prosecutor elected to charge Graham as an adult. The charges against Graham were armed burglary with assault or battery, a first-degree felony carrying a maximum penalty of life imprisonment without the possibility of parole; and attempted armed robbery, a second-degree felony carrying a maximum penalty of 15 years' imprisonment.

[Graham accepted a plea bargain and promised to obey the law; the judge withheld adjudication and placed Graham on probation with two terms of three years each, to be served concurrently. Graham was required to spend the first 12 months of his probation in jail, but he received credit for the time he had already spent in jail. Graham's promise to obey the law was broken rather quickly after his release, when he and two others were charged with a home-invasion robbery involving forcible entry and a firearm. The youth ransacked the home while holding the victims hostage, barracaded them in the closet, and left. Later that evening they attempted another robbery. One of the accomplices was shot, and Graham drove him to the hospital; the police saw Graham as he drove away and signaled him to stop. Graham sped away, crashed the car, and ran on foot, but officers apprehended and searched the car, where they found three handguns. Graham was charged with probation violation and the new crimes committed since his release. He was found guilty of these crimes and of the deferred charge of armed robbery. He was sentenced to LWOP. The Court discussed the meaning of the Eighth Amendment's prohibition against cruel and unusual punishment and continued as follows:]

As compared to adults, juveniles have a "lack of maturity and an under-developed sense of responsibility"; they "are more vulnerable or susceptible to negative influences and outside pressures, including peer pressure"; and their characters are "not as well formed." These salient characteristics mean that "[i]t is difficult even for expert psychologists to differentiate between the juvenile offender whose crime reflects unfortunate yet transient immaturity, and the rare juvenile offender whose crime reflects irreparable corruption."

Accordingly, "juvenile offenders cannot with reliability be classified among the worst offenders." A juvenile is not absolved of responsibility for his action, but his transgression "is not as morally reprehensive as that of an adult." . . .

Juveniles are more capable of change than are adults, and their actions are less likely to be evidence of "irretrievably depraved character" than are the actions of adults. It remains that "[f]rom a moral standpoint it would be misguided to equate the failings of a minor with those of an adult, for a greater possibility exists that a minor's character deficiencies will be re-formed."

The Court discussed in detail the philosophical bases for punishment: retribution, deterrence, incapacitation, and rehabilitation, rejecting the first three as reasons for imposing LWOP and noting that LWOP denies a juvenile a chance to rehabilitate. The Court also considered the lack of the use of LWOP for juveniles internationally. The Court then determined that LWOP for juveniles who commit a crime that does not involve homicide constitutes cruel and unusual punishment and thus violates the Eighth Amendment of the federal constitution.

On 25 June 2012, the U.S. Supreme Court held that mandating a life sentence without parole for a juvenile who is convicted of murder also constitutes cruel and unusual punishment and thus violates the Eighth Amendment. In *Miller v. Alabama*, along with a companion case, the Court emphasized its prior holdings recognizing the capacity for change in juveniles. Justice Elena Kagan, who delivered the Court's opinion, noted that in neither of the two cases "did the sentencing authority have any discretion to impose" a sentence other than life without parole, meaning that the young defendants would die in prison

even if a judge or jury would have thought that his youth and its attendant characteristics, along with the nature of his crime, made a lesser sentence

(Continued)

Focus 11.5 (*Continued*)

(for example, life *with* the possibility of parole) more appropriate. [In view of the "capacity for change" and the "lessened culpability" of juveniles, this process] runs afoul of our cases' requirement of individualized sentencing for defendants facing the most serious penalties.[3]

[1]*Sullivan v. Florida*, 130 S.Ct. 2059 (2010).
[2]*Graham v. Florida*, 130 S.Ct. 2011 (2010), cases and citations omitted.
[3]*Miller v. Alabama*, 2012 U.S. LEXIS 4873 (25 June 2012), emphasis in the original, together with *Jackson v. Hobbs, Director, Arkansas Department of Correction.*

the federal system have enacted **Megan's laws,** which require that released sex offenders register when they move into a community. Some jurisdictions require that the community be notified, either by the sex offender or by law enforcement authorities.

Megan Kanka was enticed into the neighbor's home with the promise of a puppy. Timmendequas, who lived in that home, along with two other sex offenders, was on parole after serving time for convictions of previous sex offenses against young girls. Megan's parents did not know about the sex offender backgrounds of Timmendequas and his housemates. Megan was murdered on 29 July 1994, and by 31 October 1994 New Jersey had enacted its Sexual Offender Registration Act. It was followed quickly by other jurisdictions.

Timmendequas was convicted of kidnapping, rape, and murder and sentenced to death. In 1997, when New Jersey abolished the death penalty, his sentence was changed to life in prison without parole for murder and a consecutive life sentence with a 25-year disqualifier for parole for the first-degree kidnapping conviction. The state supreme court upheld the convictions and sentences, and the U.S. Supreme Court refused to review them. In June 2011, the New Jersey Court of Appeals held that Timmendequas should be permitted to argue that his defense counsel was ineffective because he did not effectively prove his client's mental retardation. The court did not hold that the convictions should be reversed; the case was remanded for a hearing on evidence concerning ineffective assistance of counsel.[46]

In 2004, the nation's attention was captured by the abduction, subsequent sexual attack, and murder of Jessica Lunsford, a young Florida girl, age nine, who was taken from the home she shared with her father and her grandparents. A sex offender who had failed to register, John E. Couey, 46, was convicted of these crimes and sentenced to death. Jessica's father, along with others, pushed for stronger federal legislation on sex offender registration. One of those, the Children's Safety and Violent Crime Reduction Act, became law in 2006.[47]

The toughest state sex offender law was enacted in California after 70 percent of the state's voters approved Proposition 83, which became effective 8 November 2006 and represents that state's Jessica's law. Among other provisions, the Sexual Predator Punishment and Control Act (SPPCA) eliminates good time credits for sex offenders, increases the mandatory minimum prison term, and requires sex offenders released on parole to wear GPS monitoring systems for life. The act permits categorizing released offenders as sexually violent predators subject to civil commitment on the basis of one, rather than two, crimes and makes it illegal for released offenders to live within 2,000 feet of any school or other place where children congregate regularly. It contains provisions concerning the use of date rape drugs and providing child pornography.[48]

Federal Registration Laws

Beginning in 1994, Congress enacted a series of laws named after abducted children and aimed at the requirement that sex offenders must register with local authorities upon release from confinement. Some of these statutes included provisions designed to encourage states to enact such legislation, even making available federal funding for law enforcement for states contingent upon their adoption of a Megan's law.[49]

In 2006, Congress enacted the Adam Walsh Child Protection and Safety Act.[50] The Act was named after a six-year-old child who was abducted from a Sears department store and beheaded in 1981. It includes the Sex Offender Registration and Notification Act (SORNA), under which the federal government provides grants to assist states with registering sex offenders, provided the states follow the federal registration requirements. The SORNA also creates a new federal crime: failure to register as a sex offender when required to do so.[51] The Walsh Act was signed 25 years after the abduction of Walsh, whose father, John Walsh, became a victims' advocate who helped establish and now is in charge of the National Center for Missing and Exploited Children. He is also the anchor of the TV show *America's Most Wanted*.

On 13 October 2008, a bill entitled Keeping the Internet Devoid of Sexual Predators Act of 2008 (the KIDS Act of 2008) was passed by the Senate. The House had passed the bill the previous year. The law requires registered sex offenders to register their email and instant messenger addresses with the National Sex Offender Registry. The Department of Justice is required to make this information available to sites that can use it to block the listed predators from preying on children. The law provides that it is a crime for Internet users to misrepresent their ages for the purpose of luring children into sexual conduct. It amends the federal criminal code to impose a fine and/or prison term of up to 10 years for failure to comply with the informational provisions of the act and up to 20 years for age misrepresentation as provided by the act. The KIDS Act also requires, at a minimum, GPS monitoring of sex offenders 24/7 upon release.[52]

Constitutional and Other Challenges

There have been numerous constitutional challenges to sex offender registration laws. During its 2002–2003 term, the U.S. Supreme Court decided two cases, one from Connecticut and one from Alaska. The Alaska case raised the issue of whether the state's sex offender registration law violates the *ex post facto* prohibition of the U.S. Constitution, while the Connecticut case raised a due process issue. The Court upheld both statutes.[53]

The fact that the U.S. Supreme Court decided these two cases and upheld sex offender registration laws does not mean that all issues are resolved; it is thus important to consider some of those issues, especially the practical ones. First is the issue of whether the laws are effective. They attempt to balance the need to protect the public with the goal of reintegrating the offender back into society as a law-abiding citizen. The latter is impossible when offenders experience hostility, humiliation, threats, or, in a few cases, violence.

Sex offender registration laws are based on the presumption that if people know who sex offenders are and where they live, society will be protected from sexual abuse. This is not necessarily the case. First, in many cases the sexual abuser is a family member or friend, and even when those persons are apprehended, they are rarely prosecuted successfully, if at all. Second, law enforcement officials do not always have accurate information for posting. Third, sufficient personnel and resources for handling notification are not available in all jurisdictions. Fourth, sex offender notification will not solve the problem of notification in other communities to which sex offenders may travel to commit their crimes. In fact, one study of California's sex offender registration laws challenged residency limitations for sex offenders, concluding that there is "almost no correlation between sex offenders living near restricted areas and where they commit their offenses."[54]

Not all sex offenders register, and thus their living arrangements are not known to neighbors, as illustrated by the failure of Jessica Lunsford's abductor to register. And even when sex offenders do comply with registration requirements, they may not be apprehended when they commit subsequent crimes. Perhaps the most blatant example of California's problems with keeping up with sexual predators occurred when officials failed to apprehend Phillip Garrido, a paroled rapist, who kidnapped Jaycee Lee Dugard in 1991, when she was 11, and kept her in temporary shelters in his backyard, fathering two children by her in the 18 years that she was his captive. This case illustrates the fact that requirements that sex offenders register does not ensure that they will not commit further sexual and other crimes. Garrido not only complied with statutory requirements to register and report: he even took his victims with him to meetings with parole authorities, and they visited him in his home and did not discover Dugard and her two children. Dugard, who published a book about her 18 years in captivity, sued the U.S. government, alleging gross negligence on the part of federal parole officers. Dugard asked for unspecified damages, which she stated she would donate to the JAYC Foundation, an organization she developed to help other crime victims.[55] She and her daughters settled for $20.4 million with the state of California.

Human rights organizations have raised numerous issues about the required registration of sex offenders. Human Rights Watch, based in New York, issued a 146-page report in 2007, *No Easy Answers: Sex Offender Laws in the United States*. The two-year investigation included over 200 interviews with victims and their families, law enforcement officers, and others. The report concluded that despite the worthwhile goal of protecting children from sexual predators, current laws were poorly crafted and ill-conceived. They are based on the crimes that precipitated them and do not address the fact that few children are sexually abused and murdered by sexual predators. Rather, most abused children are victims of family members, family friends, or acquaintances. Further, the assumption that most sex offenders reoffend is not founded in research; three out of every four do not reoffend. The report noted that in many states, juveniles who are convicted of sex offenses are subject to registration as sex offenders for life. But, in many cases, their acts "while frowned upon, do not suggest a danger to the community, including consensual sex, 'playing doctor,' and exposing themselves." Indeed, requiring all sex offenders to register for life may make it impossible for law enforcement to deal with the most serious offenders, those we really do want to keep off the streets.[56]

Another human rights issue is raised by evidence that residency restrictions more negatively impact minorities than other groups.[57]

Finally, there is concern that sex offender registration laws are too harsh when applied to juveniles. Illinois amended its statute in 2007 to permit the removal of juvenile sex offenders from this requirement if they can prove to a judge that they are not a threat to society. Lawmakers overrode the governor's veto on this issue, as they used evidence from the Human Rights Watch stating that juveniles are usually not recidivists and are usually not violent offenders.[58]

Civil Commitment Procedures

Since registration requirements for released sex offenders may not be effective, some states require civil commitment of these offenders after they are eligible for release from prison. In 1997, in *Kansas v. Hendricks,* the U.S. Supreme Court upheld the Kansas civil commitment statute in the case of Leroy Hendricks, who was convicted in 1984 of indecent liberties with two 13-year-old boys. After serving most of his 10-year sentence, Hendricks was scheduled for release from prison, but a jury determined that he was a sexual predator, and the judge found that he had a mental abnormality. He was involuntarily confined indefinitely under the Kansas Sexually Violent Predator Act, which defines a *sexually violent predator* as "any person who has been convicted of or charged with a sexually violent offense and who suffers from a mental abnormality or personality disorder which makes the person likely to engage in the predatory acts of sexual violence." In a 5–4 decision, the U.S. Supreme Court upheld the civil commitment on the grounds that Hendricks was to be treated, not punished.[59]

By 2007, 20 states had civil commitment procedures in place for sex offenders who are released from prison, and approximately 2,700 such offenders were being held at that time. One newspaper pointed out that Hendricks, who at that time had been in so-called treatment for 13 years, was costing the state $185,000 per year, eight times the cost of keeping an inmate in prison in Kansas.[60]

Sex offender registration laws can be expected to continue to generate debate and controversy, especially until the U.S. Supreme Court answers all the issues surrounding these relatively new statutes.

SUMMARY

This text began with an examination of the purposes of criminal law, a discussion that included an overview of punishment philosophies. The philosophy that dominates at any given time is reflected in sentencing policies. Thus, with the trend toward retribution and deterrence came a movement away from rehabilitation and the indeterminate sentencing structure. In recent years there has been some movement back toward rehabilitation and treatment.

Allegations of legislative and judicial sentence disparity and judicial leniency resulted in public pressure to exert controls over sentencing judges and to influence legislative changes in sentence lengths. The chapter examined sentence types and sentencing guidelines. The essence of the federal mandate and subsequent proposed guidelines is to decrease sentencing discretion. Although mitigating and aggravating circumstances of a crime and characteristics of an offender may be considered in sentencing, the U.S. Sentencing Commission developed guidelines that represent an attempt to avoid the harshness of a system that sentences every offender of a particular crime to the same sentence. But it is also an attempt to eliminate extreme disparity that may result in a less structured system. The federal guidelines and the Sentencing Commission remain controversial.

The U.S. Supreme Court initially upheld the constitutionality of the commission's mandate, but in 2005, the Court ruled that the guidelines are not mandatory. Subsequent U.S. Supreme Court decisions concerning the guidelines were also discussed.

The chapter included a discussion of the recent attempts by federal and state jurisdictions to increase the penalties of multiple offenders. The resulting "three strikes and you're out" legislation was analyzed in the context of its practical and legal implications, emphasizing the U.S. Supreme Court's rulings upholding the California statute. Attempts to increase the amount of time served by inmates by enacting truth in sentencing legislation were also noted. Particular attention was given to the Fair Sentencing Act of 2010 before the chapter turned to a discussion of capital punishment.

Constitutional issues in sentencing constituted the next section of the chapter, beginning with a look at the issues concerning the execution of the mentally challenged. Issues concerning the assessment of facts submitted at the sentencing stage were noted, with the roles of the judge and the jury analyzed in the context of the most recent U.S. Supreme Court decisions. Equal protection issues surrounding sentencing on the basis of race and gender were probed. Proportionality and cruel and unusual punishment issues were discussed, with the primary emphasis on their application to capital punishment, with a focus on the recent U.S. Supreme Court decision concerning whether capital punishment for the rape but not murder of a child constitutes cruel and unusual punishment. The sentencing of juveniles was analyzed both in terms of capital punishment and the imposition of life without parole.

The final section of the chapter was devoted to a look at sex offender registration and civil commitment laws.

This completes the analysis of criminal law, a subject of great complexity and extreme importance. This text has provided only an overview of the subject; criminal law varies among jurisdictions, and in some cases that variance is significant. It is possible to gain only an introduction to the general issues, problems, and trends in such a vast, rapidly changing field. Many issues related to these discussions are left to a text in criminal procedure; some are primarily criminological in nature, whereas others relate to the correctional system. All are interrelated and important to a comprehensive understanding of U.S. criminal justice systems.

STUDY QUESTIONS

1. Explain how punishment philosophy relates to sentencing.
2. Explain the differences in these sentencing models: legislative, judicial, and administrative. Relate your answer to specific sentencing reforms discussed in this chapter.
3. What is presumptive sentencing? Give examples.
4. If sentencing guidelines are used, should they be based on a jurisdiction's previous sentencing practices or on ideal sentencing practices? If the latter, how would you propose to draft the guidelines? How much discretion would you allow?
5. Washington state legislators claim that their 1981 sentencing code revision represents a move from indeterminate to determinate sentencing. Analyze this claim.
6. Describe the U.S. Sentencing Commission, its purpose, and its problems. What are some of the constitutional issues with regard to its sentencing guidelines, and how have they been resolved, if at all?
7. Define and discuss the implications of "three strikes and you're out" and "truth in sentencing" legislation.
8. What is the nature and purpose of the Fair Sentencing Act of 2010?
9. Discuss the current status of capital punishment. Do you think this form of punishment should be abolished or retained? Give reasons for your answer.
10. What is the status of executing the mentally challenged?
11. Analyze the recent U.S. Supreme Court decisions concerning capital punishment sentencing issues and the right to a trial by jury.
12. Outline the constitutional issues concerning equal protection.
13. What is meant by *proportionality* in sentencing? What has the U.S. Supreme Court held about this concept?
14. What is the legal status of executing juveniles in the United States? What is the legal status of imposing upon them life without parole in cases that do not involve murder?
15. What are sex offender registration laws? Assess the importance, the validity, and the constitutionality of such laws.

16. What provisions are available for the civil commitment of a sex offender after that person has completed a prison sentence?

FOR DEBATE

The issue of capital punishment has become one of national importance in the last few years, with some states declaring a moratorium on its use. The extreme nature of this penalty requires that it be imposed only in rare cases. The U.S. Supreme Court has ruled that capital punishment is unconstitutional under some circumstances. With that in mind, debate the following issue:

RESOLVED: Capital punishment should be abolished in the United States because it constitutes cruel and unusual punishment and thus violates the federal Constitution.

KEY TERMS

aggravating circumstances   258
capital punishment   266
clemency   257
determinate sentence   255
indeterminate sentence   255
Megan's laws   274
mitigating circumstances   258

pardon   257
presumptive sentencing   257
sentence   255
sentence disparity   258
sentencing guidelines   257
three strikes and you're out   263
truth in sentencing   265

INTERNET ACTIVITY

1. The Sentencing Project contains valuable information on its website, http://www.sentencingproject.org (accessed 16 May 2012). Check out its discussions of topics, such as women and criminal justice systems, race and sentencing, recent state criminal justice initiatives, and drug policies.
2. The Death Penalty Information Center, http://www.deathpenaltyinfo.org (accessed 16 May 2012), contains extensive information on the death penalty. Check this source to view current data on the penalty and recent changes in the law.

NOTES

1. Tex. Penal Code, Section 12.21 *et seq.* (2012).
2. *Twentieth Century Task Force on Criminal Sentencing, Fair and Certain Punishment,* with a background paper by Alan M. Dershowitz (New York: McGraw-Hill, 1976), pp. 19–20.
3. David Boerner, *Sentencing in Washington: A Legal Analysis of the Sentencing Reform Act of 1981* (Seattle: Butterworth Legal Publishers, 1985), p. 1–1.
4. See Rev. Code Wash., Section 9.94A.535 (2012).

5. The Sentencing Reform Act was passed as part of the Comprehensive Crime Control Act of 1984, Public Law 98-473, 98 Stat. 1837, 1976 (1984), and is codified with its subsequent amendments in USCS, Title 18, Section 3551 *et seq.* (2012), and USCS, Title 28, Sections 991-998 (2012).
6. The discussion here and later of the major issues and how the commission proposes to resolve them comes from the opening statements of the proposed guidelines, which are published in the *Federal Register* 52 (13 May 1987): 18048–18053.
7. *Mistretta v. United States,* 488 U.S. 361, 367 (1989). For additional information on early challenges to federal sentencing guidelines, see *United States v. Apprendi,* 530 U.S. 466 (2000); and *Blakely v. Washington,* 542 U.S. 296 (2004). For a discussion of these cases, see Sue Titus Reid, *Criminal Law,* 9th ed. (New York: Oxford University Press, 2012), pp. 46–48, 193, 354, 355.
8. *United States v. Booker,* 543 U.S. 220 (2005). See also *United States v. Fanfan,* 543 U.S. 220 (2005), the companion case to *Booker.*
9. *Rita v. United States,* 551 U.S. 338 (2007).
10. *Claiborne v. United States,* 551 U.S. 87 (2007).
11. In 2007, the U.S. Supreme Court also decided other sentencing cases. See *Gall v. United States,* 552 U.S. 38 (2007); and *Cunningham v. California,* 549 U.S. 270 (2007), discussed in Reid, *Criminal Law,* 9th ed, pp. 355, 356. See also *Shepard v. United States,* 544 U.S. 13 (2005), discussed in Reid, *Criminal Law,* 9th ed., pp. 356–57, 365.
12. See Cal Pen Code, Section 667 (2012).
13. "Ruling on Three-Strikes Laws Could Heavily Impact Corrections," *Corrections Professional* 7, no. 15 (19 April 2002): n.p. The cases are *Ewing v. California,* 538 U.S. 11 (2003) and *Lockyer v. Andrade,* 538 U.S. 63 (2003).
14. "Aging Behind Bars: 'Three Strikes' Seven Years Later," (August 2001), http://www.sentencingproject.org (accessed 15 May 2012).
15. See *Brown v. Plata,* 131 S.Ct. 1910 (2011).
16. Violent Offender Incarceration and Truth in Sentencing Incentive Grants, USCS, Title 42, Section 13701 *et seq.* (2012).
17. The Fair Sentencing Act of 2010, 124 Stat. 2372 (2012).
18. U.S. Department of Justice, Statement of the Attorney General on Passage of the Fair Sentencing Act, Press Release (28 July 2010), http://www.justice.gov/opa/pr/2010/July/10-ag-867.html (accessed 13 July 2011).
19. "Bill Clinton Admits 'Regret' on Crack Cocaine Sentencing," (3 March 2008), quoted on the website of The Sentencing Project, http://www.sentencingproject.org (accessed 9 March 2008).
20. *United States v. Anthony Fisher,* 635 F.3d 336 (7th Cir. 2011), *vacated, remanded, Dorsey v. United States,* 132 S.Ct. 2321 (2012).
21. *Furman v. Georgia,* 408 U.S. 238 (1972).
22. See *Gregg v. Georgia,* 428 U.S. 153 (1976); and *Woodson v. North Carolina,* 428 U.S. 280 (1976).
23. *Ford v. Wainwright,* 477 U.S. 399 (1986).
24. *Penry v. Lynaugh,* 492 U.S. 302 (1989).

25. *Atkins v. Virginia*, 536 U.S. 304 (2002).
26. *Panetti v. Quarterman*, 552 U.S. 930 (2007).
27. *United States v. Apprendi*, 530 U.S. 466 (2000).
28. *Ring v. Arizona*, 534 U.S. 1103 (2002).
29. *Harris v. United States*, 536 U.S. 545 (2002).
30. *Blakely v. Washington*, 542 U.S. 296 (2004).
31. *Shepard v. United States*, 544 U.S. 13 (2005).
32. *Cunningham v. California*, 549 U.S. 270 (2007). The relevant California statutes are Cal Pen Code, Sections 288.5(a) and 1170(b)(2012).
33. *Miller-El v. Cockrell*, 537 U.S. 322 (2003), *on remand, Miller-El v. Johnson*, 330 F.3d 690 (5th Cir. 2003), *subsequent appeal, Miller-El v. Dretke*, 361 F. 3d 849 (5th Cir. 2004), *rev'd., remanded*, 545 U.S. 231 (2005), *and on remand, remanded*, 2005 U.S. App. LEXIS 15206 (5th Cir. 2005), *abrogated as stated in Davis v. Fisk Electric* Co., 268 S.W.3d 58 (Tex. 2008).
34. *Williams v. New York*, 337 U.S. 241, 247 (1949).
35. *United States v. Armstrong*, 517 U.S. 456 (1996).
36. Marc Mauer and Ryan S. King, *Uneven Justice: State Rates of Incarceration by Race and Ethnicity,"* The Sentencing Project (July 2007), p. 3, http://www .sentencingproject.org (accessed 31 July 2012).
37. *People v. Weeks*, 372 N.E.2d 163 (Ill.App.4th Dist. 1977), *appeal dismissed sub nom.*, 439 U.S. 809 (1978).
38. "Women in the Criminal Justice System," The Sentencing Project (May 2007), http://www.sentencingproject.org (accessed 31 July 2012).
39. *Coker v. Georgia*, 433 U.S. 584 (1977).
40. *Kennedy v. Louisiana*, 554 U.S. 407 (2008).
41. *Kennedy v. Louisiana*, 554 U.S. 407 (2008).
42. *Watson v. United States*, 439 F.2d 442, 473 (D.C.Cir. 1970).
43. *Thompson v. Oklahoma*, 487 U.S. 815 (1988).
44. *Stanford v. Parker*, 266 F.3d 442 (6th Cir. 2001), *cert. denied*, 537 U.S. 831 (2002); *Baldwin v. Alabama*, 472 U.S. 372 (1985).
45. *Roper v. Simmons*, 543 U.S. 551 (2005).
46. *State v. Timmendequas*, 737 A.2d 55 (N.J. 1999), *mot. granted, State v. Timmendequas*, 744 A.2d 1204 (N.J. 1999), *and subsequent appeal*, 773 A.2d 18 (N.J. 2001), *and cert. denied, Timmendequas v. New Jersey*, 534 U.S. 858 (2001). The citation for the remand is *State v. Timmendequas 2011 N.J. Super. Unpub. LEXIS* 1518 (N.J.Super.Ct.App.Div. 14 June 2011). See also "Sentence Upheld for Megan's Murderer: But Court Orders a Review of Defense," *The Star-Ledger* (Newark, N.J.) (15 June 2011), p. 11.
47. Children's Safety and Violent Crime Reduction Act, P.L. 109-248 (2012).
48. California's Jessica's law is codified at Cal Pen Code, Section 3003.5 *et seq.* (2012).
49. See, for example, the Jacob Wetterling Act, codified at USCS, Title 42, Section 14071, enacted in 1994, subsequently amended, and repealed under later statutes.
50. The Adam Walsh Child Protection and Safety Act is codified at USCS, Title 18, Section 4248 (2012).

51. The registration requirements of the Sex Offender Registration and Notification Act (SORNA) are codified at USCS, Title 42, Section 16913 (2012). The federal crime of failure to register as a sex offender is codified at USCS, Title 18, Section 2250(1)(2)(A) (2012).

52. "Rep. Pomeroy Testifies on His Bill to Keep Kids Safe from Sex Offenders on Internet," *US Fed News* (17 October 2007), n.p. The Keeping the Internet Devoid of Sexual Predators of the KIDS Act of 2008, Public Law 110-400 (2012), is codified at USCS, Title 42, Section 1690 (2012).

53. See *Smith v. Doe,* 538 U.S. 84 (2003); and *Connecticut Department of Safety v. Doe,* 538 U.S. 1 (2003).

54. See California Sex Offender Management Board (CASOMB), California Department of Mental Health, Recommendations Report (January 2010), http://www.casomb.org (accessed 9 October 2011).

55. "Jaycee Dugard Lawsuit Seen as a Long Shot," *Christian Science Monitor* (23 September 2011), n.p.

56. Human Rights Watch, *No Easy Answers: Sex Offender Laws in the United States,"* (11 September 2007), http://www.hrw.org/, accessed 9 October 2011.

57. See, for example, Lorine A. Hughes and Keri B. Burchfield, "Sex Offender Residence Restrictions in Chicago: An Environmental Injustice?" *Justice Quarterly* 25, no. 4 (December 2008): 647–673.

58. Human Rights Watch, "Illinois Amends Sex Offender Laws for Youths," http://www.hrw.org/ (accessed 9 October 2011). The Illinois statute is codified at ILCS, Chapter 730, Section 150/3-5(d) (2012).

59. Sexually Violent Predator Act, Kan. Stats. Ann., Section 59-29a01 *et seq.* (2006). The case is *Kansas v. Hendricks,* 521 U.S. 346 (1997).

60. "Doubts Rise as States Hold Sex Offenders after Prison," *New York Times* (4 March 2007), p. 1; "Wrong Turn on Sex Offenders," *New York Times* (13 March 2007), p. 18.

Glossary

A

Accessory. Subordinate; one who contributes, as in a crime, to the acts of another but in a subordinate position.

Accessory after the fact. One who, knowing that a felony has been committed, receives, relieves, comforts, or assists the felon to hinder apprehension and conviction.

Accessory before the fact. One who incites, orders, commands, or abets a crime but is not present when the crime is committed.

Accomplice. A person who participates in the responsibility for a crime but not in the criminal act itself. Such a person assumes criminal culpability in terms of his or her degree of participation in the criminal activity.

Actus reus. An act that, if combined with other elements of a crime, may lead to the arrest, trial, and conviction of the accused.

Administrative law. Rules and regulations made, through proper procedures, by agencies to which power has been delegated by a state legislature or, in the federal system, by the U.S. Congress. Administrative agencies also investigate and decide cases concerning potential violations of their rules.

Adultery. Consensual sexual intercourse between a married person and someone other than his or her spouse. Some statutes provide that the sex act constitutes adultery by both parties even if only one is married to someone else. Others limit the crime to the married party.

Adversary system. The Anglo-American system for settling disputes in court. It assumes the defendant is innocent until proven guilty. Prosecuting attorneys, representing the state, and defense attorneys, representing the defendant, try to convince a judge or jury of their version of the case. *See also* **Inquisitorial system.**

Affirmative defense. The introduction by the defense attorney of new factual allegations which, if true, constitute a complete or partial defense to the crime charged. *See also* **Defense.**

Aggravated assault. An assault committed with particular outrage or atrocity or involving a dangerous weapon; may also involve an assault with the intention of committing another crime.

Aggravating circumstances. Circumstances that are above or beyond those required for the crime but that make the crime more serious; may be used with reference to many crimes, but the concept is critical particularly in capital punishment cases, where it is required. *See also* **Mitigating circumstances.**

Aid or abet. The act of assisting or facilitating the commission of a crime.

Appeal. A step in a judicial proceeding, involving a petition to a higher court to review a lower court's decision.

Appellant. The party in a lawsuit who appeals a court's decision to a higher court, arguing that the lower court made a mistake that prejudiced the appellant, who now deserves a reversal of the decision and a new hearing. The party against whom this appeal is filed is called the **Appellee.**

Appellee. *See* **Appellant.**

Arson. Any willful or malicious burning or attempt to burn, with or without an intent to defraud, a dwelling house, public building, motor vehicle or aircraft, or the personal property of another person. Some statutes include the burning of one's own property with the intent to defraud.

Asportation. The act of moving things or people from one place to another.

Assault. Technically, an assault is a threat to commit a battery, but often the term is used to refer to a battery, which is the unauthorized, harmful touching of another person. If the unauthorized threat or touching results in serious bodily harm or the use of a weapon, the crime may be considered **aggravated assault.**

Attempt. A crime that may be defined as an act involving two basic elements: a step toward the commission of a crime and a specific intent to commit that crime.

Attendant circumstances. Facts surrounding a crime that are considered to be a part of that crime and that must be proved, along with elements of the crime.

Automatism. A defense for a defendant who has proof that he or she was unconscious or semiconscious when the crime was committed. Epilepsy, a concussion, or an emotional trauma are examples of conditions that may be used for this defense.

B

Baby Moses laws. Laws protecting mothers and fathers who abandon their unwanted newborns in ways that will ensure the health and safety of those infants. Generally, these laws permit parents to leave the infants in designated safe places and avoid prosecution for abandonment or murder. Such laws limit the applicable time period, for example, to a few hours or days or, in some jurisdictions, as long as 30 days.

Bailee. A person to whom goods are entrusted by a **bailor.**

Bailor. A person who entrusts goods to another party, known as the **bailee.**

Battered person syndrome. A syndrome arising from a cycle of abuse by a special person, often a parent or a spouse, that leads the battered person to perceive that violence against the offender is the only way to end the abuse. In some cases, the battered person murders the batterer, and in some jurisdictions, evidence of the battered person syndrome constitutes a defense to that crime.

Battery. *See* **Assault.**

Beyond a reasonable doubt. The standard of proof in criminal cases. Often the concept is not defined by courts, but it refers to evidence that is fully satisfactory, entirely convincing, and true to a moral certainty.

Bigamy. The crime of knowingly and willingly contracting a second marriage when aware that another marriage is undissolved. Some jurisdictions consider the crime one of strict liability; thus, *knowledge* of a prior marriage is not required.

Bill of attainder. Defined by the U.S. Supreme Court in 1876 as a "legislative act which inflicts punishment without a judicial trial." Originally, the phrase referred only to the death penalty, and a bill of attainder involving lesser penalties was called a *bill of pains and penalties.* Both concepts are forbidden by the U.S. Constitution.

Blackmail. Similar to **extortion**, this crime is usually associated with the unlawful demand for money or something else of value by threats to expose some embarrassing or disgraceful allegation or fact about the target, to accuse that person of a crime, or to do bodily harm to him or her or damage that person's property.

Breach of the peace. A willfully committed act that disturbs the public tranquillity or order and for which there is no legal justification.

Bribery. The offering, giving, receiving, or soliciting of anything of value to influence action by public (or in some jurisdictions, nonpublic) officials.

Burden of proof. In a legal case, the duty of proving a disputed fact. For example, in a criminal case, the state has the burden of proving the defendant guilty **beyond a reasonable doubt**.

Burglary. Under common law, breaking and entering the dwelling of another during the night time with the intent to commit a felony. Many current statutes extend the crime to any structure or time and do not require an actual breaking; an unauthorized entry will suffice.

C

CAN-SPAM Act. A federal statute containing, among other provisions, measures for the elimination of unwanted spam on computers and directing the Federal Trade Commission (FTC) to adopt a rule requiring a warning on sexually explicit spam. The FTC did that, and the provision carries civil as well as criminal penalties, with the latter including a possible prison sentence and stiff fine.

Capital punishment. Punishment by death for those who are convicted of capital murder.

Carjacking. Auto theft by force or threat of force.

Case law. The aggregate of reported judicial decisions, which are legally binding court interpretations of written statutes and previous court decisions or rules made by courts in the absence of written statutes or other sources of law.

Causation. A relationship between two phenomena in which the occurrence of the former brings about changes in the latter. In the legal sense, causation is the element of a crime that requires the existence of a causal relationship between the offender's conduct and the particular harmful consequences.

Child abuse. The physical, psychological, sexual, or emotional abuse of a child by parents, other relatives, acquaintances, or strangers. May include child pornography and child prostitution.

Circumstantial evidence. Direct evidence—such as eyewitness testimony—of facts other than those for which proof is needed but from which deductions or inferences may be drawn concerning the facts in dispute.

Civil law. In contrast to criminal law, civil law pertains to rules that are concerned with private or civil rights. The wronged person seeks compensation through civil litigation.

Clemency. Mercy, kindness, leniency; a term used to describe the actions of a governor or a president when he or she commutes a sentence—for example, from death to life—or grants a **pardon**.

Codified. Reducing customs, unwritten laws, and rules, to written statutes.

Common law. Contrasted to written law, common law consists of legally binding rules derived from judicial decisions, customs, and traditions. Broadly defined, it refers to the legal system that began in England and was followed in the United States.

Complicity. A term used to describe the actions of persons who are considered legally responsible for a crime although they did not participate in the act itself. *See also* **Accomplice.**

Computer crime. Crime committed by use of the computer. Computer criminals have developed programs that access, scramble, or erase computer files and that aid in theft, such as the stealing of a person's identity, as well as the invasion of privacy.

Condonation. The forgiving of a criminal act by a victim. Usually condonation is not a defense, but in some cases a victim of a nonserious crime may negotiate a settlement with the defendant, after which the court may drop the criminal charge.

Conspiracy. Agreeing with another to join together for the purpose of committing an unlawful act, or agreeing to use unlawful means to commit an act that would otherwise be lawful. The unlawful act does not have to be committed; the crime of conspiracy involves the *agreement* to engage in the unlawful act.

Constructive possession. A legal doctrine referring to the condition of having the power to control an item, along with having the intent to do so.

Contempt. Willfully disregarding or disobeying a public official's orders. Courts may issue civil or criminal contempt citations, referred to as *contempt of court.*

The U.S. Congress may also issue *contempt of Congress* citations to witnesses who deliberately interfere with its powers.

Controlled substances. Any drug that the statute in question has designated as such.

Conversion. The process of using the property or goods of another for one's own use and without permission.

Corpus delicti. Literally, "the body of the crime"; the body or other evidence that generally must be produced to prove that a crime has occurred.

Corroborating evidence. Additional data to support the charge of a crime, especially in rape and other cases in which there were no witnesses to the alleged act.

Crime. An act of omission or intention that violates criminal case or statutory law and is punishable by law.

Crime rate. The number of crimes per 100,000 in the population.

Crimes known to the police. All serious offenses that have been reported to the police and for which the police have sufficient evidence to believe that those crimes were actually committed.

Criminal law. The ordinances, regulations, and statutes that define behavior considered to be a threat to the well-being of society and for which legal sanctions are provided. The accused must be prosecuted by the government.

Cruel and unusual punishment. Punishment that is prohibited by the Eighth Amendment of the U.S. Constitution. Examples are torture, excessively long sentences, and the death penalty for rape without homicide. State constitutions may also prohibit cruel and (or) unusual punishment.

Culpability. Being guilty or at fault. There are four criteria that may be used to determine culpability: intention, knowledge, negligence, and recklessness. Different crimes may require different kinds of culpability to prove guilt.

Curtilage. The enclosed ground and buildings immediately surrounding a dwelling place or house; may also include grounds that are not enclosed but that are considered part of the area.

Cybercrime. Crime committed by use of computers and the Internet. It can involve many kinds of acts, ranging from creating viruses to stealing music files to bullying.

Cyberstalking. Stalking someone by use of the Internet. *See also* **Stalking.**

Cyberterrorism. The use of the Internet for terrorist threats.

D

Date rape. Forced sexual acts that occur during a social occasion. The alleged victim may have agreed to some intimacy but not to the activities defined in that jurisdiction as constituting the elements of rape.

Deadly force. Force that is likely to cause serious bodily injury or death.

Defense. A legal response by the defendant. It may consist only of a denial of the factual allegations of the prosecution. A defense that offers new factual allegations in an effort to negate the charges is an **affirmative defense.**

Defense attorney. The attorney for the defendant in a legal proceeding.

Department of Homeland Security (DHS). A federal cabinet-level position created after the 9/11 terrorist attacks; the agency combined 22 previous agencies into one organization, which coordinates the federal agencies involved in domestic preparedness, all of the federal agencies that are involved in activities for domestic preparedness, and agencies that coordinate plans for natural and person-made crises and emergency planning.

Determinate sentence. *See* **Sentence.**

Deterrence. A punishment philosophy that assumes that behavior may be controlled and criminal behavior prevented by the threat of punishment. *General deterrence* strives to discourage criminality by other people by intimidating them with the punishment of an offender. *Specific deterrence* prevents additional crimes by an offender by punishing that offender.

Discretion. Decisions based on one's judgment rather than legal rules. In criminal justice systems discretion can result in inconsistency but also in actions suitable for individual circumstances.

Disorderly conduct. Minor offenses, such as drunkenness or fighting, that disturb the peace or behavior standards of a community or shock the morality of its population.

Domestic violence. Causing physical or other types of harm or even death to members of the family, including children, parents, spouses, siblings, grandparents, and step-relatives; the concept may be extended to include nonrelatives with whom one has an intimate relationship.

Drug. A substance used to alter the body or mind of a living being. Drugs may be prescribed by doctors for medical treatment; some are legally available without prescriptions. Drugs may also be used for illegal purposes. In either case, drugs may be harmful or fatal.

Drug abuse. The chronic or periodic misuse of alcohol or other drugs. Drug abuse is considered detrimental to society as well as to the individual abuser. Drug abuse may occur even if the substance has been prescribed by the individual's physician.

Drug paraphernalia. Any item, product, or material that could be used to violate the controlled substance statutes of a particular jurisdiction.

Drug trafficking. Trading in illegal drugs.

Dual court system. System that characterizes U.S. court systems, consisting of a federal system and 50 state systems, which pass and enforce their own laws, along with municipal systems that make and enforce their own ordinances.

Due process. Constitutional principle that a person's life, liberty, or property cannot be deprived without lawful procedures. The courts interpret what due process requires in specific fact patterns.

Duress. In criminal law, a condition in which an individual is coerced or induced by the wrongful act of another to commit a criminal act. May be used as a defense.

Durham rule. A test of insanity (also known as the *product rule)* that states that "an accused is not criminally responsible if his unlawful act was the product of mental disease or mental defect."

E

Elder abuse. Violent and other types of abuse of elderly persons, including such acts as fraud, assault and battery, withholding food stamps or other economic benefits, theft of savings and Social Security checks, threats to send the person to a nursing home, and so on. The perpetrators are often family members, but crimes against the elderly are also committed by strangers.

Elements of a crime. All aspects of a criminal act that must be proved beyond a reasonable doubt by the prosecution to substantiate a conviction. This includes the concurrence of an act and a criminal state of mind that causes a harmful result. It may also include **attendant circumstances**.

Embezzlement. Misappropriation or misapplication of money or property entrusted to one's care, custody, or control.

Embracery. A common law misdemeanor meaning a corrupt attempt to influence a juror by means of promises, money, or other persuasions. Today many jurisdictions include this offense under a separate title such as "corrupt influencing of jurors" or include it within the crime of obstructing justice.

Enterprise liability. The process of holding an entire business enterprise legally liable for an event.

Entrapment. The defense that a defendant was induced by a government agent to commit a crime that the defendant would not have been inclined to commit without such inducement.

Equal protection. The constitutional principle guaranteeing that U.S. legal systems shall not deny to any person or class of persons the same treatment as other persons or classes of persons in the same or similar situations. Of particular significance are the circumstances of race, ethnicity, religion, disability, age, sexual orientation, and gender.

Espionage. Spying; that is, gathering, transmitting, or losing information about the national defense, with the expectation or knowledge that such information will be used against the country or to the advantage of a foreign country (or state).

Euthanasia. A term applied to the act of killing someone, often at that person's request, because of a terminal illness, considerable pain, or a debilitating handicap.

Excusable homicide. A killing that is accidental or is the result of self-defense or other circumstances that the law permits.

Expert testimony. Opinion evidence given at a trial by a person who possesses technical knowledge or skill that is both relevant to the case and not possessed by the average person.

***Ex post facto* law.** A law that provides punishment for an act that was not defined as a crime when the act was committed or that increases the penalty for a crime committed prior to the enactment of the statute. *Ex post facto* laws are not permitted under the U.S. Constitution.

Extortion. Obtaining property from another by wrongful use of actual or threatened force, fear, or violence, or the corrupt taking of a fee by a public officer, under color of his or her office, when that fee is not due.

F

Facilitation. Making it easier for another to commit a crime.

Factual impossibility. In the law, a defense that is possible only when there are circumstances, unknown to the actor, that prevent the commission of an offense, such as an attempt crime.

False imprisonment. The unlawful and knowing restraint of a person against his or her wishes so as to deny freedom. *See also* **Kidnapping**.

False pretense. Representation of some fact or circumstance that is not true and that is meant to mislead the other party.

False swearing. Untrue statements willfully and knowingly made under oath or equivalent affirmation inside or outside a judicial proceeding. *See also* **Perjury**.

Felony. A serious offense such as murder, armed robbery, or rape. Punishments for felonies range from one year's imprisonment to death but may also include fines, community service, or even probation.

Felony murder. An unlawful killing of a person that occurs while attempting to commit or while committing another felony, such as robbery, rape, or arson.

Fence. A person who receives stolen property from a thief and in turn disposes of it in a profitable manner.

Fetal abuse. Abusing a fetus. In some jurisdictions any resulting injury may lead to legal culpability; in some states, killing a fetus may result in a murder charge.

Fetal alcohol syndrome. Refers to a cluster of abnormalities that a fetus may have due to the fact that its mother consumed alcohol during her pregnancy. The effects include growth deficiencies, facial abnormalities, and mental retardation.

Fighting words. Words that tend to incite violence by the person to whom they are directed. Fighting words are more like a slap on the face than a communication of ideas. They are not protected by the First Amendment right to free speech.

Fleeing felon. A person trying to avoid arrest after committing a felony.

Forfeiture. The process of taking from a person accused of a crime, items (such as money, a boat, or a car) thought to be associated with illegal acts, such as drug trafficking. The property may be taken by the government and held until the case is decided; upon a conviction it may be retained by the government and sold or disposed of in some other way.

Forgery. Falsely making or altering, with the intent to defraud, a negotiable and legally enforceable instrument, such as a bank check.

Fornication. Generally, consensual sexual intercourse between two unmarried persons, but some statutes may include the act of sexual intercourse committed by an unmarried person with a married person, defining the act of the married person as *adultery*. *See also* **Adultery**.

Fraud. Falsely representing a fact, either by conduct or by words or writing, in order to induce a person to rely on the misrepresentation and surrender something of value.

G

Grand larceny. *See* **Petit larceny**.

Guilty but mentally ill (GBMI). An alternative to the insanity defense; permits finding that defendants were mentally ill but not insane at the time they committed the crimes charged. They are guilty, and they may be punished, but generally the jurisdictions that have this concept require that these defendants must receive psychiatric treatment while they are confined, often in a psychiatric facility rather than a prison.

H

Hate crime. A crime associated with evidence of prejudice based on any or all of the following, depending on the jurisdiction's approach: race, religion, disability, gender, age, national origin, sexual orientation, or ethnicity.

Home invasion robbery. Robbery that occurs when a person enters a dwelling for the purpose of committing a robbery and engages in a robbery of the occupant.

Homicide. An inclusive term that refers to all cases in which human beings—by their own acts, omissions, or procurement—kill other human beings. Homicide may be criminal (murder, manslaughter, or negligent homicide) or noncriminal (committed with justification or excuse).

I

Identity theft. The stealing of an individual's Social Security number or other important information about his or her identity and using that information to commit crimes, such as removing funds from the victim's bank account.

Incapacitation. A punishment theory and a sentencing goal, generally implemented by incarcerating offenders to prevent them from committing any other crimes. In earlier times, incapacitation involved such measures as removing the hands of thieves or castrating rapists.

Incest. Sexual relations between members of the immediate family who are too close in legal relationships to marry, such as between siblings, a parent and child, or a grandparent and grandchild.

Inchoate crimes. Crimes that are imperfect or uncompleted and that may lead to other crimes. For example, an attempt to commit rape may lead to rape, but even if it does not, the attempt is a crime.

Indeterminate sentence. *See* **Sentence**.

Infanticide. The killing of an infant at or soon after its birth.

Inference. A concept permitting the drawing of a conclusion based on other facts or logic presented in a case. The jury may use its reason and common sense to infer, for example, that based on certain evidence, a crime was committed by the defendant.

Injunction. A prohibitive remedy issued by a court and ordering someone or an agency to do something or stop doing something; based on a request by a party who petitions the court for the relief. There are several kinds of injunctions, including those that are preliminary (until a further hearing), partial, temporary, or permanent.

Inquisitorial system. A system in which the accused is presumed guilty and must prove his or her innocence.

Insanity. A state of mind that negates a defendant's responsibility for his or her actions.

Intent. State of mind referring to the willful commission of an act or the omission of an act that a person has a legal duty to perform. *See also* **Mens rea**.

Intervening act. An act that occurs after an alleged criminal act and the resulting injury; may be considered the legal cause, or at least a contributing cause, of the injury.

Intimate partner violence (IPV). Violence toward a current or former spouse, girlfriend, or boyfriend.

Intoxication. The condition that exists when a person consumes alcohol or other drugs to the extent that his or her mental or physical abilities are significantly affected.

Involuntary manslaughter. *See* **Manslaughter**.

Involuntary intoxication. Intoxication without choice or will, such as that which occurs when someone slips drugs into the food or drink of an unsuspecting person. *See also* **Voluntary intoxication**.

Irresistible impulse test. A test for insanity providing that an accused cannot be found guilty of a criminal act if he or she is unable to control the actions leading to a crime even though the accused may have known the act was wrong.

J

Judicial review. The process that occurs when appellate courts review and interpret the acts that occur in the lower courts. Those issues on review may be upheld, altered, reversed, or remanded. Appellate courts may also review acts that occur within the legislative and executive branches of government.

Jurisdiction. The lawful exercise of authority, and the geographic area (or subject matter) in which authority may be exercised. For instance, city police have legal authority only within the city limits. Courts may only hear cases for which they have jurisdiction (such as civil or criminal cases, misdemeanor or felony cases, probate, or drug cases, and so on).

Jury nullification. The power of juries to ignore the evidence and acquit even in the face of strong evidence supporting a conviction.

Justifiable homicide. A killing that is intentional but carries no evil intent and is permitted by law, such as one involving capital punishment or a killing by a law enforcement officer in the line of duty when attempting to prevent a felony.

K

Kidnapping. Restricting the freedom of a victim against his or her will and, in some jurisdictions, removing the victim from one place to another. Kidnapping is **false imprisonment** with aggravating circumstances, such as ransom, torture, extortion, prostitution, or pornography.

L

Larceny by trick. Deceptively obtaining possession of goods from a victim who surrenders possession voluntarily and without knowledge of the deceit involved.

Larceny-theft. The unlawful taking, carrying, leading, or riding away of property from the possession of another with the intent to steal. Larceny may be categorized as **petit larceny** or **grand larceny**, depending on the value of the stolen property.

Legal duty. A duty imposed by statutory or case law or through an explicit or implied contract.

Legal impossibility. Defense providing that even if the defendant's intentions, for example, to commit an attempt crime, were fully performed or set in motion, a crime would not have been committed.

Lesser included offense. A crime less serious than the one with which a defendant was charged. The lesser included offense has some but not all of the elements within the charged offense but must not include any elements that are not required for that offense.

M

Mala in se. Acts that are considered by most people to be morally wrong in themselves, such as rape, murder, or robbery.

Mala prohibita. Acts that are generally considered wrong because they are prohibited by legislation, although they may not be recognized by most people as morally wrong.

Malice aforethought. A required element of murder, providing that the killing be predetermined and intentional and without legal justification or excuse. *See also* **Premeditation.**

Malicious mischief. The malicious infliction of damage to or the destruction of the property of another.

Manslaughter. An unlawful killing without malice. It can be voluntary or involuntary. **Voluntary manslaughter** is a killing that would be murder except that it was committed in the heat of passion for which there is a reasonable explanation or excuse. **Involuntary manslaughter** is a criminal homicide that is committed recklessly but unintentionally, as when one is under the influence of alcohol or other drugs. **Negligent manslaughter** is a killing that is not lawful or justified and involves no malice–only negligence.

Marital rape. Forced sexual intercourse (or other specific sex acts, such as sodomy) with a spouse. The act is not recognized as a crime in all jurisdictions.

Mayhem. A common law offense sometimes included within the crime of assault and battery. It refers to permanent injury inflicted on a victim with the intent to injure. The act may disable or disfigure.

Megan's laws. Laws requiring the registration of sex offenders when they move into a community. Some jurisdictions require the offenders to notify neighbors; others require only that law enforcement authorities be notified.

Mercy killings. *See* **Euthanasia**.

Mens rea. The guilty intent or evil mind required for criminal culpability.

Misdemeanor. A crime that is less serious than a felony and that is punishable by a fine, probation, community service, or short confinement in a jail.

Misprision of treason. The concealment from proper officials of the known treason of another but without sufficient involvement to constitute the elements of a **principal** in the crime.

Mistake. A defense arguing that a defendant would not have committed a criminal act if he or she had possessed accurate knowledge of the law or the facts.

Mistrial. A trial declared invalid for a variety of reasons, such as the inability of a jury to reach a verdict, the death of a juror or counsel, or improper behavior by a juror or others involved in the trial.

Mitigating circumstances. Circumstances that do not justify or excuse a crime but that, because of justice and fairness, make the crime less reprehensible; may be used to reduce a crime to a lesser offense, such as to reduce murder to manslaughter. Mitigating circumstances must be considered before the death penalty is imposed. *See also* **Aggravating circumstances.**

M'Naghten rule. Also known as the *right-versus-wrong test* of insanity, the M'Naghten rule states that an accused cannot be considered guilty of a criminal act if, as a result of a defect of reason caused by a disease of the mind, the accused did not know the nature and quality of the act or did not know that the act was wrong.

Model Penal Code (MPC). The American Law Institute's systemized statement of criminal law that was proposed in 1962 and has been subsequently revised. Its provisions are suggested as models for state criminal law revisions.

Money laundering. Hiding the existence, illegal use of, or illegal source of income and making that income appear legal by disguising it.

Motive. The reason for a defendant's actions.

Murder. The unlawful and unjustified killing of another human being (or a fetus in some jurisdictions) with malice aforethought. Types of murder include the intent to kill, the intent to do great bodily harm, an act done in willful disregard of the strong likelihood that death or great injury would result, or a killing committed during the commission of another felony.

N

Necessity. Condition in which an act, though criminal in other circumstances, may not be considered criminal because of the compelling force of the circumstances.

Negligence. An act that a reasonable person would not do, or would not fail to do under similar circumstances. It does not require a criminal intent.

Negligent manslaughter. *See* **Manslaughter.**

O

Obscenity. Written or visual material that is not protected by the First Amendment because of its offensive, clear description or depiction of sexual acts; because of its lack of any political, literary, scientific, or artistic value; and because of its tendency to arouse improper sexual reactions in the average person.

Obstruction of justice. Interference with the orderly processes of civil and criminal courts, such as refusing to produce evidence, intimidating witnesses, and bribing judges. The crime may be committed by judicial and other officials and might constitute **official misconduct in office.**

Official misconduct in office. Any willful, unlawful behavior by public officials in the course of their official duties. The misconduct may be a failure to act, a wrongful act, or an improperly performed act that the official has a right to do.

P

Pandering. Procuring or securing a person, usually a female, to satisfy the lust of another, usually a male; catering to the lust of another person; also called *pimping.*

Pardon. An act by a state governor or the president of the United States that exempts an individual from punishment for a crime for which he or she was convicted and that removes the legal consequences of that conviction. Pardons may be absolute or conditional; may be individual or granted to a group or class of offenders; and may be full or partial, in which case the pardon remits only part of the punishment or removes some, but not all, of the legal disabilities resulting from conviction.

Perjury. False statements made willfully and knowingly under oath in a judicial proceeding. **Subornation of perjury** is the offense of procuring someone to commit perjury. *See also* **False swearing.**

Personal property. Technically, in law, *property* refers to anything that belongs exclusively to an individual. It is divided into two types: personal and real. *Personal property* technically refers to anything owned and to which the owner has an exclusive legal interest except real estate, in contrast to *real property*, which refers to land and items affixed to land, which cannot be moved legally.

Petit larceny. *Petit* literally means *small*. *Petit larceny*, in contrast to **grand larceny**, refers to the stealing of smaller amounts. Generally the statutes will specify the amount of money that must be stolen to move from a charge of petit to one of grand larceny.

Pinkerton rule. A rule stating that a co-conspirator may be held accountable for the acts of fellow conspirators even though the requirements of liability for the acts of accomplices are not met.

Postpartum depression (PPD) syndrome. A disorder that some women experience after giving birth.

Posttraumatic stress disorder (PTSD). A disorder in which stress is experienced by people who have suffered severe trauma, such as war trauma, rape, or other forms of traumatic abuse. Symptoms include nightmares, feelings of guilt, disorientation, and reliving the traumatic event(s). It is argued that victims of this disorder should not be held accountable for their criminal acts because they cannot control their behavior.

Premeditation. The act of planning, deliberating, designing, or thinking out in advance an intention to kill another person. *See also* **Malice aforethought**.

Preponderance of the evidence. Evidence showing that, on the whole, it supports the fact in question. This burden of proof in a civil case is less than the criminal standard of **beyond a reasonable doubt**.

Presumption. The assumption of a fact based on other facts.

Presumptive sentencing. A sentencing model in which the legislature specifies the normal sentence for each crime, and judges are permitted to deviate only under specified types of circumstances, or by giving written reasons, or both.

Principal. Under common law, the person who committed the crime, in contrast to the **accessory after the fact** or **accessory before the fact**, who assisted in the crime or who encouraged another to commit a crime. Many modern statutes do not make this distinction. Both are treated as principals, and accessories may be convicted even if the principal has not been convicted.

Principal in the first degree. The one who perpetrates the crime either through his or her own acts or by the use of inanimate objects or innocent people.

Principal in the second degree. The one who incites or abets the commission of the crime and is present actually or constructively.

Procedural law. The body of law that provides the legal methods and procedures by which **substantive law** is to be enforced.

Property crimes. Crimes that are directed toward property rather than toward the person. The four major property crimes as categorized by the FBI are burglary, larceny-theft, motor vehicle theft, and arson.

Prosecutor or prosecuting attorney. A government official whose duty is to initiate and maintain criminal proceedings on behalf of the government against persons accused of committing crimes.

Prostitution. Indiscriminate sexual acts for hire. Some statutes specify women as the offenders, but others also include men. The criminal offense may include not only the prostitute but also any persons who solicit or promote the business of prostitution or who live off the prostitute's earnings.

R

Rape. Historically defined as unlawful vaginal intercourse with a woman who was not the offender's wife. More recently, many jurisdictions have revised their rape statutes to include spouses and male victims, as well as penetration of any body opening (or specified body openings, such as the anus or the vagina) by a foreign object, including but not limited to the penis. In January 2012, the Federal Bureau of Investigation (FBI) made such changes in its definition of rape.

Rape shield statute. Statute that prohibits the introduction into a rape trial of any information concerning the past sexual experiences of the alleged victim. An exception might be the alleged victim's sexual history with the defendant, providing that information is relevant to an understanding of whether the alleged victim consented to sex in the case at issue.

Rape trauma syndrome (RTS). Stress that occurs after forced sex; now considered a **posttraumatic stress disorder (PTSD).** Evidence of the syndrome is permitted in an increasing number of courts.

Rebuttable presumption. A presumption that may be refuted by evidence.

Rehabilitation. Punishment philosophy that attempts to reform the offender through education, work, or other appropriate treatment modalities.

Retribution. The philosophy that offenders should receive the punishment they deserve in light of the crimes they committed.

Riot. *See* **Unlawful assembly.**

Robbery. The taking or attempting to take anything of value from the care, custody, or control of a person or persons by force or threat of force or violence or by putting the victim in fear.

Rout. *See* **Unlawful assembly.**

S

Sanction. A penalty or punishment that is imposed on a person in order to enforce the law.

Securities. Stocks, bonds, notes, and other documents that are representative of a share in a company or a debt of a company.

Sedition. A communication or agreement aimed at stirring up **treason** or at defaming the government.

Seduction. The act by a man who uses solicitation, persuasion, promises, bribes, or other methods to entice a woman to have unlawful sexual intercourse with him. Most seduction laws have been repealed, but those that remain generally categorize the crime as a misdemeanor and may be gender neutral.

Sentence. The judgment pronounced by the court (trial judge) and imposed on a defendant who pleads guilty or who is found guilty after a trial. A

determinate sentence is one in which the legislature has set the type and length of sentence for each crime, leaving the judge little or no discretion. An **indeterminate sentence** leaves the sentence decision up to judges or sets a minimum and maximum term and permits the judge to set the exact sentence in each case.

Sentence disparity. A term used to describe the variations and inequities that result when defendants convicted of the same crime receive varying sentences; may also refer to varying legislative sentences from state to state.

Sentencing guidelines. Guidelines established by legislatures, judges, or others (such as sentencing commissions) to be followed by judges in assessing sentences. Some divergence is allowed but usually must be accompanied by a statement of reasons.

Sexual abuse. Sexual mistreatment, which includes child pornography and the sexual molestation of children, as well as the sexual abuse of adults.

Sodomy. Generally interpreted as an act involving anal or oral sex with another person of the same or opposite sex or with an animal.

Solicitation. The asking, inciting, ordering, urgently requesting, or enticing of another person to commit a crime.

Stalking. Defined in the National Violence Against Women Survey as "a course of conduct directed at a specific person that involves repeated visual or physical proximity, nonconsensual communication, or verbal, written or implied threats, or a combination thereof, that would cause a reasonable person fear." The term *repeated* means two or more times. State statutes may vary from this definition. *See also* **Cyberstalking**.

Stare decisis. Literally, "Let the decision stand." *Stare decisis* means that although the law must be flexible and change with the times, it must also be stable and predictable, and courts are reluctant to make changes.

Statutory law. Law that originates with the legislature in a written enactment.

Statutory rape. Sexual intercourse (or, in some jurisdictions, other sexual acts as well) with an underage person even though that person consented. An underage person is deemed by law to be incapable of giving legal consent to sexual acts.

Strict liability. A legal concept that holds defendants responsible for wrongful acts even when they are not guilty of negligence, fault, or bad faith. This concept is often used in **tort** law to hold employers liable for the acts of their employees.

Subornation of perjury. *See* **Perjury**.

Substantial capacity test. Provides that persons cannot be held accountable for a criminal act if they have a mental disease or defect that results in their inability either to appreciate the fact that the act is wrong or to conform their conduct to the law.

Substantial factor. One that a reasonable person might conclude was sufficient to support the resulting damage to property or personal injury or death caused by a tort or a crime.

Substantive law. Law that defines the elements of crimes and the punishments legally available for those acts. *See also* **Procedural law.**

T

Terrorism. Violent acts or threats of violence to create fear, alarm, dread, or coercion, usually against governments.

Three strikes and you're out. Legislation enacted in recent years and designed to impose long sentences on persons who are convicted of a third serious crime.

Tort. Literally, a wrong; refers to the area of law that may lead to civil liability for negligent acts (such as automobile accidents or medical malpractice); intentional acts (such as assault, battery, libel, or slander); product liability (such as making and selling defective products or failing to warn when a warning would be reasonable); and strict liability (such as statutory rape). Some actions, such as trespassing on real property, assault and battery, or rape, may constitute crimes as well as torts.

Transportation Security Administration (TSA). Agency created by the Aviation and Transportation Security Act (ATSA) enacted in 2001. The agency was created to assume the screening functions for all commercial flights, a responsibility that previously had been under the Federal Aviation Administration (FAA), which was restructured by the statute. Originally reporting to the U.S. Department of Transportation, the TSA became part of the **Department of Homeland Security (DHS)** in March 2003.

Treason. An attempt to overthrow the government of which one is a member, or a betrayal of that government to a foreign power. Treason was thought to be such a serious offense that it was included within the U.S. Constitution, the only crime specified in that document. Under English common law the betrayal or killing of the sovereign or king was referred to as *high treason.*

Trespass. The entering or remaining unlawfully in or on the premises (including land, boats, or other vehicles) of another under certain circumstances as specified by statute.

Trespasser. One who commits a **trespass.**

Truth in sentencing. A concept requiring that actual time served by offenders is close to the time allocated for their sentences. Many jurisdictions are establishing 85 percent as their goal, meaning that offenders may not be released for any reason until they have served 85 percent of their sentences.

U

Under color of law. A phrase referring to a public official's assigned duties. For a person to be convicted of official misconduct, the person must be a public official or one acting in that capacity. The misconduct must occur during the course of that person's official duties.

Uniform Crime Reports (UCR). Official crime data, which is collected, compiled, and published by the Federal Bureau of Investigation (FBI) annually. The data are based on **crimes known to the police**—crimes that are reported to or observed by the police and that the police have reason to believe were committed. The report also publishes arrest data.

Unlawful assembly. The meeting of three or more persons to disturb the public peace with the intention of participating in a forcible and violent execution of an unlawful enterprise or of a lawful enterprise in an unauthorized manner. To constitute unlawful assembly, the group need not carry out its purpose; but if it takes steps to do so, it commits a **rout**. If it actually carries out the plan, it commits a **riot**.

USA Patriot Act. A law (the Uniting and Strengthening America by Providing Appropriate Tools Required to Intercept and Obstruct Terrorism Act of 2001) enacted after the 11 September 2001 terrorist attacks on the United States and subsequently revised and renewed. The statute was designed to provide tools for combating terrorism and other issues and has been subsequently amended.

V

Vagrancy. Under common law, an act or condition of wandering about from place to place without any visible means of support, refusing to work even though able to do so, and living off the charity of others. Many statutory vagrancy laws have been declared unconstitutional because of their vagueness and tendency to discriminate against racial and ethnic minorities and the poor.

Vicarious liability. The placing of legal liability on one person (or corporation) for the action of another. An example would be to hold the owner of a bar responsible for an employee who sold liquor to an intoxicated person who then drove a car and killed another person.

Violent crime. A crime defined by the FBI's *UCR* as a serious crime against a person. The four serious violent crimes in the *UCR* are murder and nonnegligent manslaughter, robbery, forcible rape, and aggravated assault.

Voluntary intoxication. Intoxication brought on by the free will of the individual. *See also* **Involuntary intoxication**.

Voluntary manslaughter. *See* **Manslaughter**.

W

Wharton rule. A rule stating that two people engaging in crimes such as adultery, bigamy, and incest or any other acts that require more than one person for their commission may not be prosecuted for conspiracy to commit those crimes. A third party must be involved for a conspiracy to exist. Some jurisdictions reject this rule.

Whistle-blower claims. Claims that expose a person, group, or business for engaging in illegal acts, such as fraud. Statutes have been enacted to provide protection for an employee who is fired for filing a whistle-blower claim, such as reporting financial improprieties of the company.

The Constitution of the United States: Selected Sections

[In the following printed copy of portions of the Constitution, spelling, capitalization, and punctuation conform to the text of the engrossed parchment.]

We the People of the United States, in Order to form a more perfect Union, establish Justice, insure domestic Tranquility, provide for the common defence, promote the general Welfare, and secure the Blessings of Liberty to ourselves and our Posterity, do ordain and establish this Constitution for the United States of America.

ARTICLE I.

SECTION. 1. All legislative Powers herein granted shall be vested in a Congress of the United States, which shall consist of a Senate and House of Representatives....

SECTION. 8. The Congress shall have Power To...regulate Commerce with foreign Nations, and among the several States, and with the Indian Tribes;...

To constitute Tribunals inferior to the supreme Court;...

To make all Laws which shall be necessary and proper for carrying into Execution the foregoing Powers, and all other Powers vested by this Constitution in the Government of the United States, or in any Department or Officer thereof.

SECTION. 9. The Privilege of the Writ of Habeas Corpus shall not be suspended, unless when in Cases of Rebellion or Invasion the public Safety may require it.

No Bill of Attainder or ex post facto Law shall be passed....

ARTICLE II.

SECTION. 1. The executive Power shall be vested in a President of the United States of America....

SECTION. 2. The President shall be Commander in Chief of the Army and Navy of the United States, and of the Militia of the several States, when called into the actual Service of the United States;...

He shall have Power, by and with the Advice and Consent of the Senate, to make Treaties, provided two thirds of the Senators present concur; and he shall nominate, and by and with the Advice and Consent of the Senate, shall appoint Ambassadors, other public Ministers and Consuls, Judges of the supreme Court, and all other Officers of the United States, whose Appointments are not herein otherwise provided for, and which shall be established by Law: but the Congress may by Law vest the Appointment of such inferior Officers, as they think proper, in the President alone, in the Courts of Law, or in the Heads of Departments....

SECTION. 4. The President, Vice President and all civil Officers of the United States, shall be removed from Office on Impeachment for, and Conviction of, Treason, Bribery, or other high Crimes and Misdemeanors.

ARTICLE III.

SECTION. 1. The judicial Power of the United States, shall be vested in one supreme Court, and in such inferior Courts as the Congress may from time to time ordain and establish. The Judges, both of the supreme and inferior Courts, shall hold their Offices during good Behaviour, and shall, at stated Times, receive for their Services a Compensation, which shall not be diminished during their Continuance in Office.

SECTION. 2. The judicial Power Shall extend to all Cases, in Law and Equity, arising under this Constitution, the Laws of the United States, and Treaties made, or which shall be made, under their Authority;—to all Cases affecting Ambassadors, other public Ministers and Consuls;—to all Cases of admiralty and maritime Jurisdiction;—to Controversies to which the United States shall be a Party;—to

Controversies between two or more States;—between a State and Citizens of another State;—between Citizens of different States;—between Citizens of the same State claiming Lands under Grants of different States, and between a State, or the Citizens thereof, and foreign States, Citizens or Subjects.

In all Cases affecting Ambassadors, other public Ministers and Consuls, and those in which a State shall be Party, the supreme Court shall have original Jurisdiction. In all the other Cases before mentioned, the supreme Court shall have appellate Jurisdiction, both as to Law and Fact, with such Exceptions, and under such Regulations as the Congress shall make.

The Trial of all Crimes, except in Cases of Impeachment, shall be by Jury; and such Trial shall be held in the State where the said Crimes shall have been committed; but when not committed within any State, the Trial shall be at such Place or Places as the Congress may by Law have directed.

SECTION. 3. Treason against the United States, shall consist only in levying War against them, or in adhering to their Enemies, giving them Aid and Comfort. No Person shall be convicted of Treason unless on the Testimony of two Witnesses to the same overt Act, or on Confession in open Court.

The Congress shall have Power to declare the Punishment of Treason, but no Attainder of Treason shall work Corruption of Blood, or Forfeiture except during the Life of the Person attainted.

ARTICLE IV.

SECTION. 1. Full Faith and Credit shall be given in each State to the public Acts, Records, and judicial Proceedings of every other State....

SECTION. 4. The United States shall guarantee to every State in this Union a Republican Form of Government, and shall protect each of them against Invasion; and on Application of the Legislature, or of the Executive (when the Legislature cannot be convened), against domestic Violence....

ARTICLE VI.

... This Constitution, and the Laws of the United States which shall be made in Pursuance thereof; and all Treaties made, or which shall be made, under the Authority of the United States, shall be the supreme Law of the Land; and the Judges in every State shall be bound thereby, any Thing in the Constitution or Laws of any State to the Contrary notwithstanding....

AMENDMENT I

Congress shall make no law respecting an establishment of religion, or prohibiting the free exercise thereof; or abridging the freedom of speech, or of the press; or the right of the people peaceably to assemble, and to petition the Government for a redress of grievances.

AMENDMENT II

A well regulated Militia, being necessary to the security of a free State, the right of the people to keep and bear Arms, shall not be infringed.

AMENDMENT III

No Solider shall, in time of peace be quartered in any house, without the consent of the Owner, nor in time of war, but in a manner to be prescribed by law.

AMENDMENT IV

The right of the people to be secure in their persons, houses, papers, and effects, against unreasonable searches and seizures, shall not be violated, and no Warrants shall issue, but upon probable cause, supported by Oath or affirmation, and particularly describing the place to be searched, and the persons or things to be seized.

AMENDMENT V

No person shall be held to answer for a capital, or otherwise infamous crime, unless on a presentment or indictment of a Grand Jury, except in cases arising in the land or naval forces, or in the Militia, when in actual service in time of War or public danger; nor shall any person be subject for the same offence to be twice put in jeopardy of life or limb; nor shall be compelled in any criminal case to be a witness against himself, nor be deprived of life, liberty, or property, without due process of law; nor shall private property be taken for public use, without just compensation.

AMENDMENT VI

In all criminal prosecutions, the accused shall enjoy the right to a speedy and public trial, by an impartial jury of the State and district wherein the crime shall have been committed, which district shall have been previously ascertained by law, and to be informed of the nature and cause of the accusation; to be confronted with the witnesses against him; to have compulsory process for obtaining witnesses in his favor, and to have the Assistance of Counsel for his defence.

AMENDMENT VII

In Suits at common law, where the value in controversy shall exceed twenty dollars, the right of trial by jury shall be preserved, and no fact tried by a jury, shall be otherwise re-examined in any Court of the United States, than according to the rules of the Common law.

AMENDMENT VIII

Excessive bail shall not be required, not excessive fines imposed, nor cruel and unusual punishments inflicted.

AMENDMENT IX

The enumeration in the Constitution, of certain rights, shall not be construed to deny or disparage others retained by the people.

AMENDMENT X

The powers not delegated to the United States by the Constitution, nor prohibited by it to the States, are reserved to the States respectively, or to the people.

AMENDMENT XI

The Judicial power of the United States shall not be construed to extend to any suit in law or equity, commenced or prosecuted against one of the United States by Citizens of another State, or by Citizens or Subjects of any Foreign State....

AMENDMENT XIV

SECTION. 1. All persons born or naturalized in the United States, and subject to the jurisdiction thereof, are citizens of the United States and of the State wherein they reside. No State shall make or enforce any law which shall abridge the privileges or immunities of citizens of the United States; nor shall any State deprive any person of life, liberty, or property, without due process of law; nor deny to any person within its jurisdiction the equal protection of the laws.... SECTION. 5. The Congress shall have power to enforce, by appropriate legislation, the provisions of this article....

AMENDMENT XVIII

SECTION. 1. After one year from the ratification of this article the manufacture, sale, or transportation of intoxicating liquors within, the importation thereof into, or the exportation thereof from the United States and all territory subject to the jurisdiction thereof for beverage purposes is hereby prohibited. SECTION. 2. The Congress and the several States shall have concurrent power to enforce this article by appropriate legislation. SECTION. 3. This article shall be inoperative unless it shall have been ratified as an amendment to the Constitution by the legislatures of the several States, as provided in the Constitution, within seven years from the date of the submission hereof to the States by the Congress....

AMENDMENT XXI

SECTION. 1. The eighteenth article of amendment to the Constitution of the United States is hereby repealed.

SECTION. 2. The transportation or importation into any State, Territory, or possession of the United States for delivery or use therein of intoxicating liquors, in violation of the laws thereof, is hereby prohibited....

How to Read a Court Citation

McKinney v. Anderson, 959 F.2d 853 (9th Cir. 1992), *aff'd., remanded, sub nom., Helling v. McKinney*, 509 U.S. 25 (1993), *on remand, remanded*, 5 F.3d 365 (9th Cir. 1993).

ORIGINAL CITATION

[*McKinney v. Anderson*]¹ [959]² [F.2d]³ [853]⁴ [9th Cir.]⁵ [1992]⁶.

1. Name of case
2. Volume number of reporter in which case is published
3. Name of reporter; *see* Abbreviations for Commonly Used Reporters for Court Cases
4. Page in the reporter where the decision begins
5. Court deciding the case
6. Year decided

ADDITIONAL CASE HISTORY

[*aff'd., remanded, sub nom.*]⁷ [*Helling v. McKinney*]⁸ [509]⁹ [U.S.]¹⁰ [25]¹¹ [1993]¹² [*on remand, remanded*]¹³ [5]¹⁴ [F.3d]¹⁵ [365]¹⁶ [9th Cir. 1993]¹⁷.

7. Affirmed and remanded (sent back for further proceedings) under a different name
8. The name under which the case was affirmed and remanded
9. Volume number of the reporter in which case is published
10. Abbreviated name of reporter
11. Page number on which the opinion begins
12. The year the U.S. Supreme Court decided the case [The name of the Court is not included as it is understood that the U.S. Reports contain only cases decided by the U.S. Supreme Court.]
13. Additional history—the case on remand
14. Volume number of reporter in which the remanded case is published
15. Abbreviated name of reporter
16. Page number on which the decision begins
17. Court that heard the remanded case and year it was decided

ABBREVIATIONS FOR COMMONLY USED REPORTERS FOR COURT CASES

Decisions of the U.S. Supreme Court
S.Ct.: Supreme Court Reporter
U.S.: United States Reports

Decisions from Other Courts: A Selected List
A., A.2d: Atlantic Reporter, Atlantic Reporter Second Series
Cal.Rptr: California Reporter
F.2d: Federal Reporter Second Series; F.3d, Third Series
F.Supp: Federal Supplement
N.Y.S.2d: New York Supplement Second Series
N.W., N.W.2d: North Western Reporter, North Western Reporter Second Series
N.E., N.E.2d: North Eastern Reporter, North Eastern Reporter Second Series
P., P.2d: Pacific Reporter, Pacific Reporter Second Series
S.E., S.E.2d: South Eastern Reporter, South Eastern Reporter Second Series

DEFINITIONS

Aff'd. Affirmed; the appellate court agrees with the decision of the lower court.

Aff'd. sub nom. Affirmed under a different name; the case at the appellate level has a different name from that of the trial court level.

Aff'd. per curiam. Affirmed by the court. The opinion is attributed to the entire court rather than designated as written by one of the judges or justices; a decision affirmed but no written opinion is issued.

Cert. denied. *Certiorari* denied; the U.S. Supreme Court refuses to hear and decide the case. Other courts may refuse cases also, and frequently that is referred to as *review denied*.

Concurring opinion. An opinion agreeing with the court's decision, but offering different reasons.

Dissenting opinion. An opinion disagreeing with the reasoning and result of the majority opinion.

Reh'g. denied. Rehearing denied; the court's refusal to rehear a case.

Remanded. The appellate court sending a case back to the lower court for further action.

Rev'd. Reversed, overthrown, set aside, made void. The appellate court reverses the decision of the lower court.

Rev'd. and remanded. Reversed and remanded; the appellate court reverses the decision and sends the case back for further action.

Vacated. Abandoned, set aside, made void. The appellate court sets aside the decision of the lower court.

Case Index

Name Index

General Index

criminal culpability, 59–60
defenses to criminal culpability, 83
in establishing guilt, 16–17
insanity defense, 69
proof of, 27
sentencing, 267
reasonable person standard
alcohol sales, 181
conspiracy, 47
culpability, 30
defense of property, 75
depraved heart murder, 99
manslaughter in domestic relations, 103–4
necessity defense, 62
negligence, 31
self-defense, 73
stalking, 132
statutory rape, 34
substantial factor test, 32
vagueness and overbreadth, 175
voluntary manslaughter, 103
rebuttable presumption, 60, 96
recidivism, 264, 271, 277
reckless assault, 113
reckless behavior, 30–31, 52, 62, 78, 99, 104, 107, 113,
151
reckless indifference, 100
Reducing Americans' Vulnerability to Ectasy (RAVE)
Act of 2002, 234
registration, of sex offenders, 186, 271, 274–77
rehabilitation, 4–5, 180–81, 254, 270, 278
reintegration, 187, 244, 276
religious practices, 185
renunciation defense, 41, 50
retribution, 4, 5, 270, 278
revenge. See retribution
right to counsel, 19–20
right-versus-wrong test of insanity, 66–67
riot, defined, 182
robbery, 5, 92, 101, 113–15, 136, 147–48, 161, 167
Rockefeller laws, 241–42
Rohypnol, 125, 229
roofies, 125
rout, 182
RTS (rape trauma syndrome), 82–83, 86
rule of law, 18

same-gender sexual behavior, 194. See also sodomy
sanction, 9
Sarbanes-Oxley Act (SOX) of 2002, 158
schedule of drugs in the U.S. federal system, 239,
245–46
second-degree murder, 101
second-degree sexual assault, 119
Securities Act of 1933, 157
Securities and Exchange Act of 1934, 157
Securities and Exchange Commission (SEC), 157–58
securities fraud, 157–59
sedition, 209
seduction and fornication, 190
self-defense, 73–74, 80, 93
sentence, 255
sentencing, 254–83. See also aggravating circumstances;
capital punishment; mitigating circumstances
Armed Career Criminal Act, 268
civil commitment, 275, 277

constitutional issues, 266–71
crack versus powder cocaine, 238
determination of, 5, 255–62
disparity, 257–58, 260–62, 278
driving under the influence (DUI), 181
equal protection, 269–70
Fair Sentencing Act of 2010, 265–66, 278
federal sentence guidelines, 258, 260–62, 275
guidelines, evaluation of, 262
guidelines for, 158, 165, 257–62
indeterminate, 258
judge's role in, 8, 267–68
jury's role in, 267–68
for juveniles, 63–64, 271–74
mandatory sentencing, 241–43, 263–66, 268, 273
models of, 255–57
National Drug Court Commencement Week and,
244
philosophy of, 254–55
proportionality and, 11, 260, 264, 270–71
reform measures, 263–66
sentence disparity, 260–62
Sentencing Reform Act of 1984, 258
substance abuse, state courts, 241–43, 246
Supreme Court, U.S, 260–62, 278
three strikes legislation, 263–65, 278
truth in sentencing legislation, 265
Washington Penal code, 254–55, 258–60
Sentencing Commission, U.S., 158, 165, 236–38, 240,
258, 265–66, 278
Sentencing Project, 243, 263, 269–70
Sentencing Reform Act of 1981 (Washington), 254–55,
258–60
Sex Offender Registration and Notification Act
(SORNA), 275
sex offenders, registration of, 186, 271, 274–77
sexting, 163–64
sexual abuse, 126–27, 186, 235, 259, 274, 276–77. See
also child abuse; rape, forcible
sexual assaults, 118, 129, 192
Sexual Offender Registration Act, 274
sexual orientation, 185
Sexual Predator Punishment and Control Act (SPPCA),
274–75
simple assault, 112
sin, crime and, 186
single adultery, 191
Sixth Amendment, 19, 267
skyjacking, 213
sleepwalking defense, 26–27
smuggling, of drugs, 229–30
social control, law as a form of, 2–3
Social Security numbers, theft of, 165–66
sodomy, 117, 119–21, 189–90
solicitation, 40–41, 53, 177–78, 190
SORNA (Sex Offender Registration and Notification
Act), 275
specific deterrence. See deterrence
specific intent, 28–29, 41
speech, freedom of, 12
spoofing, 165
stalking, 111, 123, 131–32, 136, 165
stand your ground statute, 74
stare decisis, 18
statutory arson, 151
statutory burglary, 149

U.S. attorney, 8
U.S. Congress, 6
USA Patriot Act, 165, 215, 217
USCS. See *United States Code*
uttering. *See* forgery

vagrancy, 177–78
vagueness doctrine, 10, 21, 47, 132, 175, 183, 189, 193, 209
vandalism, 235
vehicular and DUI manslaughter, 105, 107, 224
Veterans Affairs, Department of, 155
Viagra, 236
vicarious liability crimes, defined, 34–35
victims
    anticipatory offense and parties to crime, 53
    condonation defense, 80
    date rape, 124
    fraud against the elderly, 153
    hate crimes, 130
    incest, 126
    JAYC Foundation, 276
    kidnapping, 129, 136
    larceny-theft, 115
    liability without fault, 34
    property crimes, 167
    prosecutorial discretion, 9
    rape, forcible, 118, 120–21
    retribution, 4
    robbery, 114
    seduction, 190
    statutory rape, 34
    terrorism, 209
    Trafficking Victims Protection Act, 186–87
    voluntary manslaughter, 103
    White Collar Crime Victim Protection Act, 153
Vietnam War, 81
violation, defined, 9
violations, as crime category, 256
violence, 176, 230. *See also* domestic violence; violent crimes
Violence Against Women Act of 1984, 123
violent crimes
    aggravated assault, 92, 112–13
    carjacking, 167
    child abuse, 136

civil commitment, 277
computer crime, 164–65
crimes against the person, 111–38
    data on, 91–93
    domestic violence, 121–27
    elder abuse, 136
    homicide, 91–107
    Jacob Wetterling Crimes Against Children and Sexually Violent Offender Registration Act, 275
    kidnapping, 127, 129
    murder and nonnegligent manslaughter, 97–103
    robbery, 114
    sexual predators, 277
    sodomy, 189
    terrorism, 209, 217
    Violent Crime Control and Law Enforcement Act of 1994, 238–39
    Violent Offender Incarceration and Truth in Sentencing Incentive Grants, 265
virtual child pornography, 191–92
voluntary intoxication, 70, 78
voluntary manslaughter, 103, 107
voter fraud, 206

waivers, from juvenile to adult court, 63
war on drugs, 239–40, 246
warrants, arrest, 15, 129
Washington Penal code, 254–55
weapons of mass destruction, 211
weapons offenses, 5, 98, 112–13, 182, 193, 211, 216
Wharton rule, 48–49, 52–54
whistle-blower claims, 158
White Collar Crime Victim Protection Act, 153
White House, drug policies, 240–41
White House Office of Combating Terrorism, 215
white-collar crime, 154–55, 158, 163
wire and mail fraud, 154–55, 157–58, 164
wiretapping, 215
withdrawal defense, 50
witness tampering, 203, 206, 238

year-and-a-day rule, 95–99, 106

Zoloft, 77